THE HEALTH CARE SYSTEM

LO

ISSN 1543-2556

THE HEALTH CARE SYSTEM

Barbara Wexler

INFORMATION PLUS® REFERENCE SERIES
Formerly Published by Information Plus, Wylie, Texas

GALE
CENGAGE Learning™

Detroit • New York • San Francisco • New Haven, Conn • Waterville, Maine • London

GALE
CENGAGE Learning™

The Health Care System

Barbara Wexler

Paula Kepos, Series Editor

Project Editors: Elizabeth Manar, Kathleen J. Edgar

Rights Acquisition and Management: Edna Shy, Jhanay Williams

Composition: Evi Abou-El-Seoud, Mary Beth Trimper

Manufacturing: Cynde Bishop

Product Management: Carol Nagel

For product information and technology assistance, contact us at
Gale Customer Support, 1-800-877-4253.
For permission to use material from this text or product,
submit all requests online at **www.cengage.com/permissions.**
Further permissions questions can be e-mailed to
permissionrequest@cengage.com

Gale
27500 Drake Rd.
Farmington Hills, MI 48331-3535

ISBN-13: 978-0-7876-5103-9 (set)   ISBN-10: 0-7876-5103-6 (set)
ISBN-13: 978-1-4144-3378-3   ISBN-10: 1-4144-3378-6

ISSN 1543-2556

This title is also available as an e-book.
ISBN-13: 978-1-4144-5756-7 (set)
ISBN-10: 1-4144-5756-1 (set)
Contact your Gale sales representative for ordering information.

Printed in the United States of America
1 2 3 4 5 6 7 13 12 11 10 09

TABLE OF CONTENTS

PREFACE

The Health Care System is part of the *Information Plus Reference Series*. The purpose of each volume of the series is to present the latest facts on a topic of pressing concern in modern American life. These topics include today's most controversial and studied social issues: abortion, capital punishment, care for the elderly, crime, the environment, health care, immigration, minorities, national security, social welfare, women, youth, and many more. Even though this series is written especially for high school and undergraduate students, it is an excellent resource for anyone in need of factual information on current affairs.

By presenting the facts, it is the intention of Gale, a part of Cengage Learning, to provide its readers with everything they need to reach an informed opinion on current issues. To that end, there is a particular emphasis in this series on the presentation of scientific studies, surveys, and statistics. These data are generally presented in the form of tables, charts, and other graphics placed within the text of each book. Every graphic is directly referred to and carefully explained in the text. The source of each graphic is presented within the graphic itself. The data used in these graphics are drawn from the most reputable and reliable sources, in particular from the various branches of the U.S. government and from major independent polling organizations. Every effort has been made to secure the most recent information available. Readers should bear in mind that many major studies take years to conduct, and that additional years often pass before the data from these studies are made available to the public. Therefore, in many cases the most recent information available in 2009 is dated from 2006 or 2007. Older statistics are sometimes presented as well, if they are of particular interest and no more-recent information exists.

Even though statistics are a major focus of the *Information Plus Reference Series*, they are by no means its only content. Each book also presents the widely held positions and important ideas that shape how the book's

subject is discussed in the United States. These positions are explained in detail and, where possible, in the words of their proponents. Some of the other material to be found in these books includes historical background, descriptions of major events related to the subject, relevant laws and court cases, and examples of how these issues play out in American life. Some books also feature primary documents, or have pro and con debate sections giving the words and opinions of prominent Americans on both sides of a controversial topic. All material is presented in an even-handed and unbiased manner; readers will never be encouraged to accept one view of an issue over another.

HOW TO USE THIS BOOK

The U.S. health care system is a multifaceted establishment consisting of health care providers, patients, and treatment facilities, just to name a few components. This book examines the state of the nation's health care system, the education and training of health care providers, and the various types of health care institutions. The ever-increasing cost of health care, prevalence of insurance, mental health care, and a comparison of health care throughout the world are also covered.

The Health Care System consists of nine chapters and three appendixes. Each of the chapters is devoted to a particular aspect of the health care system in the United States. For a summary of the information covered in each chapter, please see the synopses provided in the Table of Contents at the front of the book. Chapters generally begin with an overview of the basic facts and background information on the chapter's topic, then proceed to examine subtopics of particular interest. For example, Chapter 6: Insurance: Those With and Those Without begins by describing the demographics of who was uninsured in 2006. Next, the chapter examines the consequences of not having health insurance. This is followed by a discussion of the sources of health insurance, including private insurance, Medicaid, and Medicare. Then a discussion on children not covered by health insurance is provided. The chapter concludes by examining a variety of topics that surround paying for health care, such the Health Insurance Portability and Accountability Act of 1996, health savings accounts, the rising costs of health insurance, and the pros and cons of mental health parity (that the same range and scope of insurance benefits available for other illnesses be provided for people with mental illness). Readers can find their way through a chapter by looking for the section and subsection headings, which are clearly set off from the text. Or, they can refer to the book's extensive index if they already know what they are looking for.

Statistical Information

The tables and figures featured throughout *The Health Care System* will be of particular use to readers in learning about this issue. These tables and figures represent an extensive collection of the most recent and important statistics on the health care system, as well as related issues—for example, graphics in the book cover the rate of home health care usage, the number of emergency department visits, the national health expenditure amounts, the percent of people without health insurance, and public opinion on the state of the health care system. Gale, a part of Cengage Learning, believes that making this information available to readers is the most important way to fulfill the goal of this book: to help readers understand the issues and controversies surrounding the health care system in the United States and reach their own conclusions.

Each table or figure has a unique identifier appearing above it, for ease of identification and reference. Titles for the tables and figures explain their purpose. At the end of each table or figure, the original source of the data is provided.

To help readers understand these often complicated statistics, all tables and figures are explained in the text. References in the text direct readers to the relevant statistics. Furthermore, the contents of all tables and figures are fully indexed. Please see the opening section of the index at the back of this volume for a description of how to find tables and figures within it.

Appendixes

Besides the main body text and images, *The Health Care System* has three appendixes. The first is the Important Names and Addresses directory. Here readers will find contact information for a number of government and private organizations that can provide further information on aspects of the health care system. The second appendix is the Resources section, which can also assist readers in conducting their own research. In this section, the author and editors of *The Health Care System* describe some of the sources that were most useful during the compilation of this book. The final appendix is the index. It has been greatly expanded from previous editions, and should make it even easier to find specific topics in this book.

ADVISORY BOARD CONTRIBUTIONS

The staff of Information Plus would like to extend its heartfelt appreciation to the Information Plus Advisory Board. This dedicated group of media professionals provides feedback on the series on an ongoing basis. Their comments allow the editorial staff who work on the project to make the series better and more user-friendly. Our top priorities are to produce the highest-quality and most useful books possible, and the Advisory Board's contributions to this process are invaluable.

The members of the Information Plus Advisory Board are:

- Kathleen R. Bonn, Librarian, Newbury Park High School, Newbury Park, California

- Madelyn Garner, Librarian, San Jacinto College–North Campus, Houston, Texas

- Anne Oxenrider, Media Specialist, Dundee High School, Dundee, Michigan

- Charles R. Rodgers, Director of Libraries, Pasco-Hernando Community College, Dade City, Florida

- James N. Zitzelsberger, Library Media Department Chairman, Oshkosh West High School, Oshkosh, Wisconsin

COMMENTS AND SUGGESTIONS

The editors of the *Information Plus Reference Series* welcome your feedback on *The Health Care System*. Please direct all correspondence to:

Editors
Information Plus Reference Series
27500 Drake Rd.
Farmington Hills, MI 48331-3535

CHAPTER 1
THE U.S. HEALTH CARE SYSTEM

When asked to describe the U.S. health care system, most Americans would probably offer a description of just a single facet of a huge, complex interaction of people, institutions, and technology. Like snapshots, each account offers an image, frozen in time, of one of the many health care providers and the settings in which medical care is delivered. Examples of these include:

- Physician offices: for many Americans, health care may be described as the interaction between a primary care physician and patient to address minor and urgent medical problems, such as colds, flu, or back pain. A primary care physician (usually a general practitioner, family practitioner, internist, or pediatrician) is the frontline caregiver—the first practitioner to evaluate and treat the patient. Routine physical examinations, prevention such as immunization and health screening to detect disease, and treatment of acute and chronic diseases commonly take place in physicians' offices.

- Medical clinics: these settings provide primary care services comparable to those provided in physicians' offices and may be organized to deliver specialized support such as prenatal care for expectant mothers, well-baby care for infants, or treatment for specific medical conditions such as hypertension (high blood pressure), diabetes, or asthma.

- Hospitals: these institutions contain laboratories, imaging centers (also known as radiology departments, where x-rays and other imaging studies are performed), and other equipment for diagnosis and treatment, as well as emergency departments, operating rooms, and highly trained personnel.

Medical care is provided through many other venues, including outpatient surgical centers, school health programs, pharmacies, worksite clinics, and voluntary health agencies such as Planned Parenthood, the American Red Cross, and the American Lung Association.

IS THE U.S. HEALTH CARE SYSTEM AILING?

Even though medical care in the United States is often considered the best available, some observers feel the system that delivers it is fragmented and in serious disarray. In *Crossing the Quality Chasm: A New Health System for the 21st Century* (2001, http://www.nap.edu/books/0309072808/html/), the Institute of Medicine (IOM) of the National Academies describes the nation's health care system as disjointed, inefficient, and in need of a major overhaul.

Regina E. Herzlinger of the Harvard Business School agrees with the IOM. In *Who Killed Health Care?: America's $2 Trillion Medical Problem—and the Consumer-Driven Cure* (2007), she contends that the current U.S. health care system is in crisis because it is incorrectly organized around the motives, methods, and preferences of health care providers and payers rather than aimed at meeting the needs of health care consumers. Herzlinger argues that the present orientation of the U.S. health care system is dangerously eroding patient welfare and driving costs so high that for millions of Americans, medical care is inaccessible.

Herzlinger proposes streamlining the system by eliminating insurance companies, which she believes only serve as "middlemen" between physicians and patients. She also recommends:

- Mandatory health insurance with subsidies provided for people who cannot afford to purchase it

- Establishment of small medical facilities that provide comprehensive health care services

- A national system of medical records that ensures confidentiality as well as provider access to medical information

- Compulsory performance reviews of all hospitals and health care organizations

Herzlinger asserts that in a consumer-driven model of health care delivery, providers would compete on the basis of quality, services would be timely, coordinated, and cost-effective, and innovation would be encouraged and rewarded.

Albert Fuchs, a practicing physician, offers another scathing indictment of the health care system in "Dollars to Doughnuts Diagnosis" (*Los Angeles Times*, April 16, 2008). Like Hurzlinger, he blames insurance companies for creating high-volume medical practices and compromising the time physicians can spend with patients. By dropping all of his insurance plans and seeing patients on a fee-for-service basis, Fuchs claims he can devote more time to his patients. He also believes that eliminating insurance companies from the health care equation will cause prices to drop. Fuchs asserts, "When doctors break free from the shackles of insurance companies, they can practice medicine the way they always hoped they could. And they can get back to the customer service model in which the paramount incentive is providing the best care."

In *A Second Opinion: Rescuing America's Health Care* (2007), Arnold S. Relman of Harvard Medical School explains how the commercialization of medicine harms both physicians and patients. Relman opines that the profit motive "increases costs; it may also jeopardize quality or aggravate the system's inequity." He favors a single-payer insurance program supported by a progressive health care tax to finance a delivery system in which all hospitals would be not-for-profit and most physicians would be salaried employees.

THE COMPONENTS OF THE HEALTH CARE SYSTEM

The health care system consists of all personal medical care services—prevention, diagnosis, treatment, and rehabilitation (services to restore function and independence)—plus the institutions and personnel that provide these services and the government, public, and private organizations and agencies that finance service delivery.

The health care system may be viewed as a complex consisting of three interrelated components: health care consumers (people in need of health care services), health care providers (people who deliver health care services—the professionals and practitioners), and the institutions or organizations of the health care system (the public and private agencies that organize, plan, regulate, finance, and coordinate services), which provide the systematic arrangements for delivering health care. The institutional component includes hospitals, clinics, and home-health agencies; the insurance companies and programs that pay for services, such as Blue Cross/Blue Shield, managed care plans such as health maintenance organizations, and preferred provider organizations; and entitlement programs such as Medicare and Medicaid (federal and state

government public assistance programs). Other institutions are the professional schools that train students for careers in medical, public health, dental, and allied health professions, such as nursing and laboratory technology. Also included are agencies and associations that research and monitor the quality of health care services; license and accreditation providers and institutions; local, state, and national professional societies; and the companies that produce medical technology, equipment, and pharmaceuticals.

Much of the interaction among the three components of the health care system occurs directly between individual health care consumers and providers. Other interactions are indirect and impersonal such as immunization programs or screening to detect disease, which are performed by public health agencies for whole populations. Regardless, all health care delivery depends on interactions among all three components. The ability to benefit from health care depends on an individual's or group's ability to gain entry to the health care system. The process of gaining entry to the health care system is referred to as access, and many factors can affect access to health care. This chapter provides an overview of how Americans access the health care system.

ACCESS TO THE HEALTH CARE SYSTEM

In the twenty-first century, access to health care services is a key measure of the overall health and prosperity of a nation or a population, but access and availability were not always linked to health status. In fact, many medical historians assert that until the beginning of the twentieth century, a visit with a physician was as likely to be harmful as it was helpful. Only since the early twentieth century has medical care been considered a positive influence on health and longevity.

There are three aspects of accessibility: consumer access, comprehensive availability of services, and supply of services adequate to meet community demand. Quality health care services must be accessible to health care consumers when and where they are needed. The health care provider must have access to a full range of facilities, equipment, drugs, and services provided by other practitioners. The institutional component of health care delivery—the hospitals, clinics, and payers—must have timely access to information to enable them to plan an adequate supply of appropriate services for their communities.

Consumer Access to Care

Access to health care services is influenced by a variety of factors. Characteristics of health care consumers strongly affect when, where, and how they access services. Differences in age, educational attainment, economic status, race, ethnicity, cultural heritage, and geographic location determine when consumers seek health care services, where they go to receive them, their expectations of treatment, and the extent to which they wish to participate in decisions about their own medical care.

People have different reasons for seeking access to health care services. Their personal beliefs about health and illness, motivations to obtain care, expectations of the care they will receive, and knowledge about how and where to receive care vary. For an individual to have access to quality care, there must be appropriately defined points of entry into the health care system. For many consumers, a primary care physician is the portal to the health care system. Besides evaluating the patient's presenting problem (or immediate health care need), the primary care physician also directs the consumer to other providers of care such as physician specialists or mental health professionals.

Some consumers access the health care system by seeking care from a clinic or hospital outpatient department, where teams of health professionals are available at one location. Others gain entry by way of a public health nurse, school nurse, social worker, or pharmacist, who refers them to an appropriate source, site, or health care practitioner.

Comprehensive Availability of Health Care Services

Historically, the physician was the exclusive provider of all medical services. Until the twentieth century, the family doctor served as physician, surgeon, pharmacist, therapist, adviser, and dentist. He carried all the tools of his trade in a small bag and could easily offer state-of-the-art medical care in his patient's home, because hospitals had little more to offer in the way of equipment or facilities. In the twenty-first century, it is neither practical nor desirable to ask one practitioner to serve in all these roles. It would be impossible for one professional to perform the full range of health care services, from primary prevention of disease and diagnosis to treatment and rehabilitation. Modern physicians and other health care practitioners must have access to a comprehensive array of trained personnel, facilities, and equipment so that they can, in turn, make them accessible to their patients.

Even though many medical problems are effectively treated in a single office visit with a physician, even simple diagnosis and treatment relies on a variety of ancillary (supplementary) services and personnel. To make the diagnosis, the physician may order an imaging study such as an x-ray or ultrasound that is performed by a radiology technician and interpreted by a radiologist (physician specialist in imaging techniques). Laboratory tests may be performed by technicians and analyzed by pathologists (physicians who specialize in microscopic analysis and diagnosis). More complicated medical problems involve teams of surgeons and high-tech surgical suites equipped with robotic assistants and rehabilitation programs in which highly trained physical and occupational therapists skillfully assist patients to regain function and independence.

Some health care services are more effectively, efficiently, and economically provided to groups rather than to individuals. Immunization to prevent communicable diseases and screening to detect diseases in their earliest and most treatable stages are examples of preventive services best performed as cooperative efforts of voluntary health organizations, medical and other professional societies, hospitals, and public health departments.

Access Requires Enough Health Care Services to Meet Community Needs

For all members of a community to have access to the full range of health care services, careful planning is required to ensure both the adequate supply and distribution of needed services. To evaluate community needs and effectively allocate health care resources, communities must gather demographic data and information about the social and economic characteristics of the population. They must also monitor the spread of disease and the frequency of specific medical conditions over time. All this population data must be considered in relation to available resources, including health care personnel, the distribution of facilities, equipment, and human resources (the available health care workforce), and advances in medicine and technology.

For example, a predicted shortage of nurses may prompt increased spending on nursing education; reviews of nurses' salary, benefits, and working conditions; and the cultivation of nonnursing personnel to perform specific responsibilities previously assigned to nurses. Similarly, when ongoing surveillance anticipates an especially virulent influenza (flu) season, public health officials, agencies, and practitioners intensify efforts to provide timely immunization to vulnerable populations such as older adults. Government agencies such as the Centers for Disease Control and Prevention (CDC), the National Institutes of Health, state and local health departments, professional societies, voluntary health agencies, and universities work together to research, analyze, and forecast health care needs. Their recommendations allow health care planners, policy makers, and legislators to allocate resources so that supply keeps pace with demand and to ensure that new services and strategies are developed to address existing and emerging health care concerns.

A REGULAR SOURCE OF HEALTH CARE IMPROVES ACCESS

According to the CDC, the determination of whether an individual has a regular source—a regular provider or site—of health care is a powerful predictor of access to health care services. Generally, people without regular sources have less access or access to fewer services, including key preventive medicine services such as prenatal care, routine immunization,

FIGURE 1.1

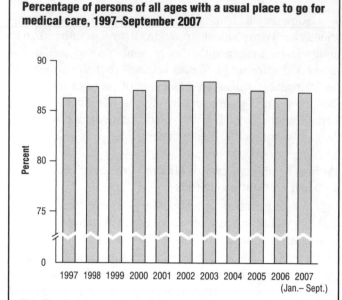

Percentage of persons of all ages with a usual place to go for medical care, 1997–September 2007

Note: The usual place to go for medical care does not include a hospital emergency room. The analyses excluded persons with an unknown usual place to go for medical care (about 0.6% of respondents each year).

SOURCE: J.S. Schiller, K.M. Heyman, and P. Barnes, "Figure 2.1. Percent of Persons of All Ages with a Usual Place to Go for Medical Care: United States, 1997–September 2007," in *Early Release of Selected Estimates Based on Data from the January–September 2007 National Health Interview Survey*, National Center for Health Statistics, March 2008, http://www.cdc.gov/nchs/data/nhis/earlyrelease/200803_02.pdf (accessed April 16, 2008)

FIGURE 1.2

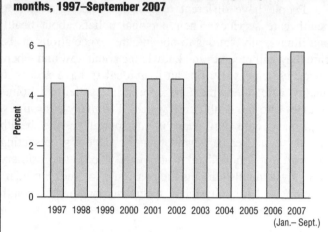

Percentage of persons of all ages who failed to obtain needed medical care due to cost at some time during the past 12 months, 1997–September 2007

Note: The analyses excluded persons with unknown responses to the question on failure to obtain needed medical care due to cost (about 0.5% of respondents each year).

SOURCE: J.S. Schiller, K.M. Heyman, and P. Barnes, "Figure 3.1. Percentage of Persons of All Ages Who Failed to Obtain Needed Medical Care Due to Cost at Some Time during the Past 12 Months: United States, 1997–September 2007," in *Early Release of Selected Estimates Based on Data from the January–September 2007 National Health Interview Survey*, National Center for Health Statistics, March 2008, http://www.cdc.gov/nchs/data/nhis/earlyrelease/200803_03.pdf (accessed April 16, 2008)

and health screening. Many factors have been found to contribute to keeping individuals from having regular sources of medical care, with income level being the best predictor of unmet medical needs or problems gaining access to health care services.

J. S. Schiller, K. M. Heyman, and P. Barnes of the National Center for Health Statistics (NCHS) analyze the 2007 National Health Interview Survey (NHIS), an annual nationwide survey of about thirty-eight thousand households in the United States, in *Early Release of Selected Estimates Based on Data from the January–September 2007 National Health Interview Survey* (March 2008, http://www.cdc.gov/ nchs/data/nhis/earlyrelease/earlyrelease200806.pdf). The researchers find that from 1997 to 2007 the percentage of people of all ages with a usual source of medical care did not substantially vary—ranging from a low of 86% in 1997 to a high of 88% in 2001. (See Figure 1.1.) From January to September 2007, 87% of people had a usual place to go for medical care.

Still, from 1998 through 2006 the percentage of people who needed medical care but did not obtain it because of financial barriers to access increased each year. The annual percentage of people who experienced this lack of access to medical care rose from 4.2% in 1998 to 5.8% in 2006 and did not change in 2007. (See Figure 1.2.)

Schiller, Heyman, and Barnes reveal that people aged eighteen to twenty-four were the least likely to have a regular source of care, but the likelihood of having a regular source of medical care increased with age among people aged eighteen years and older. (See Figure 1.3.) Children under age eighteen were more likely than adults aged eighteen to sixty-four to have a usual place to go for medical care. Among adults (aged eighteen to sixty-four), women were more likely than men to have a usual place to seek medical care. Schiller, Heyman, and Barnes indicate that not having a regular health care provider is a greater predictor of delay in seeking care than insurance status. Health care consumers with a regular physician or source of health care services are less likely to use the hospital emergency room to obtain routine nonemergency medical care and are less likely to be hospitalized for preventable illnesses.

The National Association of Community Health Centers (NACHC) is a nonprofit organization that represents the interests of federally supported and other federally qualified health centers and serves as an information source about health care for poor and medically underserved populations in the United States. In *Access Denied: A Look at America's Medically Disenfranchised* (2007, http://www.nachc.com/client/documents/research/ Access_Denied42407.pdf), the NACHC reports that fifty-six million Americans of all income levels, race, and

FIGURE 1.3

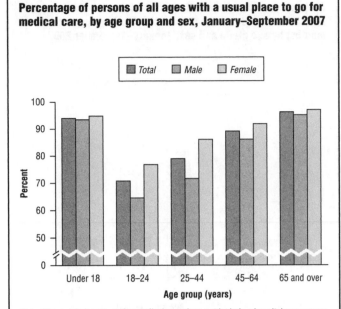

Percentage of persons of all ages with a usual place to go for medical care, by age group and sex, January–September 2007

Note: The usual place to go for medical care does not include a hospital emergency room. The analyses excluded 241 persons (1.5%) with an unknown usual place to go for medical care.

SOURCE: J.S. Schiller, K.M. Heyman, and P. Barnes, "Figure 2.2. Percentage of Persons of All Ages with a Usual Place to Go for Medical Care, by Age Group and Sex: United States, January–September 2007," in *Early Release of Selected Estimates Based on Data from the January–September 2007 National Health Interview Survey*, National Center for Health Statistics, March 2008, http://www.cdc.gov/nchs/data/nhis/earlyrelease/200803_02.pdf (accessed April 16, 2008)

FIGURE 1.4

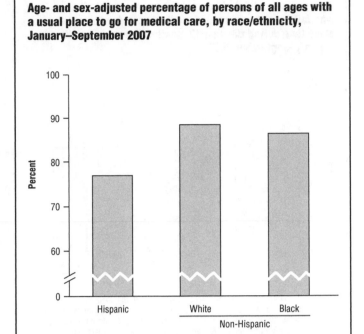

Age- and sex-adjusted percentage of persons of all ages with a usual place to go for medical care, by race/ethnicity, January–September 2007

Notes: The usual place to go for medical care does not include a hospital emergency room. The analyses excluded 241 persons (1.5%) with an unknown usual place to go for medical care. Estimates are age-sex adjusted using the projected 2000 U.S. population as the standard population and using five age groups: under 18 years, 18–24 years, 25–44 years, 45–64 years, and 65 years and over.

SOURCE: J.S. Schiller, K.M. Heyman, and P. Barnes, "Figure 2.3. Age-Sex-Adjusted Percentage of Persons of All Ages with a Usual Place to Go for Medical Care, by Race/Ethnicity: United States, January–September 2007," in *Early Release of Selected Estimates Based on Data from the January–September 2007 National Health Interview Survey*, National Center for Health Statistics, March 2008, http://www.cdc.gov/nchs/data/nhis/earlyrelease/200803_02.pdf (accessed April 16, 2008)

ethnicity were "medically disenfranchised" (at risk of inadequate access to basic medical services) in 2005 and that low-income families and minorities—populations traditionally characterized as medically underserved—were the hardest hit. The number of people considered medically disenfranchised was higher than the nearly forty-seven million Americans who lacked health insurance during the same year because the NACHC believes people lack access for a variety of additional reasons such as scarcity of health care resources, geographically inaccessible services, and health care that was not culturally sensitive or was otherwise unacceptable to health care consumers.

There Are Americans without Access to Medical Care in Every State

According to NACHC, in 2005 there were medically unserved Americans in every state, with the highest concentrations in Florida, Texas, and California. Together, these three states contained 29% of the fifty-six million. Twenty-one states were home to more than one million medically disenfranchised people and in nine states (Alabama, Alaska, Florida, Kansas, Mississippi, Missouri, Oregon, South Carolina, and Utah) two out of five residents had sharply limited or no access to the health care system. More than half (55.9%) of Alabama residents were medically disenfranchised.

In 2005 close to fifteen hundred counties in nearly every state had disenfranchised populations and did not have health centers. Health centers served fifteen million people in 2005, effectively reducing the number of medically disenfranchised people by 21%. In Hawaii, Maine, New Jersey, and Vermont, health centers reduced the number of disenfranchised by 50%; in ten other states (California, Colorado, Connecticut, Illinois, Maryland, Montana, New Mexico, New York, Pennsylvania, and South Dakota) and in the District of Columbia health centers reduced the ranks of the disenfranchised by 30%.

Race and Ethnicity Continue to Affect Access to Health Care

According to Schiller, Heyman, and Barnes, Hispanic adults continue to be less likely to have a regular source for medical care than white non-Hispanic and African-American non-Hispanic people. After adjusting for age and gender, 77% of Hispanics had a usual source of medical care, compared to 88.6% of non-Hispanic whites and 86.4% of non-Hispanic African-Americans. (See Figure 1.4.) Hispanics and non-Hispanic African-

FIGURE 1.5

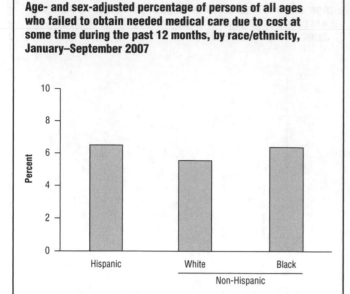

Age- and sex-adjusted percentage of persons of all ages who failed to obtain needed medical care due to cost at some time during the past 12 months, by race/ethnicity, January–September 2007

Notes: The analyses excluded 102 persons (0.2%) with unknown responses to the question on failure to obtain needed medical care due to cost. Estimates are age-sex adjusted using the projected 2000 U.S. population as the standard population and using three age groups: under 18 years, 18–64 years, and 65 years and over.

SOURCE: J.S. Schiller, K.M. Heyman, and P. Barnes, "Figure 3.3. Age-Sex-Adjusted Percentage of Persons of All Ages Who Failed to Obtain Needed Medical Care Due to Cost at Some Time during the Past 12 Months, by Race/Ethnicity: United States, January–September 2007," in *Early Release of Selected Estimates Based on Data from the January–September 2007 National Health Interview Survey*, National Center for Health Statistics, March 2008, http://www.cdc.gov/nchs/data/nhis/earlyrelease/200803_03.pdf (accessed April 16, 2008)

FIGURE 1.6

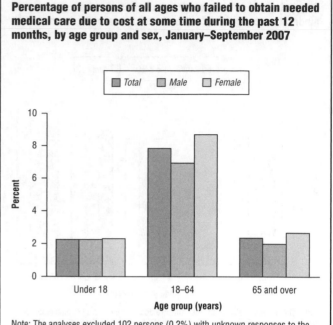

Percentage of persons of all ages who failed to obtain needed medical care due to cost at some time during the past 12 months, by age group and sex, January–September 2007

Note: The analyses excluded 102 persons (0.2%) with unknown responses to the question on failure to obtain needed medical care due to cost.

SOURCE: J.S. Schiller, K.M. Heyman, and P. Barnes, "Figure 3.2. Percentage of Persons of All Ages Who Failed to Obtain Needed Medical Care Due to Cost at Some Time during the Past 12 Months, by Age Group and Sex: United States, January–September 2007," in *Early Release of Selected Estimates Based on Data from the January–September 2007 National Health Interview Survey*, National Center for Health Statistics, March 2008, http://www.cdc.gov/nchs/data/nhis/early release/200803_03.pdf (accessed April 16, 2008)

Americans were more likely than non-Hispanic whites to suffer financial barriers to access. After adjusting for age and gender, 6.5% of Hispanics and 6.4% of non-Hispanic African-Americans were unable to obtain needed medical care because of financial barriers, compared to 5.5% of non-Hispanic whites. (See Figure 1.5.) Health educators speculate that language barriers and the lack of information about the availability of health care services may serve to widen this gap.

Women Face Additional Obstacles

In *Women and Health Care: A National Profile* (July 2005, http://www.kff.org/womenshealth/upload/Women-and-Health-Care-A-National-Profile-Key-Findings-from-the-Kaiser-Women-s-Health-Survey.pdf), Alina Salganicoff, Usha R. Ranji, and Roberta Wyn analyze data from the 2004 Kaiser Women's Health Survey. The researchers indicate that, overall, Hispanic and African-American women fared worse than white women in terms of access to health care services.

According to Salganicoff, Ranji, and Wyn, Hispanic women reported less access to care than their white counterparts. More than one-quarter (29%) of Hispanic women had not visited a health care provider in the year before the survey, compared to 16% of African-American women and

11% of white women. Uninsured women were the least likely to have had a provider visit (67%), compared to women covered by private insurance, Medicaid, or Medicare (90%, 88%, and 93%, respectively).

Schiller, Heyman, and Barnes also document gender-based disparities in access. Women aged eighteen to sixty-four and those aged sixty-five and older were more likely than men to have failed to obtain needed medical care because of financial barriers to access. (See Figure 1.6.)

Children Need Better Access to Health Care, Too

Barbara Bloom and Robin A. Cohen of the NCHS analyzed data from the 2006 NHIS to look at selected health measures, including children's access to care, and compiled their findings in *Summary Health Statistics for U.S. Children: National Health Interview Survey, 2006* (September 2007, http://www.cdc.gov/nchs/data/series/sr_10/sr10_234.pdf). Among other factors, Bloom and Cohen's analysis focused on the unmet health care needs of children under age eighteen, poverty status, insurance coverage, and usual place of medical care.

The researchers note that in 2006, 5% of children in the United States did not have a regular source of medical care. Non-Hispanic African-American children (97%) and

TABLE 1.1

Selected measures of health care access for children under age 18, by selected characteristics, 2006

Selected characteristic	All children under 18 years	Has usual place of health care[a]	Usual place of health care[b]					
			Clinic	Doctor's office	Emergency room	Hospital outpatient	Some other place	Doesn't go to one place most often
			Number in thousands[c]					
Total[d] (crude)	**73,493**	**69,626**	**15,137**	**52,879**	**419**	**673**	**233**	**202**
Sex								
Male	37,569	35,525	7,757	26,877	237	386	132	*96
Female	35,924	34,101	7,380	26,003	182	287	*101	106
Age								
0–4 years	20,410	19,704	4,648	14,644	107	217	*43	*39
5–11 years	27,776	26,417	5,673	20,157	157	245	106	*61
12–17 years	25,307	23,505	4,817	18,078	154	210	*84	*102
Race								
1 race[e]	70,976	67,245	14,606	51,132	410	601	233	180
White	55,881	52,891	11,007	40,958	260	279	169	151
Black or African American	11,455	10,964	2,747	7,778	116	242	*47	†
American Indian or Alaska Native	691	661	360	277	†	†	—	—
Asian	2,835	2,615	458	2,048	†	*62	†	†
Native Hawaiian or other Pacific Islander	114	*114	†	*72	†	—	—	—
2 or more races[f]	2,518	2,382	531	1,747	†	*72	—	†
Black or African American and white	935	868	167	680	—	†	—	†
American Indian or Alaska Native and white	572	522	206	259	—	†	—	†
Hispanic origin and race[g]								
Hispanic or Latino	14,815	13,175	4,987	7,649	158	222	†	92
Mexican or Mexican American	10,186	8,919	3,709	4,875	76	148	†	*68
Not Hispanic or Latino	58,678	56,451	10,150	45,230	260	451	184	111
White, single race	42,480	41,017	6,605	33,951	*131	*80	125	*76
Black or African American, single race	10,899	10,483	2,509	7,570	100	227	*42	†
Family structure[h]								
Mother and father	51,777	49,295	9,700	38,641	236	355	174	124
Mother, no father	17,083	16,215	4,326	11,358	148	268	*34	*71
Father, no mother	2,479	2,180	511	1,622	†	†	†	—
Neither mother nor father	2,154	1,936	600	1,258	*23	*33	†	†
Parent's education[i]								
Less than high school diploma	10,103	9,010	3,893	4,811	103	136	†	*35
High school diploma or GED[j]	16,106	15,187	3,683	11,096	128	172	*46	*61
More than high school	44,356	42,812	6,762	35,310	161	316	146	83
Family income[k]								
Less than $20,000	12,865	11,940	4,343	7,148	123	242	*22	*59
$20,000 or more	56,887	54,207	9,883	43,345	273	386	145	119
$20,000–$34,999	10,320	9,461	2,824	6,348	93	109	†	*34
$35,000–$54,999	10,843	10,161	2,100	7,854	*77	*68	*31	†
$55,000–$74,999	8,071	7,756	1,384	6,229	†	*66	†	†
$75,000 or more	17,425	17,148	2,043	14,984	†	*62	†	*17
Poverty status[l]								
Poor	11,139	10,233	3,789	6,118	79	183	†	*41
Near poor	13,098	12,082	3,332	8,364	132	170	*51	†
Not poor	32,175	31,253	4,531	26,364	*77	135	*72	*52
			Number in thousands[c]					
Health insurance coverage[m]								
Private	42,773	41,747	5,391	35,936	*60	122	131	*52
Medicaid or other public	21,407	20,670	6,991	13,128	144	326	*38	*29
Other	1,738	1,659	585	923	†	*104	†	†
Uninsured	7,251	5,269	2,050	2,760	190	121	*53	91
Place of residence								
Large MSA[n]	37,482	35,507	7,257	27,274	184	396	177	146
Small MSA[n]	23,470	22,301	4,557	17,311	181	164	*52	34
Not in MSA[n]	12,542	11,819	3,324	8,294	†	*112	†	†

non-Hispanic white children (97%) were more likely to have a regular source of care, compared to Hispanic children (89%). Bloom and Cohen also reveal a relationship between not having a usual source of medical care and family struc-ture, family income, poverty status, and health insurance coverage. The likelihood of lacking a regular source of care or having unmet needs was higher among poor and near-poor families of all races and ethnic groups. (See Table 1.1.)

TABLE 1.1

Selected measures of health care access for children under age 18, by selected characteristics, 2006 [CONTINUED]

Selected characteristic	All children under 18 years	Has usual place of health care[a]	Usual place of health care[b]					
			Clinic	Doctor's office	Emergency room	Hospital outpatient	Some other place	Doesn't go to one place most often
			Number in thousands[c]					
Region								
Northeast	13,574	13,319	2,015	10,966	88	147	†	*58
Midwest	16,708	16,080	4,252	11,616	*53	125	†	—
South	27,186	25,358	4,400	20,345	205	264	*66	*66
West	16,026	14,870	4,470	9,953	*73	*137	133	*78
Current health status								
Excellent or very good	60,121	57,195	11,668	44,385	298	404	219	172
Good	11,933	11,085	3,048	7,642	105	230	†	*25
Fair or poor	1,398	1,306	416	818	†	*39	—	†

*Estimates preceded by an asterisk have a relative standard error of greater than 30% and less than or equal to 50% and should be used with caution as they do not meet the standards of reliability or precision.

†Estimates with a relative standard error greater than 50% are indicated with a dagger, but data are not shown.

—Quantity zero.

[a]Having a usual place of health care is based on the question, "Is there a place that [child's name] USUALLY goes when [he/she] is sick or you need advice about [his/her] health?"

[b]Usual place of health care is based on the question, "What kind of place is it/what kind of place does [child's name] go to most often—clinic or health center, doctor's office or HMO, hospital emergency room, hospital outpatient department or some other place?"

[c]Unknowns for the columns are not included in the frequencies, but they are included in the "all children under 18 years" column.

[d]Total includes other races not shown separately and children with unknown family structure, parent's education, family income, poverty status, health insurance, or current health status. Additionally numbers within selected characteristics may not add to totals because of rounding.

[e]In accordance with the 1997 standards for federal data on race and Hispanic or Latino origin, the category "1 race" refers to persons who indicated only a single race group. Persons who indicated a single race other than the groups shown are included in the total for "1 race" but are not shown separately because of small sample sizes. Therefore, the frequencies for the category "1 race" will be greater than the sum of the frequencies for the specific groups shown separately. Persons of Hispanic or Latino origin may be of any race or combination of races.

[f]The category "2 or more races" refers to all persons who indicated more than one race group. Only two combinations of multiple race groups are shown because of small sample sizes for other combinations. Therefore, the frequencies for the category "2 or more races" will be greater than the sum of the frequencies for the specific combinations shown separately.

[g]Persons of Hispanic or Latino origin may be of any race or combination of races. Similarly, the category "not Hispanic or Latino" refers to all persons who are not of Hispanic or Latino origin, regardless of race.

[h]Family structure refers to parents living in the household. "Mother and father" can include biological, adoptive, step, in-law, or foster relationships. Legal guardians are classified in "neither mother nor father".

[i]Parent's education is the education level of the parent with the higher level of education, regardless of that parent's age.

[j]GED is General Educational Development high school equivalency diploma.

[k]The categories "less than $20,000" and "$20,000 or more" include both persons reporting dollar amounts and persons reporting only that their incomes were within one of these two categories. The indented categories include only those persons who reported dollar amounts.

[l]Poverty status is based on family income and family size using the Census Bureau's poverty thresholds for the previous calendar year. "Poor" persons are defined as below the poverty threshold. "Near poor" persons have incomes of 100% to less than 200% of the poverty threshold. "Not poor" persons have incomes that are 200% of the poverty threshold or greater.

[m]Classification of health insurance coverage is based on a hierarchy of mutually exclusive categories. Persons with more than one type of health insurance were assigned to the first appropriate category in the hierarchy. Persons under age 65 years and those aged 65 years and over were classified separately because of the prominence of Medicare coverage in the older population. The category "private" includes persons who had any type of private coverage either alone or in combination with other coverage. For example, for persons aged 65 years and over, "private" includes persons with only private or private in combination with Medicare. The category "uninsured" includes persons who had no coverage as well as those who had only Indian Health Service coverage or had only a private plan that paid for one type of service such as accidents or dental care.

[n]MSA is metropolitan statistical area. Large MSAs have a population size of 1,000,000 or more; small MSAs have a population size of less than 1,000,000. "Not in MSA" consists of persons not living in a metropolitan statistical area.

SOURCE: Barbara Bloom and Robin Cohen, "Table 11. Frequencies of Having a Usual Place of Health Care and Frequency Distributions of Usual Place of Health Care for Children with a Usual Place of Health Care for Children under 18 Years of Age, by Selected Characteristics: United States, 2006," in "Summary Health Statistics for U.S. Children: National Health Interview Survey, 2006," *Vital Health Stat Series*, no.10 (234), 2007, http://www.cdc.gov/nchs/data/series/sr_10/sr10_234.pdf (accessed April 16, 2008).

Having health insurance and the type of health insurance also predicted whether a child had a regular source of care. In 2006 children with no health insurance (5.3 million out of a total of 7.3 million children aged eighteen years and under, or 73%) were less likely to have a usual place for health care than children with private health insurance (41.7 million out of 42.8 million, or 98%). (See Table 1.1.)

Bloom and Cohen also find that more than twice as many children with private health insurance (35.9 million) received health care in a physician's office than children with Medicaid or other public health insurance (13.1 million). (See Table 1.1.) Children without health insurance were more likely to receive routine health care in an emergency room than were children with private or public health insurance.

In 2006, 9.5% of U.S. children had no health insurance coverage. (See Table 1.2.) Of those children who were uninsured, 13.3% lived in families with incomes of less than $20,000 per year and 16.5% lived in families with incomes ranging from $20,000 to $34,999, compared to 3% of children in households with incomes of $75,000 or more. Children from poor and near-poor families were more likely to be uninsured, have unmet medical needs, and delay seeking care because of financial barriers more frequently than children from families that were not poor. Health professionals are especially concerned about delayed or missed medical visits for children because well-child visits are not only opportunities for early detection of developmental problems and timely treatment of illnesses but also ensure that children receive the recommended schedule of immunizations.

TABLE 1.2

Age-adjusted percentages of selected measures of health care access for children under age 18, by selected characteristics, 2006

Selected characteristic	All children under 18 years	Selected measures of health care access					
		Number in thousands[d]			Percent[e]		
		Uninsured for health care[a]	Unmet medical need[b]	Delayed care due to cost[c]	Uninsured for health care[a]	Unmet medical need[b]	Delayed care due to cost[c]
Total[f] (age-adjusted)	73,492	6,921	1,792	2,942	9.5	2.4	0.4
Total[f] (crude)	73,492	6,921	1,792	2,942	9.5	2.4	0.4
Sex							
Male	37,568	3,628	963	1,511	9.7	2.6	0.4
Female	35,924	3,293	828	1,431	9.2	2.3	0.4
Age[g]							
0–4 years	20,386	1,516	455	758	7.5	2.2	3.7
5–11 years	27,830	2,624	634	1,016	9.5	2.3	3.7
12–17 years	25,276	2,782	702	1,168	11.1	2.8	4.6
Race							
1 race[h]	71,043	6,634	1,739	2,832	9.4	2.4	4.0
White	55,866	5,250	1,327	2,309	9.4	2.4	4.1
Black or African American	11,496	949	363	458	8.4	3.2	4.0
American Indian or Alaska Native	737	176	†	*18	23.7	†	*2.5
Asian	2,850	242	*38	*47	8.8	*1.4	*1.7
Native Hawaiian or other Pacific Islander	94	†	—	—	*20.6	—	—
2 or more races[i]	2,449	288	*53	*110	12.1	*2.2	*4.6
Black or African American and white	924	95	†	*40	9.5	*3.4	*4.0
American Indian or Alaska Native and white	566	137	†	*59	24.4	†	*10.3
Hispanic origin and race[j]							
Hispanic or Latino	14,815	2,850	472	704	19.9	3.2	4.8
Mexican or Mexican American	10,125	2,251	329	510	23.1	3.3	5.2
Not Hispanic or Latino	58,677	4,071	1,319	2,238	7.0	2.2	3.8
White, single race	42,454	2,633	895	1,686	6.2	2.1	3.9
Black or African American, single race	10,914	836	346	412	7.8	3.2	3.8
Family structure[k]							
Mother and father	51,768	4,664	972	1,769	9.1	1.9	3.4
Mother, no father	17,065	1,645	686	948	9.7	4.0	5.5
Father, no mother	2,469	311	*68	152	12.8	*3.5	6.7
Neither mother nor father	2,190	302	67	73	13.5	2.7	3.3
Parent's education[l]							
Less than high school diploma	9,762	2,074	337	479	21.4	3.5	4.9
High school diploma or GED[m]	16,126	1,896	497	754	11.9	3.1	4.7
More than high school	43,531	2,502	853	1,611	5.8	2.0	3.7
Family income[n]							
Less than $20,000	12,417	1,593	461	545	13.3	3.8	4.5
$20,000 or more	55,513	4,829	1,192	2,247	8.7	2.1	4.0
$20,000–$34,999	9,747	1,590	429	746	16.5	4.4	7.7
$35,000–$54,999	10,253	1,261	321	622	12.4	3.1	6.0
$55,000–$74,999	7,762	518	120	247	6.6	1.5	3.1
$75,000 or more	16,868	510	*129	360	3.0	*0.8	2.1
Poverty status[o]							
Poor	10,539	1,365	394	550	13.4	3.9	5.3
Near poor	12,379	2,052	537	920	16.8	4.4	7.5
Not poor	30,977	1,560	440	941	5.0	1.4	3.0
Health insurance coverage[p]							
Private	43,283	—	548	1,021	—	1.3	2.3
Medicaid or other public	21,027	—	368	708	—	1.9	3.5
Other	1,673	—	†	*32	—	†	*1.9
Uninsured	6,921	6,921	862	1,169	100.0	12.4	16.9
Place of residence							
Large MSA[q]	38,266	3,529	941	1,484	9.3	2.5	3.9
Small MSA[q]	22,965	2,094	539	887	9.2	2.4	3.9
Not in MSA[q]	12,261	1,299	312	572	10.6	2.5	4.6

According to Bloom and Cohen, there was significant geographic variation in insurance status, which was strongly linked to children's access to health care services. The percentage of children in the South (12.8%) and West (11.6%) who were uninsured in 2006 was nearly 50% higher than the percentage of uninsured

TABLE 1.2

Age-adjusted percentages of selected measures of health care access for children under age 18, by selected characteristics, 2006

[CONTINUED]

		Selected measures of health care access					
Selected characteristic	All children under 18 years	Uninsured for health care[a]	Unmet medical need[b]	Delayed care due to cost[c]	Uninsured for health care[a]	Unmet medical need[b]	Delayed care due to cost[c]
		Number in thousands[d]			Percent[e]		
Region							
Northeast	13,208	568	170	276	4.3	1.3	2.1
Midwest	16,757	1,044	295	704	6.3	1.8	4.2
South	27,069	3,421	878	1,221	12.8	3.2	4.5
West	16,459	1,889	449	742	11.6	2.7	4.5
Current health status							
Excellent or very good	59,370	5,172	1,199	2,079	8.8	2.0	3.5
Good	12,581	1,619	481	726	12.9	3.8	5.7
Fair or poor	1,407	125	107	133	8.8	7.6	9.5

[†]Estimates with a relative standard error greater than 50% are indicated with a dagger, but data are not shown.
[*]Estimates preceded by an asterisk have a relative standard error of greater than 30% and less than or equal to 50% and should be used with caution as they do not meet the standards of reliability or precision.
—Quantity zero.
[a]Uninsured for health care is based on the following question in the family core section of the survey: "[Are you/is anyone] covered by health insurance or some other kind of health care plan?"
[b]Unmet medical need is based on the following question in the family core section of the survey: "DURING THE PAST 12 MONTHS, was there any time when [you/someone in the family] needed medical care, but did not get it because [you/the family] couldn't afford it?"
[c]Delayed health care due to cost is based on the following question in the family core section of the survey: "DURING THE PAST 12 MONTHS, [have/has] [you/anyone in the family] delayed seeking medical care because of worry about the cost?"
[d]Unknowns for the columns are not included in the frequencies, but they are included in the "all children under 18 years" column.
[e]Unknowns for the column variables are not included in the denominators when calculating percentages.
[f]Total includes other races not shown separately and children with unknown family structure, parent's education, family income, poverty status, health insurance, or current health status. Additionally, numbers within selected characteristics may not add to totals because of rounding.
[g]Estimates for age groups are not age adjusted.
[h]In accordance with the 1997 standards for federal data on race and Hispanic or Latino origin, the category "1 race" refers to persons who indicated only a single race group. Persons who indicated a single race other than the groups shown are included in the total for "1 race" but are not shown separately because of small sample sizes. Therefore, the frequencies for the category "I race" will be greater than the sum of the frequencies for the specific groups shown separately. Persons of Hispanic or Latino origin may be of any race or combination of races.
[i]The category "2 or more races" refers to all persons who indicated more than one race group. Only two combinations of multiple race groups are shown be cause of small sample sizes for other combinations. Therefore, the frequencies for the category "2 or more races" will be greater than the sum of the frequencies for the specific combinations shown separately.
[j]Persons of Hispanic or Latino origin may be of any race or combination of races. Similarly, the category "not Hispanic or Latino" refers to all persons who are not of Hispanic or Latino origin, regardless of race. The tables in this report use the complete new Office of Management and Budget race and Hispanic origin terms.
[k]Family structure refers to parents living in the household. "Mother and father" can include biological, adoptive, step, in-law, or foster relationships. Legal guardians are classified in "neither mother nor father."
[l]Parent's education is the education level of the parent with the higher level of education, regardless of that parent's age.
[m]GED is General Educational Development high school equivalency diploma.
[n]The categories "less than $20,000" and "$20,000 or more" include both persons reporting dollar amounts and persons reporting only that their incomes were within one of these two categories. The indented categories include only those persons who reported dollar amounts.
[o]Poverty status is based on family income and family size using the Census Bureau's poverty thresholds for the previous calendar year. "Poor" persons are defined as below the poverty threshold. "Near poor" persons have incomes of 100% to less than 200% of the poverty threshold. "Not poor" persons have incomes that are 200% of the poverty threshold or greater.
[p]Classification of health insurance coverage is based on a hierarchy of mutually exclusive categories. Persons with more than one type of health insurance were assigned to the first appropriate category in the hierarchy. Persons under age 65 years and those aged 65 years and over were classified separately because of the prominence of Medicare coverage in the older population. The category "Private" includes persons who had any type of private coverage either alone or in combination with other coverage. For example, for persons aged 65 years and over, "Private" includes persons with only private or private in combination with Medicare. The category "Uninsured" includes persons who had no coverage as well as those who had only Indian Health Service coverage or had only a private plan that paid for one type of service such as accidents or dental care.
[q]MSA is metropolitan statistical area. Large MSAs have a population size of 1,000,000 or more; small MSAs have a population size of less than 1,000,000. "Not in MSA" consists of persons not living in a metropolitan statistical area.
Note: Data are based on household interviews of a sample of the civilian noninstitutionalized population.

SOURCE: Barbara Bloom and Robin Cohen, "Table 15. Frequencies and Age-Adjusted Percentages (with Standard Errors) of Selected Measures of Health Care Access for Children under 18 Years of Age, by Selected Characteristics: United States, 2006," in "Summary Health Statistics for U.S. Children: National Health Interview Survey, 2006," *Vital Health Stat Series*, no.10 (234), 2007, http://www.cdc.gov/nchs/data/series/sr_10/sr10_234.pdf (accessed April 16, 2008)

children in the Midwest (6.3%) and the Northeast (4.3%). (See Table 1.2.)

How to Reduce Disparities in Access to Care

Health care researchers believe many factors contribute to differences in access, including cultural perceptions and beliefs about health and illness, patient preferences, availability of services, and provider bias. They recommend special efforts to inform and educate minority health care consumers and increased understanding and sensitivity among practitioners and other providers of care. Besides factual information, minority consumers must overcome the belief that they are at a disadvantage because of their race or ethnicity. Along with action to dispel barriers to access, educating practitioners, policy makers, and consumers can help reduce the perception of disadvantage.

For decades, health care researchers have documented sharp differences in the ability of ethnic and racial groups to access medical services. The federal government has repeatedly called for an end to these disparities. Even though some observers believe universal health insurance coverage is an important first step in eliminating disparities, there is widespread concern that the challenge is more complicated and calls for additional analysis and action.

In "The Challenge of Eliminating Disparities in Health" (*Journal of General Internal Medicine*, vol. 17, no. 6, June 2002), Judy Ann Bigby asserts that "eliminating racial disparities ... requires an understanding of the ecology of health, the interconnectedness of biologic, behavioral, physical, and socioenvironmental factors that determine health." Bigby believes that a multifaceted approach must be used to address the many issues involved in access, including improving the physical environment, overcoming economic and social barriers, ensuring the availability of effective health services, and acting to reduce personal behavioral risk factors such as smoking, obesity, poor nutrition, substance abuse, and physical inactivity. Developing strategies to promote personal, institutional, and community change simultaneously may stimulate the sweeping reforms needed to reduce and ultimately eliminate disparities.

Managed care refers to a system of health payment or delivery in which the plan attempts to control or coordinate use of health services by its enrolled members to contain health expenditures, improve quality, or both. Research supported by the Agency for Healthcare Research and Quality (AHQR), the lead federal agency charged with improving the quality, safety, efficiency, and effectiveness of health care, suggests that managed care, with its emphasis on preventive health services, may improve ethnic disparities in access for Hispanics and whites but not for African-Americans or Asians and Pacific Islanders. Jennifer S. Haas et al. analyze in "Effect of Managed Care Insurance on the Use of Preventive Care for Specific Ethnic Groups in the United States" (*Medical Care*, vol. 40, no. 9, September 2002) data about preventive health care use by people enrolled in fee-for-service and managed care plans from the AHRQ Medical Expenditure Panel Survey of noninstitutionalized U.S. civilians.

Haas et al. consider the use of four preventive health screenings: mammography within the past two years for women aged fifty to seventy-five, breast examination, Pap smear (screening for cervical cancer) within the past two years for women aged eighteen and sixty-five, and cholesterol screening within the past five years for men and women above age twenty. Their analysis reveals that Hispanic and white women enrolled in managed care plans reported higher rates of mammography, breast exam, and Pap smear than Hispanic women with fee-for-service insurance. There were no significant differences in access to preventive care for African-Americans or Asians and Pacific Islanders by type of insurance. Haas et al. theorize

that managed care may improve access to a usual source of care for Hispanics, who are more likely to lack a usual source of care than whites.

AHRQ Report Documents Disparities in Access

In July 2003 the AHRQ released its first *National Healthcare Disparities Report* (http://www.ahrq.gov/qual/nhdr03/nhdr2003.pdf), a report requested by Congress that documented racial health disparities including access to care. Among other things, the report cited the finding that African-Americans and low-income Americans have higher mortality rates for cancer than the general population because they are less likely to receive screening tests for certain forms of the disease and other preventive services. Even though the report asserted that differential access may lead to disparities in quality and observed that opportunities to provide preventive care are often missed, it conceded that knowledge about why disparities exist is limited.

The AHRQ report generated fiery debate in the health care community and among legislators and painted a rather bleak view of disparities. The report called for detailed data to support quality improvement initiatives and observed that "community-based participatory research has numerous examples of communities working to improve quality overall, while reducing healthcare disparities for vulnerable populations."

Highlights from the *National Healthcare Disparities Report 2007*

In *National Healthcare Disparities Report 2007* (February 2008, http://www.ahrq.gov/qual/nhdr07/nhdr07.pdf), the AHRQ tracks the measures of access to care that the first report, *National Healthcare Disparities Report*, identified. These measures include factors that facilitated access, such as having a primary care provider, and factors that were barriers to access, such as having no health insurance. The AHRQ's principal findings are:

• Disparities in access persist. The AHRQ notes that disparities related to race, ethnicity, and socioeconomic status still exist in terms of access to the health care system. Table 1.3 shows the factors that account for disparities in access among members of racial and ethnic minorities, and Table 1.4 shows how socioeconomic variables—income, education, and insurance status—serve to enable or deter access. For example, African-Americans, Native Americans, Hispanics, and Alaskan Natives continued to experience worse access to care than whites, and poor people and those without insurance had less access to care than those with higher incomes. (See Table 1.3 and Table 1.4.) For Hispanics, all disparities in access—except one that related to patients' own perceptions of difficulties or delays in obtaining health care—were found to have worsened.

TABLE 1.3

Racial and ethnic differences in factors that influence access to care, 2005

Core report measure	Racial difference[a]					Ethnic difference[b]
	Black	Asian	NHOPI	AI/AN	> 1 Race	Hispanic
Health insurance coverage						
Persons under 65 with health insurance	↓	=	=	↓	=	↓
Persons uninsured all year	=	=	=	↓	=	↓
Usual source of care						
Persons who have a specific source of ongoing care	↓	=	↓	=	=	↓
Persons who have a usual primary care provider	↓	=	=	=	=	↓
Patient perceptions of need						
People who experience difficulties or delays in obtaining health care or do not receive needed care	=	↑		=	↓	↑
People who experience difficulties or delays in obtaining health care due to financial or insurance reasons	=	=			↓	↓

[a]Compared with whites.
[b]Compared with non-Hispanic whites.
NHOPI = Native Hawaiian or other Pacific Islander; AI/AN = American Indian or Alaska Native.

Key to symbols
= Group and comparison group have about same access to health care.
↑ Group has better access to health care than the comparison group.
↓ Group has worse access to health care than the comparison group.
Blank cell: Reliable estimate for group could not be made.

SOURCE: "Table 3.1a. Racial and Ethnic Differences in Facilitators and Barriers to Health Care," in *National Healthcare Disparities Report 2007*, U.S. Department of Health and Human Services, Agency for Healthcare Research and Quality, February 2008, http://www.ahrq.gov/qual/nhdr07/nhdr07.pdf (accessed April 16, 2008)

TABLE 1.4

Socioeconomic factors that influence access to health care, 2005

Core report measure	Income difference[a]			Educational difference[b]		Insurance difference[c]
	<100%	100–199%	200–399%	<HS	HS grad	Uninsured
Health insurance coverage						
Persons under 65 with health insurance	↓	↓	↑	↓	↓	
Persons uninsured all year	↓	↓	↑	↓	↓	
Usual source of care						
Persons who have a specific source of ongoing care	↓	↓	↑	↓	↓	↓
Persons who have a usual primary care provider	↓	↓	↑	↓	↓	↓
Patient perceptions of need						
People who experience difficulties or delays in obtaining health care or do not receive needed care	↓	↓	↑	↓	↓	↓

[a]Compared with persons with family incomes 400% of federal poverty thresholds or above.
[b]Compared with persons with any college education.
[c]Compared with persons under 65 with any private health insurance.
HS=High school.

Key to Symbols
=Group and comparison group have about same access to health care.
↑Group has better access to health care than the comparison group.
↓ Group has worse access to health care than the comparison group.
Blank cell: Reliable estimate for group could not be made.

SOURCE: "Table 3.1b. Socioeconomic Differences in Facilitators and Barriers to Health Care," in *National Healthcare Disparities Report 2007*, U.S. Department of Health and Human Services, Agency for Healthcare Research and Quality, February 2008, http://www.ahrq.gov/qual/nhdr07/nhdr07.pdf (accessed April 16, 2008)

- Even though some disparities are diminishing, many groups continue to face disparities in access. Socioeconomic status accounts for some differences in health insurance coverage of racial and ethnic groups but not all. Hispanics of every income and educational level remained less likely than their non-Hispanic peers to have health insurance. African-Americans, Native Americans, and Alaskan Natives who had attended college were much less likely than whites who had attended college to have health insurance.

- No group had attained the goal of 100% of Americans covered by health insurance set forth in *Healthy People 2010* (2000, http://www.healthypeople.gov/document/tableofcontents.htm), the set of national health objectives that aim to identify and reduce the most significant preventable threats to health.

ACCESS TO MENTAL HEALTH CARE

Besides the range of barriers to access faced by all Americans trying to access the health care system, people seeking mental health care face unique challenges, not the least of which is that they are even less able than people in good mental health to successfully navigate the fragmented mental health service delivery system. Furthermore, because people with serious mental illness frequently suffer from unemployment and disability, they are likely to join the ranks of the impoverished, uninsured, and homeless, which only compounds access problems. Finally, the social stigmas (deeply held negative attitudes) that promote discrimination against people with mental illness are a powerful deterrent to seeking care.

The social stigmas attached to being labeled "crazy" prevent some sufferers of mental illness from seeking and obtaining needed care. Myths about mental illness persist, especially the mistaken beliefs that mental illness is a sign of moral weakness or that an affected individual can simply choose to "wish or will away" the symptoms of mental illness. People with mental illness cannot just "pull themselves together" and will themselves well. Without treatment, symptoms can worsen and persist for months or even years.

Besides reluctance to seek care, social stigmas can have far-reaching consequences for people with mental illnesses. They may face discrimination in the workplace, in school, and in efforts to find housing. Thwarted in their efforts to maintain independence, people suffering from mental illness may become trapped in a cycle characterized by feelings of worthlessness and hopelessness and may be further isolated from the social and community supports and treatments most able to help them recover.

The President's New Freedom Commission on Mental Health describes in *Achieving the Promise: Transforming Mental Health Care in America* (2003, http://www.mentalhealthcommission.gov/reports/Finalreport/FullReport.htm) problems in the delivery of mental health care and six overarching goals related to access to mental health services. (See Table 1.5.) For example, achievement of the first goal, to improve Americans' understanding that mental health is vital for overall health, would doubtless improve access by reducing the stigmas associated with seeking treatment for mental illness. The second goal, of delivering family and consumer-driven care, would also act to improve access by

TABLE 1.5

Goals and recommendations from the President's New Freedom Commission on Mental Health for improving the mental health care system, 2003

Goal 1	Americans understand that mental health is essential to overall health.		
	Recommendations	1.1	Advance and implement a national campaign to reduce the stigma of seeking care and a national strategy for suicide prevention.
		1.2	Address mental health with the same urgency as physical health.
Goal 2	Mental health care is consumer and family driven.		
	Recommendations	2.1	Develop an individualized plan of care for every adult with a serious mental illness and child with a serious emotional disturbance.
		2.2	Involve consumers and families fully in orienting the mental health system toward recovery.
		2.3	Align relevant federal programs to improve access and accountability for mental health services.
		2.4	Create a comprehensive state mental health plan.
		2.5	Protect and enhance the rights of people with mental illnesses.
Goal 3	Disparities in mental health services are eliminated.		
	Recommendations	3.1	Improve access to quality care that is culturally competent.
		3.2	Improve access to quality care in rural and geographically remote areas.
Goal 4	Early mental health screening, assessment, and referral to services are common practice.		
	Recommendations	4.1	Promote the mental health of young children.
		4.2	Improve and expand school mental health programs.
		4.3	Screen for co-occurring mental and substance use disorders and link with integrated treatment strategies.
		4.4	Screen for mental disorders in primary health care, across the life span, and connect to treatment and supports.
Goal 5	Excellent mental health care is delivered and research is accelerated.		
	Recommendations	5.1	Accelerate research to promote recovery and resilience, and ultimately to cure and prevent mental illnesses.
		5.2	Advance evidence-based practices using dissemination and demonstration projects and create a public-private partnership to guide their implementation.
		5.3	Improve and expand the workforce providing evidence-based mental health services and supports.
		5.4	Develop the knowledge base in four understudied areas: mental health disparities, long-term effects of medications, trauma, and acute care.

offering care that is more acceptable to consumers and less likely to infringe on the rights of people with mental illnesses. Goals 3 and 6—eliminating disparities in mental health services and using technology to reach underserved populations—are clear moves to improve access. Goals 4 and 5 address the quality and effectiveness of mental health care; however, they, too, directly affect access by improving screening and detection of mental

TABLE 1.5

Goals and recommendations from the President's New Freedom Commission on Mental Health for improving the mental health care system, 2003 [CONTINUED]

Goal 6	Technology is used to access mental health care and information.	
Recommendations	6.1	Use health technology and telehealth to improve access and coordination of mental health care, especially for Americans in remote areas or in underserved populations.
	6.2	Develop and implement integrated electronic health record and personal health information systems.

SOURCE: "Goals and Recommendations in a Transformed Mental Health System," in *Achieving the Promise: Transforming Mental Health Care in America*, President's New Freedom Commission on Mental Health, 2003, http://www.mentalhealthcommission.gov/reports/Finalreport/FullReport.htm (accessed April 16, 2008)

illness and by expanding the workforce that provides mental health and support services.

Disparities in Access to Mental Health Care

The principal barriers to access of mental health care are the cost of services, the fragmented organization of these services, and the social stigmas toward mental illness. These obstacles may act as deterrents for all Americans, but for racial and ethnic minorities they are compounded by language barriers, ethnic and cultural compatibility of practitioners, and geographic availability of services.

The AHRQ finds in *National Healthcare Disparities Report 2007* that when compared to whites, minorities have less access to care and are less likely to receive needed services. The proportion of African-Americans, Hispanics, and Asian-Americans that received outpatient mental health care in 2005 was lower than whites; lower among the poor and near poor than the middle incomes; and increased with educational attainment. Some of these differences may be attributable to cultural attitudes toward mental health.

Education and income explain some but not all the racial and ethnic differences in access. According to the AHRQ, across all levels of income and education, Hispanics were less likely than non-Hispanic whites to have received mental health care in 2005, 7.8% compared to 15.1%. African-Americans with higher incomes and educational attainment were less likely to have received care than whites with comparable socioeconomic status, but the gap closes among the poor and people with less than a high school education.

IS ACCESS A RIGHT OR A PRIVILEGE?

The AHRQ and other health care researchers and policy makers observe that having health insurance does not necessarily ensure access to medical care. They contend that many other factors, including cost-containment measures put in place by private and public payers, have reduced access to care. Nonetheless, reduced access affects vulnerable populations—the poor, people with mental illness and other disabilities, and immigrants—more than others.

Health care is a resource that is rationed. In the United States and other countries without universal or national programs of health insurance, people with greater incomes and assets are more likely than low-income families to have health insurance and as a result have greater access to health care services.

A wide range of groups and organizations support the idea that health care is a fundamental human right, rather than a privilege. These organizations include Physicians for a National Health Program, the American Association of Retired Persons, National Health Care for the Homeless, Inc., and the Friends Committee on National Legislation, a Quaker public interest lobby.

Americans Are Worried about Access to Care

The Mayo Clinic Health Policy Center reports in "Health Care Reform Survey: Costs Are Top Worry" (March 10, 2008, http://www.mayoclinic.org/news2008-rst/4698.html) that in 2007 Americans were pessimistic about the likelihood that reforms to improve the health care system will occur in the coming decade. Less than half (43%) of the survey respondents said they were satisfied, very satisfied, or completely satisfied with the U.S. health care system, and the majority (80%) felt it was vitally important to improve health care quality and reduce health care costs.

According to the center, costs were the most pressing concern of health care consumers in 2007. Ninety-one percent of respondents felt that costs were excessively high. Access was identified as the second-most pressing concern by 24% of respondents. More than two-thirds of respondents called for improved access to health information and services. They want the freedom to choose their own physicians, hospitals, and insurance plans. Respondents without insurance were more likely to give failing ratings to the health care system's ability to ensure coordination of care, access, and value.

CHAPTER 2
HEALTH CARE PRACTITIONERS

The art of medicine consists of amusing the patient while nature cures the disease.

—Voltaire

One of the first duties of the physician is to educate the masses not to take medicine.

—William Osler, *Sir William Osler: Aphorisms, from His Bedside Teachings and Writings* (1950)

PHYSICIANS

Physicians routinely perform medical examinations, provide preventive medicine services, diagnose illness, treat patients suffering from injury or disease, and offer counsel about how to achieve and maintain good health. There are two types of physicians trained in traditional Western medicine: the Doctor of Medicine (MD) is schooled in allopathic medicine and the Doctor of Osteopathy (DO) learns osteopathy. Allopathy is the philosophy and system of curing disease by producing conditions that are incompatible with disease, such as prescribing antibiotics to combat bacterial infection. The philosophy of osteopathy is different; it is based on recognition of the body's capacity for self-healing, and it emphasizes structural and manipulative therapies such as postural education, manual treatment of the musculoskeletal system (osteopathic physicians are trained in hands-on diagnosis and treatment), and preventive medicine. Osteopathy is also considered a holistic practice because it considers the whole person, rather than simply the diseased organ or system.

In modern medical practice, the philosophical differences may not be obvious to most health care consumers because MDs and DOs use many comparable methods of treatment, including prescribing medication and performing surgery. In fact, the American Osteopathic Association (2008, http://www.osteopathic.org/index.cfm?PageID=aoa_main), the national medical professional society that represents more than sixty-one thousand DOs, admits that many people who seek care from osteopathic physicians

may be entirely unaware of their physician's training, which emphasizes holistic interventions or special skills such as manipulative techniques. Like MDs, DOs complete four years of medical school and postgraduate residency training; may specialize in areas such as surgery, psychiatry, or obstetrics; and must pass state licensing examinations to practice.

Medical School, Postgraduate Training, and Qualifications

Modern medicine requires considerable skill and extensive training. The road to gaining admission to medical school and becoming a physician is long, difficult, and intensely competitive. Medical school applicants must earn excellent college grades, achieve high scores on entrance exams, and demonstrate emotional maturity and motivation to be admitted to medical school. Once admitted, medical students spend the first two years primarily in laboratories and classrooms learning basic medical sciences such as anatomy (detailed understanding of body structure), physiology (biological processes and vital functions), and biochemistry. They also learn how to take medical histories, perform complete physical examinations, and recognize symptoms of diseases. During their third and fourth years, the medical students work under supervision at teaching hospitals and clinics. By completing clerkships—spending time in different specialties such as internal medicine, obstetrics and gynecology, pediatrics, psychiatry, and surgery— they acquire the necessary skills and gain experience to diagnose and treat a wide variety of illnesses.

Following medical school, new physicians must complete a year of internship, also referred to as postgraduate year one, that emphasizes either general medical practice or one specific specialty and provides clinical experience in various hospital services (e.g., inpatient care, outpatient clinics, emergency rooms, and operating rooms). In the past, many physicians entered practice after this first year of postgraduate training. In the present era of specialization, most physicians choose to continue in residency training, which lasts an additional three to six years, depending on the specialty. Those who choose a subspecialty such as cardiology, infectious diseases, oncology, or plastic surgery must spend additional years in residency and may then choose to complete fellowship training. Immediately after residency, they are eligible to take an examination to earn board certification in their chosen specialty. Fellowship training involves a year or two of laboratory and clinical research work as well as opportunities to gain additional clinical and patient care expertise.

Medical School Applicants

According to the Association of American Medical Colleges (AAMC; September 25, 2007, http://www.aamc.org/newsroom/pressrel/2007/071016.htm), the number of students entering medical school for the 2006–07 academic year was the largest ever—a 2.3% increase from the previous year—with 17,759 first-year students matriculated. The students were selected from a pool of 42,315 applicants. Applications from African-Americans and Hispanics rose by 9.2%.

Conventional and Newer Medical Specialties

Rapid advances in science and medicine and changing needs have resulted in a variety of new medical and surgical specialties, subspecialties, and concentrations. For example, geriatrics, the medical subspecialty concerned with the prevention and treatment of diseases in older adults, has developed in response to growth in this population. In 1909 Ignatz L. Nascher (1863–1944) coined the term *geriatrics* from the Greek *geras* (old age) and *iatrikos* (physician). Geriatricians are physicians trained in internal medicine or family practice who obtain additional training and certification in the diagnosis and treatment of older adults. According to the American Geriatrics Society (AGS; 2008, http://www.americangeriatrics.org/news/geria_faqs.shtml), the United States needs more geriatricians to care for its growing population of older adults. In 2008 there were only 7,590 board-certified geriatricians (one for every 2,500 Americans seventy-five and older) and 1,657 geropsychiatrists (one for every 11,451 Americans seventy-five and older). The AGS forecasts that this ratio will decrease by 2030 to one geriatrician for every 4,254 Americans seventy-five and older and one geropsychiatrist for every 20,195 Americans seventy-five or older.

Another relatively new medical specialty has resulted in physician intensivists. Intensivists, as the name indicates, are trained to staff hospital intensive care units (ICUs, which are sometimes known as critical care units), where the most critically ill patients are cared for using a comprehensive array of state-of-the-art technology and equipment. This specialty arose in response to both the increasing complexity of care provided in ICUs and the demonstrated benefits of immediate availability of highly trained physicians to care for critically ill patients. The Health Resources and Service Administration (HRSA) notes in *The Critical Care Workforce: A Study of the Supply and Demand for Critical Care Physicians* (May 6, 2006, ftp://ftp.hrsa.gov/bhpr/nationalcenter/criticalcare.pdf) that the demand for intensivists will likely fail to meet the demands of the aging population in the United States by 2020. The HRSA predicts a shortfall of forty-three hundred intensivists in 2020. According to the article "U.S. Predicts Shortage of Intensivists" (*California Healthline*, May 23, 2006), the Critical Care Workforce Partnership (an alliance of medical societies) advocates increasing medical school capacity to train intensivists and asserts that increasing the supply of intensivists could help save as many as fifty-four thousand lives per year.

The fastest-growing new specialty is hospitalists, physicians who are hospital based as opposed to office based and who provide a variety of services from caring for hospitalized patients who do not have personal physicians to explaining complex medical procedures to patients and families and coordinating many aspects of inpatient care. Robert M. Wachter reports in "The State of Hospital Medicine in 2008" (*Medical Clinics of North America*, vol. 92, no. 2, March 2008) that there were twenty thousand hospitalists in the United States in 2006 and their ranks are expected to grow in coming years. Wachter opines "that hospitalists have quickly become indispensable to their patients, their hospitals, and to the health care system as a whole. There are no indications that the situation is likely to change in the future."

More traditional medical specialties include:

- Anesthesiologist—administers anesthesia (partial or complete loss of sensation) and monitors patients in surgery

- Cardiologist—diagnoses and treats diseases of the heart and blood vessels

- Dermatologist—trained to diagnose and treat diseases of the skin, hair, and nails

- Family practitioner—delivers primary care to people of all ages and, when necessary, refers patients to other physician specialists

- Gastroenterologist—specializes in digestive system disorders

- Internist—provides diagnosis and nonsurgical treatment of a broad array of illnesses affecting adults

- Neurologist—specializes in the nervous system and provides diagnosis and treatment of brain, spinal cord, and nerve disorders

- Obstetrician-gynecologist—provides health care for women and their reproductive systems, as well as care for mothers and babies before, during, and immediately following delivery

- Oncologist—dedicated to the diagnosis and treatment of cancer

- Otolaryngologist—skilled in the medical and surgical treatment of ear, nose, and throat disorders and related structures of the face, head, and neck

- Pathologist—uses skills in microscopic chemical analysis and diagnostics to detect disease in body tissues and fluids

- Psychiatrist—specializes in the prevention, diagnosis, and treatment of mental health and emotional disorders

- Pulmonologist—specializes in diseases of the lungs and respiratory system

- Urologist—provides diagnosis as well as medical and surgical treatment of the urinary tract in both men and women as well as male reproductive health services

HIGH COSTS, LONG HOURS, AND LOW WAGES. According to the AAMC (2008, http://services.aamc.org/tsfreports/report_median.cfm?year_of_study=2008), the medical school tuition and fees during the 2007–08 academic year were $22,199 for in-state residents at public schools and $39,964 for students at private schools. The AAMC indicates in "With Debt on the Rise, Students and Schools Face an Uphill Battle" (*AAMC Reporter*, January 2008) that medical school students graduating in 2006 had incurred a median debt comparable to a home mortgage—an average of $130,000. Even though a physician's earning power is considerable, and many students are able to repay their debts during their first years of practice, some observers believe the extent of medical students' indebtedness may unduly influence their career choices. They may train for higher-paying specialties and subspecialties rather than follow their natural interests or opt to practice in underrepresented specialties or underserved geographic areas. The high cost of medical education is also believed to limit the number of minority applicants to medical school.

Historically, medical training has been difficult and involved long hours. Fiona McDonald notes in "Working to Death: The Regulation of Working Hours in Health Care" (*Law and Policy*, vol. 1, no. 1, January 2008) that residents typically work twenty-four- to thirty-six-hour shifts and more than eighty hours per week. Lack of sleep and low wages are a way of life for most medical students and residents, although the thirty-six-hour shift has come under criticism as an unnecessary, and possibly dangerous, practice. In 1995 New York State limited most residents to twenty-four-hour shifts and eighty-hour weeks. The regulations were the first of their kind in the country.

In 2003 the Accreditation Council for Graduate Medical Education, which oversees thousands of residency programs every year, adopted guidelines that limited duty hours to eighty hours per week (surgical programs were permitted to have residents work eighty-eight hours per week) for the nation's one hundred thousand physicians-in-training. In "Adapting to Duty-Hour Limits—Four Years On" (*New England Journal of Medicine*, vol. 356, no. 26, June 28, 2007), Harry H. Yoon reports that many medical residency programs have had to refashion or overhaul their programs to comply with the new standards.

The Number of Physicians in Practice Is Increasing

In 2005, of the 902,053 physicians in the United States, 300,022 were primary care physicians. (See Table 2.1.) Primary care physicians are the front line of the health care system—the first health professionals most people see for medical problems or routine care. Family practitioners, internists, pediatricians, obstetrician/gynecologists, and general practitioners are considered to be primary care physicians. Primary care physicians tend to see the same patients regularly and develop relationships with patients over time as they offer preventive services, scheduled visits, follow-up, and urgent medical care. When necessary, they refer patients for consultation with, and care from, physician specialists.

In 2005, 563,225 physicians maintained office-based practices; 155,248 were in hospital-based practices; and 95,391 physicians were residents and interns. (See Table 2.2.) Besides the growing number of graduates of U.S. medical schools, the ranks of international medical graduates grew by 46,334, from 144,306 in 1995 to 190,640 in 2005.

The number of active physicians devoted to patient care, as opposed to research, administration, or other roles, varies by geographic region and by state, from a high of 38.4 physicians per 10,000 civilian population in Massachusetts in 2005 to a low of 15.7 physicians per 10,000 people in Oklahoma. (See Table 2.3.) New England has the most physicians devoted to patient care per 10,000 population (33.4), whereas the West South Central and Mountain divisions have the fewest, 19.5 and 20, respectively.

Working Conditions

Many physicians work long, irregular hours. The Bureau of Labor Statistics (BLS; December 18, 2007, http://www.bls.gov/oco/ocos074.htm) reports that in 2006 more than one-third of full-time physicians worked sixty hours or more per week performing patient care and administrative duties such as office management. Physicians and surgeons held about 633,000 jobs in 2006, and 15% were self-employed. About 50% of physicians held salaried positions, and 18% were employed by private hospitals. Physicians in salaried positions, such as those employed by health maintenance organizations, usually have shorter and more regular hours and enjoy more flexible work schedules than those in private practice. Instead of working as solo practitioners, growing numbers of physicians work in clinics or are partners in group practices or other integrated health care systems. Medical group practices allow

TABLE 2.1

Medical doctors in primary care, by specialty, selected years 1949–2005

Specialty	1949[a]	1960[a]	1970	1980	1990	1995	2000	2002	2004	2005
					Number					
Total doctors of medicine[b]	**201,277**	**260,484**	**334,028**	**467,679**	**615,421**	**720,325**	**813,770**	**853,187**	**884,974**	**902,053**
Active doctors of medicine[c]	**191,577**	**247,257**	**310,929**	**435,545**	**559,988**	**646,022**	**737,504**	**768,498**	**792,154**	**801,742**
General primary care specialists	113,222	125,359	134,354	170,705	213,514	241,329	274,653	286,294	296,495	300,022
General practice/family medicine	95,980	88,023	57,948	60,049	70,480	75,976	86,312	89,357	91,164	91,858
Internal medicine	12,453	26,209	39,924	58,462	76,295	88,240	101,353	106,499	111,800	112,934
Obstetrics/gynecology	—	—	18,532	24,612	30,220	33,519	35,922	36,810	37,779	38,285
Pediatrics	4,789	11,127	17,950	27,582	36,519	43,594	51,066	53,628	55,752	56,945
Primary care subspecialists	—	—	3,161	16,642	30,911	39,659	52,294	57,929	62,322	65,420
Family medicine	—	—	—	—	—	236	483	627	768	835
Internal medicine	—	—	1,948	13,069	22,054	26,928	34,831	38,821	41,471	43,552
Obstetrics/gynecology	—	—	344	1,693	3,477	4,133	4,319	4,228	4,280	4,315
Pediatrics	—	—	869	1,880	5,380	8,362	12,661	14,253	15,803	16,718
					Percent of active doctors of medicine					
General primary care specialist	59.1	50.7	43.2	39.2	38.1	37.4	37.2	37.3	37.4	37.4
General practice/family medicine	50.1	35.6	18.6	13.8	12.6	11.8	11.7	11.6	11.5	11.5
Internal medicine	6.5	10.6	12.8	13.4	13.6	13.7	13.7	13.9	14.1	14.1
Obstetrics/gynecology	—	—	6.0	5.7	5.4	5.2	4.9	4.8	4.8	4.8
Pediatrics	2.5	4.5	5.8	6.3	6.5	6.7	6.9	7.0	7.0	7.1
Primary care subspecialists	—	—	1.0	3.8	5.5	6.1	7.1	7.5	7.9	8.2
Family medicine	—	—	—	—	—	0.0	0.1	0.1	0.1	0.1
Internal medicine	—	—	0.6	3.0	3.9	4.2	4.7	5.1	5.2	5.4
Obstetrics/gynecology	—	—	0.1	0.4	0.6	0.6	0.6	0.6	0.5	0.5
Pediatrics	—	—	0.3	0.4	1.0	1.3	1.7	1.9	2.0	2.1

0.0 Percent greater than zero but less than 0.05.
— Data not available.
[a]Estimated by the Bureau of Health Professions, Health Resources Administration. Active doctors of medicine (M.D.s) include those with address unknown and primary specialty not classified.
[b]Includes M.D.s engaged in federal and nonfederal patient care (office-based or hospital-based) and other professional activities.
[c]Starting with 1970 data, M.D.s who are inactive, have unknown address, or primary specialty not classified are excluded.
Notes: Data are as of December 31 except for 1990–1994 data, which are as of January 1, and 1949 data, which are as of midyear. Outlying areas include Puerto Rico, the U.S. Virgin Islands, and the Pacific islands of Canton, Caroline, Guam, Mariana, Marshall, American Samoa, and Wake. Data are based on reporting by physicians.

SOURCE: "Table 108. Doctors of Medicine in Primary Care, by Specialty: United States and Outlying Areas, Selected Years 1949–2005," in *Health, United States, 2007. With Chartbook on Trends in the Health of Americans*, U.S. Department of Health and Human Services, Centers for Disease Control and Prevention, National Center for Health Statistics, 2007, http://www.cdc.gov/nchs/data/hus/hus07.pdf#listtables (accessed April 17, 2008). Data from the American Medical Association (AMA).

physicians to have more flexible schedules, to realize purchasing economies of scale, to pool their money to finance expensive medical equipment, and to be better able to adapt to changes in health care delivery, financing, and reimbursement.

Physicians' Earnings and Opportunities

Physicians' earnings are among the highest of any profession. According to the Medical Group Management Association (MGMA), in *Physician Compensation and Production Survey: 2007 Report Based on 2006 Data* (2007, http://www.mgma.com/WorkArea/showcontent.aspx?id=14288), the median annual total compensation for primary care physicians in 2006 was $171,519, and for specialists it was $322,259. The range of salaries varies widely and is often based on a physician's specialty, the number of years in practice, the hours worked, and the geographic location. The MGMA reports that in 2006 orthopedic surgeons and invasive cardiologists were among the top earners, with median annual earnings of $446,517 and $457,563, respectively, whereas pediatricians and family practitioners earned the least: $174,209 and $164,021 per year, respectively.

Physician Visits

In 2005 Americans made 963.6 million office visits to physicians. (See Table 2.4.) Women aged eighteen to forty-four visited physicians nearly twice as often as men, and, as expected, people over seventy-five years of age of both genders saw doctors more than twice as often as most younger people.

Physician Satisfaction

Changes in the health care delivery system—particularly the shift from traditional fee-for-service practice to managed care, with its efforts to standardize medical practice, which reduces physicians' ability to manage their time, schedules, and professional relationships—have been named as factors contributing to physicians' dissatisfaction with their choice of career. Other changes, including decreasing reimbursement and an ever-increasing emphasis on documentation to satisfy government and private payers, as well as administrative requirements that infringe on time physicians would rather spend caring for patients, have also increased physician dissatisfaction.

TABLE 2.2

Medical doctors by activity and place of medical education, selected years 1975–2005

Activity and place of medical education	1975	1985	1995	2000	2002	2003	2004	2005
				Number of doctors of medicine				
Doctors of medicine	393,742	552,716	720,325	813,770	853,187	871,535	884,974	902,053
Professionally active[a]	340,280	497,140	625,443	692,368	719,431	736,211	744,143	762,438
Place of medical education:								
U.S. medical graduates	—	392,007	481,137	525,691	544,779	558,167	563,118	571,798
International medical graduates[b]	—	105,133	144,306	164,437	172,770	178,044	181,025	190,640
Activity:								
Nonfederal[c]	312,089	475,573	604,364	672,987	699,249	—	—	—
Patient care[d]	287,837	431,527	564,074	631,431	658,123	691,873	700,287	718,473
Office-based practice	213,334	329,041	427,275	490,398	516,246	529,836	538,538	563,225
General and family practice	46,347	53,862	59,932	67,534	71,696	73,508	73,234	74,999
Cardiovascular diseases	5,046	9,054	13,739	16,300	16,989	17,301	17,252	17,519
Dermatology	3,442	5,325	6,959	7,969	8,282	8,477	8,651	8,795
Gastroenterology	1,696	4,135	7,300	8,515	9,044	9,326	9,430	9,742
Internal medicine	28,188	52,712	72,612	88,699	96,496	99,670	101,776	107,028
Pediatrics	12,687	22,392	33,890	42,215	46,097	47,996	49,356	51,854
Pulmonary diseases	1,166	3,035	4,964	6,095	6,672	6,919	7,072	7,321
General surgery	19,710	24,708	24,086	24,475	24,902	25,284	25,229	26,079
Obstetrics and gynecology	15,613	23,525	29,111	31,726	32,738	33,636	33,811	34,659
Ophthalmology	8,795	12,212	14,596	15,598	16,052	16,240	16,304	16,580
Orthopedic surgery	8,148	13,033	17,136	17,367	18,118	18,423	18,632	19,115
Otolaryngology	4,297	5,751	7,139	7,581	8,001	8,103	8,160	8,206
Plastic surgery	1,706	3,299	4,612	5,308	5,593	5,725	5,845	6,011
Urological surgery	5,025	7,081	7,991	8,460	8,615	8,804	8,793	8,955
Anesthesiology	8,970	15,285	23,770	27,624	28,661	29,254	29,984	31,887
Diagnostic radiology	1,978	7,735	12,751	14,622	15,896	16,403	16,828	17,618
Emergency medicine	—	—	11,700	14,541	16,907	17,727	18,961	20,173
Neurology	1,862	4,691	7,623	8,559	9,034	9,304	9,632	10,400
Pathology, anatomical/clinical	4,195	6,877	9,031	10,267	10,103	10,209	10,653	11,747
Psychiatry	12,173	18,521	23,334	24,955	25,350	25,656	25,998	27,638
Radiology	6,970	7,355	5,994	6,674	6,916	7,010	6,900	7,049
Other specialty	15,320	28,453	29,005	35,314	34,084	34,861	36,037	39,850
Hospital-based practice	74,503	102,486	136,799	141,033	141,877	162,037	161,749	155,248
Residents and interns[e]	53,527	72,159	93,650	95,125	96,547	100,033	102,563	95,391
Full-time hospital staff	20,976	30,327	43,149	45,908	45,330	62,004	59,186	59,857
Other professional activity[f]	24,252	44,046	40,290	41,556	41,126	44,338	43,856	43,965
Federal[c]	28,191	21,567	21,079	19,381	20,182	—	—	—
Patient care	24,100	17,293	18,057	15,999	16,701	—	—	—
Office-based practice	2,095	1,156	. . .	. . .	. . .	—	—	—
Hospital-based practice	22,005	16,137	18,057	15,999	16,701	—	—	—
Residents and interns	4,275	3,252	2,702	600	390	—	—	—
Full-time hospital staff	17,730	12,885	15,355	15,399	16,311	—	—	—
Other professional activity[f]	4,091	4,274	3,022	3,382	3,481	—	—	—
Inactive	21,449	38,646	72,326	75,168	84,166	84,360	92,323	99,823
Not classified	26,145	13,950	20,579	45,136	49,067	50,447	48,011	39,304
Unknown address	5,868	2,980	1,977	1,098	523	517	497	488

— Data not available.
. . . Category not applicable.
[a]Excludes inactive, not classified, and address unknown.
[b]International medical graduates received their medical education in schools outside the United States and Canada.
[c]Starting with 2003 data, separate estimates for federal and nonfederal doctors of medicine are not available.
[d]Specialty information based on the physician's self-designated primary area of practice. Categories include generalists and specialists.
[e]Starting with 1990 data, clinical fellows are included in this category. In prior years, clinical fellows were included in the other professional activity category.
[f]Includes medical teaching, administration, research, and other. Prior to 1990, this category also included clinical fellows.
Notes: Data for doctors of medicine are as of December 31, except for 1990–1994 data, which are as of January 1. Outlying areas include Puerto Rico, the U.S. Virgin Islands, and the Pacific islands of Canton, Caroline, Guam, Mariana, Marshall, American Samoa, and Wake. Data are based on reporting by physicians.

SOURCE: "Table 107. Doctors of Medicine, by Activity and Place of Medical Education: United States and Outlying U.S. Areas, Selected Years 1975–2005," in *Health, United States, 2007. With Chartbook on Trends in the Health of Americans*, U.S. Department of Health and Human Services, Centers for Disease Control and Prevention, National Center for Health Statistics, 2007, http://www.cdc.gov/nchs/data/hus/hus07.pdf#listtables (accessed April 17, 2008). Data from the American Medical Association (AMA).

Bruce E. Landon, James Reschovsky, and David Blumenthal report in "Changes in Career Satisfaction among Primary Care and Specialist Physicians, 1997–2001" (*Journal of the American Medical Association*, vol. 289, no. 4, January 22, 2003) that even though most physicians were satisfied with their careers, there was significant geographic variation in physician satisfaction.

TABLE 2.3

Active physicians in patient care, by geographic division and state, selected years 1975–2005

Geographic division and state	Total physicians[a]				Doctors of medicine in patient care[b]			
	1975	1985	1995[c]	2005[d, e]	1975	1985	1995	2005[e]
	Number per 10,000 civilian population							
United States	15.3	20.7	24.2	26.9	13.5	18.0	21.3	23.8
New England	19.1	26.7	32.5	37.5	16.9	22.9	28.8	33.4
Connecticut	19.8	27.6	32.8	35.4	17.7	24.3	29.5	31.8
Maine	12.8	18.7	22.3	30.1	10.7	15.6	18.2	24.3
Massachusetts	20.8	30.2	37.5	42.8	18.3	25.4	33.2	38.4
New Hampshire	14.3	18.1	21.5	26.7	13.1	16.7	19.8	24.1
Rhode Island	17.8	23.3	30.4	35.8	16.1	20.2	26.7	32.0
Vermont	18.2	23.8	26.9	35.4	15.5	20.3	24.2	32.1
Middle Atlantic	19.5	26.1	32.4	35.0	17.0	22.2	28.0	30.0
New Jersey	16.2	23.4	29.3	32.6	14.0	19.8	24.9	27.6
New York	22.7	29.0	35.3	38.0	20.2	25.2	31.6	33.9
Pennsylvania	16.6	23.6	30.1	32.0	13.9	19.2	24.6	25.8
East North Central	13.9	19.3	23.3	26.6	12.0	16.4	19.8	22.8
Illinois	14.5	20.5	24.8	27.5	13.1	18.2	22.1	24.4
Indiana	10.6	14.7	18.4	21.9	9.6	13.2	16.6	19.8
Michigan	15.4	20.8	24.8	27.4	12.0	16.0	19.0	21.5
Ohio	14.1	19.9	23.8	27.7	12.2	16.8	20.0	23.4
Wisconsin	12.5	17.7	21.5	25.7	11.4	15.9	19.6	23.4
West North Central	13.3	18.3	21.8	25.0	11.4	15.6	18.9	21.7
Iowa	11.4	15.6	19.2	21.1	9.4	12.4	15.1	16.6
Kansas	12.8	17.3	20.8	23.6	11.2	15.1	18.0	20.4
Minnesota	14.9	20.5	23.4	27.9	13.7	18.5	21.5	25.7
Missouri	15.0	20.5	23.9	25.9	11.6	16.3	19.7	21.5
Nebraska	12.1	15.7	19.8	23.8	10.9	14.4	18.3	21.8
North Dakota	9.7	15.8	20.5	24.2	9.2	14.9	18.9	22.3
South Dakota	8.2	13.4	16.7	22.3	7.7	12.3	15.7	20.6
South Atlantic	14.0	19.7	23.4	26.7	12.6	17.6	21.0	23.8
Delaware	14.3	19.7	23.4	26.1	12.7	17.1	19.7	22.4
District of Columbia	39.6	55.3	63.6	75.6	34.6	45.6	53.6	65.8
Florida	15.2	20.2	22.9	25.3	13.4	17.8	20.3	22.4
Georgia	11.5	16.2	19.7	22.0	10.6	14.7	18.0	20.1
Maryland	18.6	30.4	34.1	39.9	16.5	24.9	29.9	34.4
North Carolina	11.7	16.9	21.1	24.8	10.6	15.0	19.4	22.8
South Carolina	10.0	14.7	18.9	23.0	9.3	13.6	17.6	21.3
Virginia	12.9	19.5	22.5	26.8	11.9	17.8	20.8	24.4
West Virginia	11.0	16.3	21.0	25.2	10.0	14.6	17.9	20.9
East South Central	10.5	15.0	19.2	22.8	9.7	14.0	17.8	21.0
Alabama	9.2	14.2	18.4	21.4	8.6	13.1	17.0	19.8
Kentucky	10.9	15.1	19.2	22.9	10.1	13.9	18.0	21.1
Mississippi	8.4	11.8	13.9	18.1	8.0	11.1	13.0	16.5
Tennessee	12.4	17.7	22.5	26.1	11.3	16.2	20.8	24.1
West South Central	11.9	16.4	19.5	21.8	10.5	14.5	17.3	19.5
Arkansas	9.1	13.8	17.3	20.4	8.5	12.8	16.0	18.9
Louisiana	11.4	17.3	21.7	24.5	10.5	16.1	20.3	23.2
Oklahoma	11.6	16.1	18.8	20.5	9.4	12.9	14.7	15.7
Texas	12.5	16.8	19.4	21.7	11.0	14.7	17.3	19.4
Mountain	14.3	17.8	20.2	22.8	12.6	15.7	17.8	20.0
Arizona	16.7	20.2	21.4	22.5	14.1	17.1	18.2	19.2
Colorado	17.3	20.7	23.7	26.8	15.0	17.7	20.6	23.6
Idaho	9.5	12.1	13.9	17.9	8.9	11.4	13.1	16.2
Montana	10.6	14.0	18.4	23.0	10.1	13.2	17.1	21.2
Nevada	11.9	16.0	16.7	19.6	10.9	14.5	14.6	17.5
New Mexico	12.2	17.0	20.2	23.9	10.1	14.7	18.0	21.5
Utah	14.1	17.2	19.2	21.2	13.0	15.5	17.6	19.1
Wyoming	9.5	12.9	15.3	19.4	8.9	12.0	13.9	17.7

In three separate rounds (1997–97, 1998–99, and 2000–01), Landon, Reschovsky, and Blumenthal surveyed more than twelve thousand primary care and specialist physicians who spent at least twenty hours per week in patient care. Each round found that approximately 80% of primary care and specialist physicians were somewhat or very satisfied with their careers, and about 18% were somewhat or very dissatisfied with their careers. The study also examined physician career satisfaction in twelve market regions in an effort to identify some of the underlying reasons for satisfaction and dissatisfaction.

Even though state regulations and health plan mergers, as well as changes in hospital competition and practice ownership, may have contributed to the geographic variation in physician dissatisfaction, Landon, Reschovsky, and Blumenthal find that physician independence—the freedom to make clinical decisions in the best interest

TABLE 2.3

Active physicians in patient care, by geographic division and state, selected years 1975–2005 [CONTINUED]

Geographic division and state	Total physicians[a]				Doctors of medicine in patient care[b]			
	1975	1985	1995[c]	2005[d, e]	1975	1985	1995	2005[e]
	Number per 10,000 civilian population							
Pacific	17.9	22.5	23.3	26.0	16.3	20.5	21.2	23.6
Alaska	8.4	13.0	15.7	24.1	7.8	12.1	14.2	21.3
California	18.8	23.7	23.7	25.7	17.3	21.5	21.7	23.3
Hawaii	16.2	21.5	24.8	31.2	14.7	19.8	22.8	28.2
Oregon	15.6	19.7	21.6	26.9	13.8	17.6	19.5	24.2
Washington	15.3	20.2	22.5	26.6	13.6	17.9	20.2	23.9

[a]Includes active doctors of medicine and active doctors of osteopathy.
[b]Excludes doctors of osteopathy (DOs); states with more than 3,000 active DOs are California, Florida, Michigan, New York, Ohio, Pennsylvania, and Texas. States with fewer than 100 active DOs are North Dakota, South Dakota, Vermont, Wyoming, and the District of Columbia. Excludes doctors of medicine in medical teaching, administration, research, and other non-patient care activities.
[c]Data for doctors of osteopathy are as of July 1996.
[d]Data for doctors of osteopathy are as of June 2005.
[e]Starting with 2003 data, federal and nonfederal physicians are included. Data prior to 2004 include nonfederal physicians only.
Notes: Data for doctors of medicine are as of December 31. Data for additional years are available. Data are based on reporting by physicians.

SOURCE: "Table 106. Active Physicians and Doctors of Medicine in Patient Care, by Geographic Division and State: United States, Selected Years 1975–2005," in *Health, United States, 2007. With Chartbook on Trends in the Health of Americans*, U.S. Department of Health and Human Services, Centers for Disease Control and Prevention, National Center for Health Statistics, 2007, http://www.cdc.gov/nchs/data/hus/hus07.pdf#listtables (accessed April 17, 2008). Data from the American Medical Association (AMA).

of patients, being able to spend adequate time with patients, and maintaining ongoing relationships with patients—was more important than income in predicting changes in physician satisfaction. Physicians who felt they had the greatest degree of autonomy appeared to be the most satisfied with their career choices.

REGISTERED NURSES

Registered nurses (RNs) are licensed by the state to care for the sick and to promote health. RNs supervise hospital care, administer medication and treatment as prescribed by physicians, monitor the progress of patients, and provide health education. Nurses work in a variety of settings, including hospitals, nursing homes, physicians' offices, clinics, and schools.

Education for Nurses

There are three types of education for RNs. These include associate degrees (two-year community college programs), baccalaureate programs (four years of college), and postgraduate (master's degree and doctorate) programs. The baccalaureate degree provides more knowledge of community health services, as well as the psychological and social aspects of caring for patients, than does the associate degree. Those who complete the four-year baccalaureate degree and the other advanced degrees are generally better prepared to eventually attain administrative or management positions and may have greater opportunities for upward mobility in related disciplines such as research, teaching, and public health.

Between 1999 and 2005 the number of RNs grew from 2.2 million to 2.4 million. (See Table 2.5.) In *The*

Registered Nurse Population: Findings from the March 2004 National Sample Survey of Registered Nurses (June 2006, ftp://ftp.hrsa.gov/bhpr/workforce/0306rnss.pdf), the HRSA reports that as of 2004 there were more than 2.9 million RNs working in the United States; however, just 83.2%, or 2.4 million, were working in the field of nursing. The largest percentage increases occurred among those holding baccalaureate, master's, and doctorate degrees. Figure 2.1 shows the trend from 2000 to 2004 of increasing numbers of RNs receiving master's and doctorate degrees.

NEED FOR NURSES EXCEEDS SUPPLY. Even though the number of RNs holding baccalaureate degrees increased sharply during the 1990s, there is still a shortage of nurses that is predicted to persist until 2020. Some health care experts believe the shortage is intensifying because more lucrative fields are now open to women, the traditional nursing population. In health occupations alone, the percentage of female students entering traditionally male professions continues to increase. For example, in 1980–81 women accounted for just 17% of first-year dentistry students, compared to 43.8% of the class entering in 2004–05. (See Table 2.6.) Similarly, increasing percentages of women are attending medical school and training to become optometrists, pharmacists, podiatrists, and public health care workers. Meanwhile, nursing school enrollment has declined. In "Iowa Faces Severe Nursing Shortage" (Associated Press, February 22, 2008), James Beltran reports that about 41% of registered nurses in the United States are at least fifty years old and nearing retirement. Along with relatively low wages, industry observers also attribute the shortfall to a lack of faculty in nursing programs, which has acted to limit enrollment. According to the American Association of Colleges of Nursing, in the

TABLE 2.4

Visits to physician offices by sex, age, and race, selected years 1995–2005

Age, sex, and race	All places[a]				Physician offices			
	1995	2000	2003	2005	1995	2000	2003	2005
	Number of visits in thousands							
Total	860,859	1,014,848	1,114,504	1,169,333	697,082	823,542	906,023	963,617
Under 18 years	194,644	212,165	223,724	238,389	150,351	163,459	169,392	185,186
18–44 years	285,184	315,774	331,015	324,108	219,065	243,011	251,853	247,568
45–64 years	188,320	255,894	301,558	328,564	159,531	216,783	257,258	283,180
45–54 years	104,891	142,233	164,431	170,674	88,266	119,474	138,634	145,034
55–64 years	83,429	113,661	137,126	157,890	71,264	97,309	118,624	138,146
65 years and over	192,712	231,014	258,206	278,272	168,135	200,289	227,520	247,683
65–74 years	102,605	116,505	120,655	133,334	90,544	102,447	106,424	119,061
75 years and over	90,106	114,510	137,552	144,938	77,591	97,842	121,096	128,623
	Number of visits per 100 persons							
Total, age-adjusted[b]	334	374	391	400	271	304	317	329
Total, crude	329	370	390	402	266	300	317	331
Under 18 years	275	293	307	325	213	226	232	253
18–44 years	264	291	301	294	203	224	229	224
45–64 years	364	422	442	454	309	358	377	391
45–54 years	339	385	406	405	286	323	343	344
55–64 years	401	481	494	523	343	412	428	458
65 years and over	612	706	753	792	534	612	664	705
65–74 years	560	656	667	725	494	577	588	647
75 years and over	683	766	850	865	588	654	748	768
Sex and age								
Male, age-adjusted[b]	290	325	338	352	232	261	273	289
Male, crude	277	314	329	345	220	251	264	283
Under 18 years	273	302	317	338	209	231	241	265
18–44 years	190	203	203	212	139	148	147	158
45–54 years	275	316	335	331	229	260	280	278
55–64 years	351	428	422	468	300	367	365	411
65–74 years	508	614	632	691	445	539	558	619
75 years and over	711	771	881	833	616	670	777	741
Female, age-adjusted[b]	377	420	442	445	309	345	360	367
Female, crude	378	424	449	456	310	348	368	377
Under 18 years	277	285	297	311	217	221	223	240
18–44 years	336	377	397	375	265	298	309	290
45–54 years	400	451	475	476	339	384	403	408
55–64 years	446	529	561	574	382	453	486	501
65–74 years	603	692	696	754	534	609	613	671
75 years and over	666	763	830	886	571	645	730	785
Race and age[c]								
White, age-adjusted[b]	339	380	399	413	282	315	332	347
White, crude	338	381	404	420	281	316	337	355
Under 18 years	295	306	330	348	237	243	260	280
18–44 years	267	301	308	306	211	239	242	242
45–54 years	334	386	409	416	286	330	352	362
55–64 years	397	480	500	534	345	416	439	476
65–74 years	557	641	653	727	496	568	582	656
75 years and over	689	764	844	854	598	658	747	763
Black or African American, age-adjusted	309	353	393	398	204	239	261	270
Black or African American, crude	281	324	365	369	178	214	236	243
Under 18 years	193	264	248	278	100	167	131	162
18–44 years	260	257	329	295	158	149	199	172
45–54 years	387	383	445	422	281	269	315	297
55–64 years	414	495	487	515	294	373	349	374
65–74 years	553	656	761	745	429	512	602	589
75 years and over	534	745	774	982	395	568	608	806

press release "Enrollment Growth Slows at U.S. Nursing Colleges and Universities in 2007" (December 3, 2007, http://www.aacn.nche.edu/media/NewsReleases/2007/enrl .htm), about thirty thousand applicants were denied admission to nursing schools in 2007 because of faculty shortages.

Industry observers feel this shortage results from a combination of factors including an aging population, a sicker population of hospitalized patients requiring more labor-intensive care, and public perception that nursing is a thankless, unglamorous job involving grueling physical labor, long hours, and low pay. In "Good Careers for 2006" (*U.S. News and World Report*, January 5, 2006), Marty Nemko deems nursing a "good career," with salaries ranging from $57,000 to well over $100,000 per year and with excellent job security. Observers also note that the public, particularly high school students considering careers in health care, are unaware of the many new opportunities in

ᵃAll places includes visits to physician offices and hospital outpatient and emergency departments.
ᵇEstimates are age-adjusted to the year 2000 standard population using six age groups: under 18 years, 18–44 years, 45–54 years, 55–64 years, 65–74 years, and 75 years and over.
ᶜStarting with 1999 data, the instruction for the race item on the patient record form was changed so that more than one race could be recorded. In previous years only one race could be checked. Estimates for race in this table are for visits where only one race was recorded. Because of the small number of responses with more than one racial group checked, estimates for visits with multiple races checked are unreliable and are not presented.
Notes: Rates for 1995–2000 were computed using 1990-based postcensal estimates of the civilian noninstitutionalized population as of July 1 adjusted for net underenumeration using the 1990 National Population Adjustment Matrix from the U.S. Census Bureau. Starting with 2001 data, rates were computed using 2000-based postcensal estimates of the civilian noninstitutionalized population as of July 1. The difference between rates for 2000 computed using 1990-based postcensal estimates and 2000 census counts is minimal. Rates will be overestimated to the extent that visits by institutionalized persons are counted in the numerator (for example, hospital emergency department visits by nursing home residents) and institutionalized persons are omitted from the denominator (the civilian noninstitutionalized population). Starting with Health, United States, 2005, data for physician offices for 2001 and beyond use a revised weighting scheme.
Data are based on reporting by a sample of office-based physicians, hospital outpatient departments, and hospital emergency departments.

SOURCE: Adapted from "Table 92. Visits to Physician Offices, Hospital Outpatient Departments, and Hospital Emergency Departments, by Selected Characteristics: United States, Selected Years 1995–2005," in *Health, United States, 2007. With Chartbook on Trends in the Health of Americans*, U.S. Department of Health and Human Services, Centers for Disease Control and Prevention, National Center for Health Statistics, 2007, http://www.cdc.gov/nchs/data/hus/hus07.pdf#listtables (accessed April 17, 2008)

nursing, such as advanced practice nursing, which offers additional independence and increased earning potential, and the technology-driven field of applied informatics (computer management of information).

ADVANCED PRACTICE NURSES AND PHYSICIAN ASSISTANTS

Much of the preventive medical care and treatment usually delivered by physicians may also be provided by midlevel practitioners—health professionals with less formal education and training than physicians. Advanced practice nurses make up a group that includes certified nurse midwives, nurse practitioners (NPs; RNs with advanced academic and clinical experience), and clinical nurse specialists (RNs with advanced nursing degrees who specialize in areas such as mental health, gerontology, cardiac or cancer care, and community or neonatal health). Physician assistants (PAs) are midlevel practitioners who work under the auspices, supervision, or direction of physicians. They conduct physical examinations, order and interpret laboratory and radiological studies, and prescribe medication. They even perform procedures (e.g., flexible sigmoidoscopy, biopsy, suturing, casting, and administering anesthesia) that were once performed exclusively by physicians.

The origins of each profession are key to understanding the differences between them. Nursing has the longer history, and nurses are recognized members of the health care team. For this reason, NPs were easily integrated into many practice settings.

PA is the newer of the two disciplines. PAs have been practicing in the United States since the early 1970s. The career originated as civilian employment for returning Vietnam War veterans who had worked as medics. The veterans needed immediate employment and few had the educational prerequisites, time, or resources to pursue the training necessary to become physicians. At the same time, the

United States was projecting a dire shortage of primary care physicians, especially in rural and inner-city practices. The use of PAs and NPs was seen as an ideal rapid response to the demand for additional medical services. They could be deployed quickly to serve remote communities or underserved populations for a fraction of the costs associated with physicians.

The numbers of PAs and NPs have increased dramatically since the beginning of the 1990s. The HRSA reports in *Registered Nurse Population* that in 2004 there were 240,460 advanced practice nurses—141,209 NPs (59%), 72,521 clinical nurse specialists (30%), 32,523 certified RN anesthetists (14%), and 13,684 certified nurse midwives (6%). Advanced practice nurses accounted for 8.3% of the total RN population. According to the American Academy of Physician Assistants (http://www.aapa.org/research/07census-intro.html), there were 75,260 PAs eligible to practice in 2007. When combined, midlevel practitioners outnumber primary care physicians.

Training, Certification, and Practice

Advanced practice nurses usually have considerable clinical nursing experience before completing certificate or master's degree NP programs. Key components of NP programs are instruction in nursing theory and practice as well as a period of direct supervision by a physician or NP. The American College of Nurse Practitioners (April 20, 2007, http://www.ejfhc.org/American%20College%20of%20Nurse%20Practitioners.htm) states that NPs are prepared to practice "either independently or as part of a health care team," but the NP scope of practice varies by state.

The Commission on Accreditation of Allied Health Education Programs accredits PA training programs. According to the American Academy of Physician Assistants (AAPA), in "Physician Assistants and Anesthesiologist Assistants—the Distinctions" (February 2005, http://www.aapa.org/gandp/issuebrief/aas.pdf), most students have an undergraduate

TABLE 2.5

Health personnel by occupation, selected years 1999–2005

Occupation title	1999	2000	2004	2005	1999–2005 AACP[b]	1999	2000	2004	2005	1999–2005 AACP[b]
Healthcare practitioner and technical occupations		Number of employees[a]					Mean hourly wage[c]			
Audiologists	12,950	11,530	9,810	10,030	−4.2	$21.96	$22.92	$26.47	$27.72	4.0
Cardiovascular technologists and technicians	41,490	40,080	43,540	43,560	0.8	$16.00	$16.81	$19.09	$19.99	3.8
Dental hygienists	90,050	148,460	155,810	161,140	10.2	$23.15	$24.99	$28.58	$29.15	3.9
Diagnostic medical sonographers	29,280	31,760	41,280	43,590	6.9	$21.04	$22.03	$25.78	$26.65	4.0
Dietetic technicians	29,190	28,010	24,630	23,780	−3.4	$10.09	$10.98	$11.89	$12.20	3.2
Dietitians and nutritionists	41,320	43,030	46,530	48,850	2.8	$17.96	$18.76	$21.46	$22.09	3.5
Emergency medical technicians and paramedics	172,360	165,530	187,900	196,880	2.2	$11.19	$11.89	$13.30	$13.68	3.4
Licensed practical and licensed vocational nurse	688,510	679,470	702,740	710,020	0.5	$13.95	$14.65	$16.75	$17.41	3.8
Nuclear medicine technologists	17,880	18,030	17,520	18,280	0.4	$20.40	$21.56	$29.43	$29.10	6.1
Occupational therapists	78,950	75,150	83,560	87,430	1.7	$24.96	$24.10	$27.19	$28.41	2.2
Opticians, dispensing	58,860	66,580	62,350	70,090	3.0	$12.11	$12.67	$14.37	$14.80	3.4
Pharmacists	226,300	212,660	222,960	229,740	0.3	$30.31	$33.39	$40.56	$42.62	5.8
Pharmacy technicians	196,430	190,940	255,290	266,790	5.2	$ 9.64	$10.38	$11.87	$12.19	4.0
Physical therapists	131,050	120,410	142,940	151,280	2.4	$28.05	$27.62	$30.00	$31.42	1.9
Physician assistants	56,750	55,490	59,470	63,350	1.9	$24.35	$29.17	$33.07	$34.17	5.8
Psychiatric technicians	54,560	53,350	59,010	62,040	2.2	$11.30	$12.53	$13.43	$14.04	3.7
Radiation therapists	12,340	13,100	14,470	14,120	2.3	$20.84	$25.59	$29.05	$30.59	6.6
Radiologic technologists and technicians	177,850	172,080	177,220	184,580	0.6	$17.07	$17.93	$21.41	$22.60	4.8
Recreational therapists	30,190	26,940	23,050	23,260	−4.3	$14.08	$14.23	$16.48	$16.90	3.1
Registered nurses	2,205,430	2,189,670	2,311,970	2,368,070	1.2	$21.38	$22.31	$26.06	$27.35	4.2
Respiratory therapists	80,230	82,670	91,350	95,320	2.9	$17.72	$18.37	$21.24	$22.24	3.9
Respiratory therapy technicians	33,990	28,230	24,190	22,060	−7.0	$16.07	$16.46	$18.00	$18.57	2.4
Speech-language pathologists	85,920	82,850	89,260	94,660	1.6	$22.99	$23.31	$26.71	$27.89	3.3
Healthcare support occupations										
Dental assistants	175,160	250,870	264,820	270,720	7.5	$11.60	$12.86	$13.97	$14.41	3.7
Home health aides	577,530	561,120	596,330	663,280	2.3	$ 9.04	$ 8.71	$ 9.13	$ 9.34	0.5
Massage therapists	21,910	24,620	32,200	37,670	9.5	$13.82	$15.51	$17.63	$19.33	5.8
Medical assistants	281,480	330,830	380,340	382,720	5.3	$10.89	$11.46	$12.21	$12.58	2.4
Medical equipment preparers	29,070	32,760	40,380	41,790	6.2	$10.20	$10.68	$12.14	$12.42	3.3
Medical transcriptionists	97,260	97,330	92,740	90,380	−1.2	$11.86	$12.37	$14.01	$14.36	3.2
Nursing aides, orderlies, and attendants	1,308,740	1,273,460	1,384,120	1,391,430	1.0	$ 8.59	$ 9.18	$10.39	$10.67	3.7
Occupational therapist aides	9,250	8,890	5,240	6,220	−6.4	$10.92	$11.21	$12.51	$13.20	3.2
Occupational therapist assistants	17,290	15,910	20,880	22,160	4.2	$15.97	$16.76	$18.49	$19.13	3.1
Pharmacy aides	48,270	59,890	47,720	46,610	−0.6	$ 9.14	$ 9.10	$ 9.52	$ 9.76	1.1
Physical therapist aides	44,340	34,620	41,910	41,930	−0.9	$ 9.69	$10.06	$11.14	$11.01	2.2
Physical therapist assistants	48,600	44,120	57,420	58,670	3.2	$16.20	$16.52	$18.14	$18.98	2.7
Psychiatric aides	51,100	57,680	54,520	56,150	1.6	$10.76	$10.79	$11.70	$11.47	1.1

[a]Estimates do not include self-employed workers and were rounded to the nearest 10.
[b]Average annual percent change. AACP is the American Association of Colleges of Pharmacy.
[c]The mean hourly wage rate for an occupation is the total wages that all workers in the occupation earn in an hour divided by the total employment of the occupation.
Notes: This table excludes occupations such as dentists, physicians, and chiropractors, with a large percentage of workers who are self-employed and/or not employed by establishments. Data are based on a semi-annual mail survey of nonfarm establishments.

SOURCE: "Table 109. Employees and Wages, by Selected Healthcare Occupations: United States, Selected Years 1999–2005," in *Health, United States, 2007. With Chartbook on Trends in the Health of Americans*, U.S. Department of Health and Human Services, Centers for Disease Control and Prevention, National Center for Health Statistics, 2007, http://www.cdc.gov/nchs/data/hus/hus07.pdf#listtables (accessed April 17, 2008)

degree and about forty-five months of health care experience before they enter a two-year PA training program. Graduates sit for a national certifying examination and, once certified, must earn one hundred hours of continuing medical education every two years and pass a recertification exam every six years.

PA practice is always delegated by the physician and conducted with physician supervision. The extent and nature of physician supervision varies from state to state. For example, Connecticut permits a physician to supervise up to six PAs, whereas California limits a supervising physician to two. Even though PAs work interdependently with physicians, supervision is not necessarily direct and

onsite; some PAs working in remote communities are supervised primarily by telephone.

In *2007 AAPA Physician Assistant Census Report* (October 12, 2007, http://www.aapa.org/research/07census-intro.html), the AAPA states that in 2007 the mean (average) annual income of physician assistants who were not self-employed was $86,214. New graduates (in 2006) could anticipate a mean annual income of $73,013.

Distinctions between Midlevel Practitioners Blurring

Pohla Smith reports in "Doing Doctors' Work" (*Pittsburgh Post-Gazette*, March 12, 2008) that even though their training may be different, in terms of their day-to-day job

FIGURE 2.1

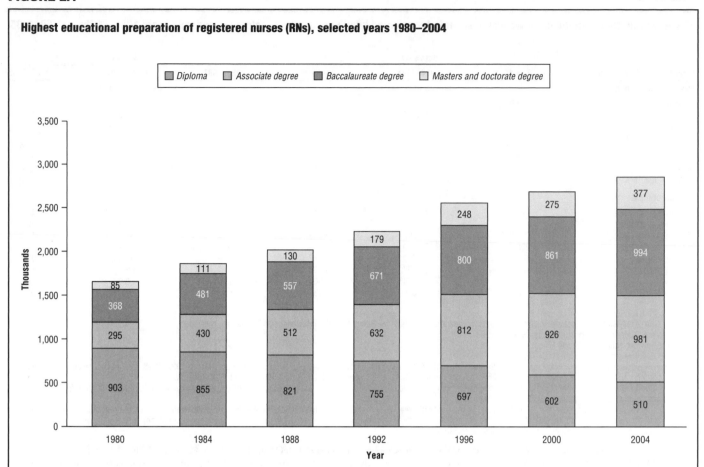

Highest educational preparation of registered nurses (RNs), selected years 1980–2004

Notes: The totals in each bar may not equal the estimated numbers of RNs in each survey year due to incomplete information provided by respondents and the effect of roundling. Only those provided initial RN educational preparation informatioin are included in the calculations used for this chart.

SOURCE: "Chart 3. Distribution of the Registered Nurse Population by Highest Nursing or Nursing-Related Educational Preparation, 1980–2004," in *The Registered Nurse Population: Findings from the March 2004 National Sample Survey of Registered Nurses*, U.S. Department of Health and Human Services, Health Resources and Services Administration, June 2006, ftp://ftp.hrsa.gov/bhpr/workforce/0306 rnss.pdf (accessed April 17, 2008)

responsibilities, NPs and PAs are becoming essentially interchangeable. Both types of practitioners diagnose and treat illness, take medical histories, and perform physical examinations. They can order diagnostic tests, prescribe medication, and assist in operating rooms and emergency departments.

DENTISTS

Dentists diagnose and treat problems of the teeth, gums, and mouth, take x-rays, apply protective plastic sealant to children's teeth, fill cavities, straighten teeth, and treat gum disease. The BLS (December 18, 2007, http://www.bls.gov/oco/ocos072.htm) reports that in 2006 there were 161,000 professionally active (as opposed to retired or employed in other fields) dentists in the United States.

Fluoridation of community water supplies and improved dental hygiene have dramatically improved the dental health of Americans. Dental caries (cavities) among all age groups have declined significantly. As a result, many dental services

are shifting focus from young people to adults. In the twenty-first century, many adults are choosing to have orthodontic services, such as straightening their teeth. In addition, the growing older adult population generally requires more complex dental procedures, such as endodontic (root canal) services, bridges, and dentures.

The overwhelming majority of dentists own solo dental practices, where only one dentist operates in each office. The BLS reports that in 2006 about one-third of dentists were self-employed, nearly all were in private practice, and that one out of seven dentists belonged to a partnership. On average, dentists work between thirty-five and forty hours per week and supervise staffers, such as dental assistants and hygienists. In *May 2007 National Occupational Employment and Wage Estimates* (May 12, 2008, http://www.bls.gov/oes/current/oes_nat.htm), the BLS notes that self-employed dentists in general practice had mean annual wages of $147,010 in 2007, whereas dental specialists' mean annual wages ranged from $120,360 to $185,340.

TABLE 2.6

First-year and total enrollment of women in schools for selected health occupations, selected academic years 1980–81 through 2004–05

Enrollment and occupation	Both sexes			Women		
	1980–1981	1990–1991	2004–2005[a]	1980–1981	1990–1991[b]	2004–2005[a]
First-year enrollment	**Number of students**			**Percent of students**		
Dentistry	6,030	4,001	4,612	19.8	38.0	—
Medicine (allopathic)[c]	17,186	16,876	17,059	28.9	38.8	49.4
Medicine (osteopathic)	1,496	1,950	3,646	22.0	34.2	50.1
Nurses, registered	110,201	113,526	—	92.7	89.3	—
Optometry[c, d]	1,258	1,239	1,429	25.3	50.6	64.9
Pharmacy[c, e]	7,377	8,267	10,437	48.4	—	65.4
Podiatry	695	561	519	—	28.0	49.0
Public health[c, f]	3,348	4,289	7,206	—	62.1	70.9
Total enrollment						
Dentistry	22,842	15,951	18,315	17.0	34.4	43.8
Medicine (allopathic)[c]	65,189	65,163	67,466	26.5	37.3	48.7
Medicine (osteopathic)	4,940	6,792	12,525	19.7	32.7	48.8
Nurses, registered	230,966	221,170	—	94.3	—	—
Optometry[c, d]	4,641	4,760	5,377	—	47.3	63.1
Pharmacy[c, e]	26,617	29,797	43,908	47.4	62.4	66.5
Podiatry	2,577	2,154	1,584	11.9	28.9	46.9
Public health[c, f]	8,486	11,386	19,434	55.2	62.5	69.6

—Data not available.
[a]Starting with 2003–2004 data, osteopathic medicine data include the students of the Edward Via Virginia College of Osteopathic Medicine.
[b]Percentage of women podiatry students is for 1991–1992.
[c]Include data from schools in Puerto Rico.
[d]2004–2005 optometry data are for 2005–2006.
[e]First-year enrollment data for pharmacy schools are for students in the first year of the final three years of pharmacy education. Prior to 1992–1993, pharmacy total enrollment data were for students in the final three years of pharmacy education. Starting in 1992–1993, pharmacy total enrollment data are for all students.
[f]For 2003–2004 data, first-year enrollment data for public health schools include Spring, Summer, and Fall enrollment. All other years of data including 2004–2005 are for Fall enrollment only and are not directly comparable to 2003–2004 data.
Notes: Total enrollment data are collected at the beginning of the academic year while first-year enrollment data are collected during the academic year. Data for chiropractic students and occupational, physical, and speech therapy students were not available for this table. Some numbers in this table have been revised and differ from previous editions of Health, United States. Data are based on reporting by health professions associations.

SOURCE: "Table 112. First-Year and Total Enrollment of Women in Schools for Selected Health Occupations: United States, Selected Academic Years 1980–81 through 2004–05," in *Health, United States, 2007. With Chartbook on Trends in the Health of Americans*, U.S. Department of Health and Human Services, Centers for Disease Control and Prevention, National Center for Health Statistics, 2007, http://www.cdc.gov/nchs/data/hus/hus07.pdffiNsttables (accessed April 17, 2008). Data from Association of American Medical Colleges, 2005, 2006, and 2007; from American Association of Colleges of Osteopathic Medicine, 2006; from Bureau of Health Professions, 1990; from American Dental Association, 2006 and unpublished data; Association of Schools and Colleges of Optometry, 2006; American Association of Colleges of Pharmacy, Fall 2005 and unpublished data; from American Association of Colleges of Podiatric Medicine, unpublished data; National League for Nursing, 1973, 1982, 1997, and unpublished data; Association of Schools of Public Health, 2005.

Dental Specialists

The ADA explains in *What Can a Career in Dentistry Offer You?* (2008, http://www.ada.org/public/careers/team/dentistry_fact.pdf) that 20% of all dentists practice in one of the nine specialty areas that the ADA recognizes. Orthodontists, who straighten teeth, make up the largest group of specialists. The next largest group, oral and maxillofacial surgeons, operates on the mouth and jaws. The balance of the specialists concentrates in pediatric dentistry (dentistry for children), periodontics (treating the gums), prosthodontics (making dentures and artificial teeth), endodontics (root canals), public health dentistry (community dental health), and oral pathology (diseases of the mouth).

According to the BLS (December 18, 2007, http://www.bls.gov/oco/ocos072.htm), as of 2006, seventeen states licensed or certified dentists who practice in specialty areas. Requirements vary by state and specialty and may include two to four years of postgraduate education and a passing score on a state-administered examination. Den-tists who teach or conduct research generally spend an additional two to five years in advanced dental training in programs operated by dental schools or university-affiliated hospitals.

Training to Become a Dentist

Entry into dental schools requires two to four years of college-level predental education—most dental students have earned excellent grades and have at least a bachelor's degree when they enter dental school. Dentists should have good visual memory, excellent judgment about space and shape, a high degree of manual dexterity, and scientific ability. Development and maintenance of a successful private practice requires business acumen, the ability to manage and organize people and materials, and strong interpersonal skills.

Dental schools require applicants to take the Dental Admissions Test (DAT). During the admission process, schools consider scores earned on the DAT, applicants' grade-point averages, and information gleaned from recommendations and interviews. Dental school usually lasts four academic years. A student begins by studying the basic sciences, including anatomy, microbiology, biochemistry, and physiology. During the last two years, students receive practical experience by treating patients, usually in dental clinics supervised by licensed dentists.

Visiting the Dentist

In 2005 more than half (57.7%) of Americans over two years of age had visited their dentists at least once in the past year. (See Table 2.7.) Children aged two to seventeen (76.2%) were more likely to have visited the dentist than any other age group, and women aged sixty-five and older were somewhat more likely to see the dentist than men. Among adults aged eighteen to sixty-four, the proportion of non-Hispanic whites (67.9%) visiting dentists was considerably higher than the proportions of non-Hispanic African-Americans (57%) and Hispanics (48.5%). People who were poor or near poor were much less likely to visit the dentist annually than those who were not poor.

SEVERE SHORTAGES OF DENTISTS IN SOME AREAS. The United States boasts the highest concentration of dentists of any country in the world. Nonetheless, health care planners caution that dentists' ranks will begin to decline during the coming decade as the number of dental school graduates—about four thousand or so annually, according to Eric S. Solomon, in "The Future of Dentistry" (*Dental Economics*, November 2004)—falls below the number of dentists retiring from the workforce. Even before this decline, residents of many states do not have adequate access to dental care, especially people in rural communities and poor urban neighborhoods, where, arguably, the need is greatest.

Even though the American Dental Hygienists' Association (ADHA) believes access to quality, affordable dental care is a right, according to the fact sheet "ADHA Access to Care Facts and Stats" (2008, http://www.adha.org/media/facts/access.htm), 40% of Americans do not receive needed care. Access to care is limited by both a shortage of practicing dentists in many communities and many Americans' inability to pay for care. In "Access to Care Position Paper, 2001" (June 9, 2008, http://www.adha.org/profissues/access_to_care.htm), the ADHS asserts that the shortage of dentists will persist and that by 2020 the number of dentists per 100,000 U.S. population will fall to 52.7. In areas where there are few practicing dentists, uninsured and low-income families have even more difficulty gaining access to already overbooked dentists.

In February 2008 the death of a twelve-year-old boy from complications resulting from an untreated dental problem underscored how lack of access to dental care has created a situation the *Oral Health in America: A Report of the Surgeon General* (September 2000, http://silk.nih.gov/public/hck1ocv.@www.surgeon.fullrpt.pdf)

calls a "silent epidemic." The report asserts that dental disease afflicts the nation's most vulnerable populations: poor children, older adults, and many members of racial and ethnic minority groups.

ALLIED HEALTH CARE PROVIDERS

Many health care services are provided by an interdisciplinary team of health professionals. The complete health care team may include physicians, nurses, midlevel practitioners, and dentists; physical and occupational therapists; audiologists and speech-language pathologists; licensed practical nurses, nurses' aides, and home health aides; and pharmacists, optometrists, podiatrists, dental hygienists, social workers, registered dieticians, and others. Table 2.8 describes some of these allied heath professions. Specific health care teams are assembled to meet the varying needs of patients. For example, the team involved in stroke rehabilitation might include a physician, a nurse, a speech-language pathologist, a social worker, and physical and occupational therapists.

Besides these allied health professionals, the HRSA asserts in *Fifth Annual Report to the Secretary of the U.S. Department of Health and Human Services and to the Congress, 2005* (November 2005, ftp://ftp.hrsa.gov/bhpr/interdisciplinary/cblreports/rpt5.pdf) that there is a growing need for other allied health personnel to fill a variety of health care professions, including epidemiologists, biostatisticians, environmental health professionals, toxicologists, public health nutritionists, preventive medicine specialists, and behavioral and mental health professionals. Other allied health care workers such as pharmacy technicians, athletic trainers, cardiovascular technologists, dispensing opticians, genetic counselors, massage therapists, and phlebotomists work in a variety of settings including hospitals, clinics, nursing homes, mental health facilities, managed care organizations, federal, state, and local government agencies, colleges and universities, public and private research organizations, and medical supply, equipment, and pharmaceutical industries.

Physical and Occupational Therapists

Physical therapists (PTs) are licensed practitioners who work with patients to preserve and restore function, improve capabilities and mobility, and regain independence following illness or injury. They also aim to prevent or limit disability and slow the progress of debilitating diseases. Treatment involves exercise to improve range of motion, balance, coordination, flexibility, strength, and endurance. PTs may also use electrical stimulation to promote healing, hot and cold packs to relieve pain and inflammation (swelling), and therapeutic massage.

According to the BLS (December 18, 2007, http://www.bls.gov/oco/ocos080.htm), PTs worked at 173,000 jobs in 2006, but some were part-time jobs and some PTs held two

TABLE 2.7

Dental visits in the past year by selected characteristics, 1997, 2004, and 2005

Characteristic	2 years and over			2–17 years			18–64 years			65 years and over[a]		
	1997	2004	2005	1997	2004	2005	1997	2004	2005	1997	2004	2005
	Percent of persons with a dental visit in the past year[b]											
2 years and over[c]	65.1	66.0	65.8	72.7	76.4	76.2	64.1	64.0	63.5	54.8	56.3	57.7
Sex												
Male	62.9	63.7	63.0	72.3	75.1	75.5	60.4	60.5	59.4	55.4	57.1	56.6
Female	67.1	68.1	68.4	73.0	77.7	77.0	67.7	67.4	67.6	54.4	55.8	58.6
Race[d]												
White only	66.4	67.0	66.8	74.0	77.3	77.1	65.7	65.2	64.8	56.8	58.6	59.9
Black or African American only	58.9	59.5	59.8	68.8	72.5	72.9	57.0	56.9	57.0	35.4	33.6	36.0
American Indian or Alaska Native only	55.1	63.4	59.3	66.8	70.3	74.8	49.9	63.4	54.1	32.2		
Asian only	62.5	66.1	62.5	69.9	73.8	70.1	60.3	64.2	60.2	53.9	58.1	60.0
Native Hawaiian or other Pacific Islander only	—	—	—	—	—	—	—	—	—	—	—	—
2 or more races	—	65.3	67.3	—	78.0	78.1	—	58.4	60.8	—	28.7	39.7
Black or African American; white	—	67.1	66.0	—	72.6	75.3	—	61.0	51.3	—	—	—
American Indian or Alaska Native; white	—	55.1	56.2	—	78.9	70.9	—	49.1	54.4	—	—	—
Hispanic origin and race[d]												
Hispanic or Latino	54.0	54.2	53.9	61.0	65.3	66.5	50.8	49.6	48.5	47.8	42.5	43.1
Not Hispanic or Latino	66.4	67.9	67.8	74.7	78.9	78.5	65.7	66.3	66.0	55.2	57.2	58.7
White only	68.0	69.5	69.4	76.4	80.9	80.4	67.5	68.1	67.9	57.2	59.8	61.2
Black or African American only	58.8	59.8	59.7	68.8	72.9	72.7	56.9	57.3	57.0	35.3	33.3	35.5
Percent of poverty level[e]												
Below 100%	50.5	49.6	50.4	62.0	65.5	66.2	46.9	44.5	44.6	31.5	30.7	34.7
100%–less than 200%	50.8	52.6	52.4	62.5	69.0	68.6	48.3	47.6	47.8	40.8	43.2	42.5
200% or more	72.5	73.0	72.6	80.1	82.2	82.0	71.2	71.3	70.5	65.9	66.4	67.8
Hispanic origin and race and percent of poverty level[d, e]												
Hispanic or Latino:												
Below 100%	45.7	47.1	47.4	55.9	61.9	64.4	39.2	38.3	36.3	33.6	29.8	37.1
100%–less than 200%	47.2	47.2	47.6	53.8	59.1	60.2	43.5	41.7	42.3	47.9	37.7	36.2
200% or more	65.1	63.7	61.9	73.7	74.2	73.6	62.3	60.4	58.2	58.8	55.4	51.8
Not Hispanic or Latino:												
White only:												
Below 100%	51.7	51.1	51.5	64.4	68.7	65.0	50.6	48.7	49.6	32.0	33.4	37.9
100%–less than 200%	52.4	54.3	54.5	66.1	73.5	72.5	50.4	50.0	50.9	42.2	45.6	45.7
200% or more	73.8	74.8	74.6	81.3	84.3	84.2	72.7	73.2	72.8	67.0	68.5	69.7
Black or African American only:												
Below 100%	52.8	49.8	52.5	66.1	68.2	71.1	46.2	42.3	44.1	27.7	21.5	24.6
100%–less than 200%	48.7	52.1	51.3	61.2	70.5	70.5	46.3	46.4	45.2	26.9	29.4	26.9
200% or more	67.7	68.2	67.6	77.1	77.7	75.9	66.1	67.0	66.7	49.8	45.0	50.7

—Data not available.

[a]Based on the 1997–2005 National Health Interview Surveys, about 25%–30% of persons 65 years and over were edentulous (having lost all their natural teeth). In 1997–2005 about 68%–70% of older dentate persons compared with 16%–20% of older edentate persons had a dental visit in the past year.

[b]Respondents were asked "About how long has it been since you last saw or talked to a dentist?"

[c]Includes all other races not shown separately.

[d]The race groups, white, black, American Indian or Alaska Native, Asian, Native Hawaiian or other Pacific Islander, and 2 or more races, include persons of Hispanic and non-Hispanic origin. Persons of Hispanic origin may be of any race. Starting with 1999 data, race-specific estimates are tabulated according to the 1997 Revisions to the Standards for the Classification of Federal Data on Race and Ethnicity and are not strictly comparable with estimates for earlier years. The five single-race categories plus multiple-race categories shown in the table conform to the 1997 standards. Starting with 1999 data, race-specific estimates are for persons who reported only one racial group; the category 2 or more races includes persons who reported more than one racial group. Prior to 1999, data were tabulated according to the 1977 standards with four racial groups, and the Asian only category included Native Hawaiian or other Pacific Islander. Estimates for single-race categories prior to 1999 included persons who reported one race or, if they reported more than one race, identified one race as best representing their race. Starting with 2003 data, race responses of other race and unspecified multiple race were treated as missing, and then race was imputed if these were the only race responses. Almost all persons with a race response of other race were of Hispanic origin.

[e]Percent of poverty level is based on family income and family size and composition using U.S. Census Bureau poverty thresholds. Missing family income data were imputed for 25%–29% of persons in 1997–1998 and 32%–35% in 1999–2005.

Notes: In 1997 the National Health Interview Survey questionnaire was redesigned.

Data are based on household interviews of a sample of the civilian noninstitutionalized population.

SOURCE: Adapted from "Table 94. Dental Visits in the Past Year by Selected Characteristics: United States, 1997, 2004 and 2005," in *Health, United States, 2007. With Chartbook on Trends in the Health of Americans*, U.S. Department of Health and Human Services, Centers for Disease Control and Prevention, National Center for Health Statistics, 2007, http://www.cdc.gov/nchs/data/hus/hus07.pdf#listtables (accessed April 18, 2008)

or more jobs at the same time. Two-thirds of practicing PTs worked in hospitals and physicians' offices; the remaining PTs were employed in outpatient rehabilitation clinics, nurs-

ing homes, and home health agencies. Even though most work in rehabilitation, PTs may specialize in areas such as sports medicine, pediatrics, or neurology. PTs often work as

TABLE 2.8

Allied health care providers

Dental hygienists provide services for maintaining oral health. Their primary duty is to clean teeth.

Emergency medical technicians (EMTs) provide immediate care to critically ill or injured people in emergency situations.

Home health aides provide nursing, household, and personal care services to patients who are homebound or disabled.

Licensed practical nurse (LPNs) are trained and licensed to provide basic nursing care under the supervision of registered nurses and doctors.

Medical records personnel analyze patient records and keep them up-to-date, complete, accurate, and confidential.

Medical technologists perform laboratory tests to help diagnose diseases and to aid in identifying their causes and extent.

Nurses' aides, orderlies, and attendants help nurses in hospitals, nursing homes, and other facilities.

Occupational therapists help disabled persons adapt to their disabilities. This may include helping a patient relearn basic living skills or modifying the environment.

Optometrists measure vision for corrective lenses and prescribe glasses.

Pharmacists are trained and licensed to make up and dispense drugs in accordance with a physician's prescription.

Physician assistants (PAs) work under a doctor's supervision. Their duties include performing routine physical exams, prescribing certain drugs, and providing medical counseling.

Physical therapists work with disabled patients to help restore function, strength and mobility. PTs use exercise, heat, cold, water, and electricity to relieve pain and restore function.

Podiatrists diagnose and treat diseases, injuries, and abnormalities of the feet. They may use drugs and surgery to treat foot problems.

Psychologists are trained in human behavior and provide counseling and testing services related to mental health.

Radiation technicians take and develop x-ray photographs for medical purposes.

Registered dietitians (RDs) are licensed to use dietary principles to maintain health and treat disease.

Respiratory therapists treat breathing problems under a doctor's supervision and help in respiratory rehabilitation.

Social workers help patients to handle social problems such as finances, housing, and social and family problems that arise out of illness or disability.

Speech pathologists diagnose and treat disorders of speech and communication.

SOURCE: "Allied Health Care Providers," U.S. Department of Commerce, Washington, DC

members of a health care team and may supervise physical therapy assistants or aides. PTs' median annual earnings were $70,920 in 2006.

Occupational therapists (OTs) focus on helping people relearn and improve their abilities to perform the "activities of daily living," meaning the tasks they perform during the course of their work and home life. Examples of activities of daily living that OTs help patients regain are dressing, bathing, and meal preparation. For people with long-term or permanent disabilities, OTs may assist them to find new ways to accomplish their responsibilities on the job, sometimes by using adaptive equipment or by asking employers to accommodate workers with special needs such as people in wheelchairs. OTs use computer programs and simulations to help patients restore fine motor skills and practice reasoning, decision making, and problem solving.

The BLS (December 18, 2007, http://www.bls.gov/oco/ocos078.htm) reports that OTs filled ninety-nine thousand jobs in 2006, with one out of ten holding more than one job at a time. The demand for OTs and PTs is expected to exceed the available supply through 2016. Besides hos-

pital and rehabilitation center jobs, it is anticipated that PTs and OTs will increasingly be involved in school program efforts to meet the needs of disabled and special education students.

Historically, a bachelor's degree in occupational therapy has been the minimum educational requirement; beginning in 2007, however, a master's degree or higher is required. According to the BLS, the median annual earnings of occupational therapists were $60,470 in 2006.

Pharmacists Provide Valuable Patient Care Services

Pharmacists are involved in many more aspects of patient care than simply compounding and dispensing medication from behind the drugstore counter. According to the American Pharmacists Association (2008, http://www.pharmacist.com/), which represents the nation's sixty thousand pharmacists (as well as pharmaceutical scientists, students, and technicians), pharmacists provide pharmaceutical care that not only improves patient adherence to prescribed drug treatment but also reduces the frequency of drug therapy mishaps, which can have serious and even life-threatening consequences.

Studies citing the value of pharmacists in patient care describe pharmacists improving rates of immunization against disease (pharmacists can provide immunization in twenty-seven states), assisting patients to better control chronic diseases such as asthma and diabetes, reducing the frequency and severity of drug interactions and adverse reactions, and helping patients effectively manage pain and symptoms of disease, especially at the end of life. Pharmacists also offer public health education programs about prescription medication safety, prevention of poisoning, appropriate use of nonprescription (over-the-counter) drugs, and medical self-care.

The BLS (December 18, 2007, http://www.bls.gov/oco/ocos079.htm) reports that pharmacists held about 243,000 jobs in 2006. About 62% worked in community pharmacies—either independently owned or part of a drugstore chain, grocery store, department store, or mass merchandiser. Most full-time salaried pharmacists worked about forty hours per week, and many self-employed pharmacists worked more than fifty hours per week. About 23% worked in hospitals in 2006. The median annual earnings of pharmacists in 2006 was $94,520.

MENTAL HEALTH PROFESSIONALS

The mental health sector includes a range of professionals—psychiatrists, psychologists, psychiatric nurses, psychiatric social workers, and marriage and family therapists—whose training, orientation, philosophy, and practice styles differ, even within a single discipline. For example, clinical psychologists may endorse and offer dramatically different forms of therapy—ranging from long-term psychoanalytic psychotherapy to short-term cognitive-behavioral therapy.

Psychiatrists

Psychiatrists are physicians who have completed residency training in the prevention, diagnosis, and treatment of mental illness, mental retardation, and substance abuse disorders. Because they are trained physicians, they are especially well equipped to care for people who have coexisting medical diseases and mental health problems and they are able to prescribe medication including psychoactive drugs. Psychiatrists may also obtain additional training that prepares them to treat selected populations such as children and adolescents or older adults (this subspecialty is called geriatric psychiatry or geropsychiatry), or they may specialize in a specific treatment modality.

Psychologists

Research psychologists investigate the physical, cognitive, emotional, or social aspects of human behavior. They work in academic and private research centers and in business, nonprofit, and governmental organizations.

Clinical psychologists help mentally and emotionally disturbed clients better manage their symptoms and behaviors. Some work in rehabilitation, treating patients with spinal cord injuries, chronic pain or illness, stroke, arthritis, and neurologic conditions. Others help people cope during times of personal crisis, such as divorce or the death of a loved one. Psychologists are also called on to help communities recover from the trauma of natural or human-made disasters, working with, for example, people who have lost their homes to earthquakes, fires, or floods, or students who have witnessed school violence.

Clinical psychologists may specialize in health psychology, neuropsychology, or geropsychology. Health psychologists promote healthy lifestyles and behaviors and provide counseling such as smoking cessation, weight reduction, and stress management to assist people to reduce their health risks. Neuropsychologists often work in stroke rehabilitation and head injury programs, and geropsychologists work with older adults in institutional and community settings.

School psychologists identify, diagnose, and address students' learning and behavior problems. They work with teachers, parents, and school personnel to improve classroom management strategies or parenting skills and design educational programs to meet the needs of students with disabilities or gifted and talented students.

Industrial-organizational psychologists aim to improve productivity and the quality of life in the workplace. They screen prospective employees and conduct training and development, counseling, and organizational development and analysis. Industrial-organizational psychologists examine aspects of work life, whereas social psychologists consider interpersonal relationships and interactions with the social environment. They work in organizational consultation, market research, systems design, or other applied psychology fields. For example, both industrial-organizational and social psychologists may be involved in efforts to understand and influence consumer-purchasing behaviors.

EDUCATION, TRAINING, LICENSURE, AND EARNINGS. Most psychologists hold a doctoral degree in psychology, which entails between five and seven years of graduate study. Clinical psychologists must usually have earned Doctor of Philosophy or Doctor of Psychology degrees and completed an internship of at least a one-year duration. An educational specialist qualifies an individual to work as a school psychologist; however, most school psychologists complete a master's degree followed by a one-year internship. People with a master's degree in psychology may work as industrial-organizational psychologists or as psychological assistants, under the supervision of doctoral-level psychologists, and conduct research or psychological evaluations. Vocational and guidance counselors usually need two years of graduate education in counseling and one year of counseling experience. A master's degree in psychology requires at least two years of full-time graduate study. People with undergraduate degrees in psychology assist psychologists and other professionals in community mental health centers, vocational rehabilitation offices, and correctional programs as well as research or administrative capacities.

Psychologists in clinical practice must be certified or licensed in all states and the District of Columbia. According to the BLS (December 18, 2007, http://www.bls.gov/oco/ocos056.htm), the median annual salary for clinical, counseling, and school psychologists was $59,449 in 2006.

Psychiatric Nurses

Psychiatric nurses have earned a degree in nursing, are licensed as RNs, and have obtained additional experience in psychiatry. Advanced practice psychiatric nurses (RNs prepared at the master's level) may prescribe psychotropic medications and conduct individual, group, and family psychotherapy as well as perform crisis intervention and case management functions. Along with primary care physicians, they are often the first points of contact for people seeking mental health help.

The American Psychiatric Nurses Association (APNA) is the professional society that represents psychiatric nurses and examines the changing profile of the profession. According to the APNA, in "About Psychiatric-Mental Health Nurses (PMHNs)" (2008, http://www.apna.org/i4a/pages/index.cfm?pageid=3292), basic-level nurses usually start at an annual salary of $35,000 to $40,000, depending on the geographic location. Advanced practice nurses' salaries start at $60,000. Nurse executives can make $100,000 or more per year. Meanwhile, faculty members average about $65,000 per year, depending on the amount of education and experience.

Clinical Social Workers

Clinical social workers are the largest group of professionally trained mental health care providers in the United States. Clinical social workers offer psychotherapy or counseling and a range of diagnostic services in public agencies, clinics, and private practice. They assist people to improve their interpersonal relationships, solve personal and family problems, and advise them about how to function effectively in their communities.

According to the BLS (April 14, 2007, http://www.bls.gov/oco/ocos060.htm), approximately 595,000 social workers were employed in the United States in 2006. Of this total, 282,000 were child, family, and school social workers, 124,000 were medical and public health social workers, and 122,000 were mental health and substance abuse social workers. In 2006 the median annual earnings of child, family, and school social workers were $37,480. Medical and public health social workers earned $43,040, and the median annual earnings of mental health and substance abuse social workers were $35,410.

EDUCATION, CERTIFICATION, AND LICENSURE. A bachelor's degree in social work is usually the minimum requirement for employment as a social worker, and an advanced degree has become the standard for many positions. A master's degree in social work is necessary for positions in health and mental health settings and is typically required for certification for clinical work. Licensed clinical social workers hold a master's degree in social work along with additional clinical training. Supervisory, administrative, and staff training positions usually require an advanced degree, and university teaching positions and research appointments normally require a doctorate in social work.

Even though all the states and the District of Columbia have licensing, certification, or registration requirements that delineate the scope of social work practice and the use of professional titles, standards for licensing vary by state. The National Association of Social Workers (2008, https://www.socialworkers.org/nasw/default.asp) is the largest membership organization of professional social workers in the world, with 150,000 members.

Counselors

Counselors assist people with personal, family, educational, mental health, and job-related challenges and problems. Their roles and responsibilities depend on the clients they serve and on the settings in which they work. According to the BLS (December 18, 2007, http://www.bls.gov/oco/ocos067.htm), more than half of all counselors have earned a master's degree. In 2006 forty-nine states and the District of Columbia had some form of

counselor credentialing, licensure, certification, or registry legislation governing counselors who practice outside schools; however, requirements vary from state to state. The American Counseling Association (ACA; 2008, http://www.counseling.org/AboutUs/), which is the world's largest association for professional counselors, represents nearly forty-five thousand professional counselors in various practice settings. The ACA has taken an active role in advocating for certification, licensure, and registry of counselors.

The BLS notes that of the 635,000 counselors employed in the United States during 2006, 260,000 were educational, vocational, and school counselors, 141,000 were rehabilitation counselors, 100,000 were mental health counselors, 83,000 were substance abuse and behavioral disorder counselors, and 25,000 were marriage and family therapists.

Working in elementary, secondary, and postsecondary schools, educational, vocational, and school counselors work with people with disabilities and help them overcome the personal, social, and vocational effects of their disabilities. They advise people with disabilities resulting from birth defects, illness or disease, accidents, or the stress of daily life.

Mental health counselors work in prevention programs to promote optimum mental health and provide a wide range of counseling services. They work closely with other mental health professionals, including psychiatrists, psychologists, clinical social workers, psychiatric nurses, and school counselors.

Substance abuse and behavioral disorder counselors help people overcome addictions to alcohol, drugs, gambling, and eating disorders. They counsel individuals, families, or groups in clinics, hospital-based outpatient treatment programs, community mental health centers, and inpatient chemical dependency treatment programs.

Marriage and family therapists use various techniques to intervene with individuals, families, and couples or to help them resolve emotional conflicts. They aim to modify perceptions and behavior, enhance communication and understanding among family members, and prevent family and individual crises. Individual marriage and family therapists may also offer psychotherapy intended to assist individuals, couples, and families to improve their interpersonal relationships.

Pastoral counselors offer a type of psychotherapy that combines spiritual resources as well as psychological understanding for healing and growth. According to the American Association of Pastoral Counselors (AAPC; 2008, http://www.aapc.org/practice.cfm), this therapeutic modality is more than simply the comfort, support, and encouragement a religious community can offer; instead, it provides "psychologically sound therapy that weaves in the religious and spiritual dimension." Typically, an

AAPC-certified counselor has obtained a bachelor's degree from a college or university, a three-year professional degree from a seminary, and a specialized master's or doctoral degree in the mental health field.

The AAPC asserts that demand for spiritually based counseling is on the rise, in part because interest in spirituality is on the rise in the United States. The organization also believes that despite increased interest in psychotherapy and increasing numbers of therapists, managed mental health care has reduced the availability of, and payment for, counseling services for many people. As a result, more people are turning to clergy for help with personal, marital, and family issues as well as with faith issues. For many working poor Americans without health insurance benefits, free or low-cost counseling from pastoral counselors is the most accessible, available, affordable, and acceptable form of mental health care.

PRACTITIONERS OF COMPLEMENTARY AND ALTERNATIVE MEDICINE

The field of complementary and alternative medicine (CAM) is attracting a growing number of professionals. The National Center for Complementary and Alternative Medicine (NCCAM; June 26, 2008, http://nccam.nih.gov/health/whatiscam/) defines alternative medicine as "a group of diverse medical and health care systems, practices, and products that are not presently considered to be part of conventional medicine." Though there is some overlap between them, the NCCAM further distinguishes complementary, alternative, and integrative medicine in the following manner:

- Alternative medicine is therapy or treatment that is used instead of conventional medical treatment.

- Complementary medicine is nonstandard therapy or treatment that is used along with conventional medicine, not in place of it. Complementary medicine appears to offer health benefits, but historically, there has been less scientific evidence to support its utility than is generally available for conventional and integrative therapies.

- Integrative medicine is the combination of conventional medical treatment and CAM therapies that have been scientifically researched and have demonstrated evidence that they are both safe and effective.

In general terms, alternative therapies are often entirely untested and unproven, whereas complementary and integrative practices that are used in conjunction with mainstream medicine have substantial scientific basis of demonstrated safety and efficacy.

Susan S. Smith indicates in "Who Uses Complementary Therapies?" (*Holistic Nursing Practice*, vol. 18, no.3, May–June 2004) that in the United States there is increasing enthusiasm for and use of CAM approaches and practices.

Multiple surveys reveal that more than four out of ten Americans use or have used some form of complementary or alternative therapy (including the services of nutritionists, Pilates and tai chi instructors, and chiropractors, among others).

Several government agencies, including the National Institutes of Health (NIH), the NCCAM, and the Centers for Disease Control and Prevention, collaborated on *The Use of Complementary and Alternative Medicine in the United States* (May 27, 2008, http://nccam.nih.gov/news/camsurvey_fs1.htm), a telephone survey of more than thirty-one thousand adults conducted in 2002. With this comprehensive study, findings of previous surveys were confirmed—that a significant proportion of Americans, as high as 74.6%, had ever used CAM therapies and products and a full 62.1% said they had used CAM therapies in the twelve months preceding the survey. (See Figure 2.2.) The survey found that the ten-most frequently used CAM therapies were:

- Prayer for own health (43%)

- Prayer by others for the respondent's health (24.4%)

- Natural products such as herbs, other botanicals, and enzymes (18.9%)

- Deep breathing exercises (11.6%)

- Participation in prayer group for own health (9.6%)

FIGURE 2.2

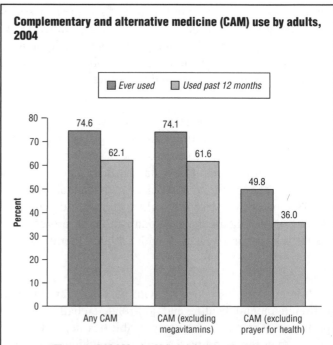

Complementary and alternative medicine (CAM) use by adults, 2004

SOURCE: "Figure 1. CAM Use by U.S. Adults," in *The Use of Complementary and Alternative Medicine in the United States*, National Institutes of Health, National Center for Complementary and Alternative Medicine, 2004, http://nccam.nih.gov/news/camsurvey_fs1.htm (accessed April 18, 2008)

- Meditation (7.6%)
- Chiropractic care (7.5%)
- Yoga (5.1%)
- Massage (5%)
- Diet-based therapies (3.5%)

Homeopathic Medicine

Homeopathic medicine (also called homeopathy) is based on the belief that "like cures like" and uses very diluted amounts of natural substances to encourage the body's own self-healing mechanisms. Homeopathy was developed by the German physician Samuel Hahnemann (1755–1843) in the 1790s. Hahnemann found that he could produce symptoms of particular diseases by injecting small doses of various herbal substances. This discovery inspired him to administer to sick people extremely diluted formulations of substances that would produce the same symptoms they suffered from in an effort to stimulate natural recovery and regeneration.

According to Kenneth R. Pelletier, a clinical professor of medicine at Stanford University School of Medicine and director of the NIH-funded Complementary and Alternative Medicine Program at Stanford, homeopathy has demonstrated effectiveness for a variety of ailments. In his book *The Best of Alternative Medicine: What Works? What Does Not?* (2000), Pelletier reports that clinical trials of homeopathy find it effective for the treatment of disorders such as seasonal allergies, asthma, childhood diarrhea, fibromyalgia, influenza, and rheumatoid arthritis.

Naturopathic Medicine

As its name suggests, naturopathic medicine (also called naturopathy) uses naturally occurring substances to prevent, diagnose, and treat disease. Even though it is now considered an alternative medicine system, it is one of the oldest medicine systems and has its origins in Native American culture and even draws from Greek, Chinese, and East Indian ideas about health and illness.

The guiding principles of modern naturopathic medicine are "first, do no harm" and "nature has the power to heal." Naturopathy seeks to treat the whole person, because disease is seen as arising from many causes rather than a single cause. Naturopathic physicians are taught that "prevention is as important as cure" and to view creating and maintaining health as equally important as curing disease. They are instructed to identify and treat the causes of diseases rather than to act only to relieve symptoms.

Naturopathic treatment methods include nutritional counseling; use of dietary supplements, herbs, and vitamins; hydrotherapy (water-based therapies, usually involving whirlpool or other baths); exercise; manipulation; massage; heat therapy; and electrical stimulation. Because naturopathy draws on Chinese and Indian medical techniques, naturopathic physicians often use Chinese herbs, acupuncture, and East Indian medicines to treat disease.

Pelletier's research finds studies demonstrating that naturopathy is effective for conditions such as asthma, atherosclerosis, back pain, some cancers, depression, diabetes, eczema (a skin condition), middle ear infections, migraine headaches, natural childbirth, and osteoarthritis. Furthermore, Pelletier asserts that licensed naturopathic physicians are among the best trained CAM practitioners and predicts that research will continue to confirm the benefits and efficacy of the safe, inexpensive, and low-risk therapies they can provide.

Traditional Chinese Medicine

Traditional Chinese medicine (TCM) uses nutrition, acupuncture, massage, herbal medicine, and Qi Gong (exercises to improve the flow of vital energy through the body) to help people achieve balance and unity of their mind, body, and spirit. Practiced for more than three thousand years by about a quarter of the world's population, TCM has been adopted by naturopathic physicians, chiropractors, and other CAM practitioners in the United States.

TCM views balancing *qi* (pronounced "chee"), the vital life force that flows over the surface of the body and through internal organs, as central to health, wellness, disease prevention, and treatment. This vital force or energy is thought to flow through the human body in meridians (channels). The Chinese believe that pain and disease develop when there is any sort of disturbance in the natural flow. TCM also seeks to balance the feminine and masculine qualities of yin and yang using other techniques such as moxibustion, which is the stimulation of acupuncture points with heat, and cupping, in which the practitioner increases circulation by putting a heated jar on the skin of a body part. Herbal medicine is the most commonly prescribed treatment.

Acupuncture

Acupuncture is a Chinese practice that dates back more than five thousand years. Chinese medicine describes acupuncture—the insertion of extremely thin, sterile needles to any of 360 specific points on the body—as a way to balance *qi*. After a diagnosis of an imbalance in the flow of energy, the acupuncturist inserts needles at specific points along the meridians (pathways of energy flow throughout the body). Each point controls a different part of the body. Once the needles are in place, they are rotated gently or are briefly charged with a small electric current.

Traditional Western medicine explains the acknowledged effectiveness of acupuncture as the result of triggering the release of pain-relieving substances called endorphins that occur naturally in the body, as well as neurotransmitters and neuropeptides that influence brain chemistry. Besides providing lasting pain relief, acupuncture has demonstrated success in helping people with substance abuse problems, relieving nausea, heightening immunity by increasing total white blood cells and T-cell production, and assisting patients to recover from stroke and other neurological impairments. Imaging techniques confirm that acupuncture acts to alter brain chemistry and function.

Chiropractic Physicians

Chiropractic physicians treat patients whose health problems are associated mainly with the body's structural and neurological systems, especially the spine. These practitioners believe that interference with these systems can impair normal functions and lower resistance to disease. Chiropractic medicine asserts that misalignment or compression of, for example, the spinal nerves can alter many important body functions. The American Chiropractic Association (2008, http://www.amerchiro.org/level2_css .cfm?T1ID=13&T2ID=61) defines the term *chiropractic* as "a health care profession that focuses on disorders of the musculoskeletal system and the nervous system, and the effects of these disorders on general health. Chiropractic care is used most often to treat neuromusculoskeletal complaints, including but not limited to back pain, neck pain, pain in the joints of the arms or legs, and headaches." Doctors of chiropractic medicine do not use or prescribe pharmaceutical drugs or perform surgery. Instead, they rely on adjustment and manipulation of the musculoskeletal system, particularly the spinal column.

Many chiropractors use nutritional therapy and prescribe dietary supplements; some employ a technique known as applied kinesiology to diagnose and treat disease. Applied kinesiology is based on the belief that every organ problem is associated with weakness of a specific muscle. Chiropractors who use this technique claim they can accurately identify organ system dysfunction without any laboratory or other diagnostic tests.

Besides manipulation, chiropractors also use a variety of other therapies to support healing and relax muscles before they make manual adjustments. These treatments include:

- Heat and cold therapy to relieve pain, speed healing, and reduce swelling

- Hydrotherapy to relax muscles and stimulate blood circulation

- Immobilization such as casts, wraps, traction, and splints to protect injured areas

- Electrotherapy to deliver deep tissue massage and boost circulation

- Ultrasound to relieve muscle spasms and reduce swelling

All states and the District of Columbia license chiropractors that meet the educational and examination requirements established by the state. According to the BLS (December 18, 2007, http://www.bls.gov/oco/ocos071 .htm), in 2006 there were about fifty-three thousand chiropractors, and most were self-employed and in solo practice. Median annual earnings of salaried chiropractors were $65,220 in 2006. Visits to chiropractors are most often for treatment of lower back pain, neck pain, and headaches.

INCREASE IN HEALTH CARE EMPLOYMENT

The number of people working in health care services increased from 12.2 million in 2000 to 14.4 million in 2006. (See Table 2.9.) Health care workers are employed in medical offices, outpatient and nursing care centers, and in patients' homes. Even though hospitals still employ a larger proportion of health workers than any other service location, more patients are now able to receive treatment in physicians' offices, clinics, and other outpatient settings.

Why Is Health Care Booming?

Three major factors appear to have influenced the escalation in health care employment: advances in technology, the increasing amounts of money spent on health care, and the aging of the U.S. population. In other sectors of the economy, technology often replaces humans in the labor force. However, health care technology has increased the demand for highly trained specialists to operate the sophisticated equipment. Because of technological advances, patients are likely to undergo more tests and diagnostic procedures, take more drugs, see more specialists, and be subjected to more aggressive treatments than ever before.

The second factor involves the amount of money the nation spends on keeping its citizens in good health. According to Kevin Freking, in "Spending on Health to Rise Dramatically" (Associated Press, February 26, 2008), the Centers for Medicare and Medicaid Services forecasts that national health expenditures will rise from an average of $7,026 per person in 2006 to $13,101 per person in 2017, which will account for 20% of the U.S. gross domestic product (the total market value of final goods and services produced within an economy in a given year). For each year that the amount of money spent on health care continues to grow, employment in the field grows as well. Some health care industry observers believe that government and private financing for the health care industry, unlike most other fields, is virtually unlimited.

The third factor contributing to the rise in the number of health care workers is the aging of the nation's population. There are greater numbers of older adults in the United States than ever before, and they are living longer. The U.S. Census Bureau (2004, http://www.census.gov/ ipc/www/usinterimproj/natprojtab02a.pdf) estimates that

TABLE 2.9

Persons employed in health service sites, by site and sex, 2000–06

Site	2000	2001	2002	2003	2004	2005	2006
Both sexes	Number of persons in thousands						
All employed civilians[a]	136,891	136,933	136,485	137,736	139,252	141,730	144,427
All health service sites[b]	12,211	12,558	13,069	13,615	13,817	14,052	14,352
Offices and clinics of physicians	1,387	1,499	1,533	1,673	1,727	1,801	1,785
Offices and clinics of dentists	672	701	734	771	780	792	852
Offices and clinics of chiropractors	120	111	132	142	156	163	163
Offices and clinics of optometrists	95	102	113	92	93	98	98
Offices and clinics of other health Practitioners[c]	143	140	149	250	274	275	292
Outpatient care centers	772	830	850	873	885	901	919
Home health care services	548	582	636	741	750	795	928
Other health care services[d]	1,027	1,101	1,188	943	976	1,045	1,096
Hospitals	5,202	5,256	5,330	5,652	5,700	5,719	5,712
Nursing care facilities	1,593	1,568	1,715	1,877	1,858	1,848	1,807
Residential care facilities, without nursing	652	668	689	601	618	615	700
Men							
All health service sites[b]	2,756	2,778	2,838	2,986	3,067	3,097	3,187
Offices and clinics of physicians	354	379	370	414	424	418	421
Offices and clinics of dentists	158	150	151	163	158	156	173
Offices and clinics of chiropractors	32	39	47	53	63	68	61
Offices and clinics of optometrists	26	27	29	29	24	27	29
Offices and clinics of other health practitioners[c]	38	41	42	63	69	80	80
Outpatient care centers	186	185	172	200	203	201	199
Home health care services	45	51	54	56	65	81	91
Other health care services[d]	304	345	362	297	314	311	344
Hospitals	1,241	1,187	1,195	1,263	1,333	1,347	1,337
Nursing care facilities	195	189	223	267	251	246	263
Residential care facilities, without nursing	177	185	193	181	164	162	189
Women							
All health service sites[b]	9,457	9,782	10,232	10,631	10,750	10,958	11,167
Offices and clinics of physicians	1,034	1,120	1,164	1,259	1,302	1,383	1,364
Offices and clinics of dentists	514	551	584	607	623	637	679
Offices and clinics of chiropractors	88	72	85	90	93	95	102
Offices and clinics of optometrists	69	75	84	64	69	71	69
Offices and clinics of other health practitioners[c]	106	99	106	186	204	195	213
Outpatient care centers	586	646	678	673	683	700	720
Home health care services	503	531	582	685	685	713	837
Other health care services[d]	723	756	826	646	662	734	752
Hospitals	3,961	4,069	4,135	4,390	4,366	4,372	4,376
Nursing care facilities	1,398	1,380	1,492	1,611	1,607	1,602	1,544
Residential care facilities, without nursing	475	483	496	420	454	453	511
Both sexes	Percent of employed civilians						
All health service sites	8.9	9.2	9.6	9.9	9.9	9.9	9.9
	Percent distribution						
All health service sites	100.0	100.0	100.0	100.0	100.0	100.0	100.0
Offices and clinics of physicians	11.4	11.9	11.7	12.3	12.5	12.8	12.4
Offices and clinics of dentists	5.5	5.6	5.6	5.7	5.6	5.6	5.9
Offices and clinics of chiropractors	1.0	0.9	1.0	1.0	1.1	1.2	1.1
Offices and clinics of optometrists	0.8	0.8	0.9	0.7	0.7	0.7	0.7
Offices and clinics of other health practitioners[c]	1.2	1.1	1.1	1.8	2.0	2.0	2.0
Outpatient care centers	6.3	6.6	6.5	6.4	6.4	6.4	6.4
Home health care services	4.5	4.6	4.9	5.4	5.4	5.7	6.5
Other health care services[d]	8.4	8.8	9.1	6.9	7.1	7.4	7.6
Hospitals	42.6	41.9	40.8	41.5	41.3	40.7	39.8
Nursing care facilities	13.0	12.5	13.1	13.8	13.4	13.2	12.6
Residential care facilities, without nursing	5.3	5.3	5.3	4.4	4.5	4.4	4.9

in 2000 there were 4.3 million Americans aged eighty-five and older; by 2050 there will be 20.9 million people over the age of eighty-five.

The increase in the number of older people is expected to boost the demand for home health care services, assisted living, and nursing home care. Many nursing homes now offer special care for stroke patients, people with Alz-heimer's disease (a progressive cognitive impairment), and people who need a respirator to breathe. To care for such patients, nursing homes need more physical therapists, nurses' aides, and respiratory therapists—three of the fastest-growing occupations. The BLS (December 18, 2007, http://www.bls.gov/oco/oco2003.htm) estimates that health care services will grow 25.4% between 2006 and 2016.

TABLE 2.9

Persons employed in health service sites, by site and sex, 2000–06 [CONTINUED]

aExcludes workers under the age of 16 years.
bData for health service sites for men and women may not sum to total for all health service sites for both sexes due to rounding.
cIncludes health service sites such as psychologists' offices, nutritionists' offices, speech defect clinics, and other offices and clinics.
dIncludes health service sites such as clinical laboratories, blood banks, CT-SCAN (computer tomography) centers, and other offices and clinics.
Notes: Annual data are based on data collected each month and averaged over the year.
Data are based on household interviews of a sample of the civilian noninstitutionalized population.

SOURCE: "Table 105. Persons Employed in Health Service Sites, by Site and Sex: United States, 2000–2006," in *Health, United States, 2007. With Chartbook on Trends in the Health of Americans*, U.S. Department of Health and Human Services, Centers for Disease Control and Prevention, National Center for Health Statistics, 2007, http://www.cdc.gov/nchs/data/hus/hus07.pdf#listtables (accessed April 18, 2008)

The fastest-growing health care occupations will be personal and home health aides, medical assistants, substance abuse and behavioral disorder counselors, skin care specialists, physical therapist assistants, pharmacy technicians, dental hygienists, mental health counselors, and mental health and substance abuse social workers. (See Figure 2.3.)

FIGURE 2.3

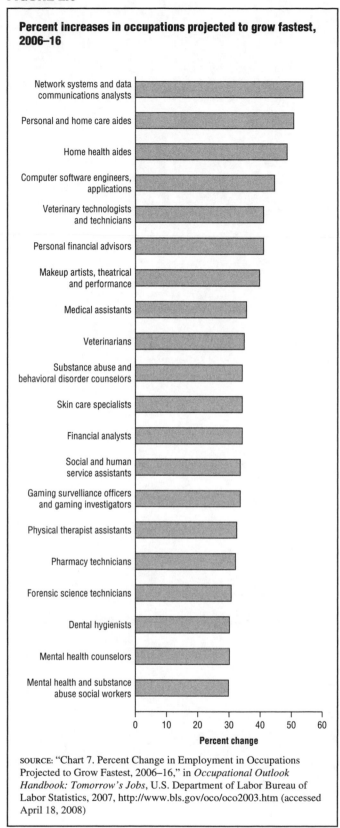

Percent increases in occupations projected to grow fastest, 2006–16

SOURCE: "Chart 7. Percent Change in Employment in Occupations Projected to Grow Fastest, 2006–16," in *Occupational Outlook Handbook: Tomorrow's Jobs*, U.S. Department of Labor Bureau of Labor Statistics, 2007, http://www.bls.gov/oco/oco2003.htm (accessed April 18, 2008)

CHAPTER 3
HEALTH CARE INSTITUTIONS

A hospital is no place to be sick.

—Samuel Goldwyn

HOSPITALS

The first hospitals in the United States were established more than two hundred years ago. No records of hospitals in the early colonies exist, but almshouses, which sheltered the poor, also cared for those who were ill. The first almshouse opened in 1662 in the Massachusetts Bay Colony. In 1756 the Pennsylvania Hospital in Philadelphia became the first U.S. institution devoted entirely to care of the sick.

Until the late 1800s, U.S. hospitals had a bad reputation. The upper classes viewed hospitals as places for the poor who could not afford home care, and the poor saw hospitalization as a humiliating consequence of personal economic failure. People from all walks of life thought hospitals were places to go to die.

TYPES OF HOSPITALS

The American Hospital Association notes in "Fast Facts on US Hospitals" (October 23, 2007, http://www.aha.org/aha/resource-center/Statistics-and-Studies/fast-facts.html) that in 2007 there were 5,747 hospitals in the United States that were described as short stay or long term, depending on the length of time a patient spends before discharge. Short-stay facilities include community, teaching, and public hospitals. Sometimes short-stay hospitals are referred to as acute care facilities because the services provided within them aim to help resolve pressing problems or medical conditions, such as a heart attack, rather than long-term chronic conditions, such as the need for rehabilitation following a head injury. Long-term hospitals are usually rehabilitation and psychiatric hospitals or facilities for the treatment of tuberculosis or other pulmonary (respiratory) diseases.

Hospitals are also distinguished by their ownership, scope of services, and whether they are teaching hospitals with academic affiliations. Hospitals may be operated as proprietary (for-profit) businesses, owned either by corporations or individuals such as the physicians on staff, or they may be voluntary—owned by not-for-profit corporations or religious organizations or operated by federal, state, or city governments. Voluntary, not-for-profit hospitals are usually governed by a board of trustees, who are selected from among community business and civic leaders and who serve without pay to oversee hospital operations.

Most community hospitals offer emergency services as well as a range of inpatient and outpatient medical and surgical services. There are more than a thousand tertiary hospitals in the United States, which provide highly specialized services such as neonatal intensive care units (for care of sick newborns), trauma services, or cardiovascular surgery programs. Most tertiary hospitals serve as teaching hospitals.

Teaching hospitals are those community and tertiary hospitals affiliated with medical schools, nursing schools, or allied-health professions training programs. Teaching hospitals are the primary sites for training new physicians, where interns and residents work under the supervision of experienced physicians. Nonteaching hospitals may also maintain affiliations with medical schools and some serve as sites for nursing and allied health professions students as well as physicians-in-training.

Community Hospitals

The most common type of hospital in the United States is the community, or general, hospital. Community hospitals, where most people receive care, are typically small, with fifty to five hundred beds. These hospitals normally provide quality care for routine medical and surgical problems. Since the 1980s many smaller hospitals have closed down because they are no longer profitable. The larger ones, usually located in cities and adjacent suburbs, are often equipped with a full complement of medical and surgical personnel and state-of-the-art equipment.

Some community hospitals are not-for-profit corporations that are supported by local funding. These include hospitals supported by religious, cooperative, or osteopathic organizations. During the 1990s increasing numbers of not-for-profit community hospitals converted their ownership status, becoming proprietary hospitals that are owned and operated on a for-profit basis by corporations. These hospitals joined investor-owned corporations because they needed additional financial resources to maintain their existence in an increasingly competitive industry. Investor-owned corporations acquire not-for-profit hospitals to build market share, expand their provider networks, and penetrate new health care markets.

Teaching Hospitals

Most teaching hospitals, which provide clinical training for medical students and other health care professionals, are affiliated with a medical school and have several hundred beds. Many of the physicians on staff at the hospital also hold teaching positions at the university affiliated with the hospital, besides teaching physicians-in-training at the bedsides of the patients. Patients in teaching hospitals understand that they may be examined by medical students and residents as well as by their primary attending physician.

One advantage of obtaining care at a university-affiliated teaching hospital is the opportunity to receive treatment from highly qualified physicians with access to the most advanced technology and equipment. A disadvantage is the inconvenience and invasion of privacy that may result from multiple examinations performed by residents and students. When compared to smaller community hospitals, some teaching hospitals have reputations for being impersonal; however, patients with complex, unusual, or difficult diagnoses usually benefit from the presence of acknowledged medical experts and more comprehensive resources available at these facilities.

Public Hospitals

Public hospitals are owned and operated by federal, state, or city governments. Many have a continuing tradition of caring for the poor. They are usually located in the inner cities and are often in precarious financial situations because many of their patients are unable to pay for services. These hospitals depend heavily on Medicaid payments supplied by local, state, and federal agencies or on grants from local governments. Medicaid is a program run by both the state and federal government for the provision of health care insurance to people younger than sixty-five years of age who cannot afford to pay for private health insurance. The federal government matches the states' contribution to provide a certain minimal level of available coverage, and the states may offer additional services at their own expense.

TREATING SOCIETY'S MOST VULNERABLE MEMBERS. Increasingly, public hospitals must bear the burden of the weaknesses in the nation's health care system. The major problems in U.S. society are readily apparent in the emergency rooms and corridors of public hospitals: poverty, drug and alcohol abuse, crime-related and domestic violence, untreated or inadequately treated chronic conditions such as high blood pressure and diabetes, and infectious diseases such as acquired immunodeficiency syndrome (AIDS) and tuberculosis.

LOSING MONEY. The typical public hospital provides millions of dollars in health care and fails to recoup these costs from reimbursement by private insurance, Medicaid, or Medicare (a program run by the federal government through which people aged sixty-five and older receive health care insurance). Joel S. Weissman notes in "The Trouble with Uncompensated Hospital Care" (*New England Journal of Medicine*, vol. 352, no. 12, March 24, 2005) that the National Association of Public Hospitals and Health Systems (NAPH) estimates that nearly half of all public hospital charges are not ultimately paid. According to Weissman, this figure has grown sharply as the number of uninsured Americans has also increased. State and local governments provide subsidies to help offset these expenses. However, even with the subsidies, the unpaid costs incurred by the nation's public hospitals add up to billions of dollars' worth of care each year.

In "Charity Care at U.S. Hospitals on the Rise as Americans with No Health Insurance Grows" (April 1, 2006, http://www.fast-health-insurance.com/health-insurance-news-archives/2006_03_26_affordable-health-insurance-news-archive.html), the PricewaterhouseCoopers Health Research Institute reports that the dollar amount of uncompensated service, of which charity care is a component, provided by U.S. hospitals rose 30% since 1999—from $20.7 billion to $27 billion in 2005. Even though approximately 70% of hospitals surveyed said they provide discounted care to the uninsured as well as charity care, many fail to communicate adequately their charity policies to patients, which results in fewer needy patients requesting financial assistance. The institute exhorts hospital leaders to "proactively report to the community and local leaders through an annual community benefit report" to defend against accusations that they are not fulfilling their charitable missions.

PROVIDING NEEDED SERVICES. The NAPH (2008, http://www.naph.org/Content/NavigationMenu/About_Our_Members/Characteristics_of_NAPH_Members/Characteristics_of_NAPH_Members.htm) believes the mission of public hospitals is to respond to the needs of their communities. As a result, most provide a broad spectrum of services. Even though the need for trauma care exists throughout the nation and across all socioeconomic levels, in thirty cities including Albuquerque, New Mexico; Las Vegas, Nevada; Memphis, Tennessee; New Orleans, Louisiana; Richmond,

Virginia; and San Francisco, California, NAPH-member hospitals are either the only providers of trauma center services or provide the highest level of trauma care.

According to Ron J. Anderson, Paul J. Boumbulian, and S. Sue Pickens, in "The Role of U.S. Public Hospitals in Urban Health" (*Academic Medicine*, vol. 79, no. 12, December 2004), almost half of NAPH-member hospitals provide prison services, and some hospitals have dedicated beds for prisoners. County and city revenues provide most, if not all, of the funds available for prison services. Many of the NAPH-member hospitals are also major academic centers, where they train medical and dental residents as well as nursing and allied health professionals. Anderson, Boumbulian, and Pickens explain that NAPH-member hospitals are just 2% of the nation's hospitals, but they provide 25% of uncompensated care.

SOME PUBLIC HOSPITALS IN PERIL OF CLOSING. New York City's cash-strapped public hospital system, the facilities that provide trauma and emergency care and are considered lifelines for the working poor, are imperiled because the bulk of their reimbursement comes from Medicaid and Medicare, which have failed to keep pace with rising inflation. In "Cabrini Medical Center Closes Its Doors" (*The Sun* [New York City, New York], March 18, 2008), E. B. Solomont reports that in 2006 a state health care commission recommended that five of the eleven public hospitals in New York City would close in the coming years. In late 2007 St. Vincent's Midtown Hospital closed and in March 2008 Cabrini Medical Center became the second hospital to close. The city's public hospital system projects an average annual deficit of $314 million between 2008 and 2012. The city has subsidized the Health and Hospitals Corporation for more than a decade. Between 2005 and 2008 the average annual subsidy was $1.2 billion, up from $290 million between 1999 and 2004.

The problems New York City faces are only compounded at the national level. In the press release "President's Budget Would Further Weaken Health Care Safety Net" (February 4, 2008, http://www.naph.org/naph/Press Room/Press_Statement_2009_Budget_02_04_09_FINAL .pdf), the NAPH decries President George W. Bush's (1946–) fiscal year 2009 budget request, explaining that cutting Medicaid expenditures by $200 billion over five years will have a disproportionate impact on public hospitals and would threaten to close more public hospitals, further compromising the nation's "safety net"—its essential role in the provision of care for uninsured Americans. Citing economic uncertainty and heightened awareness about matters of national security, the NAPH asks Congress to reject this budget, and if needed, to enact legislation to prevent President Bush from implementing a budget that "will severely damage public hospitals nationally."

Hospital Emergency Rooms: More Than They Can Handle

For many Americans, the hospital emergency room has replaced the physician's office as the place to seek health care services. With no insurance and little money, many people go to the only place that will take them without question. Insurance companies and health care planners estimate that more than half of all emergency room visits are for nonemergency treatment.

Poor or near poor children up to eighteen years of age of all races were more likely to visit emergency rooms (27.3% and 21.8%, respectively) in 2005 than those who were not poor (17.9%). (See Table 3.1.) In 2005, 28.5% of children on Medicaid visited emergency rooms at least once, as opposed to 17.4% of children who were privately insured and 18.4% of uninsured children. In the eighteen and older age group, 29.8% of poor people made one or more emergency department visits and 23.2% of the near poor made one or more visits in 2005. (See Table 3.2.) Of adults aged eighteen to sixty-four, 17.3% of people who were privately insured made one or more emergency room visits during 2005, as opposed to 40.1% of those who had Medicaid and 19.5% of those who were uninsured.

Even though any type of hospital can experience slow emergency room service, public hospitals are frequently underfunded and understaffed, and service can be exceedingly slow. All-day waits in the emergency room for initial treatment are not uncommon. Andrew P. Wilper et al. of the Harvard Medical School indicate in "Waits to See an Emergency Department Physician: U.S. Trends and Predictors, 1997–2004" (*Health Affairs*, vol. 27, no. 2, January 15, 2008) that the median waiting time to see a physician in a hospital emergency department rose from twenty-two minutes in 1997 to thirty minutes in 2004. The researchers attribute the longer waits to an increase in the number of emergency room visits and the closure of many emergency rooms. Uninsured patients and those who do not have a primary care physician account for much of the increase. When they use emergency rooms for routine care, the system becomes overburdened. At the same time, hospitals provide so much uncompensated care through emergency rooms that they end up closing or stop offering emergency care.

MAJORITY OF EMERGENCY ROOM PATIENTS HAVE HEALTH INSURANCE. Because people without health insurance or a usual source of care often resort to using hospital emergency departments, many industry observers assume that the crowding and long waits in the emergency department are at least in part caused by uninsured patients seeking care for routine illnesses such as colds, flu, or back pain. In "Characteristics of Frequent Users of Emergency Departments" (*Annals of Emergency Medicine*, vol. 48, no. 1, July 2006), Kelly A. Hunt et al. refute this hypothesis

TABLE 3.1

Emergency department visits within the past 12 months among children under 18, by selected characteristics, 1997, 2004, and 2005

Characteristic	Under 18 years			Under 6 years			6–17 years		
	1997	2004	2005	1997	2004	2005	1997	2004	2005
	Percent of children with one or more emergency department visits								
All children[a]	19.9	20.9	20.5	24.3	26.2	26.8	17.7	18.4	17.4
Race[b]									
White only	19.4	20.6	19.8	22.6	25.3	25.3	17.8	18.3	17.1
Black or African American only	24.0	23.1	23.8	33.1	31.1	31.6	19.4	19.4	20.0
American Indian or Alaska Native only	*24.1	*17.7	*32.1	*24.3	*	*	*24.0	*16.7	*
Asian only	12.6	15.8	14.6	20.8	*19.4	20.2	8.6	14.3	12.3
Native Hawaiian or other Pacific Islander only	—	*	*	—	*	*	—	*	*
2 or more races	—	27.0	24.8	—	35.7	38.3	—	21.3	17.1
Hispanic origin and race[b]									
Hispanic or Latino	21.1	20.6	19.5	25.7	26.9	28.0	18.1	16.9	14.5
Not Hispanic or Latino	19.7	21.0	20.7	24.0	26.0	26.5	17.6	18.7	18.0
White only	19.2	20.7	19.9	22.2	24.8	24.5	17.7	18.8	17.9
Black or African American only	23.6	22.8	23.8	32.7	30.7	31.8	19.2	19.1	20.0
Percent of poverty level[c]									
Below 100%	25.1	27.6	27.3	29.5	34.3	33.5	22.2	23.6	23.5
100%–less than 200%	22.0	22.3	21.8	28.0	29.5	30.8	19.0	18.6	17.4
200% or more	17.3	18.5	17.9	20.5	21.9	22.7	15.8	16.9	15.7
Hispanic origin and race and percent of poverty level[b, c]									
Hispanic or Latino:									
Percent of poverty level:									
Below 100%	21.9	23.1	21.8	25.0	29.2	28.4	19.6	19.2	17.4
100%–less than 200%	20.8	20.9	17.8	28.8	26.4	26.1	15.6	17.6	13.1
200% or more	20.4	17.9	18.8	23.4	24.8	29.3	18.7	14.4	13.5
Not Hispanic or Latino:									
White only:									
Percent of poverty level:									
Below 100%	25.5	32.3	34.1	27.2	36.6	37.3	24.4	29.9	32.2
100%–less than 200%	22.3	23.8	22.8	25.8	31.3	30.7	20.7	19.6	19.1
200% or more	17.2	18.3	17.4	20.1	20.9	20.8	15.9	17.2	15.9
Black or African American only:									
Percent of poverty level:									
Below 100%	29.3	29.2	27.1	39.5	37.5	34.8	23.0	24.1	22.6
100%–less than 200%	22.5	21.2	24.1	31.7	27.8	33.3	18.5	18.9	20.3
200% or more	17.7	18.9	20.6	22.6	25.8	27.4	15.9	15.9	17.6
Health insurance status at the time of interview[d]									
Insured	19.8	21.0	20.7	24.4	25.9	26.8	17.5	18.5	17.7
Private	17.5	18.5	17.4	20.9	21.1	21.7	15.9	17.3	15.5
Medicaid	28.2	27.2	28.5	33.0	34.3	35.5	24.1	22.3	23.6
Uninsured	20.2	20.7	18.4	23.0	28.7	26.6	18.9	17.6	15.4
Health insurance status prior to interview[d]									
Insured continuously all 12 months	19.6	20.7	20.5	24.1	25.5	26.7	17.3	18.4	17.3
Uninsured for any period up to 12 months	24.0	27.3	26.0	27.1	37.4	34.4	21.9	22.2	22.4
Uninsured more than 12 months	18.4	16.6	14.4	19.3	21.9	15.7*	18.1	15.0	14.0

and characterize frequent users of emergency medical care (adults who made four or more emergency department visits in one year) as people with both insurance (84%) and a usual source for health care (81%). Between 2000 and 2001 frequent users accounted for just 8% of emergency department users and 28% of all adult visits. Contesting the notion that frequent users were generally inappropriate users, Hunt et al. find that frequent users were sicker than less frequent users and made more health care visits to other parts of the health care system for care. They conclude that most emergency department utilization by frequent users appears to be appropriate.

HOSPITALS TRY TO EASE THE PAIN OF WAITING. In an effort to distinguish themselves from competitors and increase patient satisfaction with care, some hospitals are promising patients in the emergency department that they will not have to wait more than thirty minutes to be seen. Even though this guarantee does not apply when the emergency department has multiple critical patients or is so full that ambulances are being diverted to other hospitals, Tammie Smith notes in "Hospital Offering a Time Guarantee" (*Richmond Times-Dispatch*, March 20, 2006) that under typical circumstances participating hospitals are attempting to reduce the average waiting time

TABLE 3.1

Emergency department visits within the past 12 months among children under 18, by selected characteristics, 1997, 2004, and 2005

[CONTINUED]

Characteristic	Under 18 years			Under 6 years			6–17 years		
	1997	2004	2005	1997	2004	2005	1997	2004	2005
Percent of poverty level and health insurance status prior to interview[c, d]									
Below 100%:									
Insured continuously all 12 months	26.3	27.4	28.1	30.9	33.2	34.3	22.8	23.7	23.8
Uninsured for any period up to 12 months	26.5	35.4	31.2	29.7	47.5	39.1	24.4	29.5	*28.2
Uninsured more than 12 months	17.5	*18.9	15.7	*16.0	*	*	18.0	*	*15.6
100%–less than 200%:									
Insured continuously all 12 months	21.8	22.3	22.1	28.0	28.7	31.0	18.6	18.8	17.4
Uninsured for any period up to 12 months	24.5	27.2	27.4	29.7	39.5	41.2	21.0	21.4	21.9
Uninsured more than 12 months	19.5	16.8	14.7	*22.5	*27.3	*	18.6	13.6	*14.5
200% or more:									
Insured continuously all 12 months	17.1	18.5	17.9	20.3	21.7	22.6	15.6	17.1	15.7
Uninsured for any period up to 12 months	20.7	22.2	21.4	21.3	30.0	26.8	20.4	18.1	18.7
Uninsured more than 12 months	17.9	*13.6	*12.6	*19.2	*	*	17.3	*12.6	*

*Estimates are considered unreliable. Data preceded by an asterisk have a relative standard error (RSE) of 20%–30%. Data not shown have an RSE of greater than 30%.

— Data not available.

[a]Includes all other races not shown separately and unknown health insurance status.

[b]The race groups, white, black, American Indian or Alaska Native, Asian, Native Hawaiian or other Pacific Islander, and 2 or more races, include persons of Hispanic and non-Hispanic origin. Persons of Hispanic origin may be of any race. Starting with 1999 data, race-specific estimates are tabulated according to the 1997 Revisions to the Standards for the Classification of Federal Data on Race and Ethnicity and are not strictly comparable with estimates for earlier years. The five single-race categories plus multiple-race categories shown in the table conform to the 1997 standards. Starting with 1999 data, race-specific estimates are for persons who reported only one racial group; the category 2 or more races includes persons who reported more than one racial group. Prior to 1999, data were tabulated according to the 1977 standards with four racial groups and the Asian only category included Native Hawaiian or other Pacific Islander. Estimates for single-race categories prior to 1999 included persons who reported one race or, if they reported more than one race, identified one race as best representing their race. Starting with 2003 data, race responses of other race and unspecified multiple race were treated as missing, and then race was imputed if these were the only race responses. Almost all persons with a race response of other race were of Hispanic origin.

[c]Percent of poverty level is based on family income and family size and composition using U.S. Census Bureau poverty thresholds. Missing family income data were imputed for 21%–25% of children in 1997–1998 and 28%–31% in 1999–2005.

[d]Health insurance categories are mutually exclusive. Persons who reported both Medicaid and private coverage are classified as having private coverage. Starting in 1997 Medicaid includes state-sponsored health plans and State Children's Health Insurance Program (SCHIP). In addition to private and Medicaid, the insured category also includes military, other government, and Medicare coverage. Persons not covered by private insurance, Medicaid, SCHIP, public assistance (through 1996), state-sponsored or other government-sponsored health plans (starting in 1997), Medicare, or military plans are considered to have no health insurance coverage. Persons with only Indian Health Service coverage are considered to have no health insurance coverage.

Notes: Data are based on household interviews of a sample of the civilian noninstitutionalized population.

SOURCE: Adapted from "Table 89. Emergency Department Visits within the Past 12 Months among Children under 18 Years of Age, by Selected Characteristics: United States, 1997, 2004, and 2005," in *Health, United States, 2007. With Chartbook on Trends in the Health of Americans*, U.S. Department of Health and Human Services, Centers for Disease Control and Prevention, National Center for Health Statistics, 2007, http://www.cdc.gov/nchs/data/hus/hus07.pdf#listtables (accessed April 19, 2008)

to see a physician—46.5 minutes—to under half an hour. When the guarantees are not met and patients have to wait longer, they may be compensated with an apology and movie tickets, prepaid gas cards, restaurant gift certificates, or even free medical care.

In "Hospitals Try Pagers to Ease the Pain of Waiting" (*Pittsburgh Post-Gazette*, January 1, 2006), Christopher Snowbeck states that other hospitals issue pagers to waiting patients, which allow them to roam the hospital campus or eat in the cafeteria rather than sitting in waiting rooms anxiously awaiting diagnostic testing or appointments. Friends and family are also offered pagers so they can be summoned quickly when physicians have updated information or a patient is ready for discharge.

HOSPITALIZATION

Table 3.3 shows that the discharge rate increased among people aged sixty-five and older from 1990 to 2003. From 2003 to 2004 the rate declined and stabilized through 2005. Discharge rates for all other age groups steadily declined during this period.

In 2005 the hospital discharge rate was 116.2 per 1,000 population. The rate for females was 132 per 1,000, and for males it was 101.3 per 1,000. (See Table 3.3.) Male patients had longer average lengths of stay (ALOS) than female patients—5.2 days compared to 4.4 days. ALOS and discharge rates varied by geography—ALOS ranged from 4.2 days in the Midwest to 5.3 days in the Northeast. Furthermore, the discharge rate per 1,000 population ranged from 100.6 in the West to 124.6 in the Northeast.

Organ Transplants

Organ transplants are a viable means of saving lives, and according to the United Network for Organ Sharing's (UNOS) Organ Procurement and Transplantation Network (OPTN; August 1, 2008, http://www.optn.org/latestData/step2.asp?), in 2007, 28,354 transplants were performed. UNOS compiles data on organ transplants, distributes organ donor cards, and maintains a registry of patients awaiting organ transplants. It reports that as of August 2008, 107,280 Americans were waiting for transplants. UNOS (May 1, 2006, http://www.optn.org/AR2006/114_dh.htm?o=1&g=2&c=15) also states that in 2004 there were 153,245 people living with functioning

TABLE 3.2

Emergency department visits within the past 12 months among adults, by selected characteristics, selected years 1997–2005

Characteristic	One or more emergency department visits				Two or more emergency department visits			
	1997	2000	2004	2005	1997	2000	2004	2005
	Percent of adults with emergency department visits							
18 years and over, age-adjusted[a, b]	19.6	20.2	20.7	20.5	6.7	6.9	7.5	7.1
18 years and over, crude[a]	19.6	20.1	20.6	20.4	6.7	6.8	7.4	7.0
Age								
18–44 years	20.7	20.5	20.9	20.8	6.8	7.0	7.4	7.1
18–24 years	26.3	25.7	24.4	25.3	9.1	8.8	8.6	8.9
25–44 years	19.0	18.8	19.7	19.2	6.2	6.4	7.0	6.5
45–64 years	16.2	17.6	18.1	18.2	5.6	5.6	6.3	6.4
45–54 years	15.7	17.9	17.9	17.6	5.5	5.8	6.4	6.1
55–64 years	16.9	17.0	18.4	19.0	5.7	5.3	6.2	6.8
65 years and over	22.0	23.7	24.5	23.7	8.1	8.6	9.5	8.2
65–74 years	20.3	21.6	20.8	20.8	7.1	7.4	7.5	7.4
75 years and over	24.3	26.2	28.7	27.1	9.3	10.0	11.8	9.1
Sex[b]								
Male	19.1	18.7	19.3	18.6	5.9	5.7	6.5	5.9
Female	20.2	21.6	22.1	22.3	7.5	7.9	8.4	8.2
Race[b, c]								
White only	19.0	19.4	20.0	19.8	6.2	6.4	7.0	6.5
Black or African American only	25.9	26.5	27.0	26.3	11.1	10.8	11.2	11.9
American Indian or Alaska Native only	24.8	30.3	27.8	31.0	13.1	12.6*	12.6*	11.1*
Asian only	11.6	13.6	12.2	15.4	2.9*	3.8*	4.1	3.8*
Native Hawaiian or other Pacific Islander only	—	*	*	*	—	*	*	*
2 or more races	—	32.5	31.5	25.7	—	11.3	14.4	12.8
American Indian or Alaska Native; White	—	33.9	32.1	29.3	—	9.4*	15.8*	15.3*
Hispanic origin and race[b, c]								
Hispanic or Latino	19.2	18.3	19.2	20.1	7.4	7.0	7.0	7.1
Mexican	17.8	17.4	17.1	17.2	6.4	7.1	5.9	5.8
Not Hispanic or Latino	19.7	20.6	21.1	20.7	6.7	6.9	7.6	7.1
White only	19.1	19.8	20.4	20.1	6.2	6.4	7.0	6.4
Black or African American only	25.9	26.5	27.2	26.2	11.0	10.8	11.3	11.9
Percent of poverty level[b, d]								
Below 100%	28.1	29.0	29.3	29.8	12.8	13.3	13.8	13.7
100%–less than 200%	23.8	23.9	23.6	23.2	9.3	9.6	9.5	9.6
200% or more	17.0	18.0	18.7	18.3	4.9	5.2	6.0	5.3
Hispanic origin and race and percent of poverty level[b, c, d]								
Hispanic or Latino:								
Below 100%	22.1	22.4	22.6	24.0	9.8	9.7	10.0	9.2
100%–less than 200%	19.2	18.1	20.2	18.7	8.1	6.7	7.1	7.1
200% or more	17.6	16.8	16.9	19.6	5.4	6.1	5.4	6.1
Not Hispanic or Latino:								
White only:								
Below 100%	29.5	30.1	30.2	30.8	13.0	13.9	14.1	13.7
100%–less than 200%	24.3	25.5	25.1	24.3	9.1	10.4	10.0	9.8
200% or more	16.8	17.7	18.6	18.1	4.8	5.0	5.9	5.0
Black or African American only:								
Below 100%	34.6	35.4	38.2	35.4	17.5	17.4	19.2	18.3
100%–less than 200%	29.2	28.5	28.5	28.9	12.8	12.2	12.1	14.2
200% or more	19.7	22.6	22.5	21.6	7.2	8.0	8.1	8.5

organ transplants. Nonetheless, many patients died waiting for an organ transplant because demand for organs continued to outpace supply.

In February 2004 UNOS/OPTN revised and strengthened its policies to guard against potential medical errors in transplant candidate and donor matching. The policy revisions were developed in response to a systematic review begun after a medical error in February 2003, when a teenager named Jesica Santillan died after receiving a heart-lung transplant from a blood-type incompatible donor at Duke University Medical Center. News of this tragic error immediately prompted transplant centers throughout the United States to perform internal audits of their protocols and procedures to ensure appropriate donor-recipient matching.

The key policy revisions included stipulations that:

- The blood type of each transplant candidate and donor must be independently verified by two staff members

TABLE 3.2

Emergency department visits within the past 12 months among adults, by selected characteristics, selected years 1997–2005 [CONTINUED]

Characteristic	One or more emergency department visits				Two or more emergency department visits			
	1997	2000	2004	2005	1997	2000	2004	2005
Health insurance status at the time of interview[e, f]								
18–64 years:								
Insured	18.8	19.5	20.1	20.0	6.1	6.4	6.9	6.6
Private	16.9	17.6	18.0	17.3	4.7	5.1	5.3	4.8
Medicaid	37.6	42.2	36.8	40.1	19.7	21.0	19.8	20.1
Uninsured	20.0	19.3	19.0	19.5	7.5	6.9	7.4	8.0

*Estimates are considered unreliable. Data followed by an asterisk have a relative standard error (RSE) of 20%–30%. Data not shown have an RSE of greater than 30%.
—Data not available.
[a]Includes all other races not shown separately and unknown health insurance status.
[b]Estimates are for persons 18 years of age and over and are age-adjusted to the year 2000 standard population using five age groups: 18–44 years, 45–54 years, 55–64 years, 65–74 years, and 75 years and over.
[c]The race groups, white, black, American Indian or Alaska Native, Asian, Native Hawaiian or other Pacific Islander, and 2 or more races, include persons of Hispanic and non-Hispanic origin. Persons of Hispanic origin may be of any race. Starting with 1999 data, race-specific estimates are tabulated according to the 1997 Revision to the Standards for the Classification of Federal Data on Race and Ethnicity and are not strictly comparable with estimates for earlier years. The five single-race categories plus multiple-race categories shown in the table conform to the 1997 standards. Starting with 1999 data, race-specific estimates are for persons who reported only one racial group; the category 2 or more races includes persons who reported more than one racial group. Prior to 1999, data were tabulated according to the 1977 standards with four racial groups, and the Asian only category included Native Hawaiian or other Pacific Islander. Estimates for single-race categories pri to 1999 included persons who reported one race or, if they reported more than one race, identified one race as best representing their race. Starting with 2003 data, race responses of other race and unspecified multiple race were treated as missing, and then race was imputed if these were the only race responses. Almost all persons with a race response of other race were of Hispanic origin.
[d]Percent of poverty level is based on family income and family size and composition using U.S. Census Bureau poverty thresholds. Missing family income data were imputed for 27%–31% of persons 18 years of age and over in 1997–1998 and 33%–36% in 1999–2005.
[e]Estimates for persons 18–64 years of age are age-adjusted to the year 2000 standard population using three age groups: 18–44 years, 45–54 years, and 55–64 years of age.
[f]Health insurance categories are mutually exclusive. Persons who reported both Medicaid and private coverage are classified as having private coverage. Starting wit 1997 data, Medicaid includes state-sponsored health plans and State Children's Health Insurance Program (SCHIP). In addition to private and Medicaid, the insured category also includes military plans, other government-sponsored health plans, and Medicare, not shown separately. Persons not covered by private insurance, Medicaid, SCHIP, public assistance (through 1996), state-sponsored or other government-sponsored health plans (starting in 1997), Medicare, or military plans are considered to have no health insurance coverage. Persons with only Indian Health Service coverage are considered to have no health insurance coverage.
Note: Data are based on household interviews of a sample of the civilian noninstitutionalized population.

SOURCE: Adapted from "Table 90. Emergency Department Visits within the Past 12 Months among Adults 18 Years of Age and over, by Selected Characteristics: United States, Selected Years 1997–2005," in *Health, United States, 2007. With Chartbook on Trends in the Health of Americans*, U.S. Department of Health and Human Services, Centers for Disease Control and Prevention, National Center for Health Statistics, 2007, http://www.cdc.gov/nchs/data/hus/hus07.pdffiHsttables (accessed April 19, 2008)

---

at the institution involved at the time blood type is entered into the national database.

- Each transplant program and organ procurement organization (OPO) must establish a protocol to ensure blood-type data for transplant candidates, and donors are accurately entered into the national database and communicated to transplant teams. UNOS will verify the existence and effective use of these protocols during routine audits of OPOs and transplant programs.

- Organs must only be offered to candidates specifically identified on the computer-generated list of medically suitable transplant candidates for a given organ offer. If the organ offer is not accepted for any candidate on a given match run, an OPO may give transplant programs the opportunity to update transplant candidate data and rerun a match to see if any additional candidates are identified.

UNOS resolved to continuously review national policies and procedures for organ placement and to recommend policy and procedure enhancements to maximize the efficiency of organ placement and the safety of transplant candidates and recipients, as well as to ensure public confidence in the transplant system. As of August 2008, there had been no further reported occurrences of unintentional blood-type incompatible transplants.

The risks associated with organ transplant were, however, publicized once again in 2005 and 2006, when two transplant recipients from the same organ donor contracted West Nile virus, a potentially serious illness transmitted by mosquitoes. Even though 28,113 transplants were performed in the United States in 2005, according to the OPTN (August 1, 2008, http://www.optn.org/latestData/step2.asp?), and these two recipients were the only ones reported to have become ill from West Nile virus, they suffered the worst possible outcome. Both developed encephalitis (a brain infection), fell into coma, and died. These cases catalyzed transplant physicians and public health officials to intensify organ safety protocols and procedures. Denise Grady reports in "For Two Transplant Patients, a Dire Complication: West Nile" (*New York Times*, May 16, 2006) that Matthew Kuehnert, an authority in transfusion and transplant safety at the Centers for Disease Control and Prevention (CDC), asserts, "I think organ safety as concerns infectious disease transmission is really underappreciated. It's something that really needs to be looked at more closely."

TABLE 3.3

Hospital discharges, days of care, and average length of stay by selected characteristics, selected years 1980–2005

Characteristic	1980[a]	1985[a]	1990	1995	2000	2002	2003	2004	2005
					Discharges per 1,000 population				
Total, age-adjusted[b]	173.4	151.4	125.2	118.0	113.3	117.3	119.5	118.4	116.2
Total, crude	167 7	148.4	122.3	115.7	112.8	117.5	120.0	119.2	117.4
Age									
Under 18 years	75.6	61.4	46.4	42.4	40.3	43.4	43.6	43.0	41.1
18–44 years	155.3	128.0	102.7	91.4	84.9	90.3	91.3	91.1	89.8
45–54 years	174.8	146.8	112.4	98.5	92.1	95.6	99.5	99.7	96.4
55–64 years	215.4	194.8	163.3	148.3	141.5	146.5	145.7	143.6	140.2
65 years and over	383.7	369.8	334.1	347.7	353.4	357.5	367.9	362.9	359.6
65–74 years	315.8	297.2	261.6	260.0	254.6	254.0	265.1	259.2	262.9
75 years and over	489.3	475.6	434.0	459.4	462.0	466.6	475.2	470.2	458.8
Sex[b]									
Male	153.2	137.3	113.0	104.8	99.1	102.4	104.4	102.6	101.3
Female	195.0	167.3	139.0	131.7	127.7	132.9	135.1	134.9	132.0
Geographic region[b]									
Northeast	162.0	142.6	133.2	133.5	127.5	123.5	127.6	128.8	124.6
Midwest	192.1	158.1	128.8	113.3	110.9	113.6	117.1	114.4	117.5
South	179.7	155.5	132.5	125.2	120.9	126.7	125.8	125.6	120.2
West	150.5	145.7	100.7	96.7	89.4	99.7	103.9	101.2	100.6
					Days of care per 1,000 population				
Total, age-adjusted[b]	1,297.0	997.5	818.9	638.6	557.7	570.9	574.6	568.7	554.2
Total, crude	1,216.7	957.7	784.0	620.2	554.6	571.7	577.8	574.1	562.1
Age									
Under 18 years	341.4	281.2	226.3	184.7	179.0	195.2	195.5	193.2	191.8
18–44 years	818.6	619.2	467.7	351.7	309.4	333.9	339.7	334.9	330.5
45–54 years	1,314.9	967.8	699.7	516.2	437.4	456.7	477.2	491.1	471.1
55–64 years	1,889.4	1,436.9	1,172.3	867.2	729.1	752.2	735.9	735.2	712.4
65 years and over	4,098.3	3,228.0	2,895.6	2,373.7	2,111.9	2,085.1	2,088.3	2,048.6	1,988.3
65–74 years	3,147.0	2,437.3	2,087.8	1,684.7	1,439.0	1,411.9	1,428.9	1,405.2	1,398.5
75 years and over	5,578.8	4,381.3	4,009.1	3,247.8	2,851.9	2,795.0	2,776.1	2,714.9	2,593.9
Sex[b]									
Male	1,239.7	973.3	805.8	623.9	535.9	549.5	546.7	541.1	530.1
Female	1,365.2	1,033.1	840.5	654.9	581.0	596.0	605.2	599.6	582.9
Geographic region[b]									
Northeast	1,400.6	1,113.0	1,026.7	839.0	718.6	690.0	694.4	687.6	663.6
Midwest	1,484.8	1,078.6	830.6	590.9	500.5	502.1	507.9	498.7	495.4
South	1,262.3	957.7	820.4	666.0	592.5	618.6	609.8	614.2	583.0
West	956.9	824.7	575.5	451.1	408.2	454.7	476.4	457.5	469.0
					Average length of stay in days				
Total, age-adjusted[b]	7.5	6.6	6.5	5.4	4.9	4.9	4.8	4.8	4.8
Total, crude	7.3	6.5	6.4	5.4	4.9	4.9	4.8	4.8	4.8
Age									
Under 18 years	4.5	4.6	4.9	4.4	4.4	4.5	4.5	4.5	4.7
18–44 years	5.3	4.8	4.6	3.8	3.6	3.7	3.7	3.7	3.7
45–54 years	7.5	6.6	6.2	5.2	4.8	4.8	4.8	4.9	4.9
55–64 years	8.8	7.4	7.2	5.8	5.2	5.1	5.1	5.1	5.1
65 years and over	10.7	8.7	8.7	6.8	6.0	5.8	5.7	5.6	5.5
65–74 years	10.0	8.2	8.0	6.5	5.7	5.6	5.4	5.4	5.3
75 years and over	11.4	9.2	9.2	7.1	6.2	6.0	5.8	5.8	5.7
Sex[b]									
Male	8.1	7.1	7.1	6.0	5.4	5.4	5.2	5.3	5.2
Female	7.0	6.2	6.0	5.0	4.6	4.5	4.5	4.4	4.4

SURGICAL CENTERS AND URGENT CARE CENTERS

Ambulatory surgery centers (also called surgicenters) are equipped to perform routine surgical procedures that do not require an overnight hospital stay. A surgical center requires less sophisticated and expensive equipment than a hospital operating room. Minor surgery, such as biopsies, abortions, hernia repair, and many cosmetic surgery procedures, are performed at outpatient surgical centers. Most procedures are done under local anesthesia, and patients go home the same day.

Most ambulatory surgery centers are freestanding, but some are located on hospital campuses or are next to physicians' offices or clinics. Facilities are licensed by

TABLE 3.3

Hospital discharges, days of care, and average length of stay by selected characteristics, selected years 1980–2005 [CONTINUED]

Characteristic	1980[a]	1985[a]	1990	1995	2000	2002	2003	2004	2005
Geographic region[b]					Average length of stay in days				
Northeast	8.6	7.8	7.7	6.3	5.6	5.6	5.4	5.3	5.3
Midwest	7.7	6.8	6.5	5.2	4.5	4.4	4.3	4.4	4.2
South	7.0	6.2	6.2	5.3	4.9	4.9	4.8	4.9	4.8
West	6.4	5.7	5.7	4.7	4.6	4.6	4.6	4.5	4.7

[a]Comparisons of data from 1980–1985 with data from later years should be made with caution as estimates of change may reflect improvements in the survey design rather than true changes in hospital use.
[b]Estimates are age-adjusted to the year 2000 standard population using six age groups: under 18 years, 18–44 years, 45–54 years, 55–64 years, 65–74 years, and 75 years and over.
Notes: Excludes newborn infants. Rates are based on the civilian population as of July 1. Starting with Health, United States, 2003, rates for 2000 and beyond are based on the 2000 census. Rates for 1990–1999 use population estimates based on the 1990 census adjusted for net underenumeration using the 1990 National Population Adjustment Matrix from the U.S. Census Bureau. Rates for 1990–1999 are not strictly comparable with rates for 2000 and beyond because population estimates for 1990–1999 have not been revised to reflect the 2000 census. Data are based on a sample of hospital records.

SOURCE: "Table 99. Discharges, Days of Care, and Average Length of Stay in Nonfederal Short-Stay Hospitals, by Selected Characteristics: United States, Selected Years 1980–2005," in *Health, United States, 2007. With Chartbook on Trends in the Health of Americans*, U.S. Department of Health and Human Services, Centers for Disease Control and Prevention, National Center for Health Statistics, 2007, http://www.cdc.gov/nchs/data/hus/hus07.pdf#listtables (accessed April 19, 2008)

their state and must be equipped with at least one operating room, an area for preparing patients for procedures, a patient recovery area, and x-ray and clinical laboratory services. Surgical centers must have a registered nurse on the premises when patients are in the facility.

Urgent care centers (also called urgicenters) are usually operated by private, for-profit organizations and provide up to twenty-four-hour care on a walk-in basis. These centers fill several special needs in a community. They provide convenient, timely, and easily accessible care in an emergency when the nearest hospital is miles away. The centers are normally open during the hours when most physicians' offices are closed, and they are economical to operate because they do not provide hospital beds. They usually treat problems such as cuts that require sutures, sprains and bruises from accidents, and various infections. Many provide inexpensive immunization, and some offer routine health care for people who do not have a regular source of medical care. Urgent care may be more expensive than a visit to the family physician, but an urgent care center visit is usually less expensive than treatment from a traditional hospital emergency department.

Clinics and Urgent Care Centers in Malls and Storefronts

In *No Appointment Needed: The Resurgence of Urgent Care Centers in the United States* (September 2007, http://www.chcf.org/documents/policy/NoAppointmentNecessaryUrgentCareCenters.pdf), Robin M. Weinck and Renée M. Betancourt indicate that since 2005 there has been a resurgence in the popularity of urgent care centers and clinics in retail settings. The updated versions of such centers offer more than simply convenient locations. Many offer extended hours, flat fees for physician visits, immunizations, comfortable surroundings, and welcome walk-in patients. They emphasize unscheduled care much more

than most do most primary care practices. Most do not bill insurance companies; patients pay in cash or by credit card. Health care industry observers characterize these clinics as affordable alternatives as health care consumers assume a greater share of costs and the number of uninsured Americans continues to rise. Victoria Colliver notes in "The Instant Doctor: Health Clinics Popping up in Malls, Storefronts" (*San Francisco Chronicle*, February 21, 2006) that detractors believe the clinics undermine continuity and quality of care when the same practitioner rarely sees patients more than once and patients do not return for follow-up visits.

LONG-TERM CARE FACILITIES

Families are still the major caretakers of older, dependent, and disabled members of American society. However, the number of people aged sixty-five and older living in long-term care facilities such as nursing homes is rising because the population in this age group is increasing rapidly. Even though many older people now live longer, healthier lives, the increase in overall length of life has increased the need for long-term care facilities.

Growth of the home health care industry in the early 1990s only slightly slowed the increase in the numbers of Americans entering nursing homes. Assisted living and continuing-care retirement communities offer other alternatives to nursing home care. When it is possible, many older adults prefer to remain in the community and receive health care in their home.

Types of Nursing Homes

Nursing homes fall into three broad categories: residential care facilities, intermediate care facilities, and skilled nursing facilities. Each provides a different range and intensity of services:

- A residential care facility (RCF) normally provides meals and housekeeping for its residents, plus some basic medical monitoring, such as administering medications. This type of home is for people who are fairly independent and do not need constant medical attention but need help with tasks such as laundry and cleaning. Many RCFs also provide social activities and recreational programs for their residents.

- An intermediate care facility (ICF) offers room and board and nursing care as necessary for people who can no longer live independently. As in the RCF, exercise and social programs are provided, and some ICFs also offer physical therapy and rehabilitation programs.

- A skilled nursing facility (SNF) provides around-the-clock nursing care, plus on-call physician coverage. The SNF is for patients who need intensive nursing care, as well as services such as occupational therapy, physical therapy, respiratory therapy, and rehabilitation.

Number of Nursing Home Residents Rising

The National Nursing Home Survey (NNHS) is a continuing series of national sample surveys of nursing homes, their residents, and their staff. The surveys were conducted in 1973–74, 1977, 1985, 1995, 1997, 1999, and 2004. Even though each survey focused on different aspects of care, they all provide some common basic information about nursing homes, their residents, and their staff from two perspectives: that of the provider of services and that of the recipient. Data about the facilities include characteristics such as size, ownership, Medicare/Medicaid certification, occupancy rate, number of days of care provided, and expenses. The surveys gathered demographic data, health status, and services received by nursing home residents. The most recent NNHS for which data are available was conducted in 2004. The nursing homes included in this survey had at least three beds and were either certified (by Medicare or Medicaid) or had a state license to operate as a nursing home.

In 2004 the nation's 16,100 certified nursing homes housed more than 1.7 million beds and had occupancy rates of 86.3%. (See Table 3.4.) Nursing homes averaged 107.6 beds per facility.

In 2004, 61.5% of all nursing homes were proprietary (privately owned). (See Table 3.4.) More than half (54.2%) were affiliated with a chain, 30.8% were operated by nonprofit, volunteer organizations, and only 7.7% were operated by governmental agencies.

Most residents of nursing homes are the "oldest old" (people aged eighty-five and older). Out of the total 1.3 million nursing home residents aged sixty-five years old and older, the so-called oldest old accounted for 674,200 (51%) of all nursing home residents in 2004. (See Table 3.5.)

Diversification of Nursing Homes

To remain competitive with home health care and the increasing array of alternative living arrangements for the elderly, many nursing homes began to offer alternative services and programs. New services include adult day care and visiting nurse services for people who still live at home. Other programs include respite plans that allow caregivers who need to travel for business or vacation to leave an elderly relative in the nursing home temporarily.

One of the most popular nontraditional services is subacute care, which is comprehensive inpatient treatment for people recovering from acute illnesses such as pneumonia, injuries such as a broken hip, and chronic diseases such as arthritis that do not require intensive, hospital-level treatment. This level of care also enables nursing homes to expand their markets by offering services to younger patients.

Innovation Improves Quality of Nursing Home Care

Even though industry observers and the media frequently raise concerns about the care provided in nursing homes and publicize instances of elder abuse and other quality of care issues, several organizations have actively sought to develop models of health service delivery that improve the clinical care and quality of life for nursing home residents. In *Evaluation of the Wellspring Model for Improving Nursing Home Quality* (August 2002, http://www.cmwf.org/usr_doc/stone_wellspringevaluation.pdf), a report that examines one such model in eastern Wisconsin, Robyn I. Stone et al. of the Institute for the Future of Aging Services and the American Association of Homes and Services for the Aging evaluate the Wellspring model of nursing home quality improvement.

Wellspring is a group of eleven not-for-profit nursing homes governed by a group called the Wellspring Alliance. Founded in 1994, the alliance aims to improve simultaneously clinical care delivered to its nursing home residents and the work environment for its employees. Education and collaboration are hallmarks of the Wellspring philosophy, and this program began by equipping nursing home personnel with the skills needed to perform their jobs and by organizing employees in teams working toward shared goals. The Wellspring model of service delivery uses a multidisciplinary clinical team approach (nurse practitioners, social service, food service personnel, nursing assistants, and facility and housekeeping personnel) to solve problems and develop approaches to better meet residents' needs. Each of these teams represents an important innovation because it allows health professionals and other workers to interact as peers and share resources, information, and decision-making in a cooperative, supportive environment.

Shared resources, training, ideas, and goals have had a powerful impact on care at the Wellspring facilities.

TABLE 3.4

Number and percent of nursing homes by selected facility characteristics, 2004

Facility characteristic	Nursing homes		Beds		Current residents	
	Number	Percent distribution	Number	Beds per nursing home	Number	Occupancy rate[a]
Total	16,100	100.0	1,730,000	107.6	1,492,200	86.3
Ownership						
Proprietary	9,900	61.5	1,074,200	108.6	918,000	85.5
Voluntary nonprofit	5,000	30.8	503,600	101.6	440,300	87.4
Government and other	1,200	7.7	152,200	123.6	133,900	88.0
Certification[b]						
Certified	15,800	98.5	1,708,900	107.8	1,475,600	86.4
Medicare and Medicaid	14,100	87.6	1,599,600	113.5	1,379,700	86.3
Medicare only	*700	*4.1	*33,100	*50.6	28,100	85.0
Medicaid only	1,100	6.9	76,200	69.0	67,900	89.1
Beds						
Fewer than 50 beds	2,200	13.9	75,800	33.8	62,200	82.1
50–99 beds	6,000	37.3	454,700	75.7	422,600	92.9
100–199 beds	6,800	42.5	903,100	132.0	788,500	87.3
200 beds or more	1,000	6.2	296,400	298.2	218,900	73.9
Geographic region						
Northeast	2,800	17.4	381,500	136.0	331,300	86.8
Midwest	5,300	33.0	526,600	99.4	448,000	85.1
South	5,400	33.6	585,600	108.3	501,500	85.6
West	2,600	16.0	236,200	92.1	211,400	89.5
Location						
Metropolitan statistical area	10,900	67.7	1,290,900	118.5	1,127,800	87.4
Micropolitan statistical area	2,600	16.2	242,200	92.9	202,000	83.4
Other location	2,600	16.0	196,900	76.3	162,400	82.5
Affiliation						
Chain	8,700	54.2	939,400	107.9	812,500	86.5
Independent	7,400	45.8	790,600	107.2	679,700	86.0

*Estimate does not meet standard of reliability or precision because the sample size is less than 30. Estimates accompanied by an asterisk (*) indicate that the sample size is between 30 and 59, or the sample size is greater than 59 but has a relative standard error of 30 percent or more.
[a]Occupancy rate is calculated by dividing residents by available beds.
[b]Estimates for nursing homes that are not certified are not shown because the sample size was less than 30 and figures are unreliable.
Notes: Numbers may not add to totals because of rounding. Percentages and rates are based on the unrounded numbers.

SOURCE: "Table 1. Number and Percent Distribution of Nursing Homes by Selected Facility Characteristics, According to Number of Beds, Beds per Nursing Home, Current Residents, and Occupancy Rate: United States, 2004," in *2004 National Nursing Home Survey*, U.S. Department of Health and Human Services, Centers for Disease Control and Prevention, National Center for Health Statistics, 2006, http://www.cdc.gov/nchs/data/nnhsd/nursinghome facilities2006.pdf#01 (accessed April 21, 2008)

Stone et al. observe more cooperation, responsibility, and accountability within the teams and the institutions than what was noted at other comparable facilities. Besides finding a strong organizational culture that seemed committed to quality patient care, the researchers also document measurable improvements in specific areas including:

- Wellspring facilities had lower rates of staff turnover than comparable Wisconsin facilities during the same time period, probably because Wellspring workers felt valued by management and experienced greater job satisfaction than other nursing home personnel.

- The Wellspring model did not require additional resources to institute, and Wellspring facilities operated at lower costs than comparable facilities.

- Wellspring facilities' performance, as measured by a federal survey, improved.

- Generally, Wellspring personnel appeared more attentive to residents' needs and problems and sought to anticipate and promptly resolve problems.

Stone et al. conclude that the organizational commitment to training and shared decision making, along with improved quality of interactions and relationships among staff and between staff and residents, significantly contributed to enhanced quality of life for residents.

The ambitious social outreach programs of one of the charter Wellspring organizations, St. Paul Elder Services, which serves a community of thirteen thousand in Kaukauna, Wisconsin, are described by James Fett in "Social Accountability: Building Bonds in Our Communities" (July–August 2004, http://www.aahsa.org/pubs_resources/futureage/best _practices/documents/BP_V3N4_JUL_AUG04/DEPT _Vision-Fett_V3N4.pdf). St. Paul Elder Services provides much uncompensated care as well as programs

TABLE 3.5

Nursing home residents age 65 and older, by age, sex, and race, selected years 1973–2004

Age, sex, and race	Number of residents in hundreds					Residents per 1,000 population[a]				
	1973–1974	1985	1995	1999	2004	1973–1974	1985	1995	1999	2004
Age										
65 years and over, age-adjusted[b]	—	—	—	—	—	58.5	54.0	46.4	43.3	34.8
65 years and over, crude	9,615	13,183	14,229	14,695	13,172	44.7	46.2	42.8	42.9	36.3
65–74 years	1,631	2,121	1,897	1,948	1,741	12.3	12.5	10.2	10.8	9.4
75–84 years	3,849	509	5,096	5,176	4,689	57.7	57.7	46.1	43.0	36.1
85 years and over	4,136	5,973	7,235	7,571	6,742	257.3	220.3	200.9	182.5	138.7
Male										
65 years and over, age-adjusted[b]	—	—	—	—	—	42.5	38.8	33.0	30.6	24.1
65 years and over, crude	2,657	3,344	3,571	3,778	3,368	30.0	29.0	26.2	26.5	22.2
65–74 years	651	806	795	841	754	11.3	10.8	9.6	10.3	8.9
75–84 years	1,023	1,413	1,443	1,495	1,408	39.9	43.0	33.5	30.8	27.0
85 years and over	983	1,126	1,333	1,442	1,206	182.7	145.7	131.5	116.5	80.0
Female										
65 years and over, age-adjusted[b]	—	—	—	—	—	67.5	61.5	52.8	49.8	40.4
65 years and over, crude	6,958	9,839	10,658	10,917	9,804	54.9	57.9	54.3	54.6	46.4
65–74 years	980	1,315	1,103	1,107	988	13.1	13.8	10.7	11.2	9.8
75–84 years	2,826	3,677	3,654	3,681	3,280	68.9	66.4	54.3	51.2	42.3
85 years and over	3,153	4,847	5,902	6,129	5,536	294.9	250.1	228.1	210.5	165.2
White[c]										
65 years and over, age-adjusted[b]	—	—	—	—	—	61.2	55.5	45.8	41.9	34.0
65 years and over, crude	9,206	12,274	12,715	12,796	11,488	46.9	47.7	42.7	42.1	36.2
65–74 years	1,501	1,878	1,541	1,573	1,342	12.5	12.3	9.3	10.0	8.5
75–84 years	3,697	4,736	4,513	4,406	4,060	60.3	59.1	45.0	40.5	35.2
85 years and over	4,008	5,660	6,662	6,817	6,086	270.8	228.7	203.2	181.8	139.4
Black or African American[c]										
65 years and over, age-adjusted[b]	—	—	—	—	—	28.2	41.5	50.8	55.5	49.9
65 years and over, crude	377	820	1,229	1,459	1,454	22.0	35.0	45.5	51.0	47.7
65–74 years	122	225	296	303	345	11.1	15.4	18.5	18.2	20.2
75–84 years	134	306	475	587	546	26.7	45.3	57.8	66.5	55.5
85 years and over	121	290	458	569	563	105.7	141.5	168.2	182.8	160.7

—Category not applicable.

[a]Rates are calculated using estimates of the civilian population of the United States including institutionalized persons. Population data are from unpublished tabulations provided by the U.S. Census Bureau. The 2004 population estimates are postcensal estimates as of July 1, 2004, based on the 2000 census.

[b]Age-adjusted to the year 2000 population standard using the following three age groups: 65–74 years, 75–84 years, and 85 years and over.

[c]Starting with 1999 data, the instruction for the race item on the current resident questionnaire was changed so that more than one race could be recorded. In previous years, only one racial category could be checked. Estimates for racial groups presented in this table are for residents for whom only one race was recorded. Estimates for residents where multiple races were checked are unreliable due to small sample sizes and are not shown.

Notes: Residents are persons on the roster of the nursing home as of the night before the survey. Residents for whom beds are maintained even though they may be away on overnight leave or in a hospital are included. People residing in personal care or domiciliary care homes are excluded.

Data are based on a sample of nursing home residents.

SOURCE: "Table 104. Nursing Home Residents 65 Years of Age and over, by Age, Sex, and Race: United States, Selected Years 1973–2004," in *Health, United States, 2007. With Chartbook on Trends in the Health of Americans*, U.S. Department of Health and Human Services, Centers for Disease Control and Prevention, National Center for Health Statistics, 2007, http://www.cdc.gov/nchs/data/hus/hus07.pdf#listtables (accessed April 21, 2008)

and services to meet unmet needs of older adults in the community. Examples of these services include free blood pressure screenings at senior housing complexes, foot, nail, and ear cleaning services, adult day care for people suffering from dementia, warm-water exercise classes, diabetic menu planning classes, and continence management programs. The president of St. Paul Elder Services explains that "our community is the source of our residents, volunteers, associates and philanthropy.... Social accountability...communicates our message of commitment, performance and excellence. Through this process, we have created and strengthened a level of trust and cooperation, improving the quality of life for everyone involved."

MENTAL HEALTH FACILITIES

In earlier centuries mental illness was often considered a sign of possession by the devil or, at best, a moral weakness. A change in these attitudes began in the late eighteenth century, when mental illness was perceived to be a treatable condition. It was then that the concept of asylums was developed, not only to lock the mentally ill away but also to provide them with "relief" from the conditions they found troubling.

In the twenty-first century mental health care is provided in a variety of treatment settings by different types of organizations. The National Center for Health Statistics (NCHS) describes in "Mental Health Organization"

(January 11, 2007, http://www.cdc.gov/nchs/datawh/nchs defs/mho.htm) the following mental health organizations:

- A psychiatric hospital (public or private) provides twenty-four-hour inpatient care to people with mental illnesses in a hospital setting. It may also offer twenty-four-hour residential care and less than twenty-four-hour care, but these are not requirements. Psychiatric hospitals are operated under state, county, private for-profit, and private not-for-profit auspices.

- General hospitals with separate psychiatric services, units, or designated beds are under government or non-governmental auspices and maintain assigned staff for twenty-four-hour inpatient care, twenty-four-hour residential care, and less than twenty-four-hour care (outpatient care or partial hospitalization) to provide mental health diagnosis, evaluation, and treatment.

- Veterans Administration (VA) hospitals are operated by the U.S. Department of Veterans Affairs and include VA general hospital psychiatric services and VA psychiatric outpatient clinics that exclusively serve people entitled to VA benefits.

- Outpatient mental health clinics that provide only ambulatory mental health services. Generally, a psychiatrist has overall medical responsibility for clients and the philosophy and orientation of the mental health program.

- Community mental health centers were funded under the Federal Community Mental Health Centers Act of 1963 and subsequent amendments to the act. During the early 1980s, when the federal government reverted to funding mental health services through block grants to the states rather than by funding them directly, the federal government stopped tracking these mental health organizations individually, and statistical reports include them in the category "all other mental health organizations." This category also includes freestanding psychiatric outpatient clinics, freestanding partial care organizations, and multiservice mental health organizations such as residential treatment centers. These so-called community mental health centers have sliding scale fees and accept Medicaid, Medicare, private health insurance, and private fee-for-service payment. Mental health care is also available from not-for-profit mental health or counseling services offered by health and social service agencies, such as Catholic Social Services, family and children's service agencies, Jewish Family Services, and Lutheran Social Services, that are staffed by qualified mental health professionals to provide counseling services.

- Residential treatment centers for emotionally disturbed children serve children and youth primarily under the age of eighteen, provide twenty-four-hour residential

services, and offer a clinical program that is directed by a psychiatrist, psychologist, social worker, or psychiatric nurse who holds a master's or doctorate degree.

Where Are the Mentally Ill?

The chronically mentally ill reside either in mental hospitals or in community settings, such as with families, in boarding homes and shelters, in single-room-occupancy hotels (usually cheap hotels or boardinghouses), in prison, or even on the streets as part of the homeless population. The institutionalized mentally ill are those people with psychiatric diagnoses who have lived in mental hospitals for more than one year or those with diagnosed mental illness who are living in nursing homes.

Declining mental health expenditures have resulted in fewer available services for specific populations of the mentally ill, particularly those who could benefit from inpatient or residential care. Even for people without conditions requiring institutional care there are barriers to access. The U.S. surgeon general's landmark report *Mental Health: A Report of the Surgeon General, 1999* (1999, http://www.mentalhealth .samhsa.gov/features/surgeongeneralreport/home.asp) describes the U.S. mental health service system as largely uncoordinated and fragmented, in part because it involves so many different sectors—health and social welfare agencies, public and private hospitals, housing, criminal justice, and education—and because it is funded through many different sources. Finally, inequalities in insurance coverage for mental health, coupled with the stigma associated with mental illness and treatment, have also limited access to services.

The U.S. Department of Health and Human Services observes in *Trends in Mental Health System Transformation, 2005: The States Respond* (2006, http://download .ncadi.samhsa.gov/ken/pdf/SMA05-4115/SMA05-4115.pdf) that state-level initiatives share the common challenge of providing the most effective treatment and services in the face of diminishing resources and increasing needs.

The NCHS reveals in *Health, United States, 2007* (2007, http://www.cdc.gov/nchs/data/hus/hus07.pdf) that the number of mental health organizations for twenty-four-hour inpatient treatment steadily declined from 3,942 in 1990 to 2,891 in 2004. (See Table 3.6.) Except for Department of Veterans Affairs medical centers, all other service sites and types of organizations diminished in capacity. The number of beds per 100,000 civilian population fell from 128.5 in 1990 to just 71.2 in 2004. This decline was not necessarily a result of better treatment for the mentally ill but a consequence of reduced funding for inpatient facilities. Many of the patients who were once housed in mental institutions (including some who had been lifelong residents in these facilities) were forced to fend for themselves, on the streets or in prisons.

TABLE 3.6

Mental health organizations and beds for 24-hour hospital and residential treatment, by type of organization, selected years 1986–2004

Type of organization	1986	1990	1994	1998	2000	2002	2004
	Number of mental health organizations						
All organizations	3,512	3,942	3,853	3,741	3,211	3,044	2,891
State and county mental hospitals	285	278	270	237	229	227	237
Private psychiatric hospitals	314	464	432	347	271	255	264
Nonfederal general hospital psychiatric services	1,351	1,577	1,539	1,595	1,325	1,231	1,230
Department of Veterans Affairs medical centers[a]	139	131	136	124	134	132	—
Residential treatment centers for emotionally disturbed children	437	501	472	462	476	510	458
All other organizations[b]	986	991	1,004	976	776	689	702
	Number of beds						
All organizations	267,613	325,529	293,139	269,148	214,186	211,040	212,231
State and county mental hospitals	119,033	102,307	84,063	71,266	61,833	57,314	57,034
Private psychiatric hospitals	30,201	45,952	42,742	31,731	26,402	24,996	28,422
Nonfederal general hospital psychiatric services	45,808	53,576	53,455	54,775	40,410	40,520	41,403
Department of Veterans Affairs medical centers[a]	26,874	24,779	21,346	17,173	8,989	9,581	—
Residential treatment centers for emotionally disturbed children	24,547	35,170	32,691	32,040	33,508	39,407	33,835
All other organizations[b]	21,150	63,745	58,842	62,163	43,044	39,222	51,536
	Beds per 100,000 civilian population[c]						
All organizations	111.7	128.5	110.9	94.0	74.8	72.2	71.2
State and county mental hospitals	49.7	40.4	31.8	24.9	21.6	19.6	19.1
Private psychiatric hospitals	12.6	18.1	16.2	11.1	9.2	8.6	9.5
Nonfederal general hospital psychiatric services	19.1	21.2	20.2	19.1	14.1	13.9	13.9
Department of Veterans Affairs medical centers[a]	11.2	9.9	8.1	6.0	3.1	3.3	—
Residential treatment centers for emotionally disturbed children	10.3	13.9	12.4	11.2	11.7	13.5	11.4
All other organizations[b]	8.8	25.2	22.2	21.7	15.0	13.4	17.3

— Data not available.
[a]Department of Veterans Affairs medical centers (VA general hospital psychiatric services and VA psychiatric outpatient clinics) were dropped from the survey as of 2004.
[b]Includes freestanding psychiatric outpatient clinics, partial care organizations, and multiservice mental health organizations.
[c]Civilian population estimates for 2000 and beyond are based on the 2000 census as of July 1; population estimates for 1992–1998 are 1990 postcensal estimates.
Notes: Data for 1990, 1992, 1994, 1998, 2000, and 2002 are revised final estimates and differ from previous editions of Health, United States. Data are based on inventories of mental health organizations.

SOURCE: "Table 114. Mental Health Organizations and Beds for 24-Hour Hospital and Residential Treatment, by Type of Organization: United States, Selected Years 1986–2004," in *Health, United States, 2007. With Chartbook on Trends in the Health of Americans*, U.S. Department of Health and Human Services, Centers for Disease Control and Prevention, National Center for Health Statistics, 2007, http://www.cdc.gov/nchs/data/hus/hus07.pdf#listtables (accessed April 21, 2008)

Besides mental health units or beds in acute care medical/surgical hospitals and physicians' offices, mental health care and treatment is offered in offices of other mental health clinicians such as psychologists, clinical social workers, and marriage and family therapists, as well as in other settings. Private psychiatric hospitals provide outpatient mental health evaluation and therapy in day programs as well as inpatient care. Like acute care hospitals, these facilities are accredited by the Joint Commission on Accreditation of Health Care Organizations and may offer outpatient services by way of referral to a local network of qualified mental health providers. Figure 3.1 shows that depression, a common mental disorder, accounted for 13% of all outpatient department visits in 2005, up from 8.8% in 1995.

National Goals for Mental Health Service Delivery

Healthy People 2010 (2000, http://www.healthypeople.gov/document/tableofcontents.htm) is a set of health objectives for the United States to achieve during the first decade of the new century. Fourteen of the 467 health objectives enumerated in *Healthy People 2010* relate to mental health and mental disorders. Even though nearly all the objectives intend to reduce the incidence and prevalence of mental illness in the United States and improve access to care and treatment, several specifically address service delivery issues related to mental health professionals and treatment facilities.

Healthy People 2010 (November 2000, http://www.healthypeople.gov/document/HTML/Volume2/18Mental.htm) objectives call for system-wide improvements in mental health service delivery. For example, number 18-12 calls on the nation to "increase the number of States and the District of Columbia that track consumers' satisfaction with the mental health services they receive." Number 18-14 asks to "increase the number of States, Territories, and the District of Columbia with an operational mental health plan that addresses mental health crisis interventions, ongoing screening, and treatment services for elderly persons."

HOME HEALTH CARE

The concept of home health care began as postacute care after hospitalization, an alternative to longer, costlier lengths of stay in regular hospitals. Home health care

FIGURE 3.1

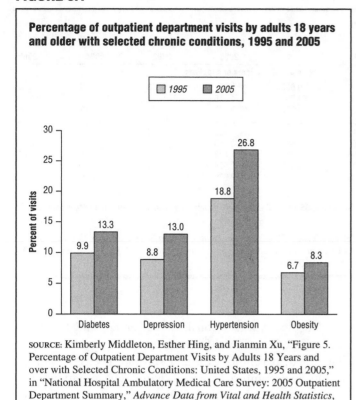

Percentage of outpatient department visits by adults 18 years and older with selected chronic conditions, 1995 and 2005

SOURCE: Kimberly Middleton, Esther Hing, and Jianmin Xu, "Figure 5. Percentage of Outpatient Department Visits by Adults 18 Years and over with Selected Chronic Conditions: United States, 1995 and 2005," in "National Hospital Ambulatory Medical Care Survey: 2005 Outpatient Department Summary," *Advance Data from Vital and Health Statistics*, no. 389, June 29, 2007, http://www.cdc.gov/nchs/data/ad/ad389.pdf (accessed April 21, 2008)

Home health care agencies provide a wide variety of services. Services range from helping with activities of daily living, such as bathing, doing light housekeeping, and making meals, to skilled nursing care, such as the nursing care needed by AIDS or cancer patients. The number of Medicare-certified home health agencies has varied in response to reimbursement, growing from 2,924 in 1980 to 10,807 in 1996, then declining to 7,519 in 2004. (See Table 3.7.) In 2005 the number rose to 8,090, the highest it has been in the twenty-first century.

In 1972 Medicare extended home care coverage to people under sixty-five years of age only if they were disabled or suffered from end-stage renal disease. Before 2000 Medicare coverage for home health care was limited to patients immediately following discharge from the hospital. By 2000 Medicare covered beneficiaries' home health care services with no requirement for previous hospitalization. There were also no limits to the number of professional visits or to the length of coverage. As long as the patient's condition warranted it, the following services were provided:

- Part-time or intermittent skilled nursing and home health aide services
- Speech-language pathology services
- Physical and occupational therapy
- Medical social services
- Medical supplies
- Durable medical equipment (with a 20% co-payment)

Over time, the population receiving home care services has changed. Since 2000 much of home health care is associated with rehabilitation from critical illnesses, and fewer users are long-term patients with chronic conditions. This changing pattern of utilization reflects a shift from longer-term care for chronic conditions to short-term, postacute care. Compared to postacute care users, the long-term patients are older, more functionally disabled, more likely to be incontinent, and more expensive to serve.

Medicare Limits Home Care Services

The Balanced Budget Act of 1997 aimed to cut approximately $16.2 billion from the federal government's home care expenditures over a period of five years. The act sought to return home health care to its original concept of short-term care plus skilled nursing and therapy services. As a result of this shift away from personal care and "custodial care" services and toward short-term, skilled nursing services, some Medicare beneficiaries who received home health care lost coverage for certain personal care services, such as assistance with bathing, dressing, and eating.

The Balanced Budget Act sharply curtailed the growth in home care spending, greatly affecting health care

services have grown tremendously since the 1980s, when prospective payment (payments made before, rather than after, care is received) for Medicare patients sharply reduced hospital lengths of stay. During the mid-1980s Medicare began to reimburse hospitals using a rate scale based on diagnosis-related groups—hospitals received a fixed amount for providing services to Medicare patients based on their diagnoses. This form of payment gave hospitals powerful financial incentives to use fewer resources because they could keep the difference between the prepayment and the amount they actually spent to provide care. Hospitals suffered losses when patients had longer lengths of stay and used more services than were covered by the standardized diagnosis-related group prospective payment.

According to the article "Home Health Care" (*Family Economics and Nutrition Review*, spring 1996), home health care grew faster in the early 1990s than any other segment of health services. Its growth may be attributable to the observation that in many cases caring for patients at home is preferable to and more cost effective than care provided in a hospital, nursing home, or some other residential facility. Oftentimes, older adults are more comfortable and much happier living in their own home or with family members. Disabled people may also be able to function better at home with limited assistance than in a residential setting with full-time monitoring.

TABLE 3.7

Medicare-certified providers and suppliers, selected years 1980–2005

Providers or suppliers	1980	1985	1990	1996	2000	2002	2004	2005
				Number of providers or suppliers				
Home health agencies	2,924	5,679	5,730	10,807	7,857	6,813	7,519	8,090
Clinical Lab Improvement Act facilities	—	—	—	164,054	171,018	173,807	189,340	196,296
End stage renal disease facilities	999	1,393	1,937	3,367	3,787	4,113	4,618	4,755
Outpatient physical therapy	419	854	1,195	2,758	2,867	2,836	2,971	2,962
Portable x-ray	216	308	443	656	666	644	608	553
Rural health clinics	391	428	551	3,673	3,453	3,283	3,536	3,661
Comprehensive outpatient rehabilitation facilities	—	72	186	531	522	524	635	634
Ambulatory surgical centers	—	336	1,197	2,480	2,894	3,371	4,136	4,445
Hospices	—	164	825	2,344	2,326	2,275	2,645	2,872

— Data not available.

Notes: Provider and supplier data for 1980–1990 are as of July 1. Provider and supplier data for 1996–2005 are as of December. Providers and suppliers certified for Medicare are deemed to meet Medicaid standards.

SOURCE: "Table 118. Medicare-Certified Providers and Suppliers: United States, Selected Years 1980–2005," in *Health, United States, 2007. With Chartbook on Trends in the Health of Americans*, U.S. Department of Health and Human Services, Centers for Disease Control and Prevention, National Center for Health Statistics, 2007, http://www.cdc.gov/nchs/data/hus/hus07.pdf#listtables (accessed April 21, 2008)

providers. Nonetheless, the aging population and the financial imperative to prevent or minimize institutionalization—hospitalization or placement in a long-term care facility—combined to generate increasing expenditures for home health care services. Medicare expenditures for home health care rose from $5.1 billion in 2003 to $7.2 billion in 2006, which represented 3.1% of Medicare expenditures. (See Table 3.8.) In contrast, payments to skilled nursing facilities accounted for 10.4% of expenditures in 2006, whereas inpatient hospital expenditures were 63.1% of the total.

HOSPICE CARE

In medieval times hospices were refuges for the sick, the needy, and travelers. The modern hospice movement developed in response to the need to provide humane care to terminally ill patients, while at the same time offering support to their families. The English physician Cicely Saunders (1918–2005) pioneered the hospice concept in Britain in the late 1960s and helped introduce it in the United States over the next decade. The care provided by hospice workers is called palliative care, and it aims to relieve patients' pain and the accompanying symptoms of terminal illness without seeking to cure the illness.

Hospice is a philosophy, an approach to care for the dying, and it is not necessarily a physical facility. Hospice may refer to a place—a freestanding facility or a designated floor in a hospital or nursing home—or to a program such as hospice home care, where a team of health professionals helps the dying patient and family at home. Hospice teams may involve physicians, nurses, social workers, pastoral counselors, and trained volunteers. The goal of hospice care is to provide support and care for people at the end of life, enabling them to remain as comfortable as possible.

Hospice workers consider the patient and family as the "unit of care" and focus their efforts on attending to emotional, psychological, and spiritual needs as well as to physical comfort and well-being. The programs provide respite care, which offers relief at any time for families who may be overwhelmed and exhausted by the demands of caregiving and may be neglecting their own needs for rest and relaxation. Finally, hospice programs work to prepare relatives and friends for the loss of their loved ones. Hospice offers bereavement support groups and counseling to help deal with grief and may even help with funeral arrangements.

The hospice concept is different from most other health care services because it focuses on care rather than on cure. Hospice workers try to minimize the two greatest fears associated with dying: fear of isolation and fear of pain. Potent, effective medications are offered to patients in pain, with the goal of controlling pain without impairing alertness so that patients may be as comfortable as possible.

Hospice care also emphasizes living life to its fullest. Patients are encouraged to stay active for as long as possible, to do things they enjoy, and to learn something new each day. Quality of life, rather than length of life, is the focus. In addition, whenever it is possible, family and friends are urged to be the primary caregivers in the home. Care at home helps both patients and family members enrich their lives and face death together.

Ira Byock, the former president of the American Academy of Hospice and Palliative Medicine, explains the concept of hospice care in *Dying Well: The Prospect for Growth at the End of Life* (1997): "Hospice care differs noticeably from the modern medical approach to dying. Typically, as a hospice patient nears death, the medical

TABLE 3.8

Medicare enrollees and expenditures by type of service, selected years 1970–2006

Medicare program and type of service	1970	1980	1990	1995	2000	2001	2002	2003	2004	2005	2006[a]
Enrollees					**Number in millions**						
Total Medicare[b]	20.4	28.4	34.3	37.6	39.7	40.1	40.5	41.2	41.9	42.6	43.2
Hospital insurance	20.1	28.0	33.7	37.2	39.3	39.7	40.1	40.7	41.4	42.2	42.9
Supplementary medical insurance[c]	19.5	27.3	32.6	35.6	37.3	37.7	38.0	38.6	—	—	—
Part B	19.5	27.3	32.6	35.6	37.3	37.7	38.0	38.6	39.1	39.7	40.3
Part D[d]	—	—	—	—	—	—	—	—	1.2	1.8	27.9
Expenditures					**Amount in billions**						
Total Medicare	$7.5	$36.8	$111.0	$184.2	$221.7	$244.8	$265.8	280.8	308.9	336.4	408.3
Total hospital insurance (HI)	5.3	25.6	67.0	117.6	131.0	143.4	152.7	154.6	170.6	182.9	191.9
HI payments to managed care organizations[e]	—	0.0	2.7	6.7	21.4	20.8	19.2	19.5	20.8	24.9	32.9
HI payments for fee-for-service utilization	5.1	25.0	63.4	109.5	105.1	117.0	129.3	134.5	146.5	154.7	155.7
Inpatient hospital	4.8	24.1	56.9	82.3	87.1	96.0	104.2	108.7	116.4	121.7	121.0
Skilled nursing facility	0.2	0.4	2.5	9.1	11.1	13.1	15.2	14.7	17.1	18.5	19.9
Home health agency	0.1	0.5	3.7	16.2	4.0	4.1	5.0	4.8	5.4	5.9	6.0
Hospice	—	—	0.3	1.9	2.9	3.7	4.9	6.2	7.6	8.6	8.9
Home health agency transfer[f]	—	—	—	—	1.7	3.1	1.2	-2.2	0.0	0.0	0.0
Administrative expenses[g]	0.2	0.5	0.9	1.4	2.8	2.5	3.0	2.8	3.3	3.3	3.3
Total supplementary medical insurance (SMI)[c]	2.2	11.2	44.0	66.6	90.7	101.4	113.2	126.1	138.3	153.4	216.4
Total Part B	2.2	11.2	44.0	66.6	90.7	101.4	113.2	126.1	137.9	152.4	169.0
Part B payments to managed care organizations[e]	0.0	0.2	2.8	6.6	18.4	17.6	17.5	17.3	18.7	22.1	31.5
Part B payments for fee-for-service utilization[h]	1.9	10.4	39.6	58.4	72.2	85.1	94.5	104.3	116.2	126.9	134.1
Physician/supplies[i]	1.8	8.2	29.6	—	—	—	—	—	—	—	—
Outpatient hospital[j]	0.1	1.9	8.5	—	—	—	—	—	—	—	—
Independent laboratory[k]	0.0	0.1	1.5	—	—	—	—	—	—	—	—
Physician fee schedule	—	—	—	31.7	37.0	42.0	44.8	48.3	54.1	57.7	58.4
Durable medical equipment	—	—	—	3.7	4.7	5.4	6.5	7.5	7.8	7.9	8.4
Laboratory[l]	—	—	—	4.3	4.0	4.4	5.0	5.5	6.0	6.5	7.1
Other[m]	—	—	—	9.9	13.6	16.0	19.6	22.6	25.0	27.5	29.3
Hospital[n]	—	—	—	8.7	8.4	12.8	13.6	15.3	17.4	20.2	23.8
Home health agency	0.0	0.2	0.1	0.2	4.5	4.5	5.0	5.1	5.9	7.1	7.2
Home health agency transfer[f]	—	—	—	—	-1.7	-3.1	-1.2	2.2	0.0	0.0	0.0
Administrative expenses[g]	0.2	0.6	1.5	1.6	1.8	1.8	2.3	2.4	2.8	3.2	3.1
Part D Transitional Assistance and Start-up costs[o]	—	—	—	—	—	—	—	—	0.2	0.7	0.0
Total Part D[d]	—	—	—	—	—	—	—	—	0.4	1.0	47.4
					Percent distribution of expenditures						
Total hospital insurance (HI)	100.0	100.0	100.0	100.0	100.0	100.0	100.0	100.0	100.0	100.0	100.0
HI payments to managed care organizations[e]	—	0.0	4.0	5.7	16.3	14.5	12.6	12.6	12.2	13.6	17.1
HI payments for fee-for-service utilization	97.0	97.9	94.6	93.1	80.2	81.6	84.7	87.0	85.9	84.6	81.1
Inpatient hospital	91.4	94.3	85.0	70.0	66.5	67.0	68.3	70.3	68.2	66.6	63.1
Skilled nursing facility	4.7	1.5	3.7	7.8	8.5	9.1	10.0	9.5	10.0	10.1	10.4
Home health agency	1.0	2.1	5.5	13.8	3.1	2.9	3.3	3.1	3.2	3.2	3.1
Hospice	—	—	0.5	1.6	2.2	2.6	3.2	4.0	4.4	4.7	4.6
Home health agency transfer[f]	—	—	—	—	1.3	2.2	0.8	-1.4	0.0	0.0	0.0
Administrative expenses[g]	3.0	2.1	1.4	1.2	2.1	1.7	2.0	1.8	2.0	1.8	1.7

details become almost automatic and attention focuses on the personal nature of this final transition—what the patient and family are going through emotionally and spiritually. In the more established system, even as people die, medical procedures remain the first priority. With hospice, they move to the background as the personal comes to the fore."

According to the National Hospice and Palliative Care Organization (NHPCO), in *NHPCO Facts and Figures: Hospice Care in America* (November 2007, http://www .nhpco.org/files/public/Statistics_Research/NHPCO_facts-and-figures_Nov2007.pdf), the use of hospice care is increasing in the United States. The NHPCO estimates that

1.3 million patients received hospice care in 2006, a 162% increase in the preceding decade. NHPCO reports that 36% of deaths in 2006 were of patients cared for in hospice programs. In 2006 Medicare and Medicaid expenditures for hospice care totaled $8.9 billion and accounted for 4.6% of Medicare expenditures. (See Table 3.8.)

MANAGED CARE ORGANIZATIONS

Managed health care is the sector of the health insurance industry in which health care providers are not independent businesses run by, for example, private medical practitioners but by administrative firms that manage

TABLE 3.8

Medicare enrollees and expenditures by type of service, selected years 1970–2006 [CONTINUED]

— Data not available.
0.0 Quantity greater than 0 but less than 0.05.
[a]Preliminary figures.
[b]Average number enrolled in the hospital insurance (HI) and/or supplementary medical insurance (SMI) programs for the period.
[c]Starting with 2004 data, the SMI trust fund consists of two separate accounts: Part B (which pays for a portion of the costs of physicians' services, outpatient hospital services, and other related medical and health services for voluntarily enrolled aged and disabled individuals) and Part D (Medicare Prescription Drug Account which pays private plans to provide prescription drug coverage).
[d]The Medicare Modernization Act, enacted on December 8, 2003, established within SMI two Part D accounts related to prescription drug benefits: the Medicare Prescription Drug Account and the Transitional Assistance Account. The Medicare Prescription Drug Account is used in conjunction with the broad, voluntary prescription drug benefits that began in 2006. The Transitional Assistance Account was used to provide transitional assistance benefits, beginning in 2004 and extending through 2005, for certain low-income beneficiaries prior to the start of the new prescription drug benefit.
[e]Medicare-approved managed care organizations.
[f]Starting with 1999 data, reflects annual home health HI to SMI transfer amounts.
[g]Includes research, costs of experiments and demonstration projects, fraud and abuse promotion, and peer review activity (changed to Quality Improvement Organization in 2002).
[h]Type-of-service reporting categories for fee-for-service reimbursement differ before and after 1991.
[i]Includes payment for physicians, practitioners, durable medical equipment, and all suppliers other than independent laboratory through 1990. Starting with 1991 data, physician services subject to the physician fee schedule are shown. Payments for laboratory services paid under the laboratory fee schedule and performed in a physician office are included under laboratory beginning in 1991. Payments for durable medical equipment are shown separately beginning in 1991. The remaining services from the physician category are included in other.
[j]Includes payments for hospital outpatient department services, skilled nursing facility outpatient services, Part B services received as an inpatient in a hospital or skilled nursing facility setting, and other types of outpatient facilities. Starting with 1991 data, payments for hospital outpatient department services, except for laboratory services, are listed under Hospital. Hospital outpatient laboratory services are included in the laboratory line.
[k]Starting with 1991 data, those independent laboratory services that were paid under the laboratory fee schedule (most of the independent lab category) are included in the laboratory line; the remaining services are included in the physician fee schedule and other lines.
[l]Payments for laboratory services paid under the laboratory fee schedule performed in a physician office, independent lab, or in a hospital outpatient department.
[m]Includes payments for physician-administered drugs; freestanding ambulatory surgical center facility services; ambulance services; supplies; freestanding end-stage renal disease (ESRD) dialysis facility services; rural health clinics; outpatient rehabilitation facilities; psychiatric hospitals; and federally qualified health centers.
[n]Includes the hospital facility costs for Medicare Part B services that are predominantly in the outpatient department, with the exception of hospital outpatient laboratory services, which are included on the laboratory line. Physician reimbursement is included on the physician fee schedule line.
[o]Part D Administrative and Transitional Start-Up Costs were funded through the SMI Part B account.
Notes: Percents are calculated using unrounded data. Totals do not necessarily equal the sum of rounded components. Estimates include service disbursements as of February 2006 for Medicare enrollees residing in the United States, Puerto Rico, Virgin Islands, Guam, other outlying areas, foreign countries, and unknown residence. Some numbers in this table have been revised and differ from previous editions of Health, United States.

SOURCE: Adapted from "Table 141. Medicare Enrollees and Expenditures and Percent Distribution, by Medicare Program and Type of Service: United States and Other Areas, Selected Years 1970–2006," in *Health, United States, 2007. With Chartbook on Trends in the Health of Americans*, U.S. Department of Health and Human Services, Centers for Disease Control and Prevention, National Center for Health Statistics, 2007, http://www.cdc.gov/nchs/data/hus/hus07.pdf#list-tables (accessed April 21, 2008)

the allocation of health care benefits. In contrast to conventional indemnity insurers that do not govern the provision of medical care services and simply pay for them, managed care firms have a significant voice in how services are administered to enable them to exert better control over health care costs. (Indemnity insurance is traditional fee-for-service coverage in which providers are paid according to the service performed.)

Managed care, which has a primary purpose of controlling service utilization and costs, represents a rapidly growing segment of the health care industry. The beneficiaries of employer-funded health plans (people who receive health benefits from their employers), as well as Medicare and Medicaid recipients, often find themselves in this type of health care program. The term *managed care organization* covers several types of health care delivery systems, such as health maintenance organizations (HMOs), preferred provider organizations (PPOs), and utilization review groups that oversee diagnoses, recommend treatments, and manage costs for their beneficiaries.

Health Maintenance Organizations

HMOs began to grow in the 1970s as alternatives to traditional health insurance, which was becoming increas-

ingly expensive. The HMO Act of 1973 was a federal law requiring employers with more than twenty-four employees to offer an alternative to conventional indemnity insurance in the form of a federally qualified HMO. The intent of the act was to stimulate HMO development, and the federal government has been promoting HMOs since the administration of President Richard M. Nixon (1913–1994), maintaining that groups of physicians following certain rules of practice can slow rising medical costs and improve health care quality.

HMOs are health insurance programs organized to provide complete coverage for subscribers' (also known as enrollees or members) health needs for negotiated, prepaid prices. The subscribers (and/or their employers) pay a fixed amount each month; in turn, the HMO group provides, at no extra charge or at a minimal charge, preventive care, such as routine checkups, screening, and immunizations, and care for any illness or accident. The monthly fee also covers inpatient hospitalization and referral services. HMO members benefit from reduced out-of-pocket costs (they do not pay deductibles), they do not have to file claims or fill out insurance forms, and they generally pay only nominal co-payments for each office visit. Members are usually locked into the plan for a specified period—usually one year. If the necessary service is available within the HMO, patients must normally use an HMO doctor. There are several types of HMOs:

- Staff model HMO—the "purest" form of managed care. All primary care physicians are employees of the HMO and practice in a centralized location such as an outpatient clinic that may also house a laboratory, pharmacy, and facilities for other diagnostic testing. The staff model offers the HMO the greatest opportunities to manage both cost and quality of health care services.

- Group model—in which the HMO contracts with a group of primary care and multispecialty health providers. The group is paid a fixed amount per patient to provide specific services. The administration of the medical group determines how the HMO payments will be distributed among the physicians and other health care providers. Group model HMOs are usually located in hospitals or in clinic settings and have on-site pharmacies. Participating physicians usually do not have any fee-for-service patients.

- Network model—in which the HMO contracts with two or more groups of health providers that agree to provide health care at negotiated prices to all members enrolled in the HMO.

- Independent practice association model (IPA)—in which the HMO contracts with individual physicians or medical groups that then provide medical care to HMO members at their own offices. The individual physicians agree to follow the practices and procedures of the HMO when caring for the HMO members; however, they generally also maintain their own private practices and see fee-for-service patients as well as HMO members. IPA physicians are paid by capitation (literally, per head) for the HMO patients and by conventional methods for their fee-for-service patients. Physician members of the IPA guarantee that the care for each HMO member for which they are responsible will be delivered within a fixed budget. They guarantee this by allowing the HMO to withhold an amount of their payments (usually about 20% per year). If at year's end the physician's cost for providing care falls within the preset amount, then the physician receives all the monies withheld. If the physician's costs of care exceed the agreed-on amount, the HMO may retain any portion of the monies it has withheld. This arrangement places physicians and other providers such as hospitals, laboratories, and imaging centers at risk for keeping down treatment costs, and this at-risk formula is the key to HMO cost-containment efforts.

Some HMOs offer an open-ended or point-of-service (POS) option that allows members to choose their own physicians and hospitals, either within or outside the HMO. However, a member who chooses an outside provider will generally have to pay a larger portion of the expenses. Physicians not contracting with the HMO but who see HMO patients are paid according to the services performed. POS members are given an incentive to seek care from contracted network physicians and other health care providers through comprehensive coverage offerings.

The number of people enrolled in HMOs more than tripled between 1980 and 1990. In 1980 HMOs covered just 4% of the U.S. population. (See Table 3.9.) By 1990, 13.4% of Americans were enrolled in HMOs. Enrollment continued to explode through the 1990s, and by 2000, 30% of the U.S. population belonged to HMOs. However, by 2006 HMO enrollment had declined to just 24.5% of the U.S population.

HMO enrollment varies by geographic region, with the highest levels of enrollment in the New England states and the far West. (See Table 3.9.) In 2006, 41.7% of the populations in Massachusetts, 49.6% in California, and 45.7% in Hawaii were enrolled in HMOs. In contrast, 0.3% of the populations of North Dakota and 0.4% in Mississippi were covered by HMOs.

HMOs Have Fans and Critics

HMOs have been the subject of considerable debate among physicians, payers, policy makers, and health care consumers. Many physicians feel HMOs interfere in the physician-patient relationship and effectively prevent them from practicing medicine the way they have traditionally practiced. These physicians claim they know their patients' conditions and are, therefore, in the best position to recommend treatment. The physicians resent being advised and overruled by insurance administrators. (Physicians can recommend the treatment they believe is best, but if the insurance company will not cover the costs, patients may be unwilling to undergo the recommended treatment.)

The HMO industry counters that its evidence-based determinations (judgments about the appropriateness of care that reflect scientific research) are based on the experiences of many thousands of physicians and, therefore, it knows which treatment is most likely to be successful. The industry maintains that, in the past, physician-chosen treatments were not scrutinized or even assessed for effectiveness, and as a result most physicians did not really know whether the treatment they prescribed was optimal for the specific medical condition.

Furthermore, the HMO industry cites the slower increase in health care expenses as another indicator of its management success. Industry spokespeople note that any major change in how the industry is run would lead to increasing costs. They claim that HMOs and other managed care programs are bringing a more rational approach to the health care industry while maintaining health care quality and controlling costs.

TABLE 3.9

HMO enrollment by geographic region, selected years 1980–2006

Geographic region and state[a]	2006[b]	1980	1985	1990	1995	1998	2000	2005	2006[b]
	Number in thousands				Percent of population				
United States[c]	72,707	4.0	7.9	13.4	19.4	28.6	30.0	23.4	24.5
New England:									
Connecticut	1,098	2.4	7.1	19.9	21.2	42.9	44.6	36.1	31.3
Maine	358	0.4	0.3	2.6	7.0	19.1	22.3	25.9	27.1
Massachusetts	2,668	2.9	13.7	26.5	39.0	54.2	53.0	37.4	41.7
New Hampshire	126	1.2	5.6	9.6	18.5	33.8	33.7	21.9	9.6
Rhode Island	283	3.7	9.1	20.6	19.6	29.8	38.1	25.9	26.3
Vermont	97	—	—	6.4	12.5	—	4.6	16.1	15.6
Mideast:									
Delaware	190	—	3.9	17.5	18.4	48.1	22.0	10.1	22.5
District of Columbia[d]	...	...	...	...	...	33.0	35.2	42.2	—
Maryland[e]	1,598	2.0	4.8	14.2	29.5	43.6	43.9	28.0	28.5
New Jersey	2,190	2.0	5.6	12.3	14.7	31.3	30.9	25.0	25.1
New York	6,268	5.5	8.0	15.1	26.6	37.8	35.8	24.0	32.6
Pennsylvania	3,346	1.2	5.0	12.5	21.5	37.1	33.9	29.8	26.9
Great Lakes:									
Illinois	2,214	1.9	7.1	12.6	17.2	20.8	21.0	15.7	17.3
Indiana	1,408	0.5	3.6	6.1	8.3	14.0	12.4	22.5	22.4
Michigan	2,746	2.4	9.9	15.2	20.5	25.3	27.1	26.3	27.1
Ohio	2,039	2.2	6.7	13.3	16.3	23.4	25.1	16.4	17.8
Wisconsin	1,375	8.5	17.8	21.7	24.0	30.8	30.2	26.8	24.8
Plains:									
Iowa	177	0.2	4.8	10.1	4.5	4.9	7.4	10.9	6.0
Kansas	264	—	3.3	7.9	4.7	14.4	17.9	16.6	9.6
Minnesota	710	9.9	22.2	16.4	26.5	32.4	29.9	25.4	13.8
Missouri	1,441	2.3	6.0	8.2	18.5	33.7	35.2	24.6	24.8
Nebraska	166	1.1	1.8	5.1	8.6	16.9	11.2	5.3	9.5
North Dakota	2	0.4	2.5	1.7	1.2	2.2	2.5	0.4	0.3
South Dakota	65	—	—	3.3	2.8	5.1	6.7	7.9	8.4
Southeast:									
Alabama	146	0.3	0.9	5.3	7.3	10.8	7.2	2.8	3.2
Arkansas	101	—	0.1	2.2	3.8	10.7	10.4	6.4	3.6
Florida	4,284	1.5	5.6	10.6	18.8	31.5	31.4	26.1	24.1
Georgia	1,952	0.1	2.9	4.8	7.6	15.5	17.4	16.4	21.5
Kentucky	310	0.9	1.6	5.7	16.1	35.1	31.5	10.2	7.4
Louisiana	460	0.6	0.9	5.4	7.2	16.6	17.0	10.7	10.2
Mississippi	12	—	—	—	0.7	3.6	1.1	0.1	0.4
North Carolina	742	0.6	1.6	4.8	8.3	17.1	17.8	10.5	8.5
South Carolina	321	0.2	1.0	1.9	5.5	9.9	9.9	7.1	7.5
Tennessee	1,701	—	1.8	3.7	12.2	24.1	33.0	14.4	28.5
Virginia[e]	1,084	—	1.1	6.1	7.7	16.9	18.5	22.2	14.3
West Virginia[e]	264	0.7	1.7	3.9	5.8	10.7	10.3	8.1	14.5
Southwest:									
Arizona	1,757	6.0	10.3	16.2	25.8	30.3	30.9	16.4	29.6
New Mexico	516	1.4	2.0	12.7	15.1	32.3	37.7	24.3	26.8
Oklahoma	248	—	2.1	5.5	7.6	13.8	14.7	7.1	7.0
Texas	2,960	0.6	3.4	6.9	12.0	17.8	18.5	11.8	12.9
Rocky Mountains:									
Colorado	1,298	6.9	10.8	20.0	23.3	36.4	39.5	25.6	27.8
Idaho	40	1.2	—	1.8	1.4	5.7	7.9	2.9	2.8
Montana	32	—	—	1.0	2.4	3.9	7.0	8.1	3.4
Utah	684	0.6	8.8	13.9	25.1	35.6	35.3	21.3	27.7
Wyoming	12	—	—	—	—	0.7	1.4	2.1	2.3

Still, many physicians resent that, with a few exceptions, HMOs are not financially liable for their decisions. When a physician chooses to forgo a certain procedure and negative consequences result, the physician may be held legally accountable. When an HMO informs a physician that it will not cover a recommended procedure and the HMO's decision is found to be wrong, it cannot be held directly liable. Many physicians assert that because HMOs make such choices, they are practicing medicine and should, therefore, be held accountable. The HMOs counter that these are administrative decisions and deny that they are practicing medicine.

The legal climate, however, began to change for HMOs during the mid-1990s. Both the Third Circuit Federal Court of Appeals in *Dukes v. U.S. Healthcare* (64 LW 2007, 1995) and the Tenth Circuit Federal Court of

TABLE 3.9

HMO enrollment by geographic region, selected years 1980–2006 [CONTINUED]

Geographic region and state[a]	2006[b]	1980	1985	1990	1995	1998	2000	2005	2006[b]
	Number in thousands				Percent of population				
Far West:									
Alaska	—	—	—	—	—	—	—	—	—
California	17,930	16.8	22.5	30.7	36.0	47.1	53.5	49.1	49.6
Hawaii	582	15.3	18.1	21.6	21.0	32.8	30.0	37.4	45.7
Nevada	627	—	5.8	8.5	15.9	26.8	23.5	25.2	26.0
Oregon	1,071	12.0	14.0	24.7	40.0	45.3	41.1	16.2	29.4
Washington	1,102	9.4	8.7	14.6	18.7	26.3	15.2	18.1	17.5

. . .Quantity less than 1,000 for number of persons and 0.02 for percent.
— Data not available.
[a]Data are shown for Bureau of Economic Analysis (BEA) regions that are constructed to show economically interdependent states. These BEA geographic regions differ from the U.S. Census Bureau geographic regions and divisions shown in some Health, United States tables.
[b]Starting with 2006 data, all managed health plans offering Medicaid products, whether licensed as HMOs or not, are included in these data. Starting with 2006 data, enrollment data for Medicare HMOs are limited to Medicare Advantage HMO plans. Previously, some other types of Medicare plans were included in the enrollment data for certain plans.
[c]HMOs in Guam are included starting in 1994; HMOs in Puerto Rico are included starting in 1998.
[d]Data for the District of Columbia (DC) not included for 1980–1996 because data not adjusted for high proportion of enrollees of DC-based HMOs living in Maryland and Virginia.
[e]Includes partial enrollment for five plans serving the District of Columbia.
Notes: Data are for midyear prior to 1990 and in 2006 and as of January 1 in all other years. Data for 1980–1990 are for pure HMO enrollment. Starting with 1994 data, pure and open-ended enrollment are included. In 1990, open-ended enrollment accounted for 3% of HMO enrollment compared with 12.5% in 2006. In 2005, 3,366 thousand enrollees in Cigna's Flexcare product were added to open-ended enrollment. Without this addition, total HMO enrollment would have continued slowly decreasing. Data are based on a census of health maintenance organizations.

SOURCE: Adapted from "Table 150. Persons Enrolled in Health Maintenance Organizations (HMOs) by Geographic Region and State: United States, Selected Years 1980–2006," in *Health, United States, 2007. With Chartbook on Trends in the Health of Americans*, U.S. Department of Health and Human Services, Centers for Disease Control and Prevention, National Center for Health Statistics, 2007, http://www.cdc.gov/nchs/data/hus/hus07.pdf#listtables (accessed April 21, 2008). Data from HealthLeaders-InterStudy.

Appeals in *PacifiCare of Oklahoma, Inc. v. Burrage* (59 F.3rd 151, 1995) agreed that HMOs were liable for malpractice and negligence claims against the HMO and HMO physicians. In *Frappier Estate v. Wishnov* (No. 95-0669, May 8, 1996), the Florida District Court of Appeals, Fourth District, agreed with the earlier findings. It seemed these decisions would be backed by new laws when both houses of Congress passed legislation (the Patients' Bill of Rights) giving patients more recourse to contest the decisions of HMOs, even though the U.S. House of Representatives and the U.S. Senate disagreed about the specific rights and the actions patients could take to enforce their rights. By August 2002 the prospects for a patients' rights law passing by the end of that year dimmed as the House and Senate failed to resolve their differences about the legislation. The central issue that stalled the negotiations about the bill was the question of how much recourse patients should have in court when they believe their HMO has not provided adequate care.

On June 21, 2004, the U.S. Supreme Court struck down a law in California and in several other states that allowed patients to sue their health plans for denying them health care services. Even though patients can still sue in federal court for reimbursement of denied benefits, they are no longer be able to sue for damages in federal or state courts.

PPOs

During the 1990s, in response to HMOs and other efforts by insurance groups to cut costs, physicians began forming or joining PPOs. PPOs are managed care organizations that offer integrated delivery systems—networks of providers—available through a wide array of health plans and are readily accountable to purchasers for access, cost, quality, and services of their networks. They use provider selection standards, utilization management, and quality assessment programs to complement negotiated fee reductions (discounted rates from participating physicians, hospitals, and other health care providers) as effective strategies for long-term cost control. Under a PPO benefit plan, covered people retain the freedom of choice of providers but are offered financial incentives such as lower out-of-pocket costs to use the preferred provider network. PPO members may use other physicians and hospitals, but they usually have to pay a higher proportion of the costs. PPOs are marketed directly to employers and to third-party administrators who then market PPOs to their employer clients.

Exclusive provider organizations (EPOs) are a more restrictive variation of PPOs in which members must seek care from providers on the EPO panel. If a member visits an outside provider who is not on the EPO panel, then the EPO will offer either limited or no coverage for the office or hospital visit.

According to HealthLeaders-InterStudy, in the press release "Boosts in Managed Care Enrollment Seen across the Board" (December 19, 2007, http://hl-is.com/index.php?p=press-archive-detailed&pr=pr_121907MMSRelease), enrollment in all types of managed care plans increased by 4.9% to 126.5 million from January 2007 to July 2007. PPO enrollment increased in California, Connecticut, Ohio, Hawaii, Iowa, Delaware, and Minnesota.

CHAPTER 4
RESEARCHING, MEASURING, AND MONITORING THE QUALITY OF HEALTH CARE

There are hundreds of agencies, institutions, and organizations dedicated to researching, quantifying (measuring), monitoring, and improving health in the United States. Some are federally funded public entities such as the many institutes and agencies governed by the U.S. Department of Health and Human Services (HHS). Others are professional societies and organizations that develop standards of care, represent the views and interests of health care providers, and ensure the quality of health care facilities such as the American Medical Association and the Joint Commission on Accreditation of Healthcare Organizations. Still other voluntary health organizations, such as the American Heart Association, the American Cancer Society, and the March of Dimes, promote research and education about prevention and treatment of specific diseases.

U.S. DEPARTMENT OF HEALTH AND HUMAN SERVICES

The HHS is the nation's lead agency for ensuring the health of Americans by planning, operating, and funding delivery of essential human services, especially for society's most vulnerable populations. According to the HHS, in "HHS: What We Do" (March 2008, http://www.hhs.gov/about/whatwedo.html/), it consists of more than three hundred programs that are operated by eleven divisions, including eight agencies in the U.S. Public Health Service and three human services agencies. It is the largest grant-making agency in the federal government, funding several thousand grants each year as well as the HHS Medicare program, the nation's largest health insurer, which processes more than one billion claims per year. For fiscal year (FY) 2009, the HHS had a budget of $736.8 billion, which is a net increase of $29 billion from FY 2008. (See Table 4.1.)

HHS Milestones

The HHS notes in "Historical Highlights" (June 19, 2005, http://www.hhs.gov/about/hhshist.html) that it began with the 1798 opening of the first Marine Hospital in Boston to care for sick and injured merchant seamen. Under President Abraham Lincoln (1809–1865) the agency that would become the U.S. Food and Drug Administration was established in 1862. The National Institutes of Health (NIH) dates back to 1887 and later became part of the Public Health Service. The 1935 enactment of the Social Security Act spurred the development of the Federal Security Agency in 1939 to direct programs in health, human services, insurance, and education. In 1946 the Communicable Disease Center, which would become the Centers for Disease Control and Prevention (CDC), was established, and nineteen years later, in 1965, Medicare (a federal health insurance program for older adults and people with disabilities) and Medicaid (state and federal health insurance for low-income people) were enacted to improve access to health care for older, disabled, and low-income Americans. That same year the Head Start program was developed to provide education, health, and social services to preschool-age children.

In 1970 the National Health Service Corps was established to help meet the health care needs of underserved areas and populations. The following year the National Cancer Act became law, which established cancer research as a national research priority. In 1984 the human immunodeficiency virus (HIV), the virus that causes the acquired immunodeficiency syndrome (AIDS), was identified by the Public Health Service and French research scientists. The National Organ Transplant Act became law in 1984, and in 1990 the Human Genome Project was initiated.

During 1994 NIH-funded research isolated the genes responsible for inherited breast cancer, colon cancer, and the most frequently occurring type of kidney cancer. In 1998 efforts were launched to eliminate racial and ethnic disparities (differences) in health, and in 2000 the human genome sequencing was published. In 2001 the Health Care Financing Administration was replaced by the Centers for

TABLE 4.1

U.S. Department of Health and Human Services budget, fiscal years 2007–09

[Dollars in millions]

	2007	2008	2009	2009 +/– 2008
Budget authority	656,726	715,790	731,407	+15,617
Outlays	670,413	707,723	736,793	+29,070
Full-time equivalents	63,748	64,750	65,630	+880

Note: May not add to the totals due to rounding.

SOURCE: "FY 2009 President's Budget for HHS," in *U.S. Department of Health and Human Services Budget in Brief, Fiscal Year 2009*, U.S. Department of Health and Human Services, 2008, http://www.hhs.gov/budget/09budget/2009BudgetInBrief.pdf (accessed April 21, 2008)

FIGURE 4.1

Cycle of health care research

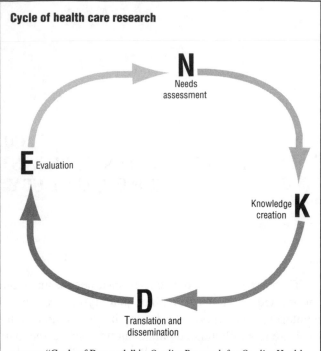

SOURCE: "Cycle of Research," in *Quality Research for Quality Health Care*, U.S. Department of Health and Human Services, Agency for Healthcare Research and Quality, March 2001, http://www.ahcpr.gov/about/qualres.pdf (accessed April 21, 2008)

Medicaid and Medicare Services, and the HHS responded to the first reported cases of bioterrorism—the 2001 anthrax attacks—and developed new strategies to prevent and detect threats of bioterrorism.

According to the Office of Management and Budget (2008, http://www.whitehouse.gov/omb/budget/fy2009/hhs.html), significant initiatives funded in the FY 2009 budget include the efforts to expand access to quality health care; prepare for the possibility of a pandemic influenza outbreak; protect the U.S population against the threat of bioterrorism; improve public health through science that protects food supplies and research that delivers new advances toward the cures in the future; and continue to address the health and human service needs of low-income children, vulnerable populations, and all Americans.

HHS Agencies and Institutes Provide Comprehensive Health and Social Services

Besides the CDC and the NIH, the HHS explains in *U.S. Department of Health and Human Services Budget in Brief, Fiscal Year 2009* (2008, http://www.hhs.gov/budget/09budget/2009BudgetInBrief.pdf) that the following agencies research, plan, direct, oversee, administer, and provide health care services:

- The Administration on Aging (AoA) provides services aimed at helping older Americans retain their independence. The AoA develops policies that support older adults and directs programs that provide transportation, in-home services, and other health and social services. For FY 2009 the AoA planned for a budget of $1.4 billion and 120 employees.

- The Administration for Children and Families (ACF) provides services for families and children in need, administers Head Start, and works with state foster care and adoption programs. The ACF planned to run about 60 programs with a budget of $45.6 billion and 1,299 employees for FY 2009.

- The Agency for Healthcare Research and Quality (AHRQ) researches access to health care, quality of care, and efforts to control health care costs. It also looks at the safety of health care services and ways to prevent medical errors. Figure 4.1 shows how the AHRQ researches health system problems by performing a continuous process of needs assessment, gaining knowledge, interpreting and communicating information, and evaluating the effects of this process on the health problem. Figure 4.2 shows the process that transforms new information about health care issues into actions to improve access, costs, outcomes (how patients fare as a result of the care they have received), and quality. For FY 2009 the AHRQ planned for a budget of $326 million and 300 employees. The AHRQ budgeted $77 million for patient safety; of this total, $45 million was invested in information technology to improve patient safety in ambulatory care settings.

- The Agency for Toxic Substances and Disease Registry (ATSDR) seeks to prevent exposure to hazardous waste. The agency's FY 2009 budget of $73 million represented a decrease of $1 million from FY 2008.

- The Centers for Medicare and Medicaid Services (CMS) administer programs that provide health insurance for about ninety-two million Americans who are either aged sixty-five and older or in financial need. It also operates the State Children's Health Insurance

FIGURE 4.2

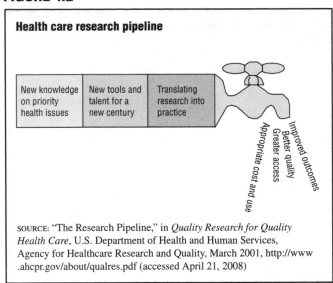

Health care research pipeline

| New knowledge on priority health issues | New tools and talent for a new century | Translating research into practice |

Improved outcomes
Better quality
Greater access
Appropriate cost and use

SOURCE: "The Research Pipeline," in *Quality Research for Quality Health Care*, U.S. Department of Health and Human Services, Agency for Healthcare Research and Quality, March 2001, http://www.ahcpr.gov/about/qualres.pdf (accessed April 21, 2008)

FIGURE 4.3

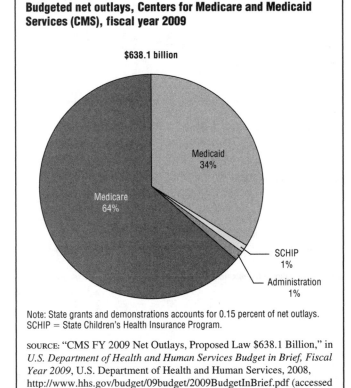

Budgeted net outlays, Centers for Medicare and Medicaid Services (CMS), fiscal year 2009

$638.1 billion

Medicaid 34%

Medicare 64%

SCHIP 1%

Administration 1%

Note: State grants and demonstrations accounts for 0.15 percent of net outlays. SCHIP = State Children's Health Insurance Program.

SOURCE: "CMS FY 2009 Net Outlays, Proposed Law $638.1 Billion," in *U.S. Department of Health and Human Services Budget in Brief, Fiscal Year 2009*, U.S. Department of Health and Human Services, 2008, http://www.hhs.gov/budget/09budget/2009BudgetInBrief.pdf (accessed April 21, 2008)

Program, which covers about ten million uninsured children, and regulates all laboratory testing, except testing performed for research purposes, in the United States. For FY 2009 the CMS planned for a $711.2 billion budget. Figure 4.3 shows the allocation of the CMS budget— roughly two-thirds (64%) was devoted to Medicare, one-third (34%) to Medicaid, and 1% each to the State Children's Health Insurance Plan and administration.

- The U.S. Food and Drug Administration (FDA) acts to ensure the safety and efficacy of dietary supplements, pharmaceutical drugs, and medical devices and monitors food safety and purity. The FDA planned for a budget of $2.4 billion in FY 2009 and 10,596 employees. The FDA budget included $287 million to protect the United States against the threat of an influenza pandemic (a worldwide epidemic), ensure the safety and security of the food supply, and provide other biodefense activities.

- The Health Resources and Services Administration (HRSA) provides services for medically underserved populations such as migrant workers, the homeless, and public housing residents. The HRSA oversees the nation's organ transplant program, directs efforts to improve maternal and child health, and delivers services to people with AIDS through the Ryan White CARE Act. In FY 2009 it planned to have 1,516 employees and a budget of $5.9 billion.

- The Indian Health Service (IHS) serves nearly 560 tribes through a network of 46 hospitals, 309 health stations, and 324 health centers. In FY 2009 the IHS planned to employ 15,131 workers and have a budget of $4.3 billion.

- The General Departmental Management provides the HHS's leadership and oversees the fifteen operating divisions of the HHS. It also advises the president about health, welfare, human service, and income security issues. In FY 2009 it was allotted 1,515 employees and a budget of $380 million.

- The Program Support Center (PSC) administers operations, financial management, and human resources for the HHS as well as for fourteen other executive departments and twenty federal agencies. The PSC staff of 1,249 processes grant payments, provides personnel and payroll services for HHS employees, and performs accounting, management, information technology, and telecommunication services.

- The Substance Abuse and Mental Health Services Administration (SAMHSA) seeks to improve access to, and availability of, substance abuse prevention and treatment programs as well as other mental health services. The SAMHSA was budgeted $3.2 billion in FY 2009 and had 528 employees.

HHS agencies work with state, local, and tribal governments as well as with public and private organizations to coordinate and deliver a wide range of services including:

- Conducting preventive health services such as surveillance to detect outbreaks of disease and immunization programs through efforts directed by the CDC and the NIH

- Ensuring food, drug, and cosmetic safety through efforts of the FDA

- Improving maternal and child health and preschool education in programs such as Head Start, which served more than one million children in 2007, according to the National Head Start Association (2007, http://www.nhsa.org/about/index.htm)

- Preventing child abuse, domestic violence, and substance abuse, as well as funding substance abuse treatment through programs directed by the ACF

- Ensuring the delivery of health care services to more than 1.9 million Native Americans and Alaskan Natives through the IHS, a network of hospitals, health centers, and other programs and facilities

- Administering Medicare and Medicaid via the CMS

- Providing financial assistance and support services for low-income and older Americans, such as home-delivered meals (Meals on Wheels) coordinated by the AoA

SUBSTANTIAL BUDGET HELPS HHS TO ACHIEVE ITS OBJECTIVES. Table 4.2 displays how the FY 2009 HHS budget was allocated and provides comparisons between 2007, 2008, and 2009 outlays. The FY 2009 budget is a net increase of $29 billion over the FY 2008 budget and aims to provide funds to help reform the health care marketplace and foster affordable choices in the health care system. It provides funds to advance the adoption of information technologies and electronic health records. The budget is also intended to increase access to care, strengthen emergency preparedness, and improve public health by intensifying prevention programs to reduce the occurrence of diabetes, asthma, and obesity. HHS agencies also continue to closely examine their expenditures to determine where they can achieve savings while continuing to provide public health activities to the nation.

U.S. PUBLIC HEALTH SERVICE COMMISSIONED CORPS. The U.S. Public Health Service Commissioned Corps (June 10, 2008, http://www.usphs.gov/aboutus/history.aspx) was originally the uniformed service component of the early Marine Hospital Service, which adopted a military model for a group of career health professionals who traveled from one marine hospital to another as their services were needed. It also assisted the Marine Hospital Service to prevent infectious diseases from entering the country by examining newly arrived immigrants and directing state quarantine (the period and place where people suspected of having contagious diseases are detained and isolated) functions. A law enacted in 1889 established this group as the Commissioned Corps, and throughout the twentieth century the corps grew to include a wide range of health professionals. Besides physicians, the corps employed nurses, dentists, research scientists, planners, pharmacists, sanitarians, engineers, and other public health professionals.

TABLE 4.2

Health and Human Services budget, by operating division, 2007–09

[Dollars in millions]

	2007	2008	2009	2009 +/− 2008
Food & Drug Administration:				
Program level	2,008	2,270	2,400	+130
Budget authority	1,574	1,720	1,771	+51
Outlays	1,563	1,394	1,728	+334
Health Resources & Services Administration:				
Budget authority	6,487	6,990	6,023	−967
Outlays	6,611	6,460	6,597	+137
Indian Health Service:				
Budget authority	3,330	3,497	3,475	−22
Outlays	3,265	3,670	3,634	−36
Centers for Disease Control & Prevention:				
Budget authority	6,082	6,179	5,746	−433
Outlays	5,586	6,567	6,105	−462
National Institutes of Health:				
Budget authority	29,128	29,457	29,457	−
Outlays	28,115	28,733	29,354	+621
Substance Abuse & Mental Health Services:				
Budget authority	3,206	3,234	3,025	−209
Outlays	3,179	3,263	3,146	−117
Agency for Healthcare Research & Quality:				
Program level	319	335	326	−9
Budget authority	—	—	—	—
Outlays	136	−88	—	+88
Centers for Medicare & Medicaid Services:				
Budget authority	557,907	615,535	633,751	+18,216
Outlays	571,560	606,929	636,179	+29,250
Administration for Children & Families:				
Budget authority	47,242	47,345	45,549	−1,796
Outlays	47,228	47,655	46,464	−1,191
Administration on Aging:				
Budget authority	1,383	1,413	1,381	−32
Outlays	1,359	1,389	1,389	−
Office of the National Coordinator:				
Budget authority	42	42	18	−24
Outlays	43	29	31	+2
Medicare Hearings and Appeals:				
Budget authority	60	64	65	+1
Outlays	54	64	65	+1
Office for Civil Rights				
Budget authority	35	34	40	+6
Outlays	31	35	39	+4
Departmental Management:				
Budget authority	365	354	380	+26
Outlays	391	303	361	+58
Public Health Social Service Emergency Fund:				
Budget authority	709	729	1,396	+667
Outlays	2,047	2,155	2,368	+213

By 1912 the Marine Hospital Service was renamed the Public Health Service (PHS) to reflect its broader scope of activities. The PHS is now part of the HHS.

TABLE 4.2

Health and Human Services budget, by operating division, 2007–09 [CONTINUED]

[Dollars in millions]

	2007	2008	2009	2009 +/− 2008
Office of Inspector General:				
Budget authority	68	68	71	+3
Outlays	112	41	79	+38
Program support center (retirement pay, medical benefits, misc. trust funds):				
Budget authority	491	518	554	+36
Outlays	516	513	549	+36
Offsetting collections:				
Budget authority	−1,383	−1,389	−1,295	+94
Outlays	−1,383	−1,389	−1,295	+94
Total, Health & Human Services:				
Budget authority	656,726	715,790	731,407	+15,617
Outlays	670,413	707,723	736,793	+29,070
Full-time equivalents	63,748	64,750	65,630	+880

SOURCE: "HHS Budget by Operating Division," in *U.S. Department of Health and Human Services Budget in Brief, Fiscal Year 2009*, U.S. Department of Health and Human Services, 2008, http://www.hhs.gov/budget/09budget/2009BudgetInBrief.pdf (accessed April 21, 2008)

PHS-commissioned officers played important roles in disease prevention and detection, acted to ensure food and drug safety, conducted research, provided medical care to underserved groups such as Native Americans and Alaskan Natives, and assisted in disaster relief programs. As one of the seven uniformed services in the United States (the other six are the U.S. Navy, U.S. Army, U.S. Marine Corps, U.S. Air Force, U.S. Coast Guard, and the National Oceanic and Atmospheric Administration Commissioned Corps), the PHS Commissioned Corps continues to perform all these functions and identifies environmental threats to health and safety, promotes healthy lifestyles for Americans, and is involved with international agencies to help address global health problems.

In 2008 the PHS Commissioned Corps numbered approximately six thousand health professionals. These people report to the U.S. surgeon general, who holds the rank of vice admiral in the PHS. Corps officers work in PHS agencies and at other agencies including the U.S. Bureau of Prisons, the U.S. Coast Guard, the Environmental Protection Agency, and the Commission on Mental Health of the District of Columbia. The surgeon general is the physician appointed by the U.S. president to serve in a medical leadership position in the nation for a four-year term of office. The surgeon general reports to the assistant secretary for health, and the Office of the Surgeon General (March 19, 2008, http://www.surgeongeneral.gov/aboutoffice.html) is part of the Office of Public Health and Science. Seventeen surgeons general have served since the 1870s. Since October

2007, Rear Admiral Steven K. Galson (1958–) has served as the acting surgeon general.

CENTERS FOR DISEASE CONTROL AND PREVENTION

The CDC is the primary HHS agency responsible for ensuring the health and safety of the nation's citizens in the United States and abroad. The CDC's responsibilities include researching and monitoring health, detecting and investigating health problems, researching and instituting prevention programs, developing health policies, ensuring environmental health and safety, and offering education and training.

The CDC (May 23, 2007, http://www.cdc.gov/about/resources/facts.htm) states that it employs over 14,000 people in 170 disciplines and in 40 countries. Besides research scientists, physicians, nurses, and other health practitioners, the CDC employs epidemiologists, who study disease in populations as opposed to individuals. Epidemiologists measure disease occurrences, such as incidence and prevalence of disease, and work with clinical researchers to answer questions about causation (how particular diseases arise and the factors that contribute to their development), whether new treatments are effective, and how to prevent specific diseases.

The CDC (January 24, 2008, http://www.cdc.gov/about/organization/research.htm) is home to twelve national centers and various institutes and offices. Among the best known are the National Center for Health Statistics, which collects vital statistics, and the National Institute for Occupational Safety and Health, which seeks to prevent workplace injuries and accidents through research and prevention. Julie Gerberding (1955–) was named the director of the CDC in 2002.

CDC Actions to Protect the Health of the Nation

The CDC is part of the first response to natural disasters, outbreaks of disease, and other public health emergencies. In the agency's role as part of an interagency National Influenza Pandemic Preparedness Task Force organized in May 2005 by the U.S. secretary of health and human services, the CDC is monitoring outbreaks and planning responses to the emerging threat of avian influenza, commonly called bird flu. Figure 4.4 shows the distribution of nations with confirmed cases of H5N1 avian influenza as of April 2008. Other examples of CDC initiatives are identification and education about effective strategies for preventing school and domestic violence as well as programs to promote a healthy diet and increase physical activity to prevent overweight and obesity.

Examples of CDC efforts to educate and communicate vital health information are its publications *Morbidity and Mortality Weekly Report* and the *Emerging Infectious Disease Journal*, which alert the medical community to

FIGURE 4.4

Nations with confirmed cases of Avian Influenza, April 2008

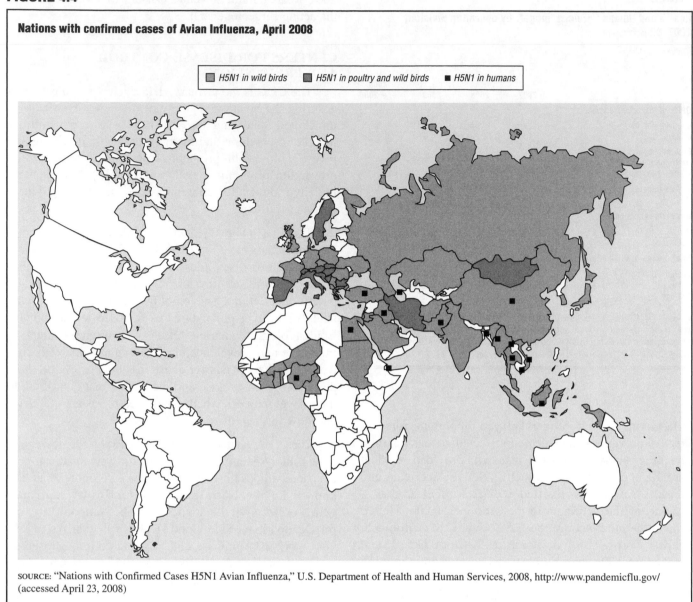

☐ *H5N1 in wild birds*　　■ *H5N1 in poultry and wild birds*　　■ *H5N1 in humans*

SOURCE: "Nations with Confirmed Cases H5N1 Avian Influenza," U.S. Department of Health and Human Services, 2008, http://www.pandemicflu.gov/ (accessed April 23, 2008)

the presence of health risks, outbreaks, and preventive measures. Besides providing vital statistics (births, deaths, and related health data), the CDC monitors Americans' health using surveys to measure the frequency of behaviors that increase health risk, such as smoking, substance abuse, and physical inactivity, and compiles data about the use of health care resources such as inpatient hospitalization rates and visits to hospital emergency departments.

The CDC partners with national, state, local, public, and private agencies and organizations to deliver services. Examples of these collaborative efforts include the global battle against HIV/AIDS by way of the Leadership and Investment in Fighting an Epidemic initiative and the CDC Coordinating Center for Health Information and Service, which was created to improve public health through increased efficiencies and to foster stronger collaboration between the CDC and international health foundations, health care practitioners,

community and philanthropic organizations, schools and universities, nonprofit and voluntary organizations, and state and local public health departments.

NATIONAL INSTITUTES OF HEALTH

The NIH (February 15, 2008, http://www.nih.gov/ about/history.htm), which began as a one-room laboratory in 1887, is the world's premier medical research center. The NIH conducts research in its own facilities and supports research in universities, medical schools, and hospitals throughout and outside the United States. The NIH trains research scientists and other investigators and serves to communicate medical and health information to professional and consumer audiences.

The NIH (July 9, 2008, http://www.nih.gov/about/ organization.htm) is composed of twenty-seven centers

FIGURE 4.5

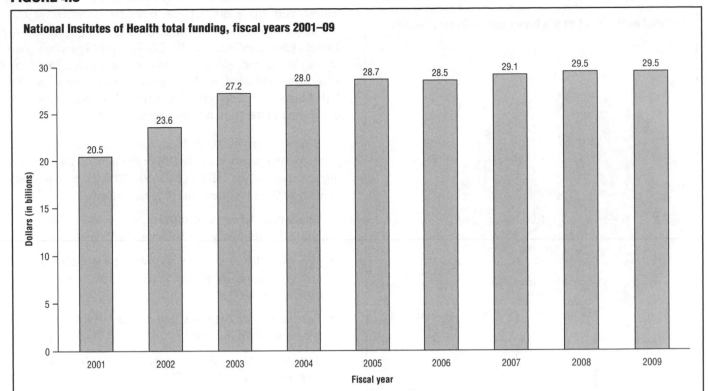

National Insitutes of Health total funding, fiscal years 2001–09

SOURCE: "NIH Total Funding," in *U.S. Department of Health and Human Services Budget in Brief, Fiscal Year 2009*, U.S. Department of Health and Human Services 2008, http://www.hhs.gov/budget/09budget/2009BudgetInBrief.pdf (accessed April 21, 2008)

and institutes and is housed in more than seventy-five buildings on a three-hundred-acre campus in Bethesda, Maryland. Among the better-known centers and institutes are the National Cancer Institute, the National Human Genome Research Institute, the National Institute of Mental Health, and the National Center for Complementary and Alternative Medicine.

The NIH explains in "Facts at a Glance" (January 9, 2006, http://clinicalcenter.nih.gov/about/welcome/fact.shtml) that patients arrive at the NIH Warren Grant Magnuson Clinical Center in Bethesda to participate in clinical research trials. About seven thousand patients per year are treated as inpatients here, and an additional one hundred thousand receive outpatient treatment. The National Library of Medicine—which produces the *Index Medicus*, a monthly listing of articles from the world's top medical journals, and maintains *MEDLINE*, a comprehensive medical bibliographic database—is in the NIH Lister Hill Center.

The NIH budget was $29.5 billion in FY 2009. Figure 4.5 shows how NIH funding has increased by more than $9 billion since 2001. The NIH (January 12, 2006, http://science .education.nih.gov/supplements/nih1/Genetic/about/about-nih.htm) works to achieve its ambitious research objectives "to acquire new knowledge to help prevent, detect, diagnose, and treat disease and disability, from the rarest genetic disorder to the common cold" by investing in promising biomedical research. The NIH makes grants and contracts

to support research and training in every state in the country, at more than two thousand institutions. The NIH allocated more than half (52.7%) of its FY 2009 budget to research project grants and nearly one-quarter to intramural research (10.6%), support research centers (10.1%), and research training (2.7%). (See Figure 4.6.)

Establishing Research Priorities

By law, all twenty-seven institutes of the NIH must be funded, and each institute must allocate its funding to specific areas and aspects of research within its domain. About half of each institute's budget is dedicated to supporting the best research proposals presented, in terms of their potential to contribute to advances that will combat the diseases the institute is charged with researching. Some of the other criteria used to determine research priorities include:

- Public health need—the NIH responds to health problems and diseases based on their incidence (the rate of development of a disease in a group during a given period), severity, and the costs associated with them. Examples of other measures used to weigh and assess need are the mortality rate (the number of deaths caused by disease), the morbidity rate (the degree of disability caused by disease), the economic and social consequences of the disease, and whether rapid action is required to control the spread of the disease.

FIGURE 4.6

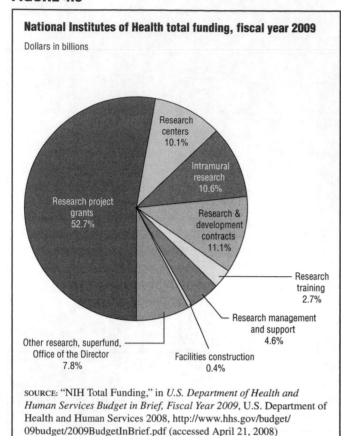

National Institutes of Health total funding, fiscal year 2009

Dollars in billions

SOURCE: "NIH Total Funding," in *U.S. Department of Health and Human Services Budget in Brief, Fiscal Year 2009*, U.S. Department of Health and Human Services 2008, http://www.hhs.gov/budget/09budget/2009BudgetInBrief.pdf (accessed April 21, 2008)

- Rigorous peer review—proposals are scrutinized by accomplished researchers to determine their potential to return on the investment of resources.

- Flexibility and expansiveness—NIH experience demonstrates that important findings for commonly occurring diseases may come from research about rarer ones. The NIH attempts to fund the broadest possible array of research opportunities to stimulate creative solutions to pressing problems.

- Commitment to human resources and technology—the NIH invests in people, equipment, and even some construction projects in the pursuit of scientific advancements.

Because not even the most gifted scientists can accurately predict the next critical discovery or stride in biomedical research, the NIH must analyze each research opportunity in terms of competition for the same resources, public interests, scientific merit, and the potential to build on current knowledge. Figure 4.7 shows all the stakeholders whose interests and opinions are considered when NIH resource allocation and grant funding decisions are made.

NIH Achievements

The HHS notes in *U.S. Department of Health and Human Services Budget in Brief, Fiscal Year 2009* that in

FY 2009 the NIH had 17,254 employees. The NIH recruits and attracts the most capable research scientists in the world. In fact, the NIH states in "The NIH Almanac—Nobel Laureates" (June 9, 2008, http://www.nih.gov/about/almanac/nobel/index.htm#scientists) that 115 scientists who conducted NIH research or were supported by NIH grants have received Nobel Prizes. Five Nobel winners made their prize-winning discoveries in NIH laboratories.

Equally important, NIH research has contributed to great improvements in the health of the nation. The following are some of the NIH's (June 19, 2007, http://www.nih.gov/about/NIHoverview.html) achievements:

- Death rates from heart disease and stroke fell by 40% and 51%, respectively, between 1975 and 2000.

- The overall five-year survival rate for childhood cancers rose to nearly 80% during the 1990s from under 60% in the 1970s.

- The number of AIDS-related deaths fell by about 70% between 1995 and 2001.

- Sudden infant death syndrome rates fell by more than 50% between 1994 and 2000.

- Infectious diseases—such as rubella, whooping cough, and pneumococcal pneumonia—that once killed and disabled millions of people are now prevented by vaccines.

- The sequencing of the human genome set a new course for developing ways to diagnose and treat diseases such as cancer, Parkinson's Disease, and Alzheimer's Disease, as well as rare diseases.

- In response to the anthrax attacks of 2001, the NIH launched and expanded research to prevent, detect, diagnose, and treat diseases caused by potential bioterrorism agents.

- New and improved imaging techniques let scientists painlessly look inside the body and detect disease in its earliest stages when it is often most effectively treated.

- Researchers aggressively pursue ways to make effective vaccines for deadly diseases such as HIV/AIDS, tuberculosis, malaria, and potential agents of bioterrorism.

- Progress in understanding the immune system may lead to new ways to treat and cure diabetes, arthritis, asthma and allergies.

- New, more precise ways to treat cancer are emerging, such as drugs that zero in on abnormal proteins in cancer cells.

- Novel research methods are being developed that can identify the causes of outbreaks, such as Severe Acute Respiratory Syndrome, in weeks rather than months or years.

FIGURE 4.7

Views taken into consideration when setting research priorities at the National Institutes of Health, 2006

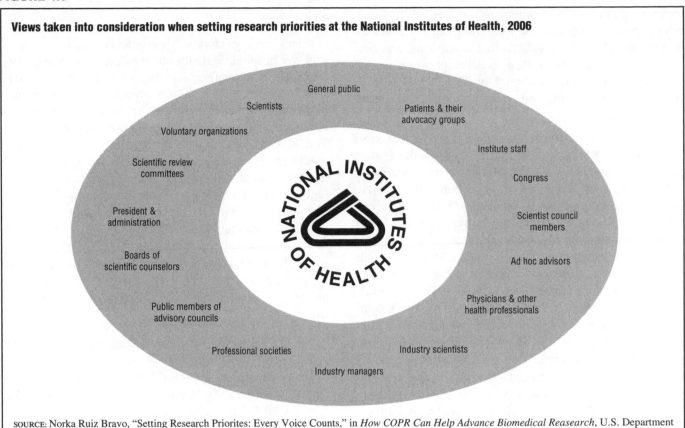

SOURCE: Norka Ruiz Bravo, "Setting Research Priorites: Every Voice Counts," in *How COPR Can Help Advance Biomedical Reasearch*, U.S. Department of Health and Human Services, National Institutes of Health, 2006, http://copr.nih.gov/presentations/bravo.pdf (accessed April 22, 2008)

Elias A. Zerhouni, the director of the NIH, explains in *NIH: A Vision for the Future* (March 6, 2007, http://www.nih.gov/about/director/budgetrequest/fy2008budge thearings.pdf) that NIH scientists have initiated and expanded the scope of their medical research and report significant findings resulting from new and ongoing research projects. Zerhouni indicates that some of these important initiatives and findings are:

- 2007 was the second consecutive year during which cancer deaths in the United States declined.

- Large-scale HIV vaccine trials are under way and new vaccine targets have been identified.

- A vaccine for the human papillomavirus (which infects more than 80% of fifteen- to fifty-year-old women and can cause cervical cancer) was approved by the FDA and is the first vaccine to protect against cancer.

- Researchers developed ways to "personalize" antico-agulant therapy—drug therapy that regulates bleeding and clotting to reduce the risk of heart attack and stroke.

ACCREDITATION

Accreditation of health care providers (facilities and organizations) provides consumers, payers, and other stake-holders with the assurance that accredited facilities and organizations have been certified as meeting or exceeding predetermined standards. Accreditation refers to both the process during which the quality of care delivered is meas-ured and the resulting official endorsement that quality standards have been met. Besides promoting accreditation to health care consumers and other purchasers of care such as employer groups, accreditation assists health care facili-ties and organizations to recruit and retain qualified staff, increase organizational efficiencies to reduce costs, identify ways to improve service delivery, and reduce liability insurance premiums.

Joint Commission on Accreditation of Healthcare Organizations

The Joint Commission on Accreditation of Healthcare Organizations (JCAHO; 2008, http://www.jointcommission .org/NewsRoom/faqs.htm) surveys and accredits more than fifteen thousand health care organizations and programs throughout the United States. The JCAHO is a not-for-profit organization and is headquartered in Oakbrook Terrace, Illinois, with a satellite office in Washington, D.C. The JCAHO (2008, http://www.jointcommission.org/AboutUs/ CareerOpportunities/default.htm) has more than one thou-sand surveyors—physicians, nurses, pharmacists, hospital and health care organization administrators, and other health professionals—who are qualified and trained to evaluate specific aspects of health care quality.

Working closely with medical and other professional societies, purchasers of health care services, and management experts as well as other accrediting organizations, the JCAHO develops the standards that health care organizations are expected to meet. Besides developing benchmarks and standards of organizational quality, the JCAHO is credited with promoting improvement in infection control, safety, and patients' rights.

THE JCAHO GROWS TO BECOME THE PREEMINENT ACCREDITING BODY. In "A Journey through the History of the Joint Commission" (2008, http://www.jointcommission.org/AboutUs/joint_commission_history.htm), the JCAHO explains that early efforts to standardize and evaluate care delivered in hospitals began in 1913 by the American College of Surgeons, a group that thirty-eight years later would start the present-day Joint Commission on Accreditation of Healthcare Organizations, originally dubbed the Joint Commission on Accreditation of Hospitals (JCAH) in 1951. In 1966 the JCAH began to offer accreditation to long-term care facilities, and in 1972 the Social Security Act was amended to require the HHS secretary to validate JCAH findings and include them in the HHS annual report to Congress. In subsequent years the JCAH's mandate was expanded to include a variety of other health care facilities, and in 1987 it was renamed the Joint Commission on Accreditation of Healthcare Organizations.

In 1992 the JCAHO instituted a requirement that accredited hospitals prohibit smoking in the hospital, and in 1993 it began performing random, surprise surveys (unannounced site visits) on 5% of accredited organizations. The JCAHO also moved to emphasize performance improvement standards, revising its policies on medical errors and instituting a hotline for complaints about quality of care.

In 1999 the JCAHO required hospitals to begin collecting and reporting data about the care they provide for five specific diagnoses: acute myocardial infarction (heart attack), congestive heart failure, pneumonia, pregnancy and related medical conditions, and surgical procedures and complications. The JCAHO calls these diagnoses "core measure data" and uses these data to compare facilities and assess the quality of service delivered. In 2002 the JCAHO moved to make its recommendations more easily understood by consumers so they could make informed choices about health care providers.

In 2006 the JCAHO shifted to an unannounced survey program—meaning that organizations receive no advanced notice of their survey date. Before this policy change, the leaders of the nation's more than forty-five hundred Medicare-participating hospitals had ample notice and time to prepare for JCAHO visits and inspections. The policy change was intended to shift hospitals' orientation from preparing for the next JCAHO survey to preparing for the next patient, and requires hospitals to conduct an annual periodic performance review using their own internal evaluators to assess their own level of standards compliance.

The hospitals must then communicate the results of their audits to the JCAHO.

This policy change, presumably implemented to improve hospital vigilance about safety, care, and quality, coincided with another, seemingly contradictory JCAHO policy change, which allows hospitals to accumulate a higher number of deficiencies (patient care lapses and other violations) before sanctions are imposed on them. The JCAHO defends this practice by explaining that it would rather identify more problems and have hospitals resolve them than deny hospitals accreditation. Charles Ornstein and Tracy Weber report in "Hospitals' Watchdog Raises Violation Threshold" (*Los Angeles Times*, April 6, 2006) that Dennis S. O'Leary, the JCAHO president, said the commission made the changes because it found that too many decent hospitals were being referred for punishment and that he expected that the number of hospitals sanctioned in 2006 would actually increase from years past.

In 2008 Amy Wilson-Stronks et al. of the JCAHO published *One Size Does Not Fit All: Meeting the Health Care Needs of Diverse Populations* (http://www.jointcommission.org/NR/rdonlyres/88C2C901-6E4E-4570-95D8-B49BD7F756CF/0/HLCOneSizeFinal.pdf), a report that exhorts health care organizations to assess and enhance their capacity to meet patients' unique cultural and language needs to better accommodate specific populations.

National Committee for Quality Assurance

The National Committee for Quality Assurance (NCQA) is another well-respected accrediting organization that focuses its attention on the managed care industry. The NCQA began surveying and accrediting managed care organizations (MCOs) in 1991. By 2008 most health maintenance organizations (HMOs) in the United States had been reviewed by the NCQA, and thirty states required licensed health maintenance organizations to report Health Plan Employer Data and Information Set (HEDIS) information or undergo NCQA accreditation. In addition, the NCQA indicates in *The State of Health Care Quality 2007* (2007, http://www.ncqa.org/Portals/0/Publications/Resource%20Library/SOHC/SOHC_07.pdf) that 141 PPOs voluntarily submitted HEDIS data to the NCQA in 2007. This represented a 76% increase from 2005, during which 80 PPOs reported.

When an MCO undergoes an NCQA survey, it is assessed by more than sixty different standards, each focusing on a specific aspect of health plan operations. The standards address access and service, the qualifications of providers, the organization's commitment to prevention programs and health maintenance, the quality of care delivered to members when they are ill or injured, and the organization's approach for helping members manage chronic diseases such as diabetes, heart disease, and asthma.

To ensure fair comparisons between managed health care plans and to track their progress and improvement over time, the NCQA considers more than sixty HEDIS measures that look at health care delivery issues such as:

- Management of asthma and effective use of medication
- Controlling hypertension (high blood pressure)
- Effective and appropriate use of antidepressant medications
- The frequency and consistency with which smokers are counseled to quit
- Rates of breast cancer screening
- The frequency and consistency with which beta blocker (drug treatment) is used following heart attack
- Rates of immunization among children and teens

The NCQA combines HEDIS data with national and regional benchmarks of quality in a national database called the Quality Compass. This national database enables employers and health care consumers to compare health plans to one another and make choices about coverage based on quality and value rather than simply on price and participating providers (physicians, hospitals, and other providers that offer services to the managed care plan members).

The NCQA issues health plan report cards that rate HMOs and MCOs, and health care consumers and other stakeholders can access them at the NCQA Web site. After the NCQA review, the MCOs may be granted the NCQA's full accreditation for three years, indicating a level of excellence that exceeds NCQA standards. Those that need some improvement are granted one-year accreditation with recommendations about areas that need improvement, and those MCOs that meet some but not all NCQA standards may be denied accreditation or granted provisional accreditation.

In 2007 the NCQA reported that health care quality had improved dramatically for the sixth consecutive year—participating health plans' performance on nearly every measure was better than the previous year's results. Furthermore, care improved regardless of payer—private employer, Medicare, or Medicaid—among health plans that measure and report quality results.

The NCQA documents in *State of Health Care Quality 2007* how improved performance saves lives. For example, successful efforts to control high blood pressure, manage cholesterol levels after patients have suffered heart attacks, and ensure that patients receive proper medication have helped prevent second heart attacks and saved the lives of thousands of Americans.

Other notable gains in quality include improved immunization rates among children and teens—80% had been immunized, which was an increase of two percentage points from the previous year; adults over age fifty were more likely to have received colon cancer screening; and rates of appropriate treatment for adults suffering from acute bronchitis and rheumatoid arthritis also rose.

Accreditation Association for Ambulatory Health Care

Another accrediting organization, the Accreditation Association for Ambulatory Health Care (AAAHC), was formed in 1979 and focuses exclusively on ambulatory (outpatient) facilities and programs. Outpatient clinics, group practices, college health services, occupational medicine clinics, and ambulatory surgery centers are among the organizations that are evaluated by the AAAHC. The AAAHC accreditation process involves a self-assessment by the organization seeking accreditation and a survey conducted by AAAHC surveyors who are all practicing professionals. The AAAHC grants accreditation for periods ranging from six months to three years.

In 2002 the AAAHC and the JCAHO signed a collaborative accreditation agreement that permits ambulatory health care organizations to use their AAAHC accreditation to satisfy JCAHO requirements. In June 2002 the CMS granted the AAAHC authority to review health plans that provide coverage for Medicare beneficiaries. HMOs, PPOs, and ambulatory surgery centers are now considered Medicare-certified on their receipt of accreditation from the AAAHC.

During 2003 and 2004 several states, including Florida, California, and Ohio, approved the AAAHC to conduct accreditation of office-based surgical centers, primary care practices, and freestanding radiology centers such as magnetic resonance imaging services. By 2008 the AAAHC (http://www.aaahc.org/eweb/dynamicpage.aspx?site=aaahc_site&webcode=about_aaahc) was accrediting over thirty-eight hundred organizations.

National Quality Forum

In 2006 two other national quality organizations, the National Quality Forum and the National Committee on Quality Health Care, merged to become a new organization, also named the National Quality Forum (NQF). The NQF is a private, not-for-profit membership organization created to develop and implement a national strategy for health care quality measurement and reporting. Its mission is to improve U.S. health care through the endorsement of consensus-based national standards for measurement and public reporting of health care performance data that provide meaningful information about whether care is safe, timely, beneficial, patient centered, equitable, and efficient.

PROFESSIONAL SOCIETIES

There are professional and membership organizations and societies for all health professionals, such as physicians, nurses, psychologists, and hospital administrators, as well as for institutional health care providers, such as hospitals, managed care plans, and medical groups. These professional organizations represent the interests and concerns of their members, advocate on their behalf, and frequently compile data and publish information about working conditions, licensing, accreditation, compensation, and scientific advancements of interest to members.

American Medical Association

The American Medical Association (AMA) is a powerful voice for U.S. physicians' interests. The AMA concerns itself with a wide range of health-related issues including medical ethics, medical education, physician and patient advocacy, and development of national health policy. The AMA publishes the highly regarded *Journal of the American Medical Association* and the *AMNews*, as well as journals in ten specialty areas called *Archives Journals*.

Founded in 1847, the AMA has worked to upgrade medical education by expanding medical school curricula and establishing standards for licensing and accreditation of practitioners and postgraduate training programs. Recent activities of the AMA are advocating for legislation to improve patient safety, opposing Medicare physician-payment cuts to ensure that older adults have access to needed medical care, and encouraging film producers, media companies, and the Motion Picture Association of America to eliminate tobacco products and their use in youth-rated films.

American Nurses Association

The American Nurses Association (ANA; 2008, http://www.nursingworld.org/FunctionalMenuCategories/AboutANA.aspx) is a professional organization that represents more than 2.9 million registered nurses (RNs) and promotes high standards of nursing practice and education as well as the roles and responsibilities of nurses in the workplace and the community. On behalf of its members, the ANA works to protect patients' rights, lobbies to advocate for nurses' interests, champions workplace safety, and provides career and continuing education opportunities. The ANA publishes the *American Journal of Nursing* and actively seeks to improve the public image of nurses among health professionals and the community at large.

American Hospital Association

The American Hospital Association (AHA; 2006, http://www.aha.org/aha/about/index.html) represents nearly five thousand hospitals, health care systems, networks, and other health care providers and thirty-seven thousand individual members. Originally established as a membership organization for hospital superintendents in 1898, the AHA eventu-ally expanded its mission to address all facets of hospital care and quality. Besides national advocacy activities and participation in the development of health policy, the AHA oversees research and pilot programs to improve health service delivery. It also gathers and disseminates hospital and other related health care data, publishes information of interest to its members, and sponsors educational opportunities for health care managers and administrators.

VOLUNTARY HEALTH ORGANIZATIONS

American Heart Association

The American Heart Association's mission is to decrease disability and death from cardiovascular diseases and stroke. The association's national headquarters is in Dallas, Texas, and twelve regional affiliate offices serve the balance of the United States. More than twenty-two million volunteers and supporters were involved with association programs and activities during 2008.

The American Heart Association (2008, http://www.americanheart.org/presenter.jhtml?identifier=10860) was started by a group of physicians and social workers in New York City in 1915. The early efforts of this group, called the Association for the Prevention and Relief of Heart Disease, were to educate physicians and the general public about heart disease. The first fund-raising efforts were launched in 1948 during a radio broadcast, and since then the association has raised millions of dollars to fund research, education, and treatment programs.

Besides research, fund-raising, and generating public awareness about reducing the risk of developing heart disease, the American Heart Association has published many best-selling cookbooks featuring heart-healthy recipes and meal planning ideas. The association is also considered one of the world's most trusted authorities about heart health among physicians and scientists. It publishes five print journals and one online professional journal, including *Circulation*, *Stroke*, *Hypertension*, and *Atherosclerosis, Thrombosis, and Vascular Biology*.

American Cancer Society

The American Cancer Society (ACS) is headquartered in Atlanta, Georgia, and has more than thirty-four hundred offices across the country. The ACS's (2008, http://www.cancer.org/docroot/AA/content/AA_1_1_ACS_Mission_Statements.asp) mission is "eliminating cancer as a major health problem by preventing cancer, saving lives, and diminishing suffering from cancer, through research, education, advocacy, and service."

The ACS is the biggest source of private, not-for-profit funding for cancer research—second only to the federal government. In "ACS Fact Sheet" (March 4, 2008, http://www.cancer.org/docroot/AA/content/AA_1_2_ACS_Fact_Sheet.asp), the ACS states that by 2008 it had invested more than $3 billion in cancer research at leading centers throughout the United States and funded forty-two Nobel Prize winners early in their careers. It also supports epidemiological research to provide cancer surveillance information about occurrence rates, risk factors, mortality, and availability of treatment services. The ACS publishes an array of patient information brochures and four clinical journals for health professionals: *Cancer*, *Cancer Cytopathology*, *CA: A Cancer Journal for Clinicians*, and *Cancer Practice*. The ACS also maintains a twenty-four-hour consumer telephone line staffed by trained cancer information specialists and a Web site with information for professionals, patients and families, and the media.

Besides education, prevention, and patient services, the ACS advocates for cancer survivors, their families, and every potential cancer patient. The ACS seeks to obtain support and passage of laws, policies, and regulations that benefit people affected by cancer. The ACS is especially concerned with developing strategies to better serve the poor and people with little formal education, who historically have been disproportionately affected by cancer.

March of Dimes

The March of Dimes was founded in 1938 by President Franklin D. Roosevelt (1882–1945) to help protect American children from polio. Besides supporting the research that produced the polio vaccine, it has advocated birth defects research and the fortification of food supplies with folic acid to prevent neural tube defects. It has also supported increasing access to quality prenatal care and the growth of neonatal intensive care units to help improve the chances of survival for babies born prematurely or those with serious medical conditions.

The March of Dimes continues to partner with volunteers, scientific researchers, educators, and community outreach workers to help prevent birth defects. It funds genetic research, investigates the causes and treatment of premature birth, educates pregnant women, and provides health care services for women and children, such as immunization, checkups, and treatment for childhood illnesses.

In 2008 the March of Dimes championed initiatives to address and reduce racial disparities in infant health outcomes, funded research to study the role genes and heredity play in premature births, and advocated for adequate funding to ensure that children receive essential, appropriate, and quality health care.

CHAPTER 5
THE INCREASING COST OF HEALTH CARE

HOW MUCH DOES HEALTH CARE COST?

American society places a high value on human life and generally wants—and expects—quality medical care. However, quality care comes with an increasingly high cost. In 1970 the United States spent 7.2% of its gross domestic product (GDP; the total market value of final goods and services produced within an economy in a given year) on health care. By 2005 health care expenditures reached 16% of the GDP. Table 5.1 shows the growth in health care expenditures, the growth in the GDP, and the annual percent change from the previous year from 1960 to 2005.

For many years the consumer price index (CPI; a measure of the average change in prices paid by consumers) increased at a greater rate for medical care than for any other commodity. From 1980 to 1990 the average annual increase in the overall CPI was 4.7%, whereas the average annual increase in the medical care index stood at 8.1%. (See Table 5.2.) By 2000 the average annual growth in the medical care index had fallen to 3.5%, but in 2006 it had risen again to 4.1%, outpacing overall inflation, which was 3.2%. The medical care index has consistently outpaced the CPI in each decade. Of all the components of health care delivery, the sharpest price increases in 2006 were in hospital services at 6.5%.

The Centers for Medicare and Medicaid Services (CMS) projects that by 2017 the national health expenditure will grow to nearly $4.3 trillion—19.5% of the GDP, from 16.3% in 2007. (See Table 5.3.) (Because the numbers in Table 5.3 are projections, they may differ from the actual numbers presented in some other tables and figures.) In "NHE Fact Sheet" (July 25, 2008, http://www.cms.hhs .gov/NationalHealthExpendData/25_NHE_Fact_Sheet.asp# TopOfPage), the CMS indicates that Medicare accounted for a staggering 18.7% of national care expenditures in 2006.

Generally, projections are most accurate for the near future and less accurate for the distant future. For exam-

ple, predictions for 2030 should be viewed more warily than predictions for 2010, because it is unlikely that the conditions on which the projections are based will remain the same. As a result, the CMS cautions that its projections should not be viewed as predictions for the future. Rather, they are intended to help policy makers evaluate the costs or savings of proposed legislative or regulatory changes.

Total Health Care Spending

The CMS, along with the Centers for Disease Control and Prevention and the U.S. Government Accountability Office, maintain most of the nation's statistics on health care costs. The CMS reports that the United States spent $2.2 trillion for health care in 2007, which was an increase of 6.7% from $2.1 trillion in 2006. (See Table 5.3.) This rate has decreased since the 9.1% increase in 2002 and is projected to remain relatively constant, although it will likely be as high as three times the rate of inflation through 2017.

Over $2.1 trillion of 2006 health care expenditures came from private funds (out-of-pocket payments, private health insurance, and other private funds), and the balance was paid with public money. (See Table 5.4.) The 2006 per capita cost for health care (the average per individual if spending was divided equally among all people in the country) was $7,026.

Of the $2.1 trillion spent on health care in 2006, close to $1.8 trillion was spent on personal health services (expenses incurred by individuals as opposed to institutions). (See Table 5.5.) Some of the services included hospital care, physician and dental services, nursing and home health care, prescription drugs, and durable medical equipment.

Table 5.5 shows the trends and annual percent changes in personal health care expenditures by category. In 2006 the nation spent $660.2 billion on professional services, by far the largest chunk of personal health care spending,

TABLE 5.1

Gross domestic product (GDP), federal, state, and local government health expenditures and average annual percent change, selected years 1960–2005

Gross domestic product, government expenditures, and national health expenditures	1960	1970	1980	1990	1995	2000	2003	2004	2005
					Amount in billions				
Gross domestic product (GDP)	$526	$1,039	$2,790	$5,803	$7,398	$9,817	$10,961	$11,713	$12,456
Federal government expenditures	$87	$201	$586	$1,254	$1,604	$1,864	$2,252	$2,383	$2,556
State and local government expenditures	40	113	329	731	978	1,270	1,515	1,606	1,704
National health expenditures	$28	$75	$254	$714	$1,017	$1,353	$1,733	$1,859	$1,988
Private	21	47	148	427	552	757	956	1,021	1,085
Public	7	28	106	287	465	596	778	838	903
Federal government	3	18	72	194	327	417	553	601	644
State and local government	4	10	35	93	138	179	225	237	259
					Amount per capita				
National health expenditures	$148	$356	$1,102	$2,813	$3,783	$4,790	$5,952	$6,322	$6,697
Private	111	222	640	1,684	2,053	2,680	3,282	3,472	3,656
Public	36	134	462	1,130	1,730	2,110	2,670	2,850	3,041
					Percent				
National health expenditures as percent of GDP	5.2	7.2	9.1	12.3	13.7	13.8	15.8	15.9	16.0
Health expenditures as a percent of total government expenditures									
Federal government	3.3	8.8	12.2	15.5	20.4	22.4	24.6	25.2	25.2
State and local government	9.8	9.2	10.6	12.7	14.1	14.1	14.8	14.8	15.2
					Percent distribution				
National health expenditures	100.0	100.0	100.0	100.0	100.0	100.0	100.0	100.0	100.0
Private	75.3	62.4	58.1	59.8	54.3	55.9	55.1	54.9	54.6
Public	24.7	37.6	41.9	40.2	45.7	44.1	44.9	45.1	45.4
					Average annual percent change from previous year shown				
Gross domestic product	—	7.0	10.4	7.6	5.0	5.8	3.7	6.9	6.3
Federal government expenditures	—	8.8	11.3	7.9	5.0	3.1	6.5	5.8	7.3
State and local government expenditures	—	10.9	11.3	8.3	6.0	5.4	6.1	6.0	6.1
National health expenditures	—	10.5	13.0	10.9	7.3	5.9	8.6	7.2	6.9
Private	—	8.5	12.2	11.2	5.2	6.5	8.1	6.8	6.3
Public	—	15.3	14.2	10.4	10.1	5.1	9.3	7.8	7.7
Federal government	—	20.0	15.0	10.5	11.0	5.0	9.8	8.6	7.2
State and local government	—	10.2	12.8	10.3	8.2	5.4	7.9	5.7	9.1
National health expenditures, per capita	—	9.2	12.0	9.8	6.1	4.8	7.5	6.2	5.9
Private	—	7.2	11.2	10.1	4.0	5.5	7.0	5.8	5.3
Public	—	13.9	13.2	9.4	8.9	4.1	8.2	6.7	6.7

—Category not applicable.

Notes: These data include revisions in health expenditures and may differ from previous editions of Health, United States. The data reflect U.S. Census Bureau resident population estimates as of July 2006, excluding the armed forces overseas and the population of outlying areas. Federal and state and local government total expenditures reflect revisions from the Bureau of Economic Analysis. Percents are calculated using unrounded data. Percents and numbers may not add to totals due to rounding.

SOURCE: "Table 121. Gross Domestic Product, Federal, and State and Local Government Expenditures, National Health Expenditures, and Average Annual Percent Change: United States, Selected Years, 1960–2005," in *Health, United States, 2007. With Chartbook on Trends in the Health of Americans*, U.S. Department of Health and Human Services, Centers for Disease Control and Prevention, National Center for Health Statistics, 2007, http://www.cdc.gov/nchs/data/hus/hus07.pdf#listtables (accessed April 24, 2008).

followed by $648.2 billion on hospital costs. This expense was followed by $447.6 billion for physician and clinical services, $216.7 billion for prescription drugs, and $177.6 billion for nursing home and home health care.

WHO PAYS THE BILL?

In general, the government is the fastest-growing payer of health care expenses. From 2002 to 2006 the public share of the nation's total health care bill rose from 45% to 46.1%, and it is projected to rise to 48.6% by 2017. (See Table 5.4.) In 2006 private health insurance, the major nongovernmental payer of health care costs, paid approximately 34.4% of all health expenditures. The share of health care spending from private, out-of-pocket (paid by the patient) funds declined from 13.2% in 2002 to 12.2% in 2006.

Personal Health Care Bill

Much of the increase in government spending has occurred in the area of personal health care. In 2002 government sources paid 43.9% of personal health care expenditures; by 2006 they covered 45.3% of the $1.8 trillion spent on personal health care services. (See Table 5.6.) Of the total expenditures, 35.1% came from the federal government and 10.2% came from state and local governments. Some of the federal increase was attributed to Medicare spending, which grew from 19.1% of all personal health care expenditures in 2002 to 21.6% in 2006.

TABLE 5.2

Consumer price index and average annual percent change for all items, selected items, and medical care costs, selected years 1960–2006

Items and medical care components	1960	1970	1980	1990	1995	2000	2003	2004	2005	2006
					Consumer price index (CPI)					
All items	29.6	38.8	82.4	130.7	152.4	172.2	184.0	188.9	195.3	201.6
All items less medical care	30.2	39.2	82.8	128.8	148.6	167.3	178.1	182.7	188.7	194.7
Services	24.1	35.0	77.9	139.2	168.7	195.3	216.5	222.8	230.1	238.9
Food	30.0	39.2	86.8	132.4	148.4	167.8	180.0	186.2	190.7	195.2
Apparel	45.7	59.2	90.9	124.1	132.0	129.6	120.9	120.4	119.5	119.5
Housing	—	36.4	81.1	128.5	148.5	169.6	184.8	189.5	195.7	203.2
Energy	22.4	25.5	86.0	102.1	105.2	124.6	136.5	151.4	177.1	196.9
Medical care	22.3	34.0	74.9	162.8	220.5	260.8	297.1	310.1	323.2	336.2
Components of medical care										
Medical care services	19.5	32.3	74.8	162.7	224.2	266.0	306.0	321.3	336.7	350.6
Professional services	—	37.0	77.9	156.1	201.0	237.7	261.2	271.5	281.7	289.3
Physicians' services	21.9	34.5	76.5	160.8	208.8	244.7	267.7	278.3	287.5	291.9
Dental services	27.0	39.2	78.9	155.8	206.8	258.5	292.5	306.9	324.0	340.9
Eye glasses and eye care[a]	—	—	—	117.3	137.0	149.7	155.9	159.3	163.2	168.1
Services by other medical professionals[b]	—	—	—	120.2	143.9	161.9	177.1	181.9	186.8	192.2
Hospital and related services	—	—	69.2	178.0	257.8	317.3	394.8	417.9	439.9	468.1
Hospital services[b]	—	—	—	—	—	115.9	144.7	153.4	161.6	172.1
Inpatient hospital services[b,c]	—	—	—	—	—	113.8	140.1	148.1	156.6	167.5
Outpatient hospital services[a,c]	—	—	—	138.7	204.6	263.8	337.9	356.3	373.0	395.0
Hospital rooms	9.3	23.6	68.0	175.4	251.2	—	—	—	—	—
Other inpatient services[a]	[b]	—	—	—	142.7	206.8	—	—	—	—
Nursing homes and adult day care[b]	—	—	—	—	—	117.0	135.2	140.4	145.0	151.0
Health insurance[d]	—	—	—	—	—	—	—	—	—	103.1
Medical care commodities	46.9	46.5	75.4	163.4	204.5	238.1	262.8	269.3	276.0	285.9
Prescription drugs and medical supplies	54.0	47.4	72.5	181.7	235.0	285.4	326.3	337.1	349.0	363.9
Nonprescription drugs and medical supplies[a]	—	—	—	120.6	140.5	149.5	152.0	152.3	151.7	154.6
Internal and respiratory over-the-counter drugs	—	42.3	74.9	145.9	167.0	176.9	181.2	180.9	179.7	183.4
Nonprescription medical equipment and supplies	—	—	79.2	138.0	166.3	178.1	178.1	179.7	180.6	183.2
				Average annual percent change from previous year shown						
All items	. . .	2.7	7.8	4.7	3.1	2.5	2.2	2.7	3.4	3.2
All items excluding medical care	. . .	2.6	7.8	4.5	2.9	2.4	2.1	2.6	3.3	3.2
All services	. . .	3.8	8.3	6.0	3.9	3.0	3.5	2.9	3.3	3.8
Food	. . .	2.7	8.3	4.3	2.3	2.5	2.4	3.4	2.4	2.4
Apparel	. . .	2.6	4.4	3.2	1.2	-0.4	-2.3	-0.4	-0.7	0.0
Housing	. . .	—	8.3	4.7	2.9	2.7	2.9	2.5	3.3	3.8
Energy	. . .	1.3	12.9	1.7	0.6	3.4	3.1	10.9	17.0	11.2
Medical care	. . .	4.3	8.2	8.1	6.3	3.4	4.4	4.4	4.2	4.0
Components of medical care										
Medical care services	. . .	5.2	8.8	8.1	6.6	3.5	4.8	5.0	4.8	4.1
Professional services	. . .	—	7.7	7.2	5.2	3.4	3.2	3.9	3.8	2.7
Physicians' services	. . .	4.6	8.3	7.7	5.4	3.2	3.0	4.0	3.3	1.5
Dental services	. . .	3.8	7.2	7.0	5.8	4.6	4.2	4.9	5.6	5.2
Eye glasses and eye care[a]	. . .	—	—	—	3.2	1.8	1.4	2.2	2.4	3.0
Services by other medical professionals[a]	. . .	—	—	—	3.7	2.4	3.0	2.7	2.7	2.9
Hospital and related services	. . .	—	—	9.9	7.7	4.2	7.6	5.9	5.3	6.4
Hospital services[b]	. . .	—	—	—	—	—	7.7	6.0	5.3	6.5
Inpatient hospital services[b,c]	. . .	—	—	—	—	—	7.2	5.7	5.7	7.0
Outpatient hospital services[a,c]	. . .	—	—	—	8.1	5.2	8.6	5.4	4.7	5.9
Hospital rooms	. . .	9.8	11.2	9.9	7.4	—	—	—	—	—
Other inpatient services[a]	. . .	—	—	—	7.7	—	—	—	—	—
Nursing homes and adult day care[b]	. . .	—	—	—	—	—	4.9	3.8	3.3	4.1
Health insurance[d]	. . .	—	—	—	—	—	—	—	—	—

WHY HAVE HEALTH CARE COSTS AND SPENDING INCREASED?

The increase in the cost of medical care is challenging to analyze, because the methods and quality of health care change constantly and as a result are often not comparable. A hospital stay in 1970 did not include the same services offered in 2008. Furthermore, the care received in a physician's office today is not comparable to that received a generation ago. One contributing factor to the rising cost of health care is the increase in biomedical technology, much of which is now available for use outside of a hospital.

Many other factors also contribute to the increase in health care costs. These include population growth, high salaries for physicians and some other health care workers, and the expense of malpractice insurance. Escalating

TABLE 5.2

Consumer price index and average annual percent change for all items, selected items, and medical care costs, selected years 1960–2006 [CONTINUED]

Items and medical care components	1960	1970	1980	1990	1995	2000	2003	2004	2005	2006
				Average annual percent change from previous year shown						
Medical care commodities	. . .	−0.1	5.0	8.0	4.6	3.1	3.3	2.5	2.5	3.6
Prescription drugs and medical supplies	. . .	−1.3	4.3	9.6	5.3	4.0	4.6	3.3	3.5	4.3
Nonprescription drugs and medical supplies[a]	. . .	—	—	—	3.1	1.2	0.6	0.2	−0.4	1.9
Internal and respiratory over-the-counter drugs	. . .	—	5.9	6.9	2.7	1.2	0.8	−0.2	−0.7	2.1
Nonprescription medical equipment and supplies	. . .	—	—	5.7	3.8	1.4	0.0	0.9	0.5	1.4

—Data not available.
. . .Category not applicable.
[a]December 1986 = 100.
[b]December 1996 = 100.
[c]Special index based on a substantially smaller sample.
[d]December 2005 = 100.
Notes: Consumer price index for all urban consumers (CPI-U) U.S. city average, detailed expenditure categories. 1982 – 1984 = 100, except where noted. Data are not seasonally adjusted. Data are based on reporting by samples of providers and other retail outlets.

SOURCE: "Table 122. Consumer Price Index and Average Annual Percent Change for All Items, Selected Items, and Medical Care Components: United States, Selected Years 1960–2006," in *Health, United States, 2007. With Chartbook on Trends in the Health of Americans*, U.S. Department of Health and Human Services, Centers for Disease Control and Prevention, National Center for Health Statistics, 2007, http://www.cdc.gov/nchs/data/hus/hus07.pdf#listtables (accessed April 24, 2008)

malpractice insurance costs and professional liability premiums have prompted some physicians and other health care practitioners to refrain from performing high-risk procedures that increase their vulnerability or have caused them to relocate to states where malpractice premiums are lower. Furthermore, to protect themselves from malpractice suits, many health care practitioners routinely order diagnostic tests and prescribe treatments that are not medically necessary and do not serve to improve their patients' health. This practice is known as defensive medicine, and even though its precise contribution to rising health care costs is difficult to gauge, industry observers agree that it is a significant factor.

Other factors include advanced biomedical procedures requiring high-technology expertise and equipment, redundant (excessive and unnecessary) technology in hospitals, cumbersome medical insurance programs and consumer demand for less restrictive insurance plans (ones that offer more choices, benefits, and coverage, but usually mean higher premiums), and consumer demand for the latest and most comprehensive testing and treatment. Legislation that increased Medicare spending and the growing number of older adults who use a disproportionate amount of health care services have also accelerated health care spending.

In "Health Spending Projections through 2017: The Baby-Boom Generation Is Coming to Medicare" (*Health Affairs*, vol. 27, no. 2, February 26, 2008), Sean Keehan et al. express a concern shared by many industry observers: "Health is projected to consume an expanding share of the economy, which means that policymakers, insurers and the public will face increasingly difficult decisions about the way health care is delivered and paid for." The researchers observe that health care will account for as much as one-fifth of the U.S. economy in the coming decade, growing at about 6.7% per year until 2017. Spending for hospital care will increase at a rate of 6.9% a year, spending for physician services will rise 5.9% annually, and spending on nursing homes will grow 5.2% a year. Much of this increase is attributable to the enormous baby-boom generation (people born between 1946 and 1964), which will soon be eligible for government-sponsored health care. The first wave of baby boomers will become eligible for Medicare in 2011. Keehan et al. predict that baby-boom Medicare enrollees will contribute 2.9 percentage points to growth in Medicare spending by 2017.

CONTROLLING HEALTH CARE SPENDING

In an effort to control health expenditures, the nation's health care system underwent some dramatic changes. Beginning in the late 1980s employers began looking for new ways to contain health benefit costs for their workers. Many enrolled their employees in managed care programs as alternatives to traditional, fee-for-service insurance. Managed care programs offered lower premiums by keeping a tighter control on costs and utilization and by emphasizing the importance of preventive care. Insurers negotiated discounts with providers (physicians, hospitals, clinical laboratories, and others) in exchange for guaranteed access to employer-insured groups. In 2006 private insurance and other private funds paid for 40.5% of the nation's health costs. (See Table 5.4.) Public sources covered 48.6% of the nation's costs, and 12.2% of the costs came directly from consumers' pockets.

TABLE 5.3

National health expenditures and annual percent change, 2002–17

										Projected						
Item	2002	2003	2004	2005	2006	2007	2008	2009	2010	2011	2012	2013	2014	2015	2016	2017
National health expenditures (billions)	$1,603.4	$1,732.4	$1,852.3	$1,973.3	$2,105.5	$2,245.6	$2,394.3	$2,555.1	$2,725.8	$2,905.1	$3,097.8	$3,305.0	$3,523.6	$3,757.0	$4,007.8	$4,277.1
National health expenditures as a percent of gross domestic product	15.3%	15.8%	15.9%	15.9%	16.0%	16.3%	16.6%	16.9%	17.1%	17.4%	17.7%	18.0%	18.4%	18.8%	19.1%	19.5%
National health expenditures per capita	$5,560	$5,952	$6,301	$6,649	$7,026	$7,439	$7,868	$8,329	$8,816	$9,322	$9,862	$10,439	$11,043	$11,684	$12,369	$13,101
Gross domestic product (billions)	$10,469.6	$10,960.8	$11,685.9	$12,433.9	$13,194.7	$13,801.7	$14,450.3	$15,158.4	$15,916.3	$16,712.1	$17,514.3	$18,320.0	$19,144.4	$20,025.0	$20,946.2	$21,909.7
Gross domestic product (billions of 2000 $)	$10,048.8	$10,301.0	$10,675.8	$11,003.4	$11,319.4	$11,557.1	$11,799.8	$12,083.0	$12,397.2	$12,719.5	$13,024.8	$13,311.3	$13,590.8	$13,889.8	$14,195.4	$14,507.7
Gross domestic product implicit price deflator (chain weighted 2000 base year)	1.042	1.064	1.095	1.130	1.166	1.196	1.220	1.248	1.278	1.309	1.340	1.372	1.405	1.439	1.473	1.509
Consumer price index (CPI-W)—1982–1984 base	1.799	1.840	1.889	1.953	2.016	2.064	2.122	2.182	2.243	2.305	2.370	2.436	2.505	2.575	2.647	2.721
CMS implicit medical price deflator[a]	1.078	1.118	1.163	1.204	1.245	1.285	1.328	1.372	1.419	1.468	1.519	1.574	1.632	1.694	1.760	1.829
U.S. population[b]	288.4	291.1	294.0	296.8	299.7	301.9	304.3	306.8	309.2	311.7	314.1	316.6	319.1	321.5	324.0	326.5
Population age less than 65 years	253.2	255.7	258.1	260.4	262.9	264.6	266.4	268.2	270.0	271.6	272.9	274.0	275.2	276.4	277.5	278.5
Population age 65 years and older	35.2	35.5	35.9	36.4	36.7	37.3	37.9	38.6	39.2	40.0	41.2	42.5	43.8	45.1	46.5	47.9
Private health insurance—NHE (billions)	$552.5	$602.8	$645.8	$685.6	$723.4	$769.4	$821.7	$878.8	$936.0	$995.4	$1,058.0	$1,124.3	$1,192.0	$1,263.4	$1,338.0	$1,415.3
Private health insurance—PHC (billions)	482.4	521.2	560.2	598.6	634.6	676.4	720.3	767.2	817.8	872.1	927.8	986.1	1,046.8	1,110.4	1,176.5	1,245.2
National health expenditures (billions)	—	8.0	6.9	6.5	6.7	6.7	6.6	6.7	6.7	6.6	6.6	6.7	6.6	6.6	6.7	6.7
National health expenditures as a percent of gross domestic product	—	3.2	0.3	0.1	0.5	2.0	1.8	1.7	1.6	1.5	1.7	2.0	2.0	1.9	2.0	2.0
National health expenditures per capita	—	7.1	5.9	5.5	5.7	5.9	5.8	5.9	5.8	5.7	5.8	5.9	5.8	5.8	5.9	5.9
Gross domestic product (billions)	—	4.7	6.6	6.4	6.1	4.6	4.7	4.9	5.0	5.0	4.8	4.6	4.5	4.6	4.6	4.6
Gross domestic product (billions of 2000 $)	—	2.5	3.6	3.1	2.9	2.1	2.1	2.4	2.6	2.6	2.4	2.2	2.1	2.2	2.2	2.2
Gross domestic product implicit price deflator (chain weighted 2000 base year)	—	2.1	2.9	3.2	3.2	2.6	2.0	2.3	2.4	2.4	2.4	2.4	2.4	2.4	2.4	2.4
Consumer price index (CPI-W)—1982–1984 base	—	2.3	2.7	3.4	3.2	2.4	2.8	2.8	2.8	2.8	2.8	2.8	2.8	2.8	2.8	2.8
CMS implicit medical price deflator[a]	—	3.7	4.1	3.5	3.4	3.2	3.4	3.3	3.4	3.5	3.5	3.6	3.7	3.8	3.9	3.9
U.S. population[b]	—	0.9	1.0	1.0	1.0	0.7	0.8	0.8	0.8	0.8	0.8	0.8	0.8	0.8	0.8	0.8
Population age less than 65 years	—	1.0	1.0	0.9	1.0	0.6	0.7	0.7	0.7	0.6	0.5	0.4	0.4	0.4	0.4	0.4
Population age 65 years and older	—	1.0	1.1	1.3	1.0	1.4	1.8	1.8	1.6	2.1	3.0	3.2	3.0	3.0	3.0	3.1
Private health insurance—NHE	—	9.1	7.1	6.2	5.5	6.4	6.8	7.0	6.5	6.3	6.3	6.3	6.0	6.0	5.9	5.8
Private health insurance—PHC	—	8.0	7.5	6.9	6.0	6.6	6.5	6.5	6.6	6.6	6.4	6.3	6.2	6.1	6.0	5.8

[a] 2000 base year. Calculated as the difference between nominal personal health care spending and real personal health care spending. Real personal health care spending is produced by deflating spending on each service type by the appropriate deflator (PPI, CPI, etc.) and adding real spending by service type. [b] July 1 Census resident based population estimates.

Notes: Numbers and percents may not add to totals because of rounding. The health spending projections were based on the 2006 version of the National Health Expenditures released in January 2008. CMS = Centers for Medicare and Medicaid Services. NHE = National Health Expenditures. PHC = Personal Health Care.

SOURCE: "Table 1. National Health Expenditures and Selected Economic Indicators, Levels and Annual Percent Change: Calendar Years 2002–2017," in *National Health Care Expenditures Projections 2007–2017*, U.S. Department of Health and Human Services, Centers for Medicare and Medicaid Services, 2006, http://www.cms.hhs.gov/NationalHealthExpendData/downloads/proj2007.pdf (accessed April 24, 2008)

TABLE 5.4

National health expenditures, by source of funds, 2002–17

Year	Total	Out-of-pocket payments	Total	Private health insurance	Other private funds	Total	Federal[a]	State and local[a]	Medicare[b]	Medicaid[c]
						Third-party payments				
							Public			
Historical estimates					**Amount in billions**					
2002	$1,603.4	$211.4	$1,392.0	$552.5	$118.4	$721.1	$508.6	$212.5	$265.1	$249.0
2003	1,732.4	224.9	1,507.6	602.8	127.4	777.3	550.7	226.6	281.5	271.6
2004	1,852.3	234.9	1,617.4	645.8	134.1	837.5	597.1	240.4	309.3	292.0
2005	1,973.3	247.1	1,726.2	685.6	143.9	896.8	639.1	257.7	338.0	313.5
2006	2,105.5	256.5	1,849.0	723.4	155.3	970.3	704.9	265.4	401.3	310.6
Projected										
2007	2,245.6	269.3	1,976.3	769.4	168.1	1,038.8	753.1	285.6	427.3	338.2
2008	2,394.3	282.6	2,111.7	821.7	180.8	1,109.3	806.8	302.5	460.7	361.2
2009	2,555.1	297.6	2,257.5	878.8	192.9	1,185.8	864.3	321.5	495.0	387.9
2010	2,725.8	314.4	2,411.4	936.0	206.3	1,269.0	926.5	342.5	531.1	417.7
2011	2,905.1	332.0	2,573.1	995.4	220.3	1,357.4	992.2	365.2	568.5	450.5
2012	3,097.8	350.6	2,747.3	1,058.0	234.6	1,454.7	1,065.3	389.4	610.5	486.0
2013	3,305.0	370.3	2,934.7	1,124.3	250.1	1,560.3	1,144.7	415.6	656.4	524.6
2014	3,523.6	391.3	3,132.3	1,192.0	266.2	1,674.1	1,230.3	443.8	705.6	566.6
2015	3,757.0	413.9	3,343.2	1,263.4	282.9	1,796.9	1,322.6	474.3	758.8	612.4
2016	4,007.8	438.1	3,569.7	1,338.0	300.2	1,931.5	1,424.3	507.2	818.1	662.3
2017	4,277.1	464.3	3,812.8	1,415.3	318.3	2,079.2	1,536.2	543.0	884.0	717.3
Historical estimates					**Per capita amount**					
2002	$5,560	$733	$4,826	$1,916	$411	$2,500	$1,763	$737	d	d
2003	5,952	773	5,179	2,071	438	2,670	1,892	779	d	d
2004	6,301	799	5,502	2,197	456	2,849	2,031	818	d	d
2005	6,649	833	5,816	2,310	485	3,022	2,153	868	d	d
2006	7,026	856	6,170	2,414	518	3,238	2,352	886	d	d
Projected										
2007	7,439	892	6,547	2,549	557	3,441	2,495	946	d	d
2008	7,868	929	6,939	2,700	594	3,645	2,651	994	d	d
2009	8,329	970	7,359	2,865	629	3,866	2,818	1,048	d	d
2010	8,816	1,017	7,799	3,027	667	4,104	2,996	1,108	d	d
2011	9,322	1,065	8,256	3,194	707	4,355	3,184	1,172	d	d
2012	9,862	1,116	8,746	3,368	747	4,631	3,391	1,240	d	d
2013	10,439	1,170	9,270	3,551	790	4,928	3,616	1,313	d	d
2014	11,043	1,226	9,817	3,736	834	5,247	3,856	1,391	d	d
2015	11,684	1,287	10,397	3,929	880	5,588	4,113	1,475	d	d
2016	12,369	1,352	11,017	4,129	926	5,961	4,396	1,565	d	d
2017	13,101	1,422	11,679	4,335	975	6,369	4,705	1,663	d	d
Historical estimates					**Percent distribution**					
2002	100.0	13.2	86.8	34.5	7.4	45.0	31.7	13.3	16.5	15.5
2003	100.0	13.0	87.0	34.8	7.4	44.9	31.8	13.1	16.2	15.7
2004	100.0	12.7	87.3	34.9	7.2	45.2	32.2	13.0	16.7	15.8
2005	100.0	12.5	87.5	34.7	7.3	45.4	32.4	13.1	17.1	15.9
2006	100.0	12.2	87.8	34.4	7.4	46.1	33.5	12.6	19.1	14.8
Projected										
2007	100.0	12.0	88.0	34.3	7.5	46.3	33.5	12.7	19.0	15.1
2008	100.0	11.8	88.2	34.3	7.5	46.3	33.7	12.6	19.2	15.1
2009	100.0	11.6	88.4	34.4	7.6	46.4	33.8	12.6	19.4	15.2
2010	100.0	11.5	88.5	34.3	7.6	46.6	34.0	12.6	19.5	15.3
2011	100.0	11.4	88.6	34.3	7.6	46.7	34.2	12.6	19.6	15.5
2012	100.0	11.3	88.7	34.2	7.6	47.0	34.4	12.6	19.7	15.7
2013	100.0	11.2	88.8	34.0	7.6	47.2	34.6	12.6	19.9	15.9
2014	100.0	11.1	88.9	33.8	7.6	47.5	34.9	12.6	20.0	16.1
2015	100.0	11.0	89.0	33.6	7.5	47.8	35.2	12.6	20.2	16.3
2016	100.0	10.9	89.1	33.4	7.5	48.2	35.5	12.7	20.4	16.5
2017	100.0	10.9	89.1	33.1	7.4	48.6	35.9	12.7	20.7	16.8

There is heightened interest in developing treatments and technologies designed to reduce the health system's dependence on expensive, inpatient hospital care. After professional services ($660.2 billion), hospital care expenditures were the single-largest spending component of total health care expenses ($648.2), accounting for 31% of all national health care expenditures in 2006. (See Table 5.5.)

The annual hospital cost growth rate was 7% in 2006 and was projected to remain at about that rate through 2017.

Physician and clinical services accounted for $447.6 billion of 2006 national health spending. (See Table 5.5.) Spending for nursing home care totaled $124.9 billion, and spending for home health care reached $52.7 billion.

TABLE 5.4

National health expenditures, by source of funds, 2002–17 [CONTINUED]

Year	Total	Out-of-pocket payments	Third-party payments						Medicare[b]	Medicaid[c]
			Total	Private health insurance	Other private funds	Public				
						Total	Federal[a]	State and local[a]		
Historical estimates			Annual percent change from previous year shown							
2002	—	—	—	—	—	—	—	—	—	—
2003	8.0	6.4	8.3	9.1	7.6	7.8	8.3	6.6	6.2	9.1
2004	6.9	4.5	7.3	7.1	5.2	7.7	8.4	6.1	9.9	7.5
2005	6.5	5.2	6.7	6.2	7.3	7.1	7.0	7.2	9.3	7.3
2006	6.7	3.8	7.1	5.5	7.9	8.2	10.3	3.0	18.7	−0.9
Projected										
2007	6.7	5.0	6.9	6.4	8.3	7.1	6.8	7.6	6.5	8.9
2008	6.6	4.9	6.9	6.8	7.5	6.8	7.1	5.9	7.8	6.8
2009	6.7	5.3	6.9	7.0	6.7	6.9	7.1	6.3	7.4	7.4
2010	6.7	5.7	6.8	6.5	6.9	7.0	7.2	6.5	7.3	7.7
2011	6.6	5.6	6.7	6.3	6.8	7.0	7.1	6.6	7.0	7.9
2012	6.6	5.6	6.8	6.3	6.5	7.2	7.4	6.6	7.4	7.9
2013	6.7	5.6	6.8	6.3	6.6	7.3	7.5	6.7	7.5	7.9
2014	6.6	5.7	6.7	6.0	6.4	7.3	7.5	6.8	7.5	8.0
2015	6.6	5.8	6.7	6.0	6.3	7.3	7.5	6.9	7.5	8.1
2016	6.7	5.9	6.8	5.9	6.1	7.5	7.7	6.9	7.8	8.2
2017	6.7	6.0	6.8	5.8	6.0	7.6	7.9	7.1	8.0	8.3

[a]Includes Medicaid State Children's Health Insurance Program (SCHIP) Expansion and SCHIP.
[b]Subset of federal funds.
[c]Subset of federal and state and local funds. Includes Medicaid SCHIP Expansion.
[d]Calculation of per capita estimates is inappropriate.
Notes: Per capita amounts based on July 1 Census resident based population estimates. Numbers and percents may not add to totals because of rounding. The health spending projections were based on the 2006 version of the National Health Expenditures (NHE) released in January 2008.

SOURCE: "Table 3. National Health Expenditures; Aggregate and per Capita Amounts, Percent Distribution and Annual Percent Change by Source of Funds: Calendar Years 2002–2017," in *National Health Care Expenditures Projections 2007–2017*, U.S. Department of Health and Human Services, Centers for Medicare and Medicaid Services, 2006, http://www.cms.hhs.gov/NationalHealthExpendData/downloads/proj2007.pdf (accessed April 24, 2008)

Nursing home expenses increased 3.5% in 2006 and were projected to rise by about 5% annually through 2017.

One of the fastest-growing components of health care is the market for prescription drugs. In 2006 Americans spent $216.7 billion on prescription medication—this was an 8.5% increase from $199.7 billion in 2005. (See Table 5.5.) A large part of the increase was financed by private insurers, who paid $47.6 billion of the drug costs in 2006, slightly lower than the previous year's $48.8 billion. (See Table 5.7.) The aging population and the fact that prescription drugs are increasingly substituted for other types of health care have fueled growth in this sector of health services. For example, antidepressant drugs have demonstrated effectiveness in place of more expensive psychotherapy.

Prescription Drug Prices Rose in 2007

In *Rx Watchdog Report Trends in Manufacturer Prices of Prescription Drugs Used by Medicare Beneficiaries 2002 to 2007* (2008, http://assets.aarp.org/rgcenter/health/2008_05_watchdog_q407.pdf), David Gross, Stephen W. Schondelmeyer, and Leigh Purvis find that pharmaceutical companies increased the prices they charge drug wholesalers for the top 220 brand-name drugs an average of 7.4% in 2007, more than two and half times the general inflation rate of 2.9%. All but four of the 220 drugs rose in price during 2007. Gross, Schondelmeyer, and Purvis note that manufacturers have increased prices of brand-name drugs used by Medicare beneficiaries since the implementation of the Medicare prescription drug benefit in 2006.

The Medicare drug benefit was intended to increase government spending for prescription drugs and provide prescription drug savings for older Americans and people with disabilities. The voluntary program allows Medicare beneficiaries to choose from dozens of plans offered by health insurers and health plans called pharmacy benefit managers.

Gross, Schondelmeyer, and Purvis observe that manufacturers' drug price increases produce higher pharmacy prices and higher out-of-pocket costs for Medicare beneficiaries who pay a percent of their drug costs as opposed to fixed copayment per prescription. The higher prices also result in higher costs for drug plans, which in turn may serve to increase the plans' premiums or cause them to reduce benefits.

HEALTH CARE FOR OLDER ADULTS, PEOPLE WITH DISABILITIES, AND THE POOR

The United States is one of the few industrialized nations that does not have a national health care program. Government-funded health care exists, and it forms a

TABLE 5.5

National health expenditures, by type of expenditures, 2002–17

Amounts (in billions of dollars)

Type of expenditure	2002	2003	2004	2005	2006	2007	2008	2009	2010	2011	2012 (Projected)	2013 (Projected)	2014 (Projected)	2015 (Projected)	2016 (Projected)	2017 (Projected)
National health expenditures	$1,603.4	$1,732.4	$1,852.3	$1,973.3	$2,105.5	$2,245.6	$2,394.3	$2,555.1	$2,725.8	$2,905.1	$3,097.8	3304.97	$3,523.6	$3,757.0	$4,007.8	$4,277.1
Health services and supplies	1,499.4	1,620.7	1,730.6	1,843.6	1,966.2	2,095.5	2,234.5	2,386.3	2,546.5	2,714.5	2,895.9	3,090.6	3,296.3	3,516.1	3,752.9	4,007.7
Personal health care	1,340.8	1,445.9	1,547.7	1,653.7	1,762.0	1,877.6	1,999.1	2,130.6	2,273.1	2,425.0	2,587.5	2,761.5	2,946.5	3,144.1	3,356.5	3,585.6
Hospital care	488.6	525.4	564.4	605.5	648.2	696.7	747.1	800.0	855.3	914.8	977.9	1,044.2	1,114.1	1,187.8	1,264.6	1,345.7
Professional services	503.1	542.9	580.7	622.2	660.2	701.1	743.1	790.6	842.5	896.4	953.3	1,014.6	1,078.6	1,146.0	1,219.2	1,297.7
Physician and clinical services	337.9	366.7	393.6	422.6	447.6	473.0	501.7	532.8	566.5	601.0	636.8	675.1	714.0	753.6	795.8	840.0
Other professional services	45.6	49.0	52.4	56.2	58.9	61.7	65.1	68.5	72.4	76.3	80.5	84.9	89.5	94.3	99.5	105.0
Dental services	73.3	76.9	81.5	86.6	91.5	96.9	102.4	108.2	114.4	120.7	127.4	134.5	142.0	150.3	159.6	169.6
Other personal health care	46.3	50.3	53.2	56.8	62.2	69.6	73.9	81.1	89.2	98.4	108.6	120.2	133.2	147.8	164.4	183.1
Nursing home and home health	139.9	148.5	157.9	168.7	177.6	187.3	198.5	210.2	222.9	236.2	250.1	264.8	280.7	297.8	316.1	336.5
Home health care	34.2	38.0	42.7	47.9	52.7	57.6	62.0	66.7	71.8	77.1	82.7	88.8	95.3	102.4	110.2	119.0
Nursing home care	105.7	110.5	115.2	120.7	124.9	129.7	136.5	143.5	151.2	159.1	167.4	176.0	185.3	195.4	206.0	217.5
Retail outlet sales of medical products	209.1	229.0	244.7	257.3	276.0	292.5	310.4	329.8	352.4	377.6	406.1	437.2	473.2	512.5	556.6	605.7
Prescription drugs	157.6	174.2	188.8	199.7	216.7	231.3	247.0	264.5	284.6	307.2	332.9	361.6	393.7	429.8	470.4	515.7
Other medical products	51.5	54.9	55.9	57.6	59.3	61.2	63.4	65.3	67.8	70.4	73.3	76.3	79.5	82.7	86.2	90.0
Durable medical equipment	20.7	22.4	22.8	23.2	23.7	24.5	25.4	26.0	27.0	28.0	29.2	30.5	31.9	33.3	34.9	36.6
Other non-durable medical products	30.8	32.4	33.1	34.4	35.6	36.7	38.0	39.3	40.9	42.4	44.0	45.8	47.6	49.3	51.3	53.4
Program administration and net cost of private health insurance	106.5	121.0	129.0	133.6	145.4	155.1	168.3	184.0	196.5	207.1	220.3	234.7	248.7	263.7	280.3	297.7
Government public health activities	52.1	53.8	53.9	56.3	58.7	62.8	67.1	71.8	76.9	82.3	88.1	94.4	101.1	108.3	116.0	124.4
Investment	104.0	111.8	121.7	129.7	139.4	150.1	159.8	168.8	179.3	190.7	201.9	214.3	227.3	240.9	254.9	269.4
Research*	32.5	35.5	38.8	40.6	41.8	42.9	44.0	45.8	48.1	50.8	53.9	57.3	60.9	64.7	68.6	72.7
Structures & equipment	71.5	76.3	83.0	89.1	97.6	107.2	115.8	122.9	131.2	139.9	148.0	157.0	166.4	176.3	186.3	196.7

Annual percent change

Type of expenditure	2002	2003	2004	2005	2006	2007	2008	2009	2010	2011	2012 (Projected)	2013 (Projected)	2014 (Projected)	2015 (Projected)	2016 (Projected)	2017 (Projected)
National health expenditures	—	8.0	6.9	6.5	6.7	6.7	6.6	6.7	6.7	6.6	6.6	6.7	6.6	6.7	6.7	6.7
Health services and supplies	—	8.1	6.8	6.5	6.6	6.6	6.6	6.8	6.7	6.6	6.7	6.7	6.7	6.7	6.7	6.8
Personal health care	—	7.8	7.0	6.8	7.0	6.6	6.5	6.6	6.9	7.0	6.7	6.8	6.7	6.7	6.8	6.8
Hospital care	—	7.5	7.4	7.3	7.0	7.5	7.2	7.1	6.9	7.0	6.9	6.8	6.7	6.6	6.4	6.4
Professional services	—	7.9	7.0	7.1	6.1	6.2	6.0	6.4	6.6	6.4	6.0	6.4	6.3	6.3	6.4	6.4
Physician and clinical services	—	8.5	7.3	7.4	5.9	5.7	6.1	6.2	6.3	6.1	6.0	6.0	5.8	5.6	5.6	5.6
Other professional services	—	7.5	7.0	7.1	4.9	5.7	5.5	5.2	5.7	5.4	5.4	5.5	5.3	5.9	5.5	5.6
Dental services	—	4.8	6.0	6.3	5.7	5.9	5.7	5.6	5.7	5.6	5.5	5.5	5.6	5.9	6.2	6.3
Other personal health care	—	8.7	5.7	6.8	9.5	11.8	6.3	9.6	10.0	10.2	10.4	10.8	11.0	11.2	11.4	...
Nursing home and home health	—	6.1	6.3	6.8	5.3	5.4	6.0	5.9	6.0	6.0	5.9	5.9	6.0	6.1	6.1	6.4
Home health care	—	11.1	12.3	12.3	9.9	9.2	7.8	7.6	7.5	7.4	7.3	7.3	7.3	7.4	7.6	8.0
Nursing home care	—	4.5	4.2	4.9	3.5	3.8	5.2	5.1	5.3	5.2	5.2	5.1	5.3	5.4	5.4	5.6
Retail outlet sales of medical products	—	9.5	6.8	5.2	7.3	6.0	6.1	6.3	6.9	7.2	7.5	7.8	8.1	8.3	8.6	8.8
Prescription drugs	—	10.5	8.4	5.8	8.5	6.7	6.8	7.1	7.6	8.0	8.3	8.6	8.9	9.2	9.4	9.6
Other medical products	—	6.5	1.8	3.1	3.0	3.2	3.6	3.0	3.9	3.8	4.1	4.2	4.1	4.1	4.3	4.4
Durable medical equipment	—	8.2	1.8	1.7	2.3	3.4	3.7	2.1	3.9	3.8	4.1	4.2	4.1	4.1	4.3	4.9
Other non-durable medical products	—	5.4	2.1	4.0	3.5	3.0	3.5	3.6	3.9	3.8	3.9	3.9	3.9	3.8	4.0	4.1
Program administration and net cost of private health insurance	—	13.6	6.6	3.6	8.8	6.6	8.5	9.3	6.8	5.4	6.4	6.5	6.0	6.1	6.3	6.2
Government public health activities	—	3.2	0.2	4.4	4.3	7.0	6.9	7.0	7.1	7.1	7.1	7.1	7.1	7.1	7.2	7.2

TABLE 5.5

National health expenditures, by type of expenditures, 2002–17 [CONTINUED]

											Projected				
Type of expenditure	2002	2003	2004	2005	2006	2007	2008	2009	2010	2011	2012	2013	2014	2015	2016	2017
Investment																
Research*	—	7.5	8.9	6.6	7.4	7.7	6.5	5.6	6.3	6.3	5.9	6.2	6.1	6.0	5.8	5.7
Structures & equipment	—	9.2	9.1	4.8	2.9	2.7	2.6	4.1	5.0	5.5	6.1	6.4	6.3	6.1	6.0	6.0
	—	6.7	8.8	7.4	9.5	9.8	8.1	6.1	6.7	6.6	5.8	6.1	6.0	5.9	5.7	5.6

*Research and development expenditures of drug companies and other manufacturers and providers of medical equipment and supplies are excluded from research expenditures. These research expenditures are implicitly included in the expenditure class in which the product falls, in that they are covered by the payment received for that product.

Notes: Numbers may not add to totals because of rounding. The health spending projections were based on the 2006 version of the National Health Expenditures (NHE) released in January 2008.

SOURCE: "Table 2. National Health Expenditure Amounts, and Annual Percent Change by Type of Expenditure: Calendar Years 2002–2017," in *National Health Care Expenditures Projections 2007–2017*, U.S. Department of Health and Human Services, Centers for Medicare and Medicaid Services, 2006, http://www.cms.hhs.gov/NationalHealthExpendData/downloads/proj2007.pdf (accessed April 24, 2008)

TABLE 5.6

Personal health expenditures, by source of funds, 2002–17

Year	Total	Out-of-pocket payments	Third-party payments			Public			Medicare[b]	Medicaid[c]
			Total	Private health insurance	Other private funds	Total	Federal[a]	State and local[a]		
Historical estimates					**Amount in billions**					
2002	$1,340.8	$211.4	$1,129.3	$482.4	$58.3	$588.7	$448.3	$140.4	$256.3	$231.9
2003	1,445.9	224.9	1,221 0	521.2	63.6	636.2	485.0	151.1	272.8	252.3
2004	1,547.7	234.9	1,312.8	560.2	64.9	687.7	525.6	162.1	298.7	271.5
2005	1,653.7	247.1	1,406.6	598.6	69.0	739.0	562.2	176.8	326.0	291.5
2006	1,762.0	256.5	1,505.5	634.6	72.7	798.2	618.1	180.1	381.0	287.5
Projected										
2007	1,877.6	269.3	1,608.4	676.4	77.0	855.0	660.3	194.7	404.7	313.1
2008	1,999.1	282.6	1,716.5	720.3	81.9	914.3	708.0	206.3	435.6	334.3
2009	2,130.6	297.6	1,833.0	767.2	87.5	978.3	758.5	219.8	467.1	359.0
2010	2,273.1	314.4	1,958.7	817.8	93.3	1,047.6	812.9	234.7	500.4	386.6
2011	2,425.0	332.0	2,093.0	872.1	99.3	1,121.5	870.6	250.9	535.2	417.0
2012	2,587.5	350.6	2,236.9	927.8	105.9	1,203.2	934.8	268.4	574.5	449.9
2013	2,761.5	370.3	2,391.2	986.1	113.0	1,292.2	1,004.8	287.4	617.5	485.7
2014	2,946.5	391.3	2,555.2	1,046.8	120.2	1,388.2	1,080.3	307.9	663.8	524.5
2015	3,144.1	413.9	2,730.2	1,110.4	127.6	1,492.2	1,162.1	330.1	713.9	566.9
2016	3,356.5	438.1	2,918.4	1,176 5	135.4	1,606.6	1,252.3	354.3	769.8	613.2
2017	3,585.6	464.3	3,121.2	1,245.2	143.5	1,732.5	1,351.8	380.6	831.9	664.2
Historical estimates					**Per capita amount**					
2002	$4,649	$733	$3,916	$1,673	$202	$2,041	$1,554	$487	d	d
2003	4,967	773	4,195	1,791	218	2,185	1,666	519	d	d
2004	5,265	799	4,466	1,906	221	2,339	1,788	551	d	d
2005	5,572	833	4,739	2,017	233	2,490	1,894	596	d	d
2006	5,880	856	5,024	2,117	243	2,663	2,062	601	d	d
Projected										
2007	6,220	892	5,328	2,241	255	2,832	2,187	645	d	d
2008	6,569	929	5,640	2,367	269	3,005	2,327	678	d	d
2009	6,945	970	5,975	2,501	285	3,189	2,473	716	d	d
2010	7,352	1,017	6,335	2,645	302	3,388	2,629	759	d	d
2011	7,781	1,065	6,716	2,798	319	3,599	2,793	805	d	d
2012	8,237	1,116	7,121	2,954	337	3,830	2,976	855	d	d
2013	8,723	1,170	7,553	3,115	357	4,082	3,174	908	d	d
2014	9,235	1,226	8,008	3,281	377	4,351	3,386	965	d	d
2015	9,778	1,287	8,491	3,453	397	4,641	3,614	1,027	d	d
2016	10,359	1,352	9,007	3,631	418	4,958	3,865	1,093	d	d
2017	10,983	1,422	9,561	3,814	440	5,307	4,141	1,166	d	d
Historical estimates					**Percent distribution**					
2002	100.0	15.8	84.2	36.0	4.3	43.9	33.4	10.5	19.1	17.3
2003	100.0	15.6	84.4	36.0	4.4	44.0	33.5	10.5	18.9	17.5
2004	100.0	15.2	84.8	36.2	4.2	44.4	34.0	10.5	19.3	17.5
2005	100.0	14.9	85.1	36.2	4.2	44.7	34.0	10.7	19.7	17.6
2006	100.0	14.6	85.4	36.0	4.1	45.3	35.1	10.2	21.6	16.3
Projected										
2007	100.0	14.3	85.7	36.0	4.1	45.5	35.2	10.4	21.6	16.7
2008	100.0	14.1	85.9	36.0	4.1	45.7	35.4	10.3	21.8	16.7
2009	100.0	14.0	86.0	36.0	4.1	45.9	35.6	10.3	21.9	16.9
2010	100.0	13.8	86.2	36.0	4.1	46.1	35.8	10.3	22.0	17.0
2011	100.0	13.7	86.3	36.0	4.1	46.2	35.9	10.3	22.1	17.2
2012	100.0	13.5	86.5	35.9	4.1	46.5	36.1	10.4	22.2	17.4
2013	100.0	13.4	86.6	35.7	4.1	46.8	36.4	10.4	22.4	17.6
2014	100.0	13.3	86.7	35.5	4.1	47.1	36.7	10.4	22.5	17.8
2015	100.0	13.2	86.8	35.3	4.1	47.5	37.0	10.5	22.7	18.0
2016	100.0	13.1	86.9	35.1	4.0	47.9	37.3	10.6	22.9	18.3
2017	100.0	13.0	87.0	34.7	4.0	48.3	37.7	10.6	23.2	18.5

major part of the health care system, but it is available only to specific segments of the U.S. population. In other developed countries government national medical care programs cover almost all their citizen's health-related costs, from maternity care to long-term care.

In the United States the major government health care entitlement programs are Medicare and Medicaid. They provide financial assistance for people aged sixty-five and older, the poor, and people with disabilities. Before the existence of these programs, many older Americans could not afford adequate medical care. For older adults who are beneficiaries, the Medicare program provides reimbursement for hospital and physician care, whereas Medicaid pays for the cost of nursing home care.

TABLE 5.6

Personal health expenditures, by source of funds, 2002–17 [CONTINUED]

Year	Total	Out-of-pocket payments	Third-party payments							
			Total	Private health insurance	Other private funds	Public			Medicare[b]	Medicaid[c]
						Total	Federal[a]	State and local[a]		
Historical estimates			Annual percent change from previous year shown							
2002	—	—	—	—	—	—	—	—	—	—
2003	7.8	6.4	8.1	8.0	9.2	8.1	8.2	7.7	6.5	8.8
2004	7.0	4.5	7.5	7.5	2.1	8.1	8.4	7.3	9.5	7.6
2005	6.8	5.2	7.1	6.9	6.4	7.5	7.0	9.0	9.1	7.4
2006	6.6	3.8	7.0	6.0	5.4	8.0	9.9	1.9	16.9	−1.4
Projected										
2007	6.6	5.0	6.8	6.6	5.8	7.1	6.8	8.1	6.2	8.9
2008	6.5	4.9	6.7	6.5	6.4	6.9	7.2	6.0	7.7	6.8
2009	6.6	5.3	6.8	6.5	6.9	7.0	7.1	6.5	7.2	7.4
2010	6.7	5.7	6.9	6.6	6.6	7.1	7.2	6.8	7.1	7.7
2011	6.7	5.6	6.9	6.6	6.5	7.1	7.1	6.9	6.9	7.9
2012	6.7	5.6	6.9	6.4	6.6	7.3	7.4	7.0	7.4	7.9
2013	6.7	5.6	6.9	6.3	6.7	7.4	7.5	7.1	7.5	7.9
2014	6.7	5.7	6.9	6.2	6.4	7.4	7.5	7.1	7.5	8.0
2015	6.7	5.8	6.8	6.1	6.1	7.5	7.6	7.2	7.5	8.1
2016	6.8	5.9	6.9	6.0	6.1	7.7	7.8	7.3	7.8	8.2
2017	6.8	6.0	6.9	5.8	6.0	7.8	8.0	7.4	8.1	8.3

[a]Includes Medicaid State Children's Health Insurance Program (SCHIP) Expansion and SCHIP.
[b]Subset of federal funds.
[c]Subset of federal and state and local funds. Includes Medicaid SCHIP Expansion.
[d]Calculation of per capita estimates is inappropriate.
Notes: Per capita amounts based on July 1 Census resident based population estimates. Numbers and percents may not add to totals because of rounding. The health spending projections were based on the 2006 version of the National Health Expenditures (NHE) released in January 2008.

SOURCE: "Table 5. Personal Health Care Expenditures; Aggregate and per Capita Amounts, Percent Distribution and Annual Percent Change by Source of Funds: Calendar Years 2002–2017," in *National Health Care Expenditures Projections 2007–2017*, U.S. Department of Health and Human Services, Centers for Medicare and Medicaid Services, 2006, http://www.cms.hhs.gov/NationalHealthExpendData/downloads/proj2007.pdf (accessed April 24, 2008)

Medicare

The Medicare program, which was enacted under Title XVIII (Health Insurance for the Aged) of the Social Security Act, was approved in July 1966. The program is composed of four parts:

- Part A provides hospital insurance. Coverage includes physicians' fees, nursing services, meals, semiprivate rooms, special-care units, operating room costs, laboratory tests, and some drugs and supplies. Part A also covers rehabilitation services, limited posthospital care in a skilled nursing facility, home health care, and hospice care for the terminally ill.

- Part B (Supplemental Medical Insurance [SMI]) is elective medical insurance; that is, enrollees must pay premiums to obtain coverage. SMI covers outpatient physicians' services, diagnostic tests, outpatient hospital services, outpatient physical therapy, speech pathology services, home health services, and medical equipment and supplies.

- Part C is the Medicare+Choice program, which was established by the Balanced Budget Act of 1997 to expand beneficiaries' options and allow them to participate in private-sector health plans.

- Part D is also elective and provides voluntary, subsidized access to prescription drug insurance coverage,

for a premium, to individuals entitled to Part A or enrolled in Part B. Part D also has provisions (premium and cost-sharing subsidies) for low-income enrollees. Part D coverage began in 2006 and includes most U.S. Food and Drug Administration (FDA) approved prescription drugs.

In general, Medicare reimburses physicians on a fee-for-service basis (paid for each visit, procedure, or treatment delivered), as opposed to per capita (per head) or per member per month. In response to the increasing administrative burden of paperwork, reduced compensation, and delays in reimbursements, some physicians opt out of Medicare participation—they do not provide services under the Medicare program and choose not to accept Medicare patients into their practices. Others still provide services to Medicare beneficiaries but do not "accept assignment," meaning that patients must pay out-of-pocket for services and then seek reimbursement from Medicare.

Because of these problems, the Tax Equity and Fiscal Responsibility Act of 1982 authorized a risk managed care option for Medicare, based on agreed-on prepayments. Beginning in 1985 the Health Care Financing Administration (now known as the CMS) could contract to pay health care providers, such as health maintenance organizations

TABLE 5.7

Prescription drug expenditures, by source of funds, 2002–17

Year	Total	Out-of-pocket payments	Third-party payments Total	Private health insurance	Other private funds	Public Total	Federal[a]	State and local[a]	Medicare[b]	Medicaid[c]
Historical estimates					**Amount in billions**					
2002	$157.6	$40.4	$117.3	$78.0	$0.0	$39.3	$23.0	$16.2	$2.4	$28.0
2003	174.2	44.2	130.0	83.5	0.0	46.5	27.6	18.9	2.3	32.8
2004	188.8	46.2	142.5	90.1	0.0	52.5	31.3	21.2	3.3	36.6
2005	199.7	48.8	150.9	95.7	0.0	55.2	32.6	22.6	3.9	37.6
2006	216.7	47.6	169.1	95.1	0.0	74.0	58.7	15.3	39.5	19.4
Projected										
2007	231.3	50.4	180.9	100.7	0.0	80.2	63.8	16.4	43.0	21.0
2008	247.0	53.5	193.5	107.1	0.0	86.4	68.9	17.5	46.7	22.3
2009	264.5	56.4	208.1	113.3	0.0	94.8	75.9	18.9	52.2	24.0
2010	284.6	59.9	224.7	120.6	0.0	104.0	83.7	20.4	58.2	26.0
2011	307.2	63.9	243.3	129.0	0.0	114.4	92.4	22.0	65.0	28.4
2012	332.9	68.3	264.6	138.2	0.0	126.3	102.5	23.8	72.9	31.0
2013	361.6	73.6	288.0	149.2	0.0	138.7	112.9	25.8	81.0	33.8
2014	393.7	79.5	314.2	161.6	0.0	152.6	124.6	28.0	90.0	36.8
2015	429.8	86.3	343.5	175.6	0.0	168.0	137.7	30.3	100.3	40.1
2016	470.4	93.9	376.4	191.3	0.0	185.1	152.4	32.7	111.9	43.5
2017	515.7	102.5	413.2	209.0	0.0	204.2	168.8	35.3	125.2	47.1
Historical estimates					**Per capita amount**					
2002	$547	$140	$407	$270	$0	$136	$80	$56	d	d
2003	598	152	446	287	0	160	95	65	d	d
2004	642	157	485	306	0	178	107	72	d	d
2005	673	164	508	322	0	186	110	76	d	d
2006	723	159	564	317	0	247	196	51	d	d
Projected										
2007	766	167	599	334	0	266	211	54	d	d
2008	812	176	636	352	0	284	226	58	d	d
2009	862	184	678	369	0	309	247	61	d	d
2010	920	194	727	390	0	336	271	66	d	d
2011	986	205	781	414	0	367	296	71	d	d
2012	1,060	217	842	440	0	402	326	76	d	d
2013	1,142	232	910	471	0	438	357	82	d	d
2014	1,234	249	985	506	0	478	391	88	d	d
2015	1,337	268	1,068	546	0	522	428	94	d	d
2016	1,452	290	1,162	591	0	571	470	101	d	d
2017	1,580	314	1,266	640	0	625	517	108	d	d
Historical estimates					**Percent distribution**					
2002	100.0	25.6	74.4	49.5	0.0	24.9	14.6	10.3	1.5	17.8
2003	100.0	25.4	74.6	47.9	0.0	26.7	15.9	10.8	1.3	18.8
2004	100.0	24.5	75.5	47.7	0.0	27.8	16.6	11.2	1.7	19.4
2005	100.0	24.4	75.6	47.9	0.0	27.6	16.3	11.3	1.9	18.8
2006	100.0	22.0	78.0	43.9	0.0	34.2	27.1	7.0	18.2	9.0
Projected										
2007	100.0	21.8	78.2	43.5	0.0	34.7	27.6	7.1	18.6	9.1
2008	100.0	21.6	78.4	43.4	0.0	35.0	27.9	7.1	18.9	9.0
2009	100.0	21.3	78.7	42.8	0.0	35.8	28.7	7.1	19.7	9.1
2010	100.0	21.1	78.9	42.4	0.0	36.6	29.4	7.2	20.5	9.1
2011	100.0	20.8	79.2	42.0	0.0	37.2	30.1	7.2	21.2	9.2
2012	100.0	20.5	79.5	41.5	0.0	38.0	30.8	7.2	21.9	9.3
2013	100.0	20.3	79.7	41.3	0.0	38.4	31.2	7.1	22.4	9.3
2014	100.0	20.2	79.8	41.0	0.0	38.8	31.7	7.1	22.9	9.3
2015	100.0	20.1	79.9	40.8	0.0	39.1	32.0	7.0	23.3	9.3
2016	100.0	20.0	80.0	40.7	0.0	39.4	32.4	7.0	23.8	9.2
2017	100.0	19.9	80.1	40.5	0.0	39.6	32.7	6.9	24.3	9.1

(HMOs) or health care prepayment plans, to serve Medicare and Medicaid patients. These groups are paid a predetermined cost per patient for their services.

Medicare-Risk HMOs Control Costs, but Some Senior Health Plans Do Not Survive

During the 1980s and 1990s the federal government, employers that provided health coverage for retiring employees, and many states sought to control costs by encouraging Medicare and Medicaid beneficiaries to enroll in HMOs. From the early 1980s through the late 1990s, Medicare-risk HMOs did contain costs because, essentially, the federal government paid the health plans that operated them with fixed fees—a predetermined dollar amount per member per month (PMPM). For this fixed fee, Medicare recipients were to receive a fairly

TABLE 5.7

Prescription drug expenditures, by source of funds, 2002–17 [CONTINUED]

| | | | Third-party payments | | | | | | | |
| | | | | | | Public | | | | |
Year	Total	Out-of-pocket payments	Total	Private health insurance	Other private funds	Total	Federal[a]	State and local[a]	Medicare[b]	Medicaid[c]
Historical estimates				Annual percent change from previous year shown						
2002	—	—	—	—	—	—	—	—	—	—
2003	10.5	9.3	10.9	7.1	—	18.4	20.1	16.2	−1.8	17.0
2004	8.4	4.7	9.6	7.9	—	12.8	13.3	12.1	40.4	11.6
2005	5.8	5.5	5.9	6.2	—	5.2	4.2	6.7	18.1	2.8
2006	8.5	−2.4	12.0	−0.7	—	34.1	80.0	−32.3	914.4	−48.3
Projected										
2007	6.7	5.8	7.0	6.0	—	8.4	8.6	7.6	8.9	8.0
2008	6.8	6.1	6.9	6.3	—	7.7	8.0	6.8	8.6	6.4
2009	7.1	5.5	7.5	5.8	—	9.7	10.2	7.5	11.9	7.4
2010	7.6	6.2	8.0	6.5	—	9.8	10.2	8.0	11.5	8.6
2011	8.0	6.6	8.3	6.9	—	9.9	10.4	8.1	11.6	9.0
2012	8.3	6.9	8.7	7.2	—	10.5	11.0	8.3	12.2	9.2
2013	8.6	7.8	8.8	7.9	—	9.8	10.2	8.3	11.0	9.1
2014	8.9	8.1	9.1	8.3	—	10.0	10.4	8.3	11.2	9.0
2015	9.2	8.5	9.3	8.7	—	10.1	10.5	8.3	11.4	8.9
2016	9.4	8.8	9.6	9.0	—	10.2	10.6	8.1	11.6	8.6
2017	9.6	9.1	9.8	9.3	—	10.3	10.8	7.9	11.9	8.2

[a]Includes Medicaid State Children's Health Insurance Program (SCHIP) Expansion and SCHIP.
[b]Subset of federal funds.
[c]Subset of federal and state and local funds. Includes Medicaid SCHIP Expansion.
[d]Calculation of per capita estimates is inappropriate.
Notes: Per capita amounts based on July 1 Census resident based population estimates. Numbers and percents may not add to totals because of rounding. The health spending projections were based on the 2006 version of the National Health Expenditures (NHE) released in January 2008.

SOURCE: "Table 11. Prescription Drug Expenditures; Aggregate and per Capita Amounts, Percent Distribution and Annual Percent Change by Source of Funds: Calendar Years 2002–2017," in *National Health Care Expenditures Projections 2007–2017*, U.S. Department of Health and Human Services, Centers for Medicare and Medicaid Services, 2006, http://www.cms.hhs.gov/NationalHealthExpendData/downloads/proj2007.pdf (accessed April 24, 2008)

comprehensive, preset array of benefits. PMPM payment provided financial incentives for Medicare-risk HMO physicians to control costs, unlike physicians who were reimbursed on a fee-for-service basis.

Even though Medicare recipients were generally pleased with these HMOs (even when enrolling meant they had to change physicians and thereby end long-standing relationships with their family doctors), many of the health plans did not fare well financially. The health plans suffered for a variety of reasons: some plans had underestimated the service utilization rates of older adults, and some were unable to provide the stipulated range of services as cost effectively as they had believed possible. Other plans found that the PMPM payment was simply not sufficient to enable them to cover all the clinical services and their administrative overhead.

Still, the health plans providing these senior HMOs competed fiercely to market to and enroll older adults. Some health plans feared that closing their Medicare-risk programs would be viewed negatively by employer groups, which, when faced with the choice of plans that offered coverage for both younger workers and retirees or one that only covered the younger workers, would choose the plans that covered both. Despite losing money, most health plans maintained their Medicare-risk programs to avoid alienating the employers they depended on to enroll workers who were younger, healthier, and less expensive to serve than the older adults.

By the mid-1990s, some of the Medicare-risk plans faced a challenge that proved daunting. Their enrollees had aged and required even more health care services than they had previously. For example, a senior HMO member who had joined as a healthy sixty-five-year-old could now be a frail seventy-five-year-old with multiple chronic health conditions requiring many costly health services. Even though the PMPM had increased over the years, for some plans it was simply insufficient to cover their costs. Some Medicare-risk plans, especially those operated by smaller health plans, were forced to end their programs abruptly, leaving thousands of older adults scrambling to join other health plans. Others endured, offering older adults comprehensive care and generating substantial cost savings for employers and the federal government.

The Balanced Budget Act of 1997 produced another plan for Medicare recipients called Medicare+Choice. This plan offers Medicare beneficiaries a wider range of managed care plan options than just HMOs—older adults may join preferred provider organizations (PPOs) and provider-sponsored organizations that generally offer greater freedom of choice of providers (physicians and hospitals) than what is available through HMO membership. These plans (as well as those formerly called Medicare-risk plans), are known as Medicare-Advantage (MA) plans. MA plans include HMOs, PPOs, private fee-for-service plans, and medical savings account plans (which deposit money from Medicare into an account that can be used to pay medical expenses). According to Abby L. Block (June 26, 2007, http://www.hhs.gov/asl/testify/2007/06/t20070626b.html) of the CMS, in his testimony before the House Energy and Commerce, Subcommittee on Oversight and Investigations in 2007, these plans had nearly 8.3 million members—one out of five Medicare beneficiaries was enrolled in a MA plan.

Medicare Faces Challenges

Higher and higher costs are being borne by fewer and fewer people. Sooner or later, this formula implodes. There is serious danger here. Medicare is drifting towards disaster. The disaster is not inevitable. If we act now, we can change the outcome. In health care, the core problem is that costs are rising significantly faster than costs in the economy as a whole.

—Michael Leavitt, the U.S. secretary of health and human services, quoted by Maggie Fox, "Medicare 'Drifting towards Disaster'" (Reuters, April 29, 2008)

The Medicare program's continuing financial viability is in jeopardy. In 1995, for the first time since 1972, the Medicare trust fund lost money, a sign that the financial condition of Medicare was worse than previously assumed. The CMS had not expected a deficit until 1997; however, income to the trust fund, primarily from payroll taxes, was less than expected and spending was higher. The deficit is significant because losses are anticipated to grow from year to year. As of 2008, there were no tax increases scheduled, and there was no reason to expect a reduction in the rate of spending.

A NATIONAL BIPARTISAN COMMISSION CONSIDERS THE FUTURE OF MEDICARE. The National Bipartisan Commission on the Future of Medicare was created by Congress in the Balanced Budget Act of 1997. The commission was chaired by Senator John B. Breaux (1944–; D-LA) and Representative William M. Thomas (1941–; R-CA) and was charged with examining the Medicare program and drafting recommendations to avert a future financial crisis and reinforce the program in anticipation of the retirement of the baby boomers.

The commission observed that much like Social Security, Medicare would suffer because there would be fewer workers per retiree to fund it. It predicted that beneficiaries' out-of-pocket costs would rise and forecast soaring Medicare enrollment.

When the commission disbanded in March 1999, it was unable to forward an official recommendation to Congress because a plan endorsed by Senator Breaux fell one vote short of the required majority needed to authorize an official recommendation. The plan backed by Senator Breaux would have changed Medicare into a premium system, where instead of Medicare directly covering beneficiaries, the beneficiaries would be given a fixed amount of money to purchase private health insurance. The plan would have also raised the age of eligibility from sixty-five to sixty-seven, as has already been done with Social Security, and provided prescription drug coverage for low-income beneficiaries, much like the Medicare Prescription Drug, Improvement, and Modernization Act of 2003.

MEDICARE PRESCRIPTION DRUG, IMPROVEMENT, AND MODERNIZATION ACT AIMS TO REFORM MEDICARE. Supported by Senator Breaux, the Medicare Prescription Drug, Improvement, and Modernization Act of 2003 was a measure intended to introduce private-sector enterprise into a Medicare model in urgent need of a reform.

The CMS explains in *Medicare and Year, 2008* (January 2008, http://www.medicare.gov/publications/pubs/pdf/10050.pdf) that older adults with substantial incomes face increasing premium costs. In 2008 older adults with annual incomes below $82,000 (or $164,000 for couples) paid a monthly premium of $96.40; individuals earning $82,001 to $102,000 (or couples earning $164,001 to $204,000) paid $122.40; those earning between $102,001 and $153,000 (or $204,001 to $306,000 for couples) paid $160.90; individuals making $153,001 to $205,000 (or $306,001 to $410,000 for couples) paid $199.70; and above $205,000 (or above $410,000 for couples) paid $238.40.

The act also expands coverage of preventive medical services. According to the CMS, new beneficiaries will receive a free physical examination along with laboratory tests to screen for heart disease and diabetes. The act also provides employers with $89 billion in subsidies and tax breaks to help offset the costs associated with maintaining retiree health benefits.

Medicare reform continues to be hotly contested. According to the article "Time Running out for Medicare Reform" (*Virginian-Pilot* [Norfolk, Virginia], March 28, 2008), the issues that attracted attention from policy makers, legislators, and the public in 2008 were the likelihood that Medicare would be in the red by 2019, drug prices, gaps in prescription drug coverage under the new legislation, access to preventive care, changes in the way physicians are reimbursed, and the role of health savings accounts and other cost sharing proposals. Health care industry observers predict that increased federal spending as a result of the new drug benefit will intensify demands for cost containment, which will increase as the baby-boom generation becomes eligible for Medicare coverage.

Medicaid

Medicaid was enacted by Congress in 1965 under Title XIX (Grants to States for Medical Assistance Programs) of the Social Security Act. It is a joint federal-state program that provides medical assistance to selected categories of low-income Americans: the aged, people who are blind or disabled, or financially struggling families with dependent children. Medicaid covers hospitalization, physicians' fees, laboratory and radiology fees, and long-term care in nursing homes. It is the largest source of funds for medical and health-related services for the poorest Americans and the second-largest public payer of health care costs, after Medicare.

In February 2006 President George W. Bush (1946–) signed the Deficit Reduction Act (DRA) into law. The DRA changes many aspects of the Medicaid program. Some of the changes are mandatory provisions that the states must enact, such as proof of citizenship and other criteria that will make it more difficult for people to qualify for or enroll in Medicaid. Other changes are optional; they allow the states to make drastic changes to the Medicaid program through state plan amendments. For example, states can choose to require anyone with a family income more than 150% of the poverty level to pay a premium of as much as 5% of their income. Before the DRA, the states had to provide a mandatory set of services to Medicaid recipients. As of March 31, 2006, the states could modify their Medicaid benefits such that they were comparable to those offered to federal and state employees, the benefits provided by the HMO with the largest non-Medicaid enrollment, or coverage approved by the secretary of health and human services.

The CMS states in the press release "Medicaid Grants to Help Improve Access to Primary Care and Avoid Unnecessary ER Visits" (April 17, 2008, http://www.cms.hhs.gov/apps/media/press/release.asp) that in 2008 Medicaid extended grants totaling $26 million to twenty states to improve access to primary care, which would help Medicaid beneficiaries avoid inappropriate use of costly hospital emergency rooms. Created by the DRA, these grants will fund initiatives to provide alternative health care settings such as community health centers.

LONG-TERM HEALTH CARE

One of the most urgent health care problems facing Americans in the twenty-first century is the growing need for long-term care. Long-term care refers to health and social services for people with chronic illnesses or mental or physical conditions so disabling that they cannot live independently without assistance—they require care daily. Longer life spans and improved life-sustaining technologies are increasing the likelihood that more people than ever before may eventually require costly, long-term care.

Limited and Expensive Options

Caring for chronically ill or elderly patients presents difficult and expensive choices for Americans: they must either provide long-term care at home or rely on nursing homes. Home health care was the fastest-growing segment of the health care industry during the first half of the 1990s. Even though the rate of growth slowed during the late 1990s, the CMS projects that the home health care sector will more than double, from $52.7 billion in 2006 to $119 billion in 2017. (See Table 5.5.)

High Cost of Long-Term Care

The options for quality, affordable long-term care in the United States are limited but improving. Nursing home costs average about $78,000 per year depending on services and location. According to MetLife, in *MetLife Market Survey of Nursing Home and Home Care Costs* (October 2007, http://www.metlife.com/FileAssets/MMI/MMIStudies2007NHAL.pdf), in 2006 nursing home care cost an average of $213 per day for a private room, or $77,745 per year. Many nursing home residents rely on Medicaid to pay these fees. In 2006 Medicaid covered 43.4% of nursing home costs for older Americans. (See Table 5.8.) The most common sources of payment at admission were Medicare (which only pays for short-term stays after hospitalization), private insurance, and other private funds. The primary source of payment changes as a stay lengthens. After their funds are exhausted, nursing home residents on Medicare shift to Medicaid.

To be eligible for Medicaid, a person must have no more than $2,500 in assets. (In the case of a married couple where only one spouse is in a nursing home, the remaining spouse can retain a house, a car, up to $75,000 in assets, and $2,000 in monthly income.) Many older adults must "spend down" to deplete their life savings to qualify for Medicaid assistance. This term refers to a provision in Medicaid coverage that provides care for seniors whose income exceeds eligibility requirements. For example, if their monthly income is $100 over the state Medicaid eligibility line, they can spend $100 per month on their medical care, and Medicaid will cover the remainder.

Nursing home care may seem cost-prohibitive, but even an unskilled caregiver who makes home visits can cost more than $25,000 per year; skilled care costs much more, and most older adults cannot afford this expense. In *Genworth Financial 2008 Cost of Care Survey* (April 2008, http://www.genworth.com/), Genworth Financial indicates that in 2008 the average hourly rates were $18 for homemaker services and $19 for home health aide services. The cost of a Medicare-certified home health aide rose 7% annually over the preceding four years to an average $38 an hour.

Lifetime savings may be exhausted long before the need for care ends. Georgetown University's Health Policy Institute estimates in "Long-Term Care May Strain U.S. Government Finances" (July 24, 2007, http://thehill.com/op-eds/long-term-care-may-strain-u.s.-government-finances-2007-07-24.html) that the total expenditure for long-term care

TABLE 5.8

Nursing home care expenditures, by source of funds, 2002–17

Year	Total	Out-of-pocket payments	Third-party payments Total	Private health insurance	Other private funds	Public Total	Federal[a]	State and local[a]	Medicare[b]	Medicaid[c]
Historical estimates						**Amount in billions**				
2002	$105.7	$29.7	$76.1	$8.7	$4.0	$63.3	$44.4	$18.9	$13.9	$47.1
2003	110.5	30.5	80.0	8.7	4.2	67.1	46.1	21.1	14.7	49.7
2004	115.2	30.8	84.3	8.7	4.2	71.5	49.3	22.2	17.0	51.5
2005	120.7	31.5	89.3	8.8	4.4	76.1	52.1	24.0	19.2	53.7
2006	124.9	32.9	92.0	9.3	4.6	78.1	53.7	24.3	20.8	54.2
Projected										
2007	129.7	34.1	95.6	9.6	4.9	81.2	56.3	24.9	22.4	55.5
2008	136.5	35.0	101.4	9.8	5.1	86.5	60.2	26.4	24.3	58.8
2009	143.5	36.6	106.9	10.2	5.3	91.5	63.7	27.7	25.9	61.7
2010	151.2	38.5	112.6	10.6	5.6	96.5	67.4	29.2	27.5	65.0
2011	159.1	40.5	118.6	10.9	5.8	101.9	71.2	30.7	29.1	68.4
2012	167.4	42.4	125.0	11.2	6.1	107.7	75.3	32.3	30.9	72.1
2013	176.0	44.2	131.8	11.5	6.4	113.8	79.8	34.1	32.8	75.9
2014	185.3	46.3	139.0	11.9	6.7	120.4	84.5	35.9	34.9	80.0
2015	195.4	48.7	146.7	12.2	7.1	127.5	89.6	37.9	37.1	84.4
2016	206.0	51.0	154.9	12.5	7.4	135.0	95.1	40.0	39.6	89.0
2017	217.5	53.6	163.8	12.8	7.9	143.2	101.0	42.2	42.4	93.9
Historical estimates						**Per capita amount**				
2002	$367	$103	$264	$30	$14	$220	$154	$66	d	d
2003	379	105	275	30	14	230	158	72	d	d
2004	392	105	287	29	14	243	168	76	d	d
2005	407	106	301	30	15	256	175	81	d	d
2006	417	110	307	31	15	261	179	81	d	d
Projected										
2007	430	113	317	32	16	269	186	83	d	d
2008	448	115	333	32	17	284	198	87	d	d
2009	468	119	349	33	17	298	208	90	d	d
2010	489	125	364	34	18	312	218	94	d	d
2011	511	130	381	35	19	327	228	99	d	d
2012	533	135	398	36	19	343	240	103	d	d
2013	556	140	416	36	20	360	252	108	d	d
2014	581	145	436	37	21	377	265	113	d	d
2015	608	151	456	38	22	396	279	118	d	d
2016	636	157	478	39	23	417	293	123	d	d
2017	666	164	502	39	24	439	310	129	d	d
Historical estimates						**Percent distribution**				
2002	100.0	28.0	72.0	8.2	3.8	59.9	42.0	17.9	13.2	44.6
2003	100.0	27.6	72.4	7.8	3.8	60.8	41.7	19.1	13.3	45.0
2004	100.0	26.8	73.2	7.5	3.7	62.1	42.8	19.3	14.8	44.7
2005	100.0	26.1	73.9	7.3	3.6	63.0	43.1	19.9	15.9	44.5
2006	100.0	26.4	73.6	7.4	3.7	62.5	43.0	19.5	16.7	43.4
Projected										
2007	100.0	26.3	73.7	7.4	3.7	62.6	43.4	19.2	17.3	42.8
2008	100.0	25.7	74.3	7.2	3.7	63.4	44.1	19.3	17.8	43.1
2009	100.0	25.5	74.5	7.1	3.7	63.7	44.4	19.3	18.1	43.0
2010	100.0	25.5	74.5	7.0	3.7	63.8	44.6	19.3	18.2	43.0
2011	100.0	25.4	74.6	6.8	3.7	64.1	44.8	19.3	18.3	43.0
2012	100.0	25.3	74.7	6.7	3.6	64.3	45.0	19.3	18.4	43.1
2013	100.0	25.1	74.9	6.6	3.6	64.7	45.3	19.4	18.6	43.1
2014	100.0	25.0	75.0	6.4	3.6	65.0	45.6	19.4	18.8	43.2
2015	100.0	24.9	75.1	6.3	3.6	65.2	45.8	19.4	19.0	43.2
2016	100.0	24.8	75.2	6.1	3.6	65.6	46.2	19.4	19.2	43.2
2017	100.0	24.7	75.3	5.9	3.6	65.9	46.5	19.4	19.5	43.2

services for older adults in 2005 (excluding the value of donated care from relatives and friends) was $206.6 billion—$129.8 billion on nursing home care and $76.8 billion on home care.

The U.S. Census Bureau (March 18, 2004, http://www .census.gov/population/www/projections/usinterimproj/ natprojtab02b.pdf) projects that the population over age eighty-five (those most likely to require long-term care) will nearly triple by 2050. Even though disability rates among older adults have declined in recent years, reducing somewhat the need for long-term care, the Congressional Budget Office anticipates that the growing population of people likely to require long-term care will no doubt increase spending commensurate with this growth.

TABLE 5.8

Nursing home care expenditures, by source of funds, 2002–17 [CONTINUED]

Year	Total	Out-of-pocket payments	Third-party payments			Public			Medicare[b]	Medicaid[c]
			Total	Private health insurance	Other private funds	Total	Federal[a]	State and local[a]		
Historical estimates			Annual percent change from previous year shown							
2002	—	—	—	—	—	—	—	—	—	—
2003	4.5	2.9	5.1	−0.2	3.2	6.0	3.7	11.4	5.7	5.5
2004	4.2	1.0	5.5	−0.2	1.9	6.5	6.9	5.4	16.0	3.6
2005	4.9	2.1	5.9	2.2	3.3	6.4	5.7	8.0	12.9	4.4
2006	3.5	4.7	3.0	4.9	5.9	2.6	3.2	1.5	8.1	0.9
Projected										
2007	3.8	3.5	4.0	3.3	4.9	4.0	4.7	2.4	7.9	2.3
2008	5.2	2.8	6.1	2.6	4.3	6.6	6.9	5.8	8.2	5.9
2009	5.2	4.4	5.4	3.5	4.8	5.7	6.0	5.1	6.9	5.1
2010	5.3	5.4	5.3	3.8	4.7	5.5	5.7	5.2	5.9	5.2
2011	5.3	5.1	5.3	3.1	4.4	5.6	5.7	5.3	5.9	5.3
2012	5.2	4.8	5.3	2.9	4.7	5.7	5.8	5.3	6.1	5.3
2013	5.1	4.3	5.4	3.0	4.9	5.7	5.9	5.4	6.2	5.4
2014	5.3	4.8	5.5	3.0	5.1	5.8	5.9	5.4	6.3	5.4
2015	5.4	5.0	5.6	2.9	5.3	5.8	6.0	5.5	6.4	5.4
2016	5.4	4.8	5.6	2.3	5.2	5.9	6.1	5.5	6.6	5.5
2017	5.6	5.1	5.7	2.1	5.9	6.1	6.3	5.5	7.0	5.5

[a]Includes Medicaid State Children's Health Insurance Program (SCHIP) Expansion and SCHIP.
[b]Subset of federal funds.
[c]Subset of federal and state and local funds. Includes Medicaid SCHIP Expansion.
[d]Calculation of per capita estimates is inappropriate.
Notes: Per capita amounts based on July 1 Census resident based population estimates. Numbers and percents may not add to totals because of rounding. The health spending projections were based on the 2006 version of the National Health Expenditures (NHE) released in January 2008.

SOURCE: "Table 13. Nursing Home Care Expenditures; Aggregate and per Capita Amounts, Percent Distribution and Annual Percent Change by Source of Funds: Calendar Years 2002–2017," in *National Health Care Expenditures Projections 2007–2017*, U.S. Department of Health and Human Services, Centers for Medicare and Medicaid Services,2006, http://www.cms.hhs.gov/NationalHealthExpendData/downloads/proj2007.pdf (accessed April 24, 2008)

MENTAL HEALTH SPENDING

In *National Expenditures for Mental Health and Substance Abuse Treatment 1993–2003* (2007, http://www.csat .samhsa.gov/IDBSE/spendEst/reports/SAMHSAFINAL9303 .pdf), a study funded by the Substance Abuse and Mental Health Services Administration (SAMHSA), Tami L. Mark et al. find that spending for mental health and substance abuse (alcohol and chemical dependency) treatment in the United States totaled $121 billion in 2003, representing 7.5% of all health care spending. Between 1993 and 2003 the annual rate of spending grew about 5.6%, almost 1% less than the growth rate for all health care (6.5%) during the same period. Medicaid is the single largest payer for mental health care, and prescription drugs are the fastest-growing component of mental health expenditures. Figure 5.1 shows that in 2003 Medicaid paid 45% of the $58 billion spent by public payers for mental health services.

Mark et al. also report that:

- Mental health spending rose from $205 to $345 per capita in inflation-adjusted dollars. This increase reflects the growing number of people treated for mental health conditions.

FIGURE 5.1

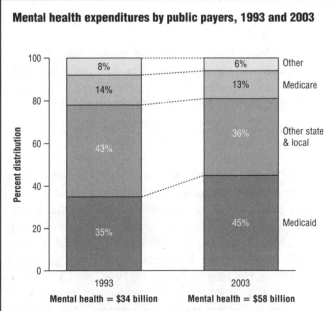

Mental health expenditures by public payers, 1993 and 2003

SOURCE: Tami L. Mark et al., "Figure 4.3. Distribution of Public MH Expenditures by Public Payer, 1993 and 2003," in *National Expenditures for Mental Health Services and Substance Abuse Treatment 1993–2003*, Substance Abuse and Mental Health Services Administration, 2007, http://www.csat.samhsa.gov/IDBSE/spendEst/ reports/SAMHSAFINAL9303.pdf (accessed April 29, 2008)

FIGURE 5.2

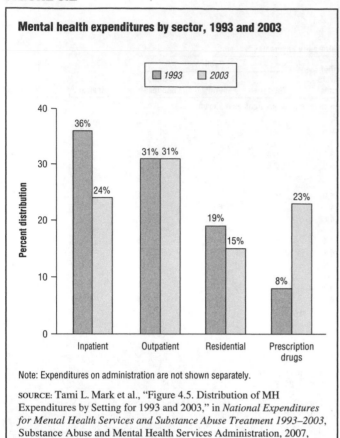

Mental health expenditures by sector, 1993 and 2003

Note: Expenditures on administration are not shown separately.

SOURCE: Tami L. Mark et al., "Figure 4.5. Distribution of MH Expenditures by Setting for 1993 and 2003," in *National Expenditures for Mental Health Services and Substance Abuse Treatment 1993–2003*, Substance Abuse and Mental Health Services Administration, 2007, http://www.csat.samhsa.gov/IDBSE/spendEst/reports/SAMHSAFINAL 9303.pdf (accessed April 29, 2008)

- Out-of pocket spending for mental health care rose by 7.2% from 1993 to 2003, compared to a 4.6% increase for other health care.

- Prescription drug spending for mental health patients increased 18.8% annually between 1993 and 2003, and was responsible for 42% of the increase in mental health spending during the same period.

- Mental health spending for inpatient services dropped from 41% in 1986 to 24% in 2003.

Health care industry observers attribute the decrease in mental health inpatient services to increased emphasis on drug treatment of mental health disorders, the increasing frequency of outpatient treatment, closure of psychiatric hospitals, and cost containment efforts of managed care. Figure 5.2 shows how retail drugs were just 8% of expenditures for mental health in 1993 but by 2003 had nearly tripled, accounting for 23% of mental health expenditures. Despite the higher spending for these psychoactive prescription drugs, some industry observers feel the increased availability of effective drug therapy actually served to contain mental health spending by enabling providers to offer drug therapy instead of more costly inpatient treatment.

SAMHSA Spending

In *U.S. Department of Health and Human Services Budget in Brief, Fiscal Year 2009* (2008, http://www.hhs.gov/budget/09budget/2009BudgetInBrief.pdf), the U.S. Department of Health and Human Services (HHS) states that the fiscal year (FY) 2009 budget request for SAMHSA was $3.2 billion, $198 million less than the FY 2008 budget. The funds were used to continue to expand suicide prevention programs and reduce youth drug use, prevent youth violence, and help people with mental illness who face homelessness.

State Mental Health Agency Expenditures

A number of court rulings during the 1970s and an evolution in professional thinking prompted the release of many people with serious mental illness from institutions to community treatment programs. The census (the number of patients or occupants, which is frequently referred to as a rate) of public mental hospitals sharply declined, and there was increasing pressure on the states to deliver community-based treatment.

State mental health agencies (SMHAs) operate the public mental health system that acts as a safety net for poor, uninsured, and otherwise indigent people suffering from mental illness. In "Key Elements of the National Statistical Picture" (2000, http://www.mentalhealth.samhsa.gov/publications/allpubs/SMA01-3537/chapter16.asp), Ted Lutterman and Michael Hogan characterize these public mental health systems "as a safety valve for an inadequate private sector response to mental illness." SMHAs vary from state to state—some purchase, regulate, administer, manage, and provide care and treatment; others simply purchase care using public funds that include general state revenues and federal funds. Generally, the federal funds are Medicare and Medicaid payments made to state-owned or state-operated facilities, although SMHAs also administer additional Medicaid payments when the state Medicaid agency grants the SHMA control of all Medicaid mental health expenditures.

Similar to the movement of privately insured people into managed care, during the 1990s state Medicaid programs turned to managed care organizations (MCOs) and behavioral health services in an effort to contain costs. More than half the states have separated the administration and financing of physical health and mental health in their MCO contracts.

SMHAs manage funds from the SAMHSA Mental Health Block Grant (MHBG) program. The MHBG was created in 1982 and its flexible funding enables states to innovate, develop, and expand successful community-based programs. Block grants (lump sums of money) are awarded based on a formula that considers each state's population, service costs, income, and taxable resources, and the funds enable the states to finance community mental health treatment programs. According to Lutterman and Hogan, MHBG expenditures dropped by 49% in inflation-adjusted dollars during the 1990s, but in 1999 Congress appropriated an additional $13.4 million to the MHBG. The FY 2009 budget request included $421 million in block grant funding.

HIGH COSTS OF RESEARCH

Medical and pharmaceutical research, disease prevention research, and the work to develop and conduct clinical trials of new drugs are expensive. The National Institutes of Health (NIH) reports in "Estimates of Funding for Various Diseases, Conditions, Research Areas" (February 5, 2008, http://www.nih.gov/news/fundingresearchareas.htm) that its FY 2009 budget allocated an estimated $2.9 billion for human immunodeficiency virus (HIV) and acquired immunodeficiency syndrome (AIDS) research, compared to $660 million to investigate obesity prevention and treatment. Pharmaceutical manufacturers also spend billions of dollars every year researching and developing new medicines. For example, according to the Pharmaceutical Research and Manufacturers of America (PhRMA; 2008, http://www.phrma.org/about_phrma/), U.S. pharmaceutical companies spent $58.8 billion in 2007. By contrast, the entire NIH FY 2007 budget was $29.1 billion. (See Figure 4.5 in Chapter 4.)

Decisions about how much is spent to research a particular disease are not based solely on how many people develop the disease or die from it. Rightly or wrongly, economists base the societal value of an individual on his or her earning potential and productivity (the ability to contribute to society as a worker). The bulk of the people who die from heart disease, stroke, and cancer are older adults. Many have retired from the workforce, and their potential economic productivity is usually low or nonexistent. (This is not an observation about how society values older adults; instead, it is simply an economic measure of present and future financial productivity.)

In contrast, AIDS patients are often much younger and die in their twenties, thirties, and forties. Until they developed AIDS, their potential productivity, measured in economic terms, was high. The number of work years lost when they die is considerable. Using this economic equation to determine how disease research should be funded, it may be considered economically wise to invest more money to research AIDS because the losses, which are measured in potential work years rather than in lives, is so much greater.

Once a new drug receives FDA approval, its manufacturer is ordinarily allowed to hold the patent on the drug to recoup its investment. During that time, the drug is priced much higher than if other manufacturers were allowed to compete by producing generic versions of the same drug. After the patent expires, competition between pharmaceutical manufacturers generally lowers the price. In contrast, HIV/AIDS drugs are granted only seven years of exclusivity under legislation to encourage research and promote development of new treatments.

In *What Goes into the Cost of Prescription Drugs? . . . and Other Questions about Your Medicines* (June 2005, http://www.phrma.org/files/Cost_of_Prescription_Drugs .pdf), PhRMA explains that the pharmaceutical manufacturer must cover the cost not only of research and development for the approximately three out of ten drugs that succeed but also for many—seven out of ten—that have failed. In contrast, the producer of generic drugs has the formula and must simply manufacture the drugs properly. On average, manufacturers spend over $800 million to bring brand-name drugs to market, including the expense of twelve to fifteen years of product development. The generic manufacturer does not have to pay for successful and unsuccessful research and development of new drugs, nor does it have to pursue the complicated, time-consuming process of seeking and obtaining FDA approval. Generic manufacturers' FDA submissions need only reference the original manufacturer's clinical data supporting the safety and efficacy of the drug.

HARDSHIP OF HIGH HEALTH CARE COSTS ON FAMILIES

Families USA is a national health care advocacy organization that is dedicated to achieving affordable, quality health care and long-term care for all American families. The organization describes itself as "the voice for American consumers" and contends that American families pay about two-thirds of the nation's health care bill, whereas American businesses pay the other third. This ratio is based on the premise that families and businesses pay for health care in several ways:

- Directly, through out-of-pocket payments and insurance expenses. These include premiums, deductibles (annual amounts that must be paid by the employee before the insurance plan begins paying), and co-payments.

- Indirectly, through Medicare payroll, income, and other federal, state, and local taxes that support public health programs. These include veterans' health benefits, military health benefits, the Medicaid program, and a variety of smaller public health programs.

As a result, Families USA estimates of per capita health care spending differ from other reports, such as those from the CMS and the U.S. Census Bureau, which take into account only direct payments.

Families also purchase insurance themselves when they work for employers that do not offer group health insurance or when insurers refuse to insure certain groups they consider to be at high risk (such as people with chronic diseases). Workers who retire before reaching age sixty-five and are not yet eligible for Medicare coverage must also purchase insurance on their own. Furthermore, many

Medicare beneficiaries pay insurance premiums for supplemental (Medigap) insurance to cover the difference in charges that Medicare does not pay, as well as uncovered costs, such as durable medical equipment.

Reed Abelson and Milt Freudenheim report in "Even the Insured Feel the Strain of Health Costs" (*New York Times*, May 4, 2008) that even some of the 158 million people with health insurance in 2008 found it challenging to pay for their health care. Some faced higher premiums, less extensive coverage, and higher out-of-pocket deductibles and co-payments. Abelson and Freudenheim note that Helen Darling, the president of the National Business Group on Health, said, "It's a bad-news situation when an individual or household has to pay out-of-pocket three, four or five times as much for their health plan as they would have at the time of the last recession. Americans have been giving their pay raise to the health care system."

High Cost of Prescription Drugs

Even though it has slowed somewhat in recent years, spending for prescription drugs remains the fastest-growing component of health care spending. In 2006 prescription drug expenditures reached $216.7 billion and were projected to more than double to $515.7 billion by 2017. (See Table 5.7.) The editorial "When Drug Costs Soar beyond Reach" (*New York Times*, April 15, 2008) observes that many patients who require costly prescription drugs, which can cost thousands or even hundreds of thousands of dollars per year, are being forced to pay as much as 33% of the drug costs. Insurance companies defend this practice by explaining that having these patients bear the brunt of their exceedingly high drug costs enables the insurance companies to control the cost of monthly premiums. Critics of this practice believe it is not only unfair but also short-sighted. They observe that if sick patients are forced to forgo their medicines, they will doubtless become sicker and incur even higher medical care costs.

To control prescription drug expenditures, many hospitals, health plans, employers, and other group purchasers have attempted to obtain discounts and rebates for bulk purchases from pharmaceutical companies. Some have developed programs to encourage health care practitioners and consumers to use less costly generic drugs, and others have limited, reduced, or even eliminated prescription drug coverage.

The Henry J. Kaiser Family Foundation explains in *Prescription Drug Trends* (May 2007, http://www.kff.org/rxdrugs/upload/3057_06.pdf) that consumers are attempting to reduce their prescription drug costs by asking their physicians for less expensive or generic drugs, comparison shopping to find the best prices for their prescription drugs, using mail-order pharmacies, purchasing drugs from vendors on the Internet, buying drugs in bulk, using over-the-counter drugs instead of prescription medications, and participating in pharmaceutical company- and state-sponsored drug assistance programs. Some consumers are ordering less expensive pharmaceuticals from Canada.

The report *USA Today/Kaiser Family Foundation/ Harvard School of Public Health Survey: The Public on Prescription Drugs and Pharmaceutical Companies: Toplines* (March 2008, http://www.kff.org/kaiserpolls/upload/7747.pdf) reveals that in 2008 cost had prompted 29% of survey respondents not to fill a prescription in the past two years and 23% said they cut pills in half or skipped doses to make their medications last longer.

Consumers also consider pharmaceutical companies as major contributors to rising health care costs. In 2008, 79% of adults named profits made by drug companies as a "very important" factor contributing to rising drug costs, and 70% said drug companies are "too concerned about making profits and not concerned enough about helping people."

Generic Drugs Promise Cost Savings

When patents expire on popular brand-name drugs, the entry of generic versions of these drugs to the market promises cost savings for consumers and payers as well as increased profits for pharmacies. Generic drugs usually cost 10% to 30% less when they first enter the market and even less once additional generic manufacturers join in the competition. According to the article "RxWatch: Generics in 2008" (November 6, 2007, http://www.calendarlive.com/media/acrobat/2008-03/36768569.pdf), among the drugs with patents that were set to expire in 2008 were fexofenadine (for seasonal allergy congestion relief), alendronate (for prevention of bone loss), bupropion (an antidepressant), and zaleplon (for people with sleeping problems). Industry observers predict that consumers can expect to pay $5 to $20 less per prescription when they opt for generic rather than brand-name drugs and payers.

RATIONING HEALTH CARE

When health care rationing (allocating medical resources) is defined as "all care that is expected to be beneficial is not always available to all patients," most health care practitioners, policy makers, and consumers accept that rationing has been, and will continue to be, a feature of the U.S. health care system. Most American opinion leaders and industry observers accept that even a country as wealthy as the United States cannot afford all the care that is likely to benefit its citizens. The practical considerations of allocating health care resources involve establishing priorities and determining how these resources should be rationed.

Opponents of Rationing

There is widespread agreement among Americans that rationing according to patients' ability to pay for health care services or insurance is unfair. Ideally, health care should be equitably allocated on the basis of need and the potential benefit derived from the care. Those who argue against rationing fear that society's most vulnerable populations—older adults, the poor, and people with chronic illnesses—suffer most from the present rationing of health care.

Many observers believe improving the efficiency of the U.S. health care system will save enough money to supply basic health care services to all Americans. They suggest that because expenditures for the same medical procedures vary greatly in different areas of the country, standardizing fees and costs could realize great savings. They also believe that money could be saved if greater emphasis was placed on preventive care and on effective strategies to prevent or reduce behaviors that increase health risk such as smoking, alcohol and drug abuse, and unsafe sexual practices. Furthermore, they insist that the high cost of administering the U.S. health system could be streamlined with a single payer for health care—as in the Canadian system.

Supporters of Rationing

Those who endorse rationing argue that the spiraling cost of health care stems from more than simple inefficiency. They attribute escalating costs to the aging population, rapid technological innovation, and the increasing price tags for labor and supplies.

Not everyone who supports rationing thinks the U.S. health care system is working well. Some rationing supporters believe that the nation's health care system charges too much for the services it delivers and that it fails altogether to deliver to millions of uninsured. In fact, they point out that the United States already rations health care by not covering the uninsured. Other health care–rationing advocates argue that the problem is one of basic cultural assumptions, not the economics of the health care industry. Americans value human life, believe in the promise of health and quality health care for all, and insist that diseases can be cured. They contend that the issue is not whether health care should be rationed but how care is rationed. They believe that the United States spends too much on health compared to other societal needs, too much on the old rather than on the young, more on curing and not enough on caring, and too much on extending the length of life and not enough on enhancing the quality of life. Supporters of rationing argue instead for a system that guarantees a minimally acceptable level of health care for all, while reining in the expensive excesses of the current system, which often acts to prolong life at any cost.

The Oregon Health Plan: An Experiment in Rationing

In 1987 Oregon designed a new, universal health care plan that would simultaneously expand coverage and contain costs by limiting services. Unlike other states, which trimmed budgets by eliminating people from Medicaid eligibility, Oregon chose to eliminate low-priority services. Michael Janofsky reports in "Oregon Starts to Extend Health Care" (*New York Times*, February 19, 1994) that the Oregon Health Plan, which was approved in August 1993, aimed to provide Medicaid to 120,000 additional residents living below the federal poverty level. The plan also established a high-risk insurance pool for people who were refused health insurance coverage because of preexisting medical conditions, offered more insurance options for small businesses, and improved employees' abilities to retain their health insurance benefits when they changed jobs. A gradual increase in the state cigarette tax was expected to provide $45 million annually, which would help fund the additional estimated $200 million needed over the next several years.

Oregon developed a table of health care services and performed a cost-benefit analysis to rank them. It was decided that Oregon Medicaid would cover the top 565 services on a list of 696 medical procedures. Janofsky notes that services that fell below the cutoff point were "not deemed to be serious enough to require treatment, like common colds, flu, mild food poisoning, sprains, cosmetic procedures and experimental treatments for diseases in advanced stages."

When setting the priorities, those making the list decided that disease prevention and quality of life were the factors that most influenced the ranking of the treatments. Quality of life (quality of well-being [QWB] in the Oregon plan) drew fire from those who felt such judgments could not be decided subjectively. Active medical or surgical treatment of terminally ill patients also ranked low on the QWB scale, whereas comfort and hospice care ranked high. The Oregon Health Services Commission (HSC) emphasized that its QWB judgments were not based on an individual's quality of life at a given time; such judgments were considered ethically questionable. Instead, it focused on the potential for change in an individual's life, posing questions such as: "After treatment, how much better or worse off would the patient be?"

Critics countered that the plan obtained its funding by reducing services that were currently offered to Medicaid recipients (often poor women and children) rather than by emphasizing cost control. Others objected to the ranking and the ethical questions raised by choosing to support some treatments over others.

In "Oregon Falters on a New Path to Health Care" (*New York Times*, January 3, 1999), Peter T. Kilborn notes that by 1998 the Oregon Health Plan had encountered major problems. The state was no longer promising universal care, physicians were seeking and finding ways to get around the rationing restrictions, and friction with federal Medicaid regulators was blocking Oregon's efforts to deny more treatments. A plan to require that employers insure all their workers or contribute to a fund to cover them failed. Spending for the health plan climbed to $2.1 billion in the 1997–99 state budget period, up from $1.7 billion in the 1995–97 period. Higher cigarette taxes did not offset the increase, thereby requiring more money from the state's general fund.

According to the Jonathan Oberlander of the University of North Carolina, Chapel Hill, in "Health Reform Interrupted: The Unraveling of the Oregon Health Plan" (*Health Affairs*, vol. 26, no. 1, 2007), the Oregon Health Plan initially did serve to reduce the percentage of uninsured Oregonians from 18% in 1992 to 11% in 1996, but its early success proved difficult to sustain. By 2003 the Oregon plan was not even close to achieving its goal of having no uninsured people in the state. In fact, the ranks of the uninsured were growing and by 2003 would again reach 17%. An economic downturn in the state and the state's strategy of explicit rationing are cited as reasons for the ambitious plan's failure to achieve its goals.

The Oregon HSC continued to modify the plan's covered benefits. The HSC's most recent effort to refine the list of covered services began in January 2002. The HSC sought to reduce the overall costs of the plan by eliminating less effective treatments and determining if any covered medical conditions could be more effectively treated using standardized clinical practice guidelines (step-by-step instructions for diagnosis and treatment of specific illnesses or disorders) while preserving basic coverage. The benefit review process will be ongoing with the HSC submitting a new prioritized list of benefits on July 1 of each even-numbered year for review by legislative assembly. In April 2008 the HSC (http://www.oregon .gov/OHPPR/HSC/docs/Apr08Plist.pdf) issued an updated prioritized list of health services (medical conditions and treatments) for 2008 and 2009.

Rationing by HMOs

Until 2000, steadily increasing numbers of Americans received their health care from HMOs or other managed care systems. According to the Kaiser Foundation (http://www .statehealthfacts.org/comparemaptable.jsp?ind=348&cat=7), by July 2007 national enrollment in HMOs was 66.8 million, which was more than four times the enrollment rate two decades earlier (15.1 million). However, the number of enrollees has steadily declined since 2000. By contrast, the number of HMOs operating in the United States has risen slightly, from 560 in July 2000 to 602 in July 2007.

Managed care programs have sought to control costs by limiting coverage for experimental, duplicative, and unnecessary treatments. Before physicians can perform experimental procedures or prescribe new treatment plans, they must obtain prior authorization (approval from the patient's managed care plan) to ensure that the expenses will be covered.

Increasingly, patients and physicians are battling HMOs for approval to use and receive reimbursement for new technology and experimental treatments. Judges and juries, moved by the desperate situations of patients, have frequently decided cases against HMOs, regardless of whether the new treatment has been shown to be effective.

"SILENT RATIONING." Physicians and health care consumers are concerned that limiting coverage for new, high-cost technology will discourage research and development for new treatments before they have even been developed. This has been called "silent rationing," because patients will never know what they have missed.

In an effort to control costs, some HMOs have discouraged physicians from informing patients about certain treatment options—those that are extremely expensive or not covered by the HMO. This has proved to be a highly controversial issue, both politically and ethically. In December 1996 the HHS ruled that HMOs and other health plans cannot prevent physicians from telling Medicare patients about all available treatment options.

Could Less Health Care Be Better Than More?

Even though health care providers and consumers fear that rationing sharply limits access to medical care and will ultimately result in poorer health among affected Americans, researchers are also concerned about the effects of too much care on the health of the nation. Several studies suggest that an oversupply of medical care may be as harmful as an undersupply.

Frank W. Young of Cornell University asserts in "An Explanation of the Persistent Doctor-Mortality Association" (*Journal of Epidemiology and Community Health*, February 2001) that supply appears to drive demand in areas with more physicians and hospitals—people visit physicians more often and spend more days in hospitals with no apparent improvement in their health status.

In *Geography and the Debate over Medicare Reform* (February 13, 2002, http://content.healthaffairs.org/cgi/re print/hlthaff.w2.96v1), John E. Wennberg, Elliott S. Fisher, and Jonathan S. Skinner find tremendous regional variation in both utilization and the cost of health care that they believe is explained, at least in part, by the distribution of health care providers. They also suggest that variations in physicians' practice styles—whether they favor outpatient treatment over hospitalization for specific procedures such as biopsies (surgical procedures to examine tissue to detect cancer cells)—greatly affects demand for hospital care.

Variation in demand for health care services in turn produces variation in health care expenditures. Wennberg, Fisher, and Skinner report wide geographic variation in Medicare spending. Medicare paid more than twice as much to care for a sixty-five-year-old in Miami, where the supply of health care providers is overabundant, than it spent on care for a sixty-five-year-old in Minneapolis, a city with an average supply of health care providers. To be certain that the difference was not simply higher fees and charges in Miami, the investigators also compared rates of utilization and found that older adults in Miami visited physicians and hospitals much more often than their counterparts in Minneapolis.

Wennberg, Fisher, and Skinner also wanted to be sure that the differences were not caused by the severity of illness, so they compared care during the last six months of life to control for any underlying regional differences in the health of the population. Remarkably, the widest variations were observed in care during the last six months of life, when older adults in Miami saw physician specialists six times as often as those in Minneapolis. The researchers assert that higher expenditures, particularly at the end of life, do not purchase better care. Instead, they finance generally unpleasant and futile interventions intended to prolong life rather than improve the quality of patients' lives. Wennberg, Fisher, and Skinner conclude that areas with more medical care, higher utilization, and higher costs fared no better in terms of life expectancy, morbidity, or mortality, and that the care that people received was no different in quality from care received by people in areas with average supplies of health care providers.

In "The Care of Patients with Severe Chronic Illness: A Report on the Medicare Program by the Dartmouth Atlas Project" (2006, http://www.dartmouthatlas.org/atlases/2006_Chronic_Care_Atlas.pdf), John E. Wennberg et al. detail differences in the management of Medicare enrollees with severe chronic illnesses. The investigators find that average utilization and health care spending varied by state, region, and even by hospital in the same region. Expenditures were not linked with rates of illness in different parts of the country; instead, they reflected how intensively selected resources (e.g., acute care hospital beds, specialist physician visits, tests, and other services) were used to care for patients who were very ill but could not be cured. Because other research demonstrates that, for these chronically ill Americans, receiving more services does not result in improved health outcomes, and because most Americans say they prefer to avoid excessively high-tech end-of-life care, the investigators conclude that Medicare spending for the care of the chronically ill could be reduced by as much as 30%, while improving quality, patient satisfaction, and outcomes. Wennberg et al.'s research and similar studies pose two important and as yet unanswered questions: How much health care is needed to deliver the best health to a population? Are Americans getting the best value for the dollars spent on health care?

CHAPTER 6
INSURANCE: THOSE WITH AND THOSE WITHOUT

In 1798 Congress established the U.S. Marine Hospital Services for seamen. It was the first time an employer offered health insurance in the United States. Payments for hospital services were deducted from the sailors' salaries.

In the twenty-first century many factors affect the availability of health insurance, including employment, income, personal health status, and age. As a result, an individual's or family's health insurance status often changes as circumstances change. In 2006 nearly six out of ten (59.7%) Americans were covered during all or some part of the year by private insurance through their employers. (See Figure 6.1.) Medicare, the federal health insurance program for older adults and people with disabilities, covered 13.6% of Americans, and Medicaid, the federal health insurance program for the poor, covered 12.9%. Another 15.8% of Americans were without health coverage.

In 2006 the 15.8% of the American population without health coverage was up from 2005, and was equal to the peak in 1998. (See Figure 6.2.) In *Income, Poverty, and Health Insurance Coverage in the United States: 2006* (August 2007, http://www.census.gov/prod/2007pubs/p60-233.pdf), Carmen DeNavas-Walt, Bernadette D. Proctor, and Jessica Smith of the U.S. Census Bureau report that after the 1998 high, the rate dropped slightly. From 2002 it varied little before stabilizing at about 16%.

According to Robin A. Cohen, Michael E. Martinez, and Heather L. Free of the National Center for Health Statistics (NCHS), in *Health Insurance Coverage: Early Release of Estimates from the National Health Interview Survey, January–September 2007* (March 2008, http://www.cdc.gov/nchs/data/nhis/earlyrelease/insur200803.pdf), 2007 marked the sixth consecutive yearly rise in the number of American adults without health insurance coverage. The researchers indicate that from January through September 2007 there were 54.5 million (18.4%) people who were uninsured for at least part of the twelve months preceding the survey. Approximately 43.7 million (14.7%) people of all ages were uninsured adults, and 43.4 million (16.7%) were under age sixty-five. About 36.7 million (19.6%) people aged eighteen to sixty-four were uninsured, as were 6.8 million (9.2%) children under age eighteen. Figure 6.3 shows the percentages of children and adults aged eighteen to sixty-four that were uninsured at the time of the survey, at least part of the year, and for more than a year, as well as the percentages of children and adults covered by public and private insurance.

WHO WAS UNINSURED IN 2006?

Not surprisingly, in 2006 people with lower household incomes—below $25,000 and from $25,000 to $49,999—were more than twice as likely as to be uninsured than those with higher incomes. In 2006, 24.9% of people with an income less than $25,000 and 21.1% of those with earnings between $25,000 and $49,999 lacked insurance, compared to 14.4% of those with incomes ranging from $50,000 to $74,999 and just 8.5% of those with incomes more than $75,000. (See Table 6.1.)

The proportion of people who did not have health insurance in 2006 varied by geography. It was greatest in the South (19%) and West (17.9%), and less in the Northeast (12.3%) and Midwest (11.4%). (See Table 6.1.) Hispanics (34.1%) and African-Americans (20.5%) were more likely to have been uninsured in 2006 than Asian-Americans (15.5%) or whites (10.8%).

The Uninsured by Gender and Age

Among people under sixty-five years old, the percentage of people without insurance in 2007 was highest among young adults aged eighteen to twenty-four (28.1%) and lowest among young people less than eighteen years old (9.2%). (See Figure 6.4.) Among adults aged eighteen to forty-four, men were more likely than women to be uninsured.

FIGURE 6.1

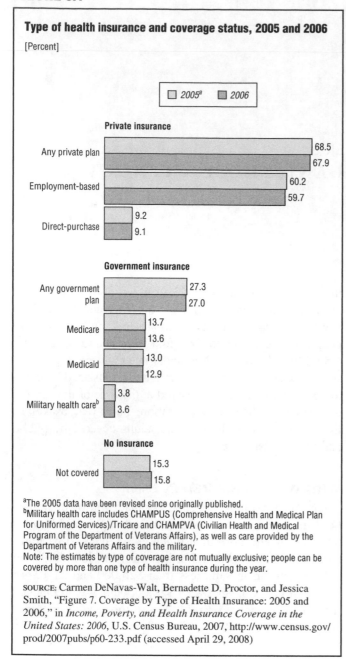

Type of health insurance and coverage status, 2005 and 2006

[Percent]

☐ 2005ᵃ ■ 2006

Private insurance

Any private plan: 68.5 / 67.9
Employment-based: 60.2 / 59.7
Direct-purchase: 9.2 / 9.1

Government insurance

Any government plan: 27.3 / 27.0
Medicare: 13.7 / 13.6
Medicaid: 13.0 / 12.9
Military health careᵇ: 3.8 / 3.6

No insurance

Not covered: 15.3 / 15.8

ᵃThe 2005 data have been revised since originally published.
ᵇMilitary health care includes CHAMPUS (Comprehensive Health and Medical Plan for Uniformed Services)/Tricare and CHAMPVA (Civilian Health and Medical Program of the Department of Veterans Affairs), as well as care provided by the Department of Veterans Affairs and the military.
Note: The estimates by type of coverage are not mutually exclusive; people can be covered by more than one type of health insurance during the year.

SOURCE: Carmen DeNavas-Walt, Bernadette D. Proctor, and Jessica Smith, "Figure 7. Coverage by Type of Health Insurance: 2005 and 2006," in *Income, Poverty, and Health Insurance Coverage in the United States: 2006,* U.S. Census Bureau, 2007, http://www.census.gov/prod/2007pubs/p60-233.pdf (accessed April 29, 2008)

LACK OF INSURANCE HAS SIGNIFICANT CONSEQUENCES

In *Sicker and Poorer: The Consequences of Being Uninsured* (May 2002, http://www.kff.org/uninsured/upload/Full-Report.pdf), a landmark report prepared for the Kaiser Commission on Medicaid and the Uninsured, Jack Hadley of the Urban Institute discusses an exhaustive review of the literature detailing the major findings of more than twenty-five years of health services research on the effects of health insurance. Hadley notes that the uninsured receive less preventive care, are diagnosed at more advanced stages of disease, and receive less treatment as measured in terms of pharmaceutical and surgical interventions.

Besides receiving less medical care and treatment, uninsured people often pay more for medical care. Lara Jakes Jordan reports in "Uninsured Patients Pay Far More for Care" (Associated Press, June 25, 2004) that hospitals routinely overcharge people without health insurance—as much as four times more than insured hospital patients are charged. The overcharging is attributed to hospitals' efforts to recoup the costs of providing care to people who are poor.

Hadley concludes that if the uninsured were provided with health insurance, their mortality rates would be reduced by between 10% and 15%. The reduction in mortality would largely result from improved access to timely and appropriate care. This finding supports the Institute of Medicine, which estimates in *Insuring America's Health: Principles and Recommendations* (2004) that eighteen thousand Americans die each year because they lack health insurance. Furthermore, Hadley notes that better health would enable uninsured people to improve their annual earnings by 10% to 30% and would also act to increase their educational attainment.

In *Dying for Coverage* (April 2008, http://familiesusa.org/issues/uninsured/publications/dying-for-coverage.html), Families USA, a national health care advocacy organization, provides the first-ever state-level estimates of the number of deaths attributable to the lack of health insurance. For example, the organization asserts that at least 8 Californians die each day because they are uninsured and that between 2000 and 2006 an estimated 19,900 Californians aged twenty-five to sixty-five died from lack of health insurance. During this same period over sixty-one hundred people between the ages of twenty-five and sixty-four in Illinois and ninety-nine hundred New Yorkers of the same age died because they had no health care coverage. Ron Pollack, the executive director of Families USA, observes in the press release "Reports Shows How Many People Are Likely to Die in Each State Due to Lack of Health Coverage" (April 8, 2008, http://www.familiesusa.org/resources/newsroom/press-releases/2008-press-releases/dying-4-coverage-nat.html) that "health insurance really matters in how people make their health care decisions. We know that people without insurance often forgo checkups, screenings, and other preventive care." Pollack laments the reports' tragic conclusion, that "a lack of health coverage is a matter of life and death for many people."

SOURCES OF HEALTH INSURANCE
People under Age Sixty-Five

For people under age sixty-five, there are two principal sources of health insurance coverage: private insurance (from employers or private policies) and Medicaid. From 1997 to 2007 the proportion of those covered by private insurance declined from 70.8% to

FIGURE 6.2

Number and percentage of uninsured, 1987–2006

[Numbers in millions, rates in percent]

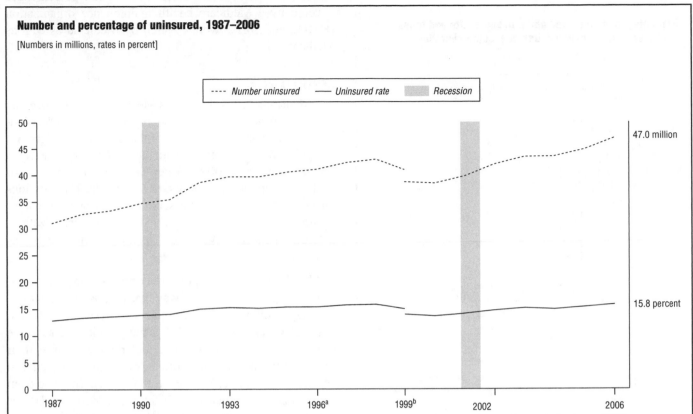

- - - - Number uninsured ——— Uninsured rate ▓ Recession

aThe series starting in 1996 reflects an approximation of the impact of an editing error that was corrected in the 2005 Annual Socialand Economic Supplement (ASEC) (2004 coverage).
bImplementation of Census 2000-based population controls occurred for the 2000 ASEC, which collected data for 1999. These estimates also reflect the results of follow-up verification questions that were asked of people who responded "no" to all questions about specific types of health insurance coverage in order to verify whether they were actually uninsured. This change increased the number and percentage of people covered by health insurance, bringing the Current Population Survey (CPS) more in line with estimates from other national surveys.
Notes: Respondents were not asked detailed health insurance questions before the 1988 CPS.
The data points are placed at the midpoints of the respective years.

SOURCE: Carmen DeNavas-Walt, Bernadette D. Proctor, and Jessica Smith, "Figure 6. Number Uninsured and Uninsured Rate: 1987 to 2006," in *Income, Poverty, and Health Insurance Coverage in the United States: 2006*, U.S. Census Bureau, 2007, http://www.census.gov/prod/2007pubs/p60-233.pdf (accessed April 29, 2008)

66.4%. (See Table 6.2.) During this same period the percentage covered by public health plans grew from 13.6% in 1997 to 18.4% in 2007.

DeNavas-Walt, Proctor, and Smith report that the percentage of people covered by employment-based health insurance dropped from 60.2% in 2005 to 59.7% in 2006. (See Figure 6.1.) In contrast, during the 1980s close to 70% of workers obtained private insurance through their employers. This decline is consistent with the continuing decline in all forms of private health coverage, which dropped from 68.5% in 2005 to 67.9% in 2006. For people under age sixty-five, the overall decline in private health insurance coverage between 1997 and 2005 was just 4.4%, from 70.8% to 66.4%, but among people who were near poor the percentage covered by private insurance fell 16.6%, from 53.5% to 36.9%. (See Table 6.3.)

Two major factors contributed to the long-term decline in private health insurance. The first is the rising cost of health care, which frequently leads to greater cost

sharing between employers and employees. Some workers simply cannot afford the higher premiums and co-payments (the share of medical bills the employee pays for each health service). The second factor is the shift in U.S. commerce from the goods-producing sector, where health benefits have traditionally been provided, to the service sector, where many employers do not offer health insurance.

People Aged Sixty-five and Older

There are three sources of health insurance for people aged sixty-five and older: private insurance, Medicare, and Medicaid. Medicare is the federal government's primary health program for those sixty-five years old and older, and all people in this age group are eligible for certain basic benefits under Medicare. Medicaid is the federal program for the poor and people with disabilities. In 2006 a scant 1.5% of adults aged sixty-five and older went without some type of health insurance. (See Table 6.1.)

FIGURE 6.3

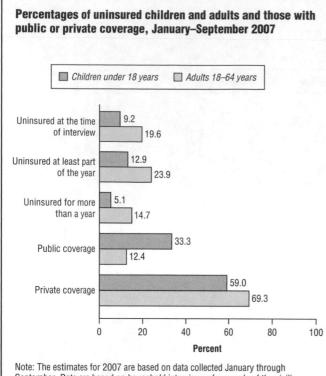

Percentages of uninsured children and adults and those with public or private coverage, January–September 2007

Children under 18 years ☐ Adults 18–64 years

Category	Children under 18 years	Adults 18–64 years
Uninsured at the time of interview	9.2	19.6
Uninsured at least part of the year	12.9	23.9
Uninsured for more than a year	5.1	14.7
Public coverage	33.3	12.4
Private coverage	59.0	69.3

Percent

Note: The estimates for 2007 are based on data collected January through September. Data are based on household interviews of a sample of the civilian noninstitutionalized population.

SOURCE: Adapted from Robin A. Cohen, Michael E. Martinez, and Heather L. Free, "Figure 2. Percentage of Persons without Health Insurance, by Three Measurements and Age Group, and Percentage of Persons with Health Insurance, by Coverage Type and Age Group: United States, January–September 2007," and "Table 1. Percentage of Persons Who Lacked Health Insurance Coverage at the Time of Interview, for at Least Part of the Past Year, or for More Than a Year, by Age Group: United States, January–September 2007," in *Health Insurance Coverage: Early Release of Estimates from the National Health Interview Survey, January–September 2007*, Centers for Disease Control and Prevention, National Center for Health Statistics, March 2008, http://www.cdc.gov/nchs/data/nhis/earlyrelease/insur200803.pdf (accessed April 29, 2008)

Older adults may be covered by a combination of private health insurance and Medicare, or Medicare and Medicaid, depending on their income and level of disability. Almost all adults over age sixty-five are covered by Medicare. In *Health, United States, 2007* (2007, http://www.cdc.gov/nchs/data/hus/hus07.pdf), the NCHS reports that in 2005, 36.4% of older adults obtained their private insurance through the workplace. Fourteen and a half percent were covered by a Medicare health maintenance organization (HMO), and 10.1% were covered by Medicaid as well as Medicare.

Older adults may be covered by a combination of private health insurance and Medicare, or Medicare and Medicaid, depending on their income and level of disability. In *Health, United States, 2007* (2007, http://www.cdc.gov/nchs/data/hus/hus07.pdf), the NCHS reports that in 2005, 36.4% of older adults obtained their private insurance

through the workplace. Fourteen and a half percent were covered by a Medicare health maintenance organization (HMO), and 10.1% were covered by Medicaid as well as Medicare.

MEDICARE C

Medicare C, also known as Medicare+Choice, became available to Medicare recipients on January 1, 1999. Medicare C came about as a result of the Balanced Budget Act of 1997 and was designed to supplement Medicare Parts A and B. Medicare C offers beneficiaries a wider variety of health plan options than previously available. These options include traditional (fee-for-service) Medicare, provider-sponsored organizations, preferred provider organizations (PPOs), Medicare HMOs, and medical savings accounts (MSAs).

Medicare provider-sponsored organizations are organized and operated the same way that HMOs are. However, they are administered by providers—physicians and hospitals. PPOs are similar to HMOs but permit patients to see providers outside the network and do not require their members to choose a network primary care physician to coordinate their care. Patients in PPOs may seek care from any physician associated with the plan. Medicare HMOs are more like traditional Medicare, except patients may pay more out-of-pocket expenses. MSAs have two parts: an insurance policy and a savings account. Medicare pays the insurance premium and deposits a fixed amount in an MSA each year to pay for an individual's health care.

CHANGING MEDICARE REIMBURSEMENT

Medicare reimbursement varies in different parts of the country, although everyone pays the same amount to Medicare through taxes. As a result, older adults in some geographic regions have access to a more comprehensive range of services such as coverage for nursing home care and eyeglasses, whereas those in other areas do not receive these benefits.

Describing this practice as unfair and outdated, legislators have repeatedly called for more equitable reimbursement formulas. For example, since 2002 the Medi-Fair Act (previously called the Medicare Fairness in Reimbursement Act), intended to improve the provision of items and services provided to Medicare beneficiaries residing in rural areas in part by improving reimbursement, has repeatedly failed to pass. Senator Patty Murray (1950–; D-WA) and Representative Adam Smith (1965–; D-WA) reintroduced the legislation in May 2008 in an effort to raise Washington State's Medicare reimbursement rates to the national average and ensure that all states receive at least the national average of per-patient spending. The Medicare Improvements for Patients and Providers Act of 2008 aimed to stem declining reimbursement by postponing a provision to reduce some

TABLE 6.1

People with or without insurance coverage by selected characteristics, 2005 and 2006

[Numbers in thousands. People as of March of the following year.]

| Characteristic | Uninsured | | | | Change (2006 less 2005)[a] | | |
| | 2005[b] | | 2006 | | Uninsured | | Insured |
	Number	Percentage	Number	Percentage	Number	Percentage	Number
People							
Total	44,815	15.3	46,995	15.8	2,180	0.6	810
Family status							
In families	34,643	14.3	36,230	14.8	1,587	0.5	1,223
Householder	10,401	13.4	10,770	13.7	370	0.3	667
Related children under 18	7,585	10.5	8,303	11.4	717	0.9	−204
Related children under 6	2,434	10.2	2,690	11.1	255	0.9	35
In unrelated subfamilies	377	30.9	341	25.0	−36	−5.9	183
Unrelated individual	9,794	19.5	10,423	20.7	629	1.2	−596
Race[c] and Hispanic origin							
White	33,946	14.4	35,486	14.9	1,540	0.5	448
White, not Hispanic	20,909	10.7	21,162	10.8	253	0.1	107
Black	7,006	19.0	7,652	20.5	646	1.5	−242
Asian	2,161	17.2	2,045	15.5	−116	−1.6	711
Hispanic origin (any race)	13,954	32.3	15,296	34.1	1,342	1.8	344
Age							
Under 18 years	8,050	10.9	8,661	11.7	611	0.8	−494
18 to 24 years	8,201	29.3	8,323	29.3	123	—	317
25 to 34 years	10,161	25.7	10,713	26.9	553	1.1	−165
35 to 44 years	7,901	18.3	8,018	18.8	117	0.4	−476
45 to 64 years	10,053	13.6	10,738	14.2	685	0.6	1,190
65 years and older	449	1.3	541	1.5	92	0.2	438
Nativity							
Native	33,034	12.8	34,380	13.2	1,346	0.5	24
Foreign born	1 1,781	33.0	12,615	33.8	834	0.8	786
Naturalized citizen	2,385	17.2	2,384	16.4	−1	−0.8	655
Not a citizen	9,396	43.1	10,231	45.0	835	1.8	131
Region							
Northeast	6,353	11.7	6,648	12.3	295	0.5	−295
Midwest	7,330	11.3	7,458	11.4	128	0.1	249
South	19,143	18.0	20,486	19.0	1,343	1.0	340
West	1,988	17.6	12,403	17.9	415	0.4	515
Metropolitan status							
Inside metropolitan statistical areas	37,718	15.3	39,421	15.8	1,704	0.5	1,154
Inside principal cities	17,149	18.2	18,107	19.0	958	0.8	83
Outside principal cities	20,569	13.5	21,314	13.8	745	0.3	1,071
Outside metropolitan statistical areas[d]	7,097	15.0	7,574	16.0	477	1.0	−344
Household income							
Less than $25,000	14,452	24.2	13,933	24.9	−520	0.7	−3,222
$25,000 to $49,999	14,651	20.1	15,319	21.1	669	1.0	−952
$50,000 to $74,999	7,826	13.3	8,459	14.4	633	1.2	−1,127
$75,000 or more	7,886	7.7	9,283	8.5	1,398	0.7	6,111
Work experience							
Total, 18 to 64 years old	36,315	19.7	37,792	20.2	1,477	0.5	866
Worked during year	26,293	18.0	27,627	18.7	1,335	0.7	470
Worked full-time	20,780	17.2	22,010	17.9	1,230	0.7	1,037
Worked part-time	5,513	22.1	5,618	22.9	104	0.8	−568
Did not work	10,022	26.1	10,165	26.1	143	—	396

—Represents or rounds to zero.
[a]Details may not sum to totals because of rounding.
[b]The 2005 data have been revised since originally published.
[c]Federal surveys now give respondents the option of reporting more than one race. Therefore, two basic ways of defining a race group are possible. A group such as Asian may be defined as those who reported Asian and no other race (the race-alone or single-race concept) or as those who reported Asian regardless of whether they also reported another race (the race-alone-or-in-combination concept). This table shows data using the first approach (race alone). The use of the single-race population does not imply that it is the preferred method of presenting or analyzing data. The Census Bureau uses a variety of approaches. Information on people who reported more than one race, such as white and American Indian and Alaska Native or Asian and black or African American, is available from Census 2000 through American FactFinder. About 2.6 percent of people reported more than one race in Census 2000. Data for American Indians and Alaska Natives, Native Hawaiians and other Pacific Islanders, and those reporting two or more races are not shown separately.
[d]The "outside metropolitan statistical areas" category includes both micropolitan statistical areas and territory outside of metropolitan and micropolitan statistical areas.

SOURCE: Carmen DeNavas-Walt, Bernadette D. Proctor, and Jessica Smith, "Table 6. People with or without Health Insurance Coverage by Selected Characteristics: 2005 and 2006," in *Income, Poverty, and Health Insurance Coverage in the United States: 2006*, U.S. Census Bureau, 2007, http://www.census.gov/prod/2007pubs/p60–233.pdf (accessed April 29, 2008)

FIGURE 6.4

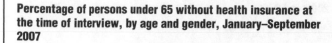

TABLE 6.2

Percentage of persons under 65 without health insurance at the time of interview, by age and gender, January–September 2007

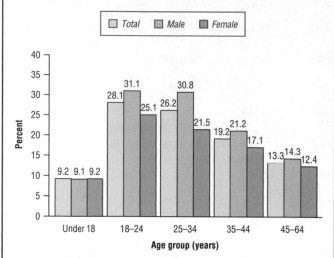

Note: The estimates for 2007 are based on data collected January through September. Data are based on household interviews of a sample of the civilian noninstitutionalized population.

SOURCE: Robin A. Cohen, Michael E. Martinez, and Heather L. Free, "Figure 4. Percentage of Persons under 65 Years of Age without Health Insurance Coverage at the Time of Interview, by Age Group and Sex: United States, January–September 2007," in *Health Insurance Coverage: Early Release of Estimates from the National Health Interview Survey, January–September 2007*, Centers for Disease Control and Prevention, National Center for Health Statistics, March 2008, http://www.cdc.gov/nchs/data/nhis/earlyrelease/insur200803.pdf (accessed April 29, 2008)

Percentage of persons without health insurance at time of interview, by age group, 1997–September 2007

Type of coverage and year	Under 65 years	Under 18 years	18–64 years
		Percent	
Public health plan coverage[a]			
1997	13.6	21.4	10.2
1998	12.7	20.0	9.5
1999	12.4	20.4	9.0
2000	12.9	22.0	9.1
2001	13.6	23.6	9.4
2002	15.2	27.1	10.3
2003	16.0	28.6	10.9
2004 (method 1)[c]	16.1	28.5	11.1
2004 (method 2)[c]	16.2	28.7	11.1
2005[c]	16.8	29.9	11.5
2006[c,d]	18.1	32.3	12.4
2007 (Jan.–Sept.)[c]	18.4	33.3	12.4
Private health insurance coverage[b]			
1997	70.8	66.2	72.8
1998	72.0	68.5	73.5
1999	73.1	69.1	74.7
2000	71.8	67.1	73.8
2001	71.6	66.7	73.7
2002	69.8	63.9	72.3
2003	68.2	62.6	70.6
2004[c]	68.6	63.1	70.9
2005[c]	68.4	62.4	70.9
2006[c,d]	66.5	59.7	69.2
2007 (Jan.–Sept.)[c]	66.4	59.0	69.3

[a]The health plan category "public health plan coverage" includes Medicaid, State Children's Health Insurance Program (SCHIP), state-sponsored or other government-sponsored health plan, Medicare (disability), and military plans.
[b]The health plan category "private health insurance coverage" excludes plans that paid for only one type of service such as accidents or dental care. A small number of persons were covered by both public and private plans and were included in both categories.
[c]Beginning in the third quarter of 2004, two additional questions were added to the National Health Interview Survey (NHIS) insurance section to reduce potential errors in reporting Medicare and Medicaid status. Persons aged 65 years and over not reporting Medicare coverage were asked explicitly about Medicare coverage, and persons under 65 years old with no reported coverage were asked explicitly about Medicaid coverage. Estimates of uninsurance for 2004 are calculated without using the additional information from these questions (noted as method 1) and with the responses to these questions (noted as method 2). Respondents who were reclassified as covered by the additional questions received the appropriate followup questions concerning periods of noncoverage for insured respondents. The two additional questions added beginning in the third quarter of 2004 did not affect the estimates of private coverage. Beginning in 2005, all estimates calculated using method 2.
[d]In 2006, NHIS underwent a sample redesign. The impact of the new sample design on estimates presented in this report is expected to be minimal.
Note: The estimates for 2007 are based on data collected in January through September. Data are based on household interviews of a sample of the civilian noninstitutionalized population.

SOURCE: Robin A. Cohen, Michael E. Martinez, and Heather L. Free, "Table 3. Percentage of Persons under the Age of 65 Years with Public Health Plan or Private Health Insurance Coverage at the Time of Interview, by Age Group: United States, 1997–September 2007," in *Health Insurance Coverage: Early Release of Estimates from the National Health Interview Survey, January–September 2007*, Centers for Disease Control and Prevention, National Center for Health Statistics, March 2008, http://www.cdc.gov/nchs/data/nhis/earlyrelease/insur200803.pdf (accessed April 29, 2008)

Medicare reimbursement rates. On July 15, 2008, President George W. Bush (1946–) vetoed the act; however, on the same day the U.S. House of Representatives and the U.S. Senate voted to override the president's veto of the bill.

Medicare Prescription Drug, Improvement, and Modernization Act

In December 2003 President Bush signed the Medicare Prescription Drug, Improvement, and Modernization Act into law. Heralded as landmark legislation, the act provides older adults and people with disabilities with a prescription drug benefit, more choices, and improved benefits under Medicare. On June 1, 2004, seniors and people with disabilities began using their Medicare-approved drug discount cards to obtain savings on prescription medicines. Low-income beneficiaries qualified for a $600 credit to help pay for their prescriptions. Besides providing coverage for prescription drugs, this legislation offers seniors the opportunity to choose the coverage and care that best meets their needs. For example, some older adults may opt for traditional Medicare coverage along with the new prescription benefit. Others may wish to obtain dental or eyeglass coverage or to enroll in managed care plans that reduce their out-of-pocket costs.

The legislation stipulated that as of 2005 all newly enrolled Medicare beneficiaries would be covered for a complete physical examination and other preventive services, such as blood tests to screen for diabetes. The

TABLE 6.3

Percentage of persons under age 65 with private health insurance at the time of interview, by age group and poverty status, 1997–September 2007

Age group and year	Total	Poverty status[a]			
		Poor	Near poor	Not poor	Unknown
		Percent of persons with private health insurance coverage[b]			
Under 65 years					
1997	70.8	22.9	53.5	87.6	66.7
1998	72.0	23.1	53.0	88.1	67.1
1999	73.1	26.1	50.9	88.9	68.0
2000	71.8	25.2	49.1	87.4	68.8
2001	71.6	25.5	48.4	87.2	67.8
2002	69.8	26.0	46.5	86.0	63.9
2003	68.2	23.4	42.3	85.8	64.1
2004[c]	68.6	20.0	44.9	85.0	66.3
2005	68.4	22.1	43.2	84.7	66.2
2006[d]	66.5	20.6	40.6	84.1	65.7
2007 (Jan.–Sept.)[e]	66.4	18.5	36.9	84.0	61.6
Under 18 years					
1997	66.2	17.5	55.0	88.9	61.7
1998	68.5	19.3	56.3	89.9	62.1
1999	69.1	20.2	52.1	90.6	63.8
2000	67.1	19.5	48.8	88.4	64.2
2001	66.7	18.1	48.4	88.4	62.2
2002	63.9	17.2	44.9	86.9	56.3
2003	62.6	14.4	39.9	86.5	58.8
2004[c]	63.1	12.6	43.0	86.4	60.0
2005	62.4	15.0	40.0	85.6	59.3
2006[d]	59.7	13.1	36.9	85.9	57.8
2007 (Jan.–Sept.)[e]	59.0	12.0	32.5	85.1	54.4
18–64 years					
1997	72.8	26.8	52.6	87.1	68.6
1998	73.5	25.8	50.9	87.4	69.1
1999	74.7	30.4	50.2	88.2	69.7
2000	73.8	29.2	49.3	87.1	70.6
2001	73.7	31.7	48.4	86.8	69.9
2002	72.3	31.8	47.5	85.7	66.9
2003	70.6	29.0	43.7	85.5	66.0
2004[c]	70.9	24.9	46.0	84.6	68.6
2005	70.9	26.8	45.0	84.4	68.7
2006[d]	69.2	25.5	42.6	83.6	68.6
2007 (Jan.–Sept.)[e]	69.3	23.0	39.6	83.6	64.0

[a]Poverty status is based on family income and family size using the U.S. Census Bureau's poverty thresholds. "Poor" persons are defined as those below the poverty threshold, "near poor" persons have incomes of 100% to less than 200% of the poverty threshold, and "not poor" persons have incomes of 200% of the poverty threshold or greater. The percentage of respondents with unknown poverty status was 19.1% in 1997, 23.6% in 1998, 26.4% in 1999, 27.0% in 2000, 27.1% in 2001, 28.1% in 2002, 31.5% in 2003, 29.6% in 2004, 28.9% in 2005, 30.7% in 2006 and 17.9% in the first three quarters of 2007. Estimates may differ from estimates based on both reported and imputed income.
[b]The category "private health insurance" excludes plans that paid for only one type of service such as accidents or dental care. A small number of persons were covered by both public and private plans and, thus, were included in both categories.
[c]These estimates were recalculated and may differ from those previously published. In 2004, a much larger than expected proportion of respondents reported a family income of "$2." Based on extensive review, these "$2" responses were coded to "Not ascertained" for the final data files. For this report, a decision was made to re-run the 2004 estimates to reflect this editing decision.
[d]In 2006, the National Health Interview Survey (NHIS) underwent a sample redesign. The impact of the new sample design on estimates presented in this report is expected to be minimal.
[e]In 2007, the income section of the NHIS was redesigned and estimates by poverty may not be directly comparable with earlier years.
Note: The estimates for 2007 are based on data collected in January through September. Data are based on household interviews of a sample of the civilian noninstitutionalized population.

SOURCE: Robin A. Cohen, Michael E. Martinez, and Heather L. Free, "Table 6. Percentage of Persons under the Age of 65 Years with Private Health Insurance Coverage at the Time of Interview, by Age Group and Poverty Status: United States, 1997–September 2007," in *Health Insurance Coverage: Early Release of Estimates from the National Health Interview Survey, January–September 2007*, Centers for Disease Control and Prevention, National Center for Health Statistics, March 2008, http://www.cdc.gov/nchs/data/nhis/earlyrelease/insur200803.pdf (accessed April 29, 2008)

new law also aimed to assist all Americans in paying out-of-pocket health costs by enabling the creation of health savings accounts, which allow Americans to set aside up to $4,500 every year, tax free, to save for medical expenses.

Medicare Drug Plans Face Rising Costs

In "Should Drug Prices Be Negotiated under Part D of Medicare? And If So, How?" (*Health Affairs*, vol. 27, no. 1, January–February 2008), Richard G. Frank and Joseph P. Newhouse of Harvard University question whether drug purchasing for the millions of older adults enrolled in Medicare Part D (the prescription drug benefit) is cost-effective. The researchers report that the prices of medicines heavily used by older adults have risen more than 24% since June 2006 and that as a result many Medicare enrollees are facing higher costs. For example, many Part D plans assign selected drugs to a "specialty tier," which means the enrollee must pay from 25% to 33% of the price of the drug. Medicare also feels the pinch of higher prices because after enrollees reach their cap of $5,726 out-of-pocket, they pay just 5% of the price. The drug plan bears 15% of the cost and Medicare bears the brunt—80%.

Frank and Newhouse suggest there is strong evidence that some Part D drug prices need to be renegotiated. They assert the government should be negotiating prices with pharmaceutical manufacturers, and they even provide a proposal, which includes terms for arbitration to resolve disputes, for how to improve purchasing of prescription drugs in Medicare.

CHILDREN

In 2007, 9.2% of children under the age of eighteen were uninsured at the time of the National Health Interview Survey (NHIS), 12.9% had been uninsured for part of the year preceding the interview, and 5.1% had been uninsured for more than a year. (See Figure 6.3.) Children living in poverty were much more likely to be uninsured—19.3% compared to the 11.7% of all children who were uninsured in 2006. (See Figure 6.5.) Hispanic children (22.1%) were the most likely to be uninsured,

followed by African-American children (14.1%) and Asian-American children (11.4%). Just 7.3% of non-Hispanic white children had no health care coverage, making them the least likely children to be uninsured in 2006. Older children aged twelve through seventeen (12.6%) were more likely to be uninsured than children under age six (11.3%) and children aged six to eleven (11.1%).

In 2007, 59% of American children were insured under private health insurance plans, either privately purchased or obtained through their parents' workplace. (See Table 6.3.) According to Cohen, Martinez, and Free, from January through September 2007 about one-third (33.3%) of American children were covered by public health coverage. More than three-quarters (77.8%) of poor children and 54.2% of near-poor children were covered by a public health plan at the time of the NHIS.

Some health care industry observers believed the 1996 welfare reform law, the Personal Responsibility and Work Opportunity Reconciliation Act, would reduce enrollment in Medicaid. Under the 1996 law, federal money once dispensed through the Aid to Families with Dependent Children program was now given as a block grant (a lump sum of money) to states. In addition, the law no longer required that children who received cash assistance were automatically enrolled in the Medicaid program. The law gave states greater leeway in defining their requirements for aid, and in a few states some families were no longer eligible for Medicaid. Regardless, Table 6.4 shows that enrollment in Medicaid actually increased, rather than decreased, from 26.6 million in 1995 to 33.2 million in 2005. During this same period the percentage of children covered by Medicaid also rose, from 21.5% to 27.2%.

Some industry analysts attributed the declining proportion of uninsured children and children covered by Medicaid in the late 1990s to expansion of the State Children's Health Insurance Program, which targeted children from low-income families and was instituted during the late 1990s. Others believed the economic boom of the late 1990s may have played a role in preventing enrollment growth in Medicaid and predicted that the economic downturn and uncertainty of the early years of the twenty-first century would reverse the downward trend in both the share of the population without health insurance and Medicaid enrollment.

In 2008 many health care advocacy groups, including the American Academy of Pediatrics, continued to agitate for federal legislation such as the MediKids Health Insurance Act (S.1303/H.R.3055) to provide health insurance for all children in the United States by 2012 regardless of family income level.

FIGURE 6.5

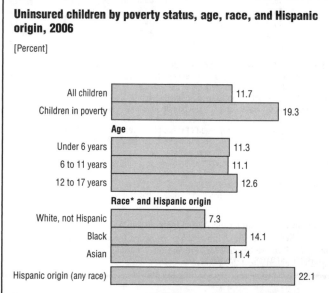

Uninsured children by poverty status, age, race, and Hispanic origin, 2006

[Percent]

Note: Federal surveys now give respondents the option of reporting more than one race. Therefore, two basic ways of defining a race group are possible. A group such as Asian may be defined as those who reported Asian and no other race (the race-alone or single-race concept) or as those who reported Asian regardless of whether they also reported another race (the race-alone-or-in-combination concept). This table shows data using the first approach (race alone).

SOURCE: Carmen DeNavas-Walt, Bernadette D. Proctor, and Jessica Smith, "Figure 8. Uninsured Children by Poverty Status, Age, and Race, and Hispanic Origin: 2006," in *Income, Poverty, and Health Insurance Coverage in the United States: 2006*, U.S. Census Bureau, 2007, http://www.census.gov/prod/2007pubs/p60-233.pdf (accessed April 29, 2008)

TABLE 6.4

Medicaid coverage of persons under 65, by selected characteristics, selected years 1984–2005

[Data are based on household interviews of a sample of the civilian noninstitutionalized population]

Characteristic	1984	19S9	1995	1997[a]	2000	2002	2003	2004(1)[b]	2004(2)[b]	2005[b]
					Number in millions					
Total[c]	14.0	15.4	26.6	22.9	23.2	29.4	30.9	31.1	31.6	33.2
					Percent of population					
Total[c]	6.8	7.2	11.5	9.7	9.5	11.8	12.3	12.3	12.5	12.9
Age										
Under 18 years	11.9	12.6	21.5	18.4	19.6	24.8	26.0	25.9	26.4	27.2
Under 6 years	15.5	15.7	29.3	24.7	24.7	30.0	32.3	31.8	32.4	34.0
6–17 years	10.1	10.9	17.4	15.2	17.2	22.3	23.0	23.1	23.4	23.9
18–14 years	5.1	5.2	7.8	6.6	5.6	7.1	7.4	7.5	7.7	8.3
18–24 years	6.4	6.8	10.4	8.8	8.1	9.9	9.6	10.3	10.4	11.3
25–34 years	5.3	5.2	8.2	6.8	5.5	6.6	7.8	7.6	7.8	8.0
35–44 years	3.5	4.0	5.9	5.2	4.3	5.9	5.6	5.7	5.8	6.6
45–64 years	3.4	4.3	5.6	4.6	4.5	5.3	5.3	5.4	5.5	5.5
45–54 years	3.2	3.8	5.1	4.0	4.2	5.1	5.0	5.4	5.5	5.2
55–64 years	3.6	4.9	6.4	5.6	4.9	5.8	5.8	5.4	5.5	5.8
Sex										
Male	5.4	5.7	9.6	8.4	8.2	10.6	10.9	10.8	11.0	11.6
Female	8.1	8.6	13.4	11.1	10.8	13.0	13.6	13.7	13.9	14.3
Race[d]										
White only	4.6	5.1	8.9	7.4	7.1	9.3	10.4	10.2	10.4	11.0
Black or African American only	20.5	19.0	28.5	22.4	21.2	23.2	23.7	24.5	24.9	24.9
American Indian or Alaska Native only	28.2	29.7	19.0	19.6	15.1	21.1	18.5	18.0	18.4	24.2
Asian only	8.7	8.8	10.5	9.6	7.5	9.8	8.0	9.6	9.8	8.2
Native Hawaiian or other Pacific Islander only	—	—	—	—	—	—	—	—	—	—
2 or more races	—	—	—	—	19.1	21.6	23.5	19.0	19.3	22.0
Hispanic origin and race[d]										
Hispanic or Latino	13.3	13.5	21.9	17.6	15.5	20.8	21.8	21.9	22.5	22.9
Mexican	12.2	12.4	21.6	17.2	14.0	20.2	21.7	21.9	22.4	23.0
Puerto Rican	31.5	27.3	33.4	31.0	29.4	29.0	31.0	28.5	29.1	31.9
Cuban	4.8	7.7	13.4	7.3	9.2	14.9	13.8	17.9	17.9	17.7
Other Hispanic or Latino	7.9	11.1	18.2	15.3	14.5	19.6	19.3	19.9	20.8	19.7
Not Hispanic or Latino	6.2	6.6	10.2	8.7	8.5	10.3	10.6	10.5	10.7	11.1
White only	3.7	4.2	7.1	6.1	6.1	7.7	8.0	7.8	7.9	8.5
Black or African American only	20.7	19.0	28.1	22.1	21.0	23.2	23.4	24.1	24.6	24.8
Age and percent of poverty level[e]										
All ages:										
Below 100%	33.0	37.6	48.4	40.5	38.4	42.8	43.2	44.2	45.0	45.7
100%–less than 150%	7.7	10.9	19.1	17.9	20.7	27.6	26.9	26.5	27.1	28.7
150%–less than 200%	3.2	5.1	8.3	8.3	11.5	16.1	17.1	16.6	16.9	18.1
200% or more	0.6	1.1	1.7	1.8	2.3	3.1	3.3	3.5	3.5	3.7
Under 18 years:										
Below 100%	43.2	47.9	66.0	58.0	58.5	66.4	67.5	69.2	70.7	71.2
100%–less than 150%	9.0	12.3	27.2	28.7	35.0	47.1	49.1	46.6	47.6	49.0
150%–less than 200%	4.4	6.1	13.1	13.0	21.3	29.1	33.6	31.9	32.4	35.3
200% or more	0.8	1.8	3.3	3.1	5.1	7.2	7.6	8.0	8.0	8.3

HEALTH INSURANCE PORTABILITY AND ACCOUNTABILITY ACT OF 1996

In August 1996 President Bill Clinton (1946–) signed the Health Insurance Portability and Accountability Act (HIPAA). This legislation aimed to provide better portability (transfer) of employer-sponsored insurance from one job to another. HIPAA ensured that people who had employer-sponsored health coverage would be able to maintain their health insurance even if they lost their job or moved to a different company. They would, of course, have to continue to pay for their insurance. However, they no longer had to fear that they would be denied coverage because of preexisting medical conditions, or be forced to go without health insurance for prolonged waiting periods.

Industry observers and policy makers viewed HIPAA as an important first step in the federal initiative to significantly reduce the number of uninsured people in the United States. Besides its portability provisions, HIPAA changed tax laws to make it easier for Americans to pay for medical care, and initiated a pilot program of MSAs that would grow into a significant new initiative in paying for health care.

HEALTH SAVINGS ACCOUNTS

The Health Insurance Portability and Accountability Act of 1996 authorized a pilot program—a five-year demonstration project designed to test the concept of MSAs, which are similar to individual retirement accounts.

TABLE 6.4

Medicaid coverage of persons under 65, by selected characteristics, selected years 1984–2005 [CONTINUED]

[Data are based on household interviews of a sample of the civilian noninstitutionalized population]

— Data not available.
[a]Starting with 1997 data, the National Health Interview Survey (NHIS) was redesigned, and changes to the questions on health insurance coverage were made.
[b]Beginning in quarter 3 of the 2004 NHIS, persons under 65 years with no reported coverage were asked explicitly about Medicaid coverage. Estimates were calculated without and with the additional information from this question in the columns labeled 2004(1) and 2004(2), respectively, and estimates were calculated with the additional information in 2005.
[c]Includes all other races not shown separately and, in 1984 and 1989, with unknown poverty level.
[d]The race groups, white, black, American Indian or Alaska Native, Asian, Native Hawaiian or other Pacific Islander, and 2 or more races, include persons of Hispanic and non-Hispanic origin. Persons of Hispanic origin may be of any race. Starting with 1999 data, race-specific estimates are tabulated according to the 1997 revisions to the Standards for the Classification of Federal Data on Race and Ethnicity and are not strictly comparable with estimates for earlier years. The five single-race categories plus multiple-race categories shown in the table conform to the 1997 standards. Starting with 1999 data, race-specific estimates are for persons who reported only one racial group; the category 2 or more races includes persons who reported more than one racial group. Prior to 1999, data were tabulated according to the 1977 standards with four racial groups and the Asian only category included Native Hawaiian or other Pacific Islander. Estimates for single-race categories prior to 1999 included persons who reported one race or, if they reported more than one race, identified one race as best representing their race. Starting with 2003 data, race responses of other race and unspecified multiple race were treated as missing, and then race was imputed if these were the only race responses. Almost all persons with a race response of other race were of Hispanic origin.
[e]Percent of poverty level is based on family income and family size and composition using U.S. Census Bureau poverty thresholds. Poverty level was unknown for 10%–11% of persons under 65 years of age in 1984 and 1989. Missing family income data were imputed for 15%–16% of persons under 65 years of age in 1994–1996, 24% in 1997, and 28%–33% in 1998–2005.
Notes: Medicaid includes other public assistance through 1996. Starting with 1997 data, state-sponsored health plan coverage is included as Medicaid coverage. Starting with 1999 data, coverage by the State Children's Health Insurance Program (SCHIP) is included as Medicaid coverage. In 2005, 10.2% of persons under 65 years of age were covered by Medicaid, 1.3% by state-sponsored health plans, and 1.5% by SCHIP.

SOURCE: Adapted from "Table 138. Medicaid Coverage among Persons under 65 Years of Age, by Selected Characteristics: United States, Selected Years 1984–2005," in *Health, United States, 2007. With Chartbook on Trends in the Health of Americans*, U.S. Department of Health and Human Services, Centers for Disease Control and Prevention, National Center for Health Statistics, 2007, http://www.cdc.gov/nchs/data/hus/hus07.pdf#listtables (accessed April 24, 2008)

Beginning on January 1, 1997, about 750,000 people with high-deductible health plans (HDHPs; high-deductible plans were defined as those that carried a deductible of $1,600 to $2,400 for an individual or $3,200 to $4,800 for families) could make tax-deductible contributions into interest-bearing savings accounts. The funds deposited into these accounts could be used to purchase health insurance policies and pay co-payments and deductibles. People using MSAs could also deduct any employer contributions into the accounts as tax-deductible income. Any unspent money remaining in the MSA at the end of the year was carried over to the next year, thereby allowing the account to grow.

To be eligible to create an MSA, individuals had to be less than sixty-five years old, self-employed, and uninsured or had to work in firms with fifty or fewer employees that did not offer health care coverage. Withdrawals to cover out-of-pocket medical expenses were tax free and the money invested grew on a tax-deferred basis. Using MSA funds for any purpose unrelated to medical care or disability resulted in a 15% penalty. However, when MSA users reached age sixty-five, the money could be withdrawn for any purpose and was taxed at the same rate as ordinary income.

Supporters of MSAs believed consumers would be less likely to seek unnecessary or duplicative medical care if they knew they could keep the money left in their accounts for themselves at the end of the year. Experience demonstrated that MSAs could simultaneously help contain health care costs, allow consumers greater control and freedom of choice of health care providers, enable consumers to save for future medical and long-term care expenses, and improve access to medical care.

In February 2001 President Bush advocated more liberal rules governing MSAs and proposed making them permanently available to all eligible Americans. Congress reviewed the president's proposed reforms and during its 2001–02 session lowered the minimum annual deductible to increase the number of eligible Americans, allowed annual MSA contributions up to 65% of the maximum deductible for individuals and 75% for families, and extended the availability of MSAs through December 31, 2003.

The Medicare Modernization Act of 2003 included provisions to establish health savings accounts (HSAs) for the general population. Like the MSA program it replaced, HSA accounts offer a variety of benefits, including more choice, greater control, and individual ownership. Specific features of HSAs include:

- Permanence and portability

- Availability to all individuals with a qualified high-deductible plan

- Minimum deductible of $1,000 per individual plan and $2,000 per family plan

- Allowing annual contributions to equal 100% of the deductible

- Allowing both employer and employee contributions

- Not placing a cap on taxpayer participation

- Allowing tax-free rollover of up to $500 in unspent flexible spending accounts

As of 2008, HSAs enable individuals to deposit up to $2,900 ($5,800 for families) per year in the accounts tax-free, and the funds roll over from year to year. Funds can be withdrawn to pay for medical bills or saved for future needs, including retirement.

Pros and Cons of HSAs

Catherine Hoffman and Jennifer Tolbert of the Henry J. Kaiser Family Foundation reveal in *Health Savings Accounts and High Deductible Health Plans: Are They an Option for Low-Income Families?* (October 2006, http://www.kff.org/uninsured/upload/7568.pdf) that most low-income families do not benefit from consumer-directed coverage such as HSAs linked to high-deductible health plans because they already have low levels of tax liability. Furthermore, greater cost sharing may reduce health care utilization among people with low incomes, especially those with chronic conditions or disabilities and others with high-cost medical needs.

Nonetheless, America's Health Insurance Plans (AHIP), an industry trade association, indicates in *January 2008 Census Shows 6.1 Million People Covered by HSA/High-Deductible Health Plans* (April 2008, http://www.ahipresearch.org/pdfs/2008_HSA_Census.pdf) that by 2008, 6.1 million people had opened an HSA. This was an increase of 1.6 million since January 2007 and twice the number predicted in 2006. The AHIP notes that 27% of new enrollees in HDHPs paired with HSAs previously had been uninsured. HSA plan enrollment also varied by geography with the highest percentages in Minnesota (9.2%), Louisiana (9%), Washington, D.C. (8.7%), Vermont (7.5%), and Colorado (7.1%).

In *Health Savings Accounts: Participation Increased and Was More Common among Individuals with Higher Incomes* (April 2008, http://www.gao.gov/new.items/d08474r.pdf), the U.S. Government Accountability Office (GAO) confirms that in 2006 the number of U.S. residents enrolled in consumer-directed health plans combined with HSAs accounted for a small (2%) but growing share of the 202 million Americans with private health insurance. In 2005 people enrolled in HDHPs with HSAs had an average adjusted gross income of $139,000, compared to $57,000 for other taxpayers. The GAO also finds that more than four out of ten people who purchased high-deductible plans did not open HSAs, even though they were eligible to do so. People who did not open HSAs said they lacked information, could not afford to open them, or felt they did not need the accounts. The GAO attributes the rise in growth and popularity of consumer-directed plans to the rising cost of health care coverage.

Advocates of HSAs include not only President Bush but also the AHIP. They believe that by having consumers assume an increasing burden of escalating medical care costs, HSAs will stimulate comparison shopping for health care providers and services and competition that will ultimately reduce the rate at which costs are rising. According to M. P. McQueen, in "HSA Users Find Hassles Amid Savings" (*Wall Street Journal*, May 1, 2008), Karen Ignagni, the president and chief executive officer of AHIP, explains that "newer data indicate that individuals are not storing assets in these account but using them for health-care services."

However, other industry analysts question whether employer cost savings are the result of HSA enrollees' decisions to forgo needed medical care. According to McQueen, Michael Thompson, a principal at PricewaterhouseCoopers, asserts that "there is a lot of evidence that suggests that when patients pay a higher percentage of the cost of their care they get less of it."

Eric Sabo reports in "A Million Little Health Savings Accounts" (February 1, 2006, http://globalrph.healthology.com/healthcare/article788.htm) that Uwe Reinhardt, a health economist at Princeton University, believes HSAs will not solve the problems of the U.S. health care system. To date, shifting more expenses to consumers has neither reduced medical costs, nor has it substantially reduced the numbers of uninsured Americans. HSAs will not help the poor or near poor, which means that county hospitals, emergency departments, and the government will have to underwrite their care. The GAO confirms that as of 2008 the low- and middle-income Americans (who are the most likely to be uninsured) were not using HSAs. Instead, those with average incomes that are nearly three times those of average tax filers had embraced them.

HEALTH INSURANCE COSTS CONTINUE TO SKYROCKET

According to the Kaiser Foundation, in *Employer Health Insurance Costs and Worker Compensation* (March 2008, http://www.kff.org/insurance/snapshot/chcm030808oth.cfm), health insurance premiums continued to increase much faster than inflation and wages, growing a cumulative 78% between 2001 and 2007 and far outpacing cumulative wage growth of 19% during the same period. Premiums averaged $4,479 for individual coverage and $12,106 for family coverage. According to Gary Claxton et al., in *Employer Health Benefits: 2007 Annual Survey* (2007, http://www.kff.org/insurance/7672/upload/76723.pdf), in 2007 the average annual premium for a family was $12,106. Workers paid an average of $694 per year toward the premium for individual coverage and $3,281 per year toward the premium for family coverage, significantly higher than the amounts reported in 2006.

Claxton et al. find that most covered workers incur a separate deductible, co-payment, or coinsurance for each hospital admission. Annual deductibles for individual coverage ranged from $401 for HMO members to $1,729 for those in HDHPs. The majority (79%) of covered workers incurred co-payments for office visits and prescription drugs. Three-quarters of workers were enrolled in plans with co-payments for prescription drugs.

This increase was attributed to larger insurance claims resulting from higher prices for hospital care and prescription drugs, coupled with increasing consumer demand for, and utilization of, health care services. Claxton et al. indicate that 10% of employers offered workers a high-deductible plan in 2007. Firms with 1,000 or more workers were more likely to offer high-deductible plans (18%) than those with 3 to 999 employees (10%).

According to Claxton et al., 45% of firms said they were likely to increase the amount workers contribute to premiums, 42% would increase office visit cost sharing, 41% wanted to increase the amount employees pay for prescription drugs, and 37% planned to increase deductible amounts. Claxton et al. and other industry analysts observe that even though employers and employees benefited from continued moderation in the rate of premium increases, if there is no relief from premium increases soon, despite employers' stated reluctance to drop employee health care coverage, many may stop offering health benefits to their employees and some workers may be forced to drop their coverage because they are unable to contribute their share of the costs. Between 2000 and 2007 the percentage of employers offering health coverage declined from 69% to 60%. Industry observers and policy makers fear that this trend, fueled by rising insurance premiums, will swell the ranks of Americans without insurance coverage.

MENTAL HEALTH PARITY

In terms of mental health care, parity refers to the premise that the same range and scope of insurance benefits available for other illnesses should be provided for people with mental illness. Historically, private health insurance plans have provided less coverage for mental illness than for other medical conditions. Coverage for mental health was more restricted and often involved more cost sharing (higher co-payments and deductibles) than coverage for medical care. As a result, many patients with severe mental illness, who frequently required hospitalizations and other treatment, quickly depleted their mental health coverage.

The Center for Policy Alternatives explains in "Mental Health Parity" (2007, http://www.cfpa.org/issues/issue.cfm/issue/MentalHealthParity.xml) that during the 1990s there was growing interest in parity of mental health with other health services. The Mental Health Parity Act of 1996 sought to bring mental health benefits closer to other health benefits. The act amended the 1974 Employee Retirement Income Security Act and the 1944 Public Health Service Act by requiring parity for annual and lifetime dollar limits but did not place restrictions on other plan features such as hospital and office visit limits. It also imposed federal standards on the mental health coverage offered by employers through group health plans. By 2007 thirty-six state laws governing mental health parity were more compre-

hensive in scope than the federal legislation, and one-third of the states required full parity.

Attempts to Legislate Mental Health Parity in 2007 and 2008

On September 18, 2007, the Mental Health Parity Act of 2007 (S. 558) was unanimously passed by the U.S. Senate. The act would prohibit group health plans and group health insurance companies from imposing treatment limitations or financial requirements for coverage of mental health that are different from those used for medical and surgical benefits. On October 17, 2007, it was sent to the House Education and Labor and referred to the Subcommittee on Health, Employment, Labor, and Pensions. In the U.S. House of Representatives comparable legislation, the Paul Wellstone Mental Health and Addictions Equity Act (H.R. 1424), was passed on March 5, 2008.

In *Cost Estimate: S. 558 Mental Health Parity Act of 2007* (March 20, 2007, http://www.cbo.gov/ftpdocs/78xx/doc7894/s558.pdf), the Congressional Budget Office (CBO) estimates that passage of S. 558 would reduce federal tax revenues by $1 billion from 2009 to 2012 and by $3 billion from 2009 to 2017. The CBO further estimates that implementation of the bill would cost $322 million from 2008 to 2017.

The CBO estimates in *Cost Estimate: H.R. 1424 Paul Wellstone Mental Health and Addiction Equity Act of 2007* (November 21, 2007, http://www.cbo.gov/ftpdocs/88xx/doc8837/hr1424ec.pdf) that enactment of H.R. 1424 would reduce federal tax revenues by $1.1 billion from 2008 to 2012 and by $3.1 billion from 2009 to 2017. The bill would produce higher premiums for employer-sponsored health benefits, and higher premiums would result in more of an employee's compensation taking the form of nontaxable employer-paid premiums and less taxable wages. This in turn would reduce federal income and payroll tax revenues. The CBO estimates that implementation of the bill would cost $820 million from 2008 to 2017. Social Security payroll taxes would account for about 35% of these totals.

Opinions about the Costs of Parity

Critics of parity legislation express concern that the Mental Health Parity Act of 1996 will sharply increase costs. However, several studies, including those performed by the CBO, and projections made by private actuarial and accounting firms, forecast cost increases of about 1% for parity in terms of dollar limits.

Research conducted before the implementation of parity legislation estimated that the cost of providing the same level of outpatient mental health care would be about twice as much as for general medical care. As a result of these estimates, traditional indemnity (fee-for-service) insurers projected that providing insurance protection against the risks of mental illness would be substantially more costly than for other medical problems. Insurers also feared "adverse selection"—that plans with comprehensive mental health benefits would attract a disproportionate number of people with severe mental illness who would be costly to treat. Similarly, in the absence of mandated minimum mental health benefits, insurers could offer poor mental health benefits to deter people in need of treatment from enrolling in their plans.

Managed care plans may be as compelled as indemnity insurers to discourage people with potentially costly illnesses from enrolling in their plans; however, they have different utilization and cost controls than indemnity insurers. Rather than reducing the demand for services by increasing cost sharing, managed care regulates treatment decision making. For example, managed care plans may direct consumers to outpatient services as opposed to inpatient services or to peer counseling programs instead of mental health professionals. By controlling treatment and related services, managed care plans are able to extend coverage and benefits to more people at little or no additional cost.

Access to Care under Parity

In *Insurance Parity for Mental Health: Cost, Access, and Quality* (June 2000, http://www.nimh.nih.gov/publi cat/nimhparity.pdf), Ruth L. Kirschstein of the National Institutes of Health considers the effects of parity on costs, utilization, and access for employers with more than 150,000 employees. The four-year study that began one year before parity went into effect finds that by the third year of parity the proportion of people receiving mental health services grew from less than 5% to more than 7% and costs were reduced by half. The cost reductions were attributed to substantial declines in inpatient utilization, reduced lengths of stay, lower per diem (by the day) costs, and lower costs for mental health care for children and adolescents.

Kirschstein asserts that parity does not necessarily improve access to mental health care because managed care and behavioral health plans control access and counter some of the gains made as a result of parity. Managed

behavioral health "carve-out" arrangements appear to influence access by offering more people access to basic mental health care than what is available through traditional fee-for-service practice. To offset the costs of this increased access, these plans generally reduce the intensity of more costly services, primarily inpatient treatment and long-term psychotherapy.

PARITY MAY NOT SOLVE ALL ACCESS PROBLEMS. According to Richard G. Frank, Howard H. Goldman, and Thomas G. McGuire, in "Will Parity in Coverage Result in Better Mental Health Care?" (*New England Journal of Medicine*, vol. 345, no. 23, December 6, 2001), parity alone will not eliminate all obstacles to gaining access to mental health care. The researchers opine that most private insurance does not cover vital components of effective mental health services. For example, private insurance does not usually cover day-hospital programs, case management, psychosocial rehabilitation, or residential treatment, nor does it cover services such as supervised housing or supported employment. Frank, Goldman, and McGuire contend that true parity would require an expanded concept of health insurance and would necessitate coverage of all services deemed necessary for optimally effective mental health care.

Actual Effects of Federal Mental Health Parity Legislation on Employers

Howard H. Goldman et al. confirm in "Behavioral Health Insurance Parity for Federal Employees" (*New England Journal of Medicine*, vol. 354, no. 13, March 30, 2006) that costs are not likely to increase when workers are given the same coverage for mental health and substance abuse treatment as they are for other medical care. The researchers consider seven Federal Employees Health Benefits plans that offer mental health and substance abuse benefits on a par with medical benefits beginning in January 2001. Among people who used mental health services, spending attributable to parity decreased significantly for three plans and did not change significantly for the four remaining plans. The institution of parity was also associated with significant reductions in out-of-pocket spending in five of the seven plans. Goldman et al. conclude that offering parity "can improve insurance protection without increasing total costs."

CHAPTER 7

INTERNATIONAL COMPARISONS OF HEALTH CARE

International comparisons are often difficult to interpret because definitions of terms and reliability of data as well as cultures and values differ. What is important in one society may be unimportant or even nonexistent in another. A political or human right that is important in one nation may be meaningless in a neighboring state. Evaluating the quality of health care systems is an example of the difficulties involved in comparing one culture to another.

Even within the United States there are cultural and regional variations in health care delivery. A visit to a busy urban urgent care center might begin with the patient completing a brief medical history, followed by five or ten minutes with a nurse who measures and records the patient's vital signs (pulse, respiration, and temperature), and conclude with a fifteen-minute visit during which the physician diagnoses the problem and prescribes treatment. In contrast, on the islands of Hawaii, a visit with a healer may last several hours and culminate with a prayer, song, or an embrace. Hawaiian healers, called kahunas, are unhurried and offer an array of herbal remedies, bodywork (massage, touch, and manipulative therapies), and talk therapies (counseling and guidance), because they believe that the healing quality of the encounter, independent of any treatment offered, improves health and well-being.

Even though comparing the performance of health care systems and health outcomes (how people fare as a result of receiving health care services) is of benefit to health care planners, administrators, and policy makers, the subjective nature of such assessments should be duly considered.

A COMPARISON OF HEALTH CARE SPENDING, RESOURCES, AND UTILIZATION

The Organization for Economic Cooperation and Development (OECD) provides information about, and to, thirty member countries that are governed democratically and participate in the global market economy. It collects and publishes data about a wide range of economic and social issues including health and health care policy. The OECD member nations are generally considered the wealthier, more developed nations in the world. The OECD (2008, http://www.oecd.org/document/58/0,3343,en_2649 _34483_1889402_1_1_1_1,00.html) notes that its member countries are Australia, Austria, Belgium, Canada, the Czech Republic, Denmark, Finland, France, Germany, Greece, Hungary, Iceland, Ireland, Italy, Japan, Korea, Luxembourg, Mexico, the Netherlands, New Zealand, Norway, Poland, Portugal, the Slovak Republic, Spain, Sweden, Switzerland, Turkey, the United Kingdom, and the United States.

Percentage of Gross Domestic Product Spent on Health Care

Even though health has always been a concern for Americans, the growth in the health care industry since the mid-1970s has made it a major factor in the U.S. economy. For many years the United States has spent a larger proportion of its gross domestic product (GDP; the total market value of final goods and services produced within an economy in a given year) on health care than have other nations with similar economic development. In 2005 U.S. health expenditures were 15.3% of the GDP, the highest rate in the OECD. (See Figure 7.1.) Other nations that spent large percentages of GDP on health care in 2003 included Switzerland (11.6%), France (11.1%), Germany (10.7%), Belgium (10.3%), Portugal (10.2%), Austria (10.2%), Greece (10.1), Canada (9.8%), Iceland (9.5%), and Australia (9.5%). Of the member nations that reported health care expenditure data in 2005, Korea (6%), Poland (6.2%), Mexico (6.4%), and the Slovak Republic (7.1%) spent the least in the OECD.

Per Capita Spending on Health Care

In 2005 the United States also experienced the highest per capita spending for health care services, spending an average of $6,401 per citizen. (See Figure 7.2.) No

FIGURE 7.1

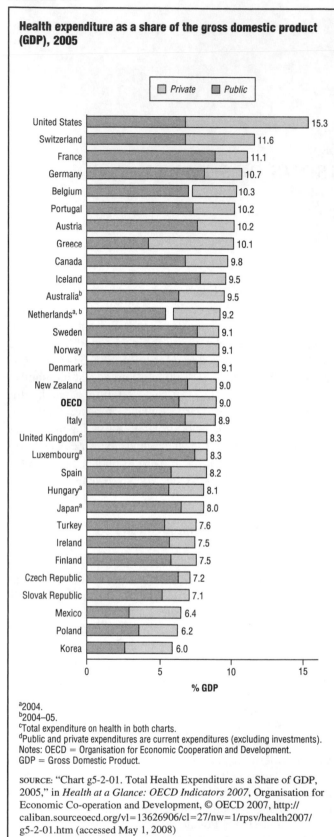

Health expenditure as a share of the gross domestic product (GDP), 2005

Legend: □ Private ■ Public

Country	% GDP
United States	15.3
Switzerland	11.6
France	11.1
Germany	10.7
Belgium	10.3
Portugal	10.2
Austria	10.2
Greece	10.1
Canada	9.8
Iceland	9.5
Australia[b]	9.5
Netherlands[a, b]	9.2
Sweden	9.1
Norway	9.1
Denmark	9.1
New Zealand	9.0
OECD	9.0
Italy	8.9
United Kingdom[c]	8.3
Luxembourg[a]	8.3
Spain	8.2
Hungary[a]	8.1
Japan[a]	8.0
Turkey	7.6
Ireland	7.5
Finland	7.5
Czech Republic	7.2
Slovak Republic	7.1
Mexico	6.4
Poland	6.2
Korea	6.0

% GDP

[a]2004.
[b]2004–05.
[c]Total expenditure on health in both charts.
[d]Public and private expenditures are current expenditures (excluding investments).
Notes: OECD = Organisation for Economic Cooperation and Development.
GDP = Gross Domestic Product.

SOURCE: "Chart g5-2-01. Total Health Expenditure as a Share of GDP, 2005," in *Health at a Glance: OECD Indicators 2007*, Organisation for Economic Co-operation and Development, © OECD 2007, http://caliban.sourceoecd.org/vl=13626906/cl=27/nw=1/rpsv/health2007/g5-2-01.htm (accessed May 1, 2008)

Iceland, $3,443; Belgium, $3,389; France, $3,374; Canada, $3,326; Germany, $3,287; and Australia, $3,128. In 2005 Turkey spent the least per capita of any OECD nation on health care ($586), followed by Mexico ($675), Poland ($867), and the Slovak Republic ($1,137).

Who Pays for Health Care?

Public expenditures for health care services, as a percentage of GDP, vary widely between the OECD member nations. Public spending on health accounted for about 73% of total health spending on average across OECD countries in 2005, and the remaining 27% of spending was paid by private sources, mainly private insurance and individuals. (See Figure 7.3.) In the United States public funding accounted for 45% of total health spending. By contrast, public sources in Luxembourg and the Czech Republic accounted for 91% and 89%, respectively, of total health spending. Other nations with above-average contributions of public funding to health expenditures included the United Kingdom (87%), Sweden (85%), Denmark (84%), Norway (84%), Iceland (83%), Japan (82%), France (80%), New Zealand (78%), Ireland (78%), Finland (78%), and Germany (77%). Public expenditures on health per capita were lowest in Greece (43%) the United States (45%), Mexico (45%), Korea (53%), and Switzerland (60%).

Of the OECD nations that reported out-of-pocket payments as a share of total health expenditures in 2005, the United States was slightly below average, at 13%. (See Figure 7.4.) In the Netherlands, France, and Luxembourg, out-of-pocket payments as a share of total health expenditures were 10% or less. In contrast, out-of-pocket spending as a share of total health care spending was 57% in Greece and 51% in Mexico. Figure 7.4 reveals that out-of-pocket spending as a share of total health care spending was also high in Korea, Switzerland, Poland, and Hungary.

Private health insurance fills the gap between public expenditures and out-of-pocket costs. Among the OECD countries declaring private insurance as a percentage of total expenditures for health in 2005, the United States far exceeded the others. At 37%, the U.S. private insurance expenditure was nearly two times that of the Netherlands (20%) and far outstripped all other countries. (See Figure 7.4.) Because the United States is the only developed country without a national health care program, U.S. private insurance expenditures cover the costs generally assumed by government programs that finance health care delivery in comparable OECD member nations.

Spending for Hospitalization and Pharmaceutical Drugs

Interestingly, even though the United States spent more on health care than other OECD nations in 2005, it devoted a smaller percentage of total health expendi-

other country came close to spending this amount per capita in 2005: Luxembourg spent $5,352 per citizen; Norway, $4,364; Switzerland, $4,177; Austria, $3,519;

FIGURE 7.2

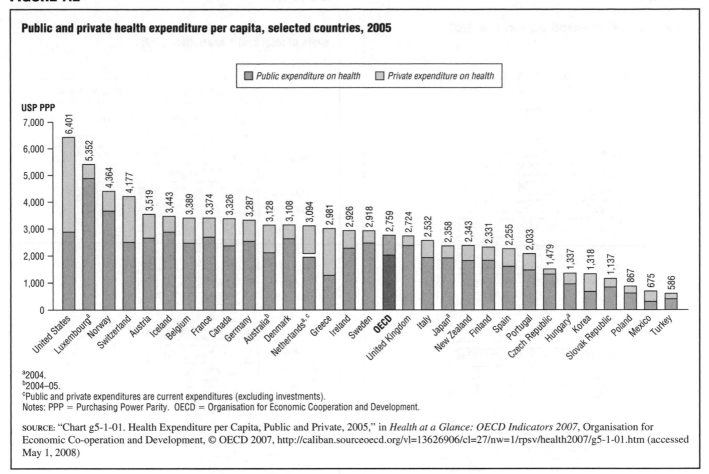

Public and private health expenditure per capita, selected countries, 2005

a2004.
b2004–05.
cPublic and private expenditures are current expenditures (excluding investments).
Notes: PPP = Purchasing Power Parity. OECD = Organisation for Economic Cooperation and Development.

SOURCE: "Chart g5-1-01. Health Expenditure per Capita, Public and Private, 2005," in *Health at a Glance: OECD Indicators 2007*, Organisation for Economic Co-operation and Development, © OECD 2007, http://caliban.sourceoecd.org/vl=13626906/cl=27/nw=1/rpsv/health2007/g5-1-01.htm (accessed May 1, 2008)

tures (30%) to inpatient curative-rehabilitative care (acute and rehabilitation hospital stays) than all the other countries in 2005. (See Figure 7.5.) This finding is attributable to lower rates of hospitalization, shorter average lengths of stay, and a rise in outpatient hospital and other ambulatory care services in the United States.

In 2005 the United States spent much more per person ($792) on pharmaceutical drugs than any other OECD country. (See Figure 7.6.) Per capita pharmaceutical spending was also high in Canada ($589), France ($554), Spain ($517), Italy ($509), Germany ($498), and Luxembourg ($465). In contrast, Mexico spent $144 and Poland $243 per capita on pharmaceuticals.

Hospital Utilization Statistics

The number of acute hospital beds is a gross measure of resource availability; however, it is important to remember that it does not reflect capacity to provide emergency or outpatient hospital care. In general, it also does not measure the number of beds devoted to nonacute or other long-term care, although it is known that in Japan many of the beds designated as acute care are actually used for long-term care. Of the OECD countries reporting acute care hospital beds per 1,000 population, Japan (8.2), Korea (6.5), Germany (6.4), Austria (6.1),

and the Czech Republic (5.7) had the highest number of acute care beds in 2005. (See Figure 7.7.) The United States was among the lowest, at 2.7 beds per 1,000 population in 2005, trailed only by Spain (2.6), Sweden (2.2), Turkey (2), and Mexico (1).

Hospital lengths of stay have consistently declined since 1960, in part because increasing numbers of illnesses can be treated as effectively in outpatient settings and because many countries have reduced inpatient hospitalization rates and average length of stay (ALOS) to control health care costs. In 2005 Japan had the longest acute care ALOS of the OECD nations, at (19.8 days), followed by Korea (10.6 days), and Germany (8.6 days), Switzerland (8.5 days), and the Czech Republic (8 days). (See Figure 7.8.) The shortest hospital stays in 2005 occurred in Denmark (3.5 days), Mexico (4 days), and Sweden (4.6 days). The United States' ALOS was 5.6 days in 2005, which was on par with France and Iceland, both at 5.4 days.

Medical practice, particularly the types and frequency of procedures performed, also varies from one country to another. The OECD looked at rates of cesarean section (delivery of a baby through an incision in the abdomen as opposed to vaginal delivery) per one hundred births

FIGURE 7.3

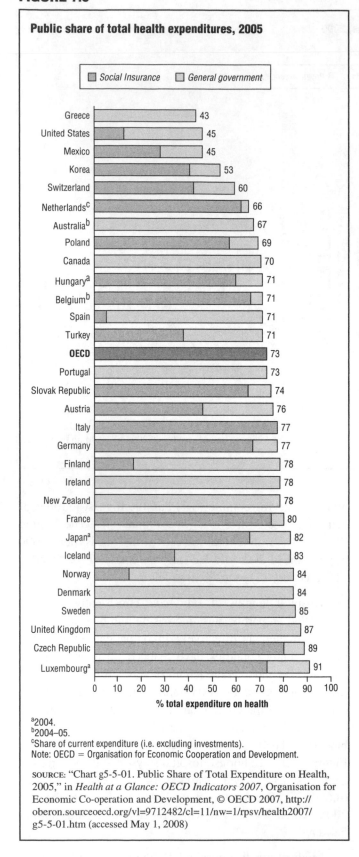

Public share of total health expenditures, 2005

☐ Social Insurance   ☐ General government

% total expenditure on health

[a]2004.
[b]2004–05.
[c]Share of current expenditure (i.e. excluding investments).
Note: OECD = Organisation for Economic Cooperation and Development.

SOURCE: "Chart g5-5-01. Public Share of Total Expenditure on Health, 2005," in *Health at a Glance: OECD Indicators 2007*, Organisation for Economic Co-operation and Development, © OECD 2007, http://oberon.sourceoecd.org/vl=9712482/cl=11/nw=1/rpsv/health2007/g5-5-01.htm (accessed May 1, 2008)

FIGURE 7.4

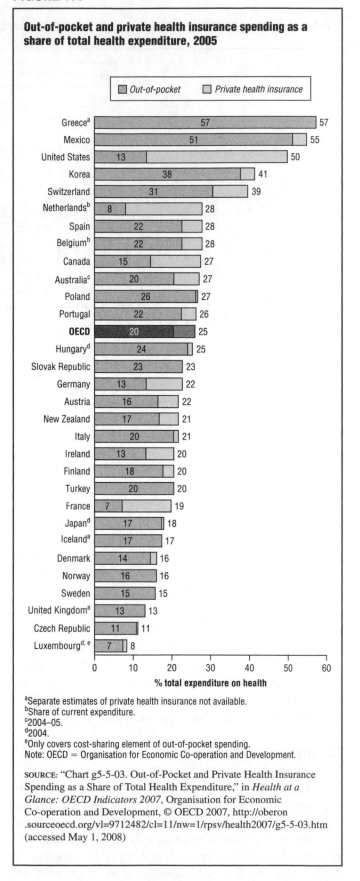

Out-of-pocket and private health insurance spending as a share of total health expenditure, 2005

☐ Out-of-pocket   ☐ Private health insurance

% total expenditure on health

[a]Separate estimates of private health insurance not available.
[b]Share of current expenditure.
[c]2004–05.
[d]2004.
[e]Only covers cost-sharing element of out-of-pocket spending.
Note: OECD = Organisation for Economic Co-operation and Development.

SOURCE: "Chart g5-5-03. Out-of-Pocket and Private Health Insurance Spending as a Share of Total Health Expenditure," in *Health at a Glance: OECD Indicators 2007*, Organisation for Economic Co-operation and Development, © OECD 2007, http://oberon.sourceoecd.org/vl=9712482/cl=11/nw=1/rpsv/health2007/g5-5-03.htm (accessed May 1, 2008)

and found both growth in the rates of cesarean section (as a percentage of all births) and considerable variation in the rates for this surgical procedure. In 2004 the highest rates

for cesarean sections per 100 live births were reported in Mexico (37.9), Italy (37.5), Korea (35.2), Australia (29.1),

FIGURE 7.5

FIGURE 7.6

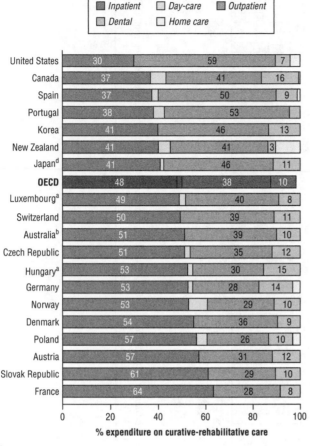

Curative-rehabilitative expenditures by site of care, 2005

Legend: Inpatient, Day-care, Outpatient, Dental, Home care

% expenditure on curative-rehabilitative care

aExcluding dental care.
b2004.
Note: OECD = Organisation for Economic Co-operation and Development.

SOURCE: "Chart g5-3-02. Curative-Rehabilitative Expenditure by Mode of Production, 2005," in *Health at a Glance: OECD Indicators 2007*, Organisation for Economic Co-operation and Development, © OECD 2007, http://puck.sourceoecd.org/vl=10591543/cl=11/nw=1/rpsv/health 2007/g5-3-02.htm (accessed May 1, 2008)

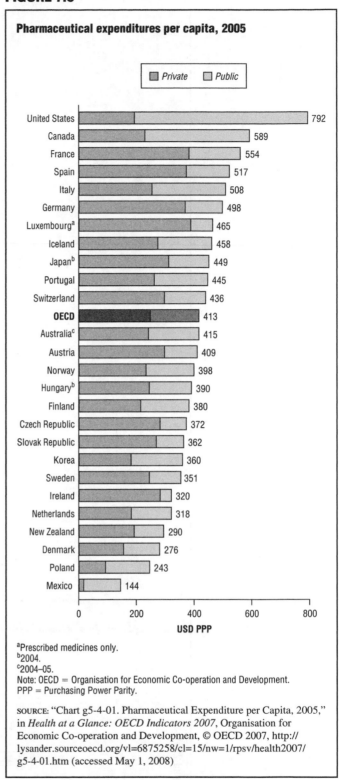

Pharmaceutical expenditures per capita, 2005

Legend: Private, Public

USD PPP

aPrescribed medicines only.
b2004.
c2004–05.
Note: OECD = Organisation for Economic Co-operation and Development.
PPP = Purchasing Power Parity.

SOURCE: "Chart g5-4-01. Pharmaceutical Expenditure per Capita, 2005," in *Health at a Glance: OECD Indicators 2007*, Organisation for Economic Co-operation and Development, © OECD 2007, http:// lysander.sourceoecd.org/vl=6875258/cl=15/nw=1/rpsv/health2007/ g5-4-01.htm (accessed May 1, 2008)

the United States (29.1), and Luxembourg (27.2). (See Figure 7.9.) Because cesarean section is performed in the hospital and generally involves at least an overnight stay, the frequency with which it and other surgical procedures are performed contributes to hospitalization rates and expenditures.

Physicians' Numbers Are Increasing

Since 1960 the OECD member nations have all enjoyed growing physician populations. In 2005 Greece and Belgium reported the highest ratio of practicing physicians, 4.9 and 4 per 1,000 population, respectively, with most countries ranging between 2 and 4 physicians per 1,000 population. (See Figure 7.10.) The countries that had the fewest practicing physicians were in Turkey (1.5 per 1,000 population), followed by Korea (1.6),

Mexico (1.8), and Japan (2). The United States, the United Kingdom, and Finland all reported data showing 2.4 physicians per 1,000 population.

The ratio of physicians to population is a limited measure of health care quality, because many other factors, such as the availability of other health care providers as well as accessibility and affordability of health care

FIGURE 7.7

Acute care hospital beds, 1990 and 2005

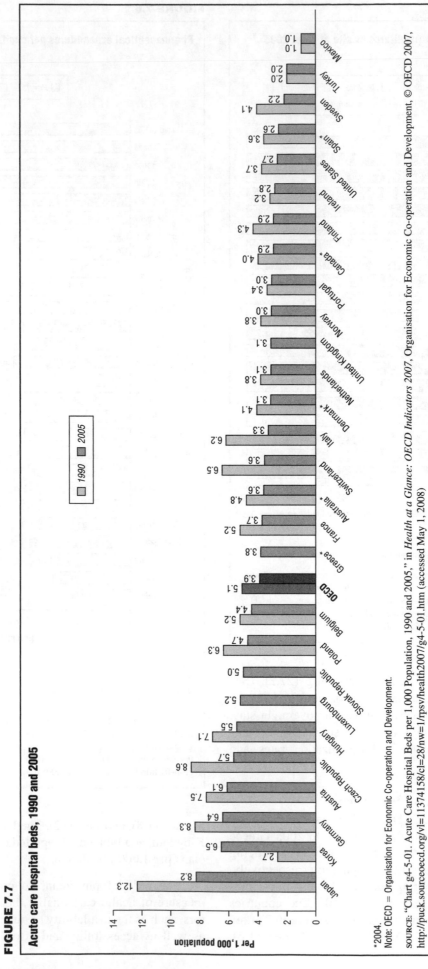

*2004.

Note: OECD = Organisation for Economic Co-operation and Development.

SOURCE: "Chart g4-5-01. Acute Care Hospital Beds per 1,000 Population, 1990 and 2005," in *Health at a Glance: OECD Indicators 2007*, Organisation for Economic Co-operation and Development, © OECD 2007, http://puck.sourceoecd.org/vl=11374158/cl=28/nw=1/rpsv/health2007/g4-5-01.htm (accessed May 1, 2008)

FIGURE 7.8

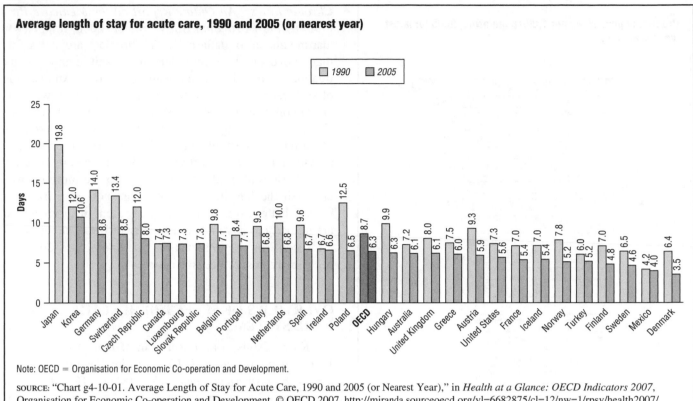

Average length of stay for acute care, 1990 and 2005 (or nearest year)

Note: OECD = Organisation for Economic Co-operation and Development.

SOURCE: "Chart g4-10-01. Average Length of Stay for Acute Care, 1990 and 2005 (or Nearest Year)," in *Health at a Glance: OECD Indicators 2007*, Organisation for Economic Co-operation and Development, © OECD 2007, http://miranda.sourceoecd.org/vl=6682875/cl=12/nw=1/rpsv/health2007/g4-10-01.htm (accessed May 1, 2008)

FIGURE 7.9

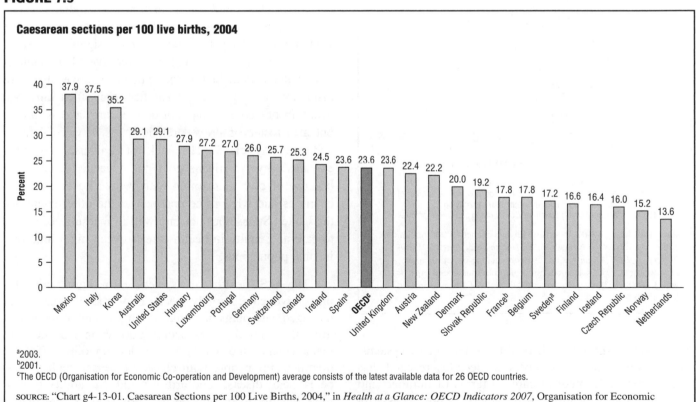

Caesarean sections per 100 live births, 2004

[a]2003.
[b]2001.
[c]The OECD (Organisation for Economic Co-operation and Development) average consists of the latest available data for 26 OECD countries.

SOURCE: "Chart g4-13-01. Caesarean Sections per 100 Live Births, 2004," in *Health at a Glance: OECD Indicators 2007*, Organisation for Economic Co-operation and Development, © OECD 2007, http://caliban.sourceoecd.org/vl=4089754/cl=26/nw=1/rpsv/health2007/g4-13-01.htm (accessed May 1, 2008)

FIGURE 7.10

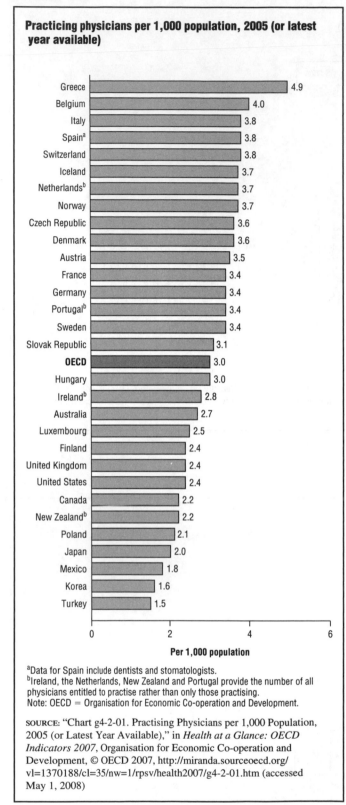

Practicing physicians per 1,000 population, 2005 (or latest year available)

Country	Per 1,000 population
Greece	4.9
Belgium	4.0
Italy	3.8
Spain[a]	3.8
Switzerland	3.8
Iceland	3.7
Netherlands[b]	3.7
Norway	3.7
Czech Republic	3.6
Denmark	3.6
Austria	3.5
France	3.4
Germany	3.4
Portugal[b]	3.4
Sweden	3.4
Slovak Republic	3.1
OECD	3.0
Hungary	3.0
Ireland[b]	2.8
Australia	2.7
Luxembourg	2.5
Finland	2.4
United Kingdom	2.4
United States	2.4
Canada	2.2
New Zealand[b]	2.2
Poland	2.1
Japan	2.0
Mexico	1.8
Korea	1.6
Turkey	1.5

Per 1,000 population

[a]Data for Spain include dentists and stomatologists.
[b]Ireland, the Netherlands, New Zealand and Portugal provide the number of all physicians entitled to practise rather than only those practising.
Note: OECD = Organisation for Economic Co-operation and Development.

SOURCE: "Chart g4-2-01. Practising Physicians per 1,000 Population, 2005 (or Latest Year Available)," in *Health at a Glance: OECD Indicators 2007*, Organisation for Economic Co-operation and Development, © OECD 2007, http://miranda.sourceoecd.org/vl=1370188/cl=35/nw=1/rpsv/health2007/g4-2-01.htm (accessed May 1, 2008)

services, also influence the quality of health care systems. Furthermore, during the last two decades research has shown that more medical care, in terms of numbers and concentration of health care providers, is not necessarily linked to better health status for the population. John E. Wennberg et al. of the Dartmouth Atlas of Health Care

Working Group find in *The Care of Patients with Severe Chronic Illness: An Online Report on the Medicare Program by the Dartmouth Atlas Project* (2006, http://www.dartmouthatlas.org/atlases/2006_Chronic_Care_Atlas.pdf) that an oversupply of providers may result in unnecessary treatment, procedures, and health care costs. An example of such research is the Dartmouth Atlas Project, which is an ongoing examination of information and analysis about national, regional, and local markets, as well as of individual hospitals and their affiliated physicians, to provide a basis for improving health and health systems. Wennberg et al. find that patients who see more doctors and visit the hospital more often are not more likely to receive better care, have no improvement in survival, and are unlikely to have a better quality of life. The researchers reconfirm the observation that more care does not necessarily ensure better outcomes.

OVERVIEWS OF SELECTED HEALTH CARE SYSTEMS

Karen Davis et al. observe in *Mirror, Mirror on the Wall: An International Update on the Comparative Performance of American Health Care* (May 2007, http://www.commonwealthfund.org/usr_doc/1027_Davis_mirror_mirror_international_update_final.pdf?section=4039) that despite having the most costly health system in the world, the United States does not compare favorably to other countries on most dimensions of performance.

Davis et al. look at six nations: Australia, Canada, Germany, New Zealand, the United Kingdom, and the United States. They find that the most significant difference between the United States and the five other countries is that the United States does not have universal health insurance coverage. The researchers opine that universal health insurance coverage not only ensures access to care but also fosters improved relationships between patients and the physicians. The lack of universal coverage explains why Americans go without needed health care because of cost more often than people do in the other countries and why, in comparison to the other countries, the United States does not fare well in measures of access to care and equity in health care between high- and low-income populations.

The U.S. health care system earns high marks for preventive care, largely because of the emphasis that managed care plans have placed on preventive medicine. Still, the United States scores poorly on chronic care management—the ability to provide ongoing, effective treatment for people with chronic diseases such as diabetes, heart disease, and arthritis and "its ability to promote healthy lives, and on the provision of care that is safe and coordinated, as well as accessible, efficient, and equitable."

Other key findings include:

- The other countries are ahead of the United States in using information technology.

- Germany had the highest scores on access to care, especially on nights and weekends as well as on the ability of primary care practices to make arrangements for patients to receive care after-hours when medical offices are closed.

- Americans with health insurance have timely access to specialized health care services. In the United Kingdom and Canada, patients often endure long wait times for specialized services. The United States and Canada rank lowest on the prompt scheduling of appointments with physicians, with patients more likely to report waiting six or more days for an appointment.

- The United States ranks last among the six countries in terms of efficient delivery of health care, with the United Kingdom and New Zealand in first and second place, respectively. Along with poor scores on measures of national health expenditures and administrative costs, the United States lagged behind in its use of multidisciplinary teams to deliver health care services. In Germany and New Zealand, patients who could be treated in a physician's office were less likely to use an emergency room for care than those in the United States.

- The United States came in last on three key indicators of healthy lives: deaths that could have been prevented with timely, effective care; infant mortality; and healthy life expectancy. The United States and the United Kingdom had much higher death rates from conditions amenable to medical care—as much as 25% to 50% higher than Canada and Australia. Australia ranks highest on healthy lives, scoring first or second on all the indicators.

The United States

The U.S. health care financing system is based on the consumer sovereignty, or private insurance, model. Employer-based health insurance is tax subsidized—that is, health insurance premiums are a tax-deductible business expense and are not generally taxed as employee compensation. The premiums for individually purchased policies purchased by self-employed Americans became fully tax deductible in 2003. Benefits, premiums, and provider reimbursement methods differ among private insurance plans and among public programs as well.

Most physicians who provide both ambulatory care (hospital outpatient service and office visits) and inpatient hospital care are generally reimbursed on either a fee-for-service basis or per capita (literally, per head, but in managed care frequently per member per month), and

payment rates vary among insurers. Increasing numbers of physicians are salaried; they are employees of the government, hospital, and health care delivery systems, universities, and private industry.

The nation's hospitals are paid on the basis of charges, costs, negotiated rates, or diagnosis-related groups, depending on the patient's insurer. There are no overall global budgets or expenditure limits. Nevertheless, managed care (oversight by some group or authority to verify the medical necessity of treatments and to control the cost of health care) has assumed an expanding role. Health maintenance organizations, preferred provider organizations, and other managed care plans and payers (government and private health insurance) now exert greater control over the practices of individual health care providers in an effort to control costs. To the extent that they govern reimbursement, managed care organizations are viewed by many physicians and other industry observers as dictating the methods, terms, and quality of health care delivery.

IS THE UNITED STATES SPENDING MORE AND GETTING LESS? A primary indicator of the quality of health care delivery in any nation is the health status of its people. Many factors can affect the health of individuals and populations: heredity, race and ethnicity, gender, income, education, geography, violent crime, environmental agents, and exposure to infectious diseases, as well as access to and availability of health care services.

Still, in the nation that spends the most on the health of its citizens, it seems reasonable to expect to see tangible benefits of expenditures for health care—that is, measurable gains in health status. This section considers three health outcomes (measures used to assess the health of a population)—life expectancy at birth, infant mortality, and the incidence of cancer—to determine the extent to which U.S. citizens derive health benefits from record-high outlays for medical care.

Overall, life expectancy at birth consistently increased in all thirty OECD member nations since 1960; however, historically, U.S. life expectancy has remained slightly below the OECD median (half were higher and half were lower). (See Figure 7.11.) Infant mortality also declined sharply during this period, but the United States fared far worse than most OECD countries—in 2005 the United States had the fourth-highest infant mortality rate. (See Figure 7.12.) Despite the well-funded U.S. battle against cancer, in 2004 the United States came in seventh for its cancer mortality rates (140 deaths of females and 203 deaths of males per 100,000 population). (See Figure 7.13.) Finally, one OECD finding that is surprising in view of the low rank of the United States on many measures and indicators of health status is that after New Zealand, the United States boasts the highest percentage of adults

FIGURE 7.11

FIGURE 7.12

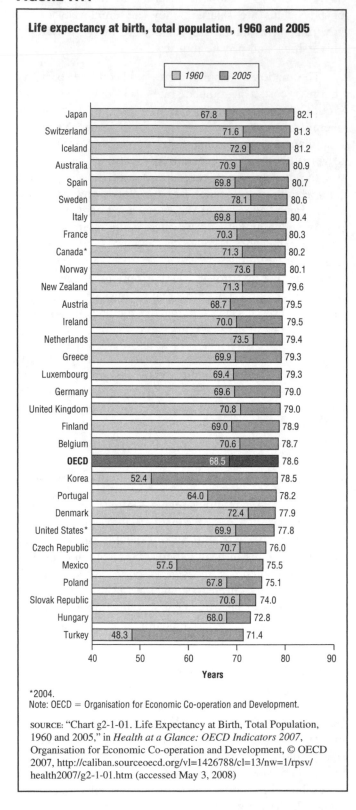

Life expectancy at birth, total population, 1960 and 2005

□ 1960　■ 2005

Country	1960	2005
Japan	67.8	82.1
Switzerland	71.6	81.3
Iceland	72.9	81.2
Australia	70.9	80.9
Spain	69.8	80.7
Sweden	78.1	80.6
Italy	69.8	80.4
France	70.3	80.3
Canada*	71.3	80.2
Norway	73.6	80.1
New Zealand	71.3	79.6
Austria	68.7	79.5
Ireland	70.0	79.5
Netherlands	73.5	79.4
Greece	69.9	79.3
Luxembourg	69.4	79.3
Germany	69.6	79.0
United Kingdom	70.8	79.0
Finland	69.0	78.9
Belgium	70.6	78.7
OECD	68.5	78.6
Korea	52.4	78.5
Portugal	64.0	78.2
Denmark	72.4	77.9
United States*	69.9	77.8
Czech Republic	70.7	76.0
Mexico	57.5	75.5
Poland	67.8	75.1
Slovak Republic	70.6	74.0
Hungary	68.0	72.8
Turkey	48.3	71.4

Years

*2004.
Note: OECD = Organisation for Economic Co-operation and Development.

SOURCE: "Chart g2-1-01. Life Expectancy at Birth, Total Population, 1960 and 2005," in *Health at a Glance: OECD Indicators 2007*, Organisation for Economic Co-operation and Development, © OECD 2007, http://caliban.sourceoecd.org/vl=1426788/cl=13/nw=1/rpsv/health2007/g2-1-01.htm (accessed May 3, 2008)

Infant mortality rates, 2005

Country	Deaths per 1,000 live births
Iceland	2.3
Sweden	2.4
Luxembourg	2.6
Japan	2.8
Finland	3.0
Norway	3.1
Czech Republic	3.4
Portugal	3.5
France	3.6
Belgium	3.7
Greece	3.8
Germany	3.9
Ireland	4.0
Spain	4.1
Switzerland	4.2
Austria	4.2
Denmark	4.4
Italy	4.7
Netherlands	4.9
Australia	5.0
United Kingdom	5.1
New Zealand	5.1
Korea[a]	5.3
Canada[b]	5.3
OECD	5.4
Hungary	6.2
Poland	6.4
United States[b]	6.8
Slovak Republic	7.2
Mexico	18.8
Turkey	23.6

Deaths per 1,000 live births

[a]In Canada, Japan, the United States and some of the Nordic countries, very premature babies with a low chance of survival are registered as live births, resulting in higher reported rates compared to countries that do not do so.
[b]2002.
Note: OECD = Organisation for Economic Co-operation and Development.

SOURCE: "Chart g2-8-01. Infant Mortality Rates, 2005," in *Health at a Glance: OECD Indicators 2007*, Organisation for Economic Co-operation and Development, © OECD 2007, http://lysander.sourceoecd.org/vl=2300343/cl=26/nw=1/rpsv/health2007/g2-8-01.htm (accessed May 3, 2008)

(89%) who consider themselves to be in good health. (See Figure 7.14.)

Cathy Schoen et al. find in "Toward Higher-Performance Health Systems: Adults' Health Care Experiences in Seven Countries, 2007" (*Health Affairs* vol. 26, no. 6, October 31, 2007), a seven-nation survey of Australia, Canada,

Germany, the Netherlands, New Zealand, the United Kingdom, and the United States, wide-ranging differences in access, after-hours care, and coordination but also common concerns.

In 2007 U.S. health care consumers faced the highest out-of-pocket costs, were least able to schedule timely

FIGURE 7.13

Cancer mortality rates for males and females, 2004

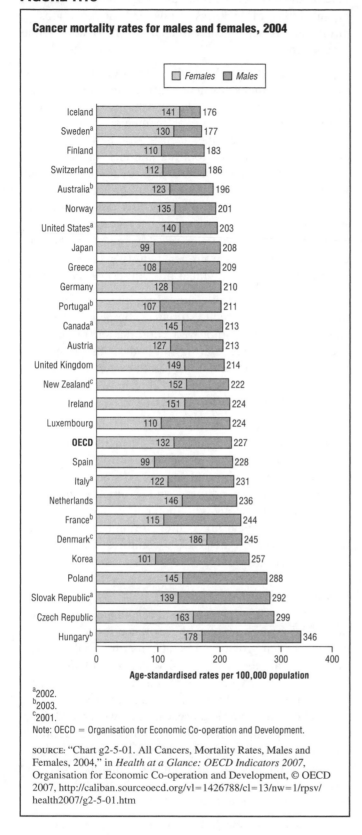

a 2002.
b 2003.
c 2001.
Note: OECD = Organisation for Economic Co-operation and Development.

SOURCE: "Chart g2-5-01. All Cancers, Mortality Rates, Males and Females, 2004," in *Health at a Glance: OECD Indicators 2007*, Organisation for Economic Co-operation and Development, © OECD 2007, http://caliban.sourceoecd.org/vl=1426788/cl=13/nw=1/rpsv/ health2007/g2-5-01.htm

FIGURE 7.14

Percentage of adults who say they are in good health, 2005

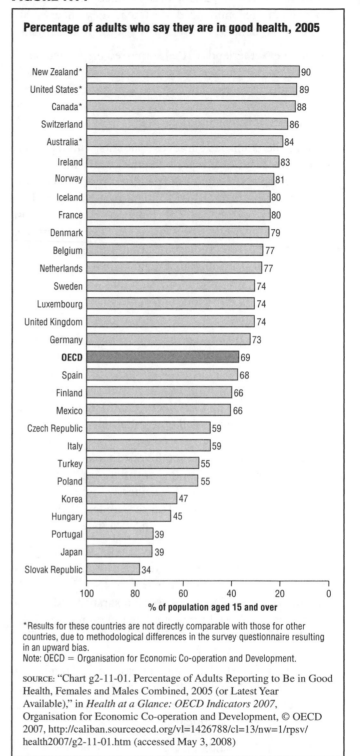

*Results for these countries are not directly comparable with those for other countries, due to methodological differences in the survey questionnaire resulting in an upward bias.
Note: OECD = Organisation for Economic Co-operation and Development.

SOURCE: "Chart g2-11-01. Percentage of Adults Reporting to Be in Good Health, Females and Males Combined, 2005 (or Latest Year Available)," in *Health at a Glance: OECD Indicators 2007*, Organisation for Economic Co-operation and Development, © OECD 2007, http://caliban.sourceoecd.org/vl=1426788/cl=13/nw=1/rpsv/ health2007/g2-11-01.htm (accessed May 3, 2008)

appointments with their physicians, and along with Canadians were the most likely to seek nonemergency care in emergency rooms. They reported the highest rates of safety issues including lab test errors, medical or medication errors, medical record and test delays, perceptions

of waste, and excessive time devoted to administrative paperwork. There were also many examples of inefficiencies and uncoordinated, fragmented care including:

• Twenty-three percent of Americans—the highest rate of any country in the survey—said they experienced coordination problems, either unavailability of medical records during physician office visits or duplication of tests

- Twenty percent of Americans recounted instances when physicians recommended treatment they thought had little or no benefit; this rate was also high in Germany

- Only the Netherlands (31%) surpassed the United States (24%) for patient reports of time spent on paperwork or resolving disputes related to medical bills or insurance. In the other countries, fewer than 15% of patients expressed this concern.

In all the countries surveyed, patients with a primary source of medical care reported significantly more favorable experiences, including spending more time with their physicians, greater involvement in health care decision making, and better coordination of care. These patients were also much less likely to have experienced medical errors, received conflicting information from different doctors, or found that diagnostic tests or medical records were unavailable at the time of care.

Germany

The German health care system is based on the social insurance model. Statutory sickness funds and private insurance cover the entire population. In "Health Care in Germany" (2005, http://www.civitas.org.uk/pubs/bb3 Germany.php), David G. Green, Ben Irvine, and Ben Cackett state that 90% of the population receives health care through the country's statutory health insurance program. Employees and employers finance these sickness funds through payroll contributions. Nearly all employers, including small businesses and low-wage industries, must participate. The remainder of the population is covered by private health insurance.

During the late 1990s Germany had the second-highest per capita health care expenditures, but by 2005 it ranked tenth in health expenditures per capita. (See Figure 7.2.) Public funds, a combination of social insurance and general government funds, paid for more than three-quarters (77%) of total expenditures for health care. (See Figure 7.3.) According to the OECD, in *Health at a Glance: OECD Indicators 2007* (2007, http://miranda.sourceoecd.org/vl=360 4819/cl=25/nw=1/rpsv/health2007/g5-5-02.htm), 79% of all medical care expenditures were publicly funded, as were 73% of pharmaceuticals.

Unlike U.S. health insurance, which is not always portable, losing or changing jobs does not affect health insurance protection in Germany among the sickness fund members. The German government does not require its wealthiest citizens to purchase health insurance, but almost all of them do so voluntarily.

Ambulatory (outpatient) and inpatient care operate in completely separate spheres in the German health care system. German hospitals are public and private, operate for profit and not-for-profit, and generally do not have outpatient departments. Ambulatory care physicians are paid on the basis of fee schedules negotiated between the organizations of sickness funds and organizations of physicians. A separate fee schedule for private patients uses a similar scale.

In 1993 Germany's Health Care Reform Law went into effect. Among its many provisions, the law tied increases in physician, dental, and hospital expenditures to the income growth rate of members of the sickness funds. It also limited the licensing of new ambulatory care physicians (based on the number of physicians already in an area) and set a cap for overall pharmaceutical outlays. Still, in 2005 Germany boasted 3.4 practicing physicians per 1,000 population, a higher ratio than well over half the OECD countries reporting. (See Figure 7.10.) The 1993 legislation also changed the hospital compensation system from per diem (per day) payments to specific fees for individual procedures and conditions.

Other German health care reform measures instituted in the 1990s also served to stimulate competition between sickness funds and improved coordination of inpatient and ambulatory care. During the mid-1990s the government also attempted to control health care costs by reducing health benefits, such as limiting how often patients could visit health spas to recuperate.

The health care reforms were not, however, successful at containing health care costs. Growth in health care spending was attributed to the comparatively high level of health care activity and resources, along with rising pharmaceutical expenditures and efforts to meet the health care needs of an aging population. Discharge rates and selected surgical procedures are higher in Germany than in relation to other OECD countries, and Germany has above-average levels of resources.

Canada

The Canadian system has been characterized as a provincial government health insurance model, in which each of the ten provinces operates its own health system under general federal rules and with a fixed federal contribution. All provinces are required to offer insurance coverage for all medically necessary services, including hospital care and physician services. However, additional services and benefits may be offered at the discretion of each province. Most provinces cover preventive services, routine dental care for children, and outpatient drugs for older adults (with a co-payment) and the poor. No restrictions are placed on a patient's choice of physicians.

Canadian citizens have equal access to medical care, regardless of their ability to pay. Entitlement to benefits is linked to residency, and the system is financed through general taxation. Private insurance is prohibited from covering the same benefits covered by the public system, yet a majority of Canadians are covered by private supplemental insurance policies. These policies generally cover services such as adult dental care, cosmetic surgery, and private or semiprivate hospital rooms. Seventy percent of all health expenditures are public, 7% are funded by private health insurance, and consumers pay about 15% of health care expenditures out of pocket. (See Figure 7.3 and Figure 7.4.)

Most hospitals are not-for-profit and are funded on the basis of global institution-specific or regional budgets. (A global institution-specific budget allocates a lump sum of money to a large department or area. Then all the groups in that department or area must negotiate to see how much of the total money each group receives.) Physicians in both inpatient and outpatient settings are paid on a negotiated, fee-for-service basis. The systems vary somewhat from province to province, and certain provinces, such as Quebec, have also established global budgets for physician services. Some provinces, including British Columbia, Alberta, and Ontario, require health care premiums for services; however, the Canada Health Act prohibits denial of health services on the basis of inability to pay premiums. The federal government's contribution to Canada's health care bill has progressively declined in the past two decades. The Canadian Institute for Health Information explains in *Exploring the 70/30 Split: How Canada's Health Care System Is Financed* (2005, http://secure.cihi .ca/cihiweb/products/FundRep_EN.pdf) that during the early 1980s the federal government paid a historic high of 50% of the total health care bill, but by 1998 it paid less than 20%. The resulting shift in costs has increased expenditures by the provinces and territories as well as out-of-pocket expenses paid by Canadians. The delivery system is largely composed of community hospitals and self-employed physicians. Nearly all of Canadian hospital beds are public; private hospitals do not participate in the public insurance program.

FINANCIAL PROBLEMS. During the 1990s public revenues did not increase rapidly enough in Canada to cover rising health care costs. The Canadian government attributed many of the financial problems to lower revenue from taxes, higher prices for biomedical technology, and relatively long hospital stays. In 1993, for the first time since Canada instituted universal health insurance twenty-seven years earlier, Canadians were required to pay for common services, such as throat cultures to test for streptococcal infections (the bacterial cause of strep throat).

As a result of cutbacks and inadequate equipment, waiting times for nonemergency surgery, such as hip replacement, and high-technology diagnostic tools, such as computerized tomography scans, could amount to months or even years. Even though Canadians generally still support their present system, physicians and consumers have expressed growing dissatisfaction with the rising costs and long waiting periods for diagnostic tests and nonemergency treatment.

SAFETY VALVE TO THE SOUTH. Some Canadians cross the border to the United States to avoid the waiting lines in their hospitals, clinics, and physicians' offices. Canadian physicians have been known to refer seriously ill patients in need of immediate medical attention to U.S. hospitals in nearby cities such as Buffalo, New York; Cleveland, Ohio; and Detroit, Michigan. In fact, many U.S. hospitals market medical services, most notably cardiac care and addiction treatment, to Canadians. Overall, however, there has been little border crossing to seek health care services. In "Phantoms in the Snow: Canadians' Use of Health Care Services in the United States" (*Health Affairs*, vol. 21, no. 3, May–June 2002), Steven J. Katz et al. indicate that Canadians account for very little U.S. hospital and health care service utilization.

CONTROLLING COSTS. The consensus is that no one wants to disassemble what has become Canada's most popular social program, but most agree that change is inevitable. In "Government/Social Health Insurance" (June, 14, 2008, http://www.ecosante.fr/OCDEENG/620010 .html), Eco-Santé states that the Ontario Health Insurance Plan insures about 80% of all Ontario residents. It has managed to cut costs in several ways, such as:

- Reducing fees to commercial laboratories and allowing them to bill patients directly for tests performed

- Stopping payment for certain services connected with employment; for example, many Canadians must pay out of pocket for preemployment physical examinations

- Ending coverage of selected services and reviewing coverage of services and procedures such as psychoanalysis, vasectomies, newborn circumcision, in vitro fertilization, as well as chiropractic, podiatric, and osteopathic services

- Increasing co-payments—the amounts patients must pay for prescriptions covered under the Ontario Drug Benefit Plan, which is used mainly by people over age sixty-five

Similarly, in an effort to cut hospital costs, British Columbia prepared health service redesign plans and instituted budget management and health care planning strategies in 2003 and 2004. A variety of initiatives including cutbacks in covered services, caps on physicians' fees and hospital budgets, and controlling the use of expensive medical technology enable this popular system to continue to offer affordable and sustainable health care.

The United Kingdom

The United Kingdom employs the National Health Service (NHS), or Beveridge, model to finance and deliver health care. The entire population is covered under a system that is financed primarily from general taxation.

There is minimal cost sharing. In 2005, 87% of all health spending was from public funds. (See Figure 7.3.)

Of the United Kingdom's hospital beds, 90% are public and generally owned by the NHS. In 2005 there were 3.1 beds per 1,000 population—more than the United States (2.7 per 1,000) but fewer than other European nations including France (3.7) and Italy (3.3). (See Figure 7.7.) Laura Donnelly reports in "NHS Hospitals Lose 32,000 Beds in a Decade" (*Telegraph* [London, England], May 25, 2008) that from 1997 to 2007 the number of NHS hospital beds declined from 198,848 to 167,019.

Services are organized and managed by regional and local public authorities. General practitioners serve as primary care physicians and are reimbursed on the basis of a combination of capitation payments (payments for each person served), fee-for-service, and other allowances. Hospitals receive overall budget allotments from district health authorities, and hospital-based physicians are salaried. Private insurance reimburses both physicians and hospitals on a fee-for-service basis.

Self-employed general practitioners are considered independent contractors, and salaried hospital-based physicians are public employees. The United Kingdom continues to face acute physician shortages: there are fewer physicians per capita (2.4 per 1,000 population in 2005) than in most other OECD countries. (See Figure 7.10.) In 1991 it became possible for large physician practices to become "budget holders" and receive larger capitation payments. Similarly, individual hospitals may become "self-governing trust hospitals," enabling them to compete for patients and market their services. Even though emergency health service is immediate, people requiring elective surgery, such as hip replacement, may end up on waiting lists for months or even years.

Since 2000 the NHS has experienced considerable change. The private sector has assumed a role in funding both buildings and services within the NHS. The authority to make decisions about local health care needs, priorities, and budgets has been delegated to local communities in some areas.

The NHS pioneered many cost-containment measures that are currently used by the United States and other countries seeking to slow escalating health care expenditures. These approaches to evaluating and managing health care costs include:

- Cost-effective analysis: calculated as a ratio, and often expressed as the cost per year per life saved, the cost-effectiveness analysis of a drug or procedure relates the cost of the drug or procedure to the health benefits it produces. This analysis enables delivery of clinically efficient, cost-effective care.

- Cost-minimization analysis: primarily applied to the pharmaceutical industry, this technique identifies the lowest cost among pharmaceutical alternatives that provide clinically comparable health outcomes.

- Cost-utility analysis: this measures the costs of therapy or treatment. Economists use the term *utility* to describe the amount of satisfaction a consumer receives from a given product or service. This analysis measures outcomes in terms of patient preference and is generally expressed as quality-adjusted life years. For example, an analysis of cancer chemotherapy drugs considers the various adverse side effects of these drugs because some patients may prefer a shorter duration of symptom-free survival rather than a longer life span marked by pain, suffering, and dependence on others for care.

France

The French health care system is based on the social insurance, or Bismarck, model. Virtually the entire population is covered by a legislated, compulsory health insurance plan that is financed through the social security system. Three major programs, and several smaller ones, are quasi-autonomous, nongovernmental bodies. The system is financed through employee and employer payroll tax contributions. In *Health at a Glance* (2007, http://fiordiliji.sourceoecd.org/vl=19658532/cl=14/nw=1/rpsv/health2007/g5-6-02.htm), the OECD notes that 87.2% of the population had private health insurance.

The public share of total health spending is 80%, and 7% of expenditures represent direct, out-of-pocket payments. (See Figure 7.3 and Figure 7.4.) Physicians practicing in municipal health centers and public hospitals are salaried, but physicians in private hospitals and in ambulatory care settings are typically paid on a negotiated, fee-for-service basis. Public hospitals are granted lump-sum budgets, and private hospitals are paid on the basis of negotiated per diem payment rates. In *Health Care Systems: An International Comparison* (May 2001, http://www.pnrec.org/2001papers/DaigneaultLajoie.pdf), Strategic Policy and Research Intergovernmental Affairs indicates that 65% of hospital beds are public, and the remaining 35% are private (and equally divided between profit and nonprofit).

In April 1996 the French government announced major reforms aimed at containing rising costs in the national health care system. The new system monitored each patient's total health costs and penalized physicians if they overran their budgets for specific types of care and prescriptions. In addition, French citizens were required to consult general practitioners before going to specialists. Initially, physicians—specialists, in particular—denounced the reforms and warned that they could lead to rationing and compromise the quality of health care.

Over time, however, these cost-containment efforts met with less resistance from physicians and consumers. By 2007 physicians and hospitals were generally accepting of moderate fee schedules, cost-sharing arrangements, and global budgeting to control costs.

Japan

Japan's health care financing is also based on the social insurance model and, in particular, on the German health care system. Eighty-two percent of health expenditures are from public funds. (See Figure 7.3.) Three general programs cover the entire population: Employee Health Insurance, Community Health Insurance, and Health and Medical Services for the Aged. Adam Dougherty of the Insure the Uninsured Project states in "Japan: The Health Care System" (July 9, 2008, http://www.itup .org/Reports/Fresh%20Thinking/Japan.pdf) that 63% of the population obtain coverage through eighteen hundred not-for-profit, nongovernmental, employer-sponsored plans. Small businesses, the self-employed, and farmers are covered through Community Health Insurance, which is administered by a conglomeration of local governmental and private bodies. Older adults are covered by a separate plan that largely pools funds from the other plans. The Japanese health expenditure is below the expected level for a country with Japan's standard of living, and its emphasis is on the government, as opposed to business, bearing the major financial burden for the nation's health care.

The health system is financed through employer and employee income-related premiums. There are different levels of public subsidization of the three different programs. Limited private insurance exists for supplemental coverage, which is purchased by about a third of the population and accounts for 1% of health expenditures, whereas out-of-pocket expenses account for 17%. (See Figure 7.4.)

Physicians and hospitals are paid on the basis of national, negotiated fee schedules. Japan manages with fewer physicians per capita than most OECD countries—just two physicians per one thousand population. (See Figure 7.10.) Physicians practicing in public hospitals are salaried, whereas those practicing in physician-owned clinics and private hospitals are reimbursed on a fee-for-service basis. The amount paid for each medical procedure is rigidly controlled. Physicians not only diagnose, treat, and manage illnesses but they also prescribe and dispense pharmaceuticals, and a considerable portion of a physician's income is derived from dispensing prescription drugs.

A close physician-patient relationship is unusual in Japan; the typical physician tries to see as many patients as possible in a day to earn a living. A patient going to a clinic for treatment may have to wait many hours in a crowded facility. As a result, health care is rarely a joint physician-patient effort. Instead, physicians tend to dictate treatment without fully informing patients about their conditions or the tests, drugs, and therapy that have been ordered or prescribed.

According to Dougherty, about 80% of Japan's hospitals are privately operated (and often physician owned) and the remaining 20% are public. Hospitals are paid according to a uniform fee schedule, and for-profit hospitals are prohibited. Even though hospital admissions are less frequent, hospital stays are typically far longer than in the United States or in any other developed member nation of the OECD, allowing hospitals and physicians to overcome the limitations of the fee schedules.

The health status of the Japanese is one of the best in the world. Japanese men and women are among the longest living in the world. In 2005 life expectancy was 82.1 years. (See Figure 7.11.) The Japanese infant and neonatal mortality rate in 2005, at 2.8 deaths per 1,000 live births, was bested only by Iceland, Sweden, and Luxembourg. (See Figure 7.12.) These two statistics are usually considered reliable indicators of a successful health care system. It should be noted, though, that Japan does not have a large impoverished class, as the United States does, and its diet is considered to be among the healthiest in the world.

Even though Japan's health care system has no doubt contributed to this preeminent health status, the current state of research in health economics does not permit the determination of the extent of its contribution. The Japanese system, which is based on social insurance, has provided both basic care and free choice of doctors to every citizen at affordable costs. It has become increasingly clear, however, that the system has not succeeded in its efforts to allocate resources properly, ensure financial equity, and adapt to changing patterns of demand.

CHAPTER 8
CHANGE, CHALLENGES, AND INNOVATION IN HEALTH CARE DELIVERY

Since the 1970s the U.S. health care system has experienced rapid and unprecedented change. The sites where health care is delivered have shifted from acute inpatient hospitals to outpatient settings, such as ambulatory care and surgical centers, clinics, and physicians' offices, and long-term care and rehabilitation facilities. Patterns of disease have changed from acute infectious diseases that require episodic care to chronic conditions that require ongoing care. Even threats to U.S. public health have changed—for example, epidemics of infectious diseases have largely been replaced by epidemics of chronic conditions such as obesity, diabetes, and mental illness. At the end of 2001 the threat of bioterrorism became an urgent concern of health care planners, providers, policy makers, and the American public; in 2006 the nation prepared for the possibility of pandemic influenza; and in 2008 the nation continued to discuss ways to address the nation's growing numbers of people without health care coverage.

There are new health care providers—midlevel practitioners (advance practice nurses, certified nurse midwives, physician assistants, and medical technologists)—and new modes of diagnosis such as genetic testing. Furthermore, the rise of managed care, the explosion of biotechnology, and the availability of information on the Internet have dramatically changed how health care is delivered.

Some health care industry observers suggest the speed at which these changes have occurred has further harmed an already complicated and uncoordinated health care system. There is concern that the present health care system cannot keep pace with scientific and technological advances. Many worry that the health care system is already unable to deliver quality care to all Americans and that it is so disorganized that it will be unable to meet the needs of the growing population of older Americans or to respond to the threat of a pandemic or bioterrorism.

This chapter considers several of the most pressing challenges and opportunities faced by the U.S. health care system. These include:

- Safety: ensuring safety by protecting patients from harm or injury inflicted by the health care system (e.g., preventing medical errors, reducing hospital-acquired infections, and safeguarding consumers from medical fraud). Besides actions to reduce problems caused by the health care system, safety and quality may be ensured by providers' use of clinical practice guidelines (e.g., standardized plans for diagnosis and treatment of disease and the effective application of technology to information and communication systems).

- Information management: information technology (IT), including the Internet, can provide health care providers and consumers with timely access to medical data, patient information, and the clinical expertise of specialists. For example, Gerard F. Anderson et al. discuss in "Health Care Spending and Use of Information Technology in OECD Countries" (*Health Affairs*, vol. 25, no. 3, May–June 2006) that effective deployment of IT can also reduce health care expenditures. Reliable public sources of consumer and provider health information on the Internet include the National Institutes of Health, the Centers for Disease Control and Prevention (CDC), and MEDLINE. Using this technology effectively is a health system challenge, especially in terms of protecting patient privacy and confidentiality and ensuring that consumers have access to accurate and reliable health information.

- Innovation: widespread use of innovations in health care delivery should be recommended only after objective analysis has demonstrated that the innovation will measurably benefit the safety, effectiveness, efficiency, or timeliness of health service delivery. Innovations should also be considered if they have the potential to reduce waste of equipment, supplies, or personnel time or if they have the capacity to allocate or distribute health care more equitably. Equitable distribution refers to access to care that does not vary in quality based on the characteristics, such as race, gender, ethnicity, or socioeconomic status, of the population served.

SAFETY

Even though the United States is generally viewed as providing quality health care services to its citizens, the Institute of Medicine (IOM) estimates in the landmark report *To Err Is Human: Building a Safer Health System* (1999, http://www.nap.edu/books/0309068371/html/) that as many as ninety-eight thousand American deaths per year are the result of preventable medical errors. More than seven thousand of these deaths are estimated to be due to preventable medication errors.

In 2008 HealthGrades, Inc., an independent health care quality research organization that grades hospitals based on a range of criteria and provides hospital ratings to health plans and other payers, issued its fifth update to the 1999 IOM report. In *Fifth Annual Patient Safety in American Hospitals Study* (April 2008, http://www.healthgrades.com/media/dms/pdf/PatientSafetyInAmericanHospitalsStudy2008.pdf), HealthGrades finds that even though participation in patient safety initiatives to reduce the frequency of medical errors has increased, there is still considerable variation in patient safety in U.S. hospitals.

HealthGrades looks at forty-one million Medicare patient records and nearly every one of the nation's five thousand hospitals to assess the mortality and economic impact of medical errors and injuries that occurred during hospital admissions nationwide from 2004 through 2006. The organization finds that about 1.1 million patient safety incidents occurred in nearly 41 million Medicare hospitalizations.

Some of the most significant patient safety findings are:

- If all the nation's hospitals performed as well as the top 15% identified in the study, then a staggering 220,106 patient safety incidents, 37,214 deaths of Medicare patients, and $2 billion in costs could have been avoided during the three-year period.

- One out of every five Medicare patients hospitalized from 2004 through 2006 who experienced a patient-safety incident died. This rate was lower than the previous year when it was one out of four.

- Patient-safety incidents with the highest rates per one thousand hospitalizations were failure to rescue (this indicator identifies patients who die following the development of a complication and assumes that quality hospitals identify these complications promptly and treat them aggressively), decubitus ulcer (bedsores), and postoperative respiratory failure (failure of lung function

following surgical procedures), which accounted for 63.4% of all documented patient-safety incidents.

- Compared to the 2004 research results, the rates of ten out of sixteen key patient safety indicators improved from 2004 to 2006.

Strengthening Safety Measures

In response to a request from the U.S. Department of Health and Human Services (HHS), the Committee on Data Standards for Patient Safety of the IOM created a detailed plan to develop standards for the collection, coding, and classification of patient safety information. The 550-page plan, *Patient Safety: Achieving a New Standard for Care* (2004), called on the HHS to assume the lead in establishing a national health information infrastructure that would provide immediate access to complete patient information and decision support tools, such as clinical practice guidelines, and capture patient safety data for use in designing ever-improving and safer health care delivery systems.

The IOM plan exhorted all health care settings to develop and implement comprehensive patient safety programs and recommended that the federal government launch patient safety research initiatives aimed at increasing knowledge, developing tools, and disseminating results to maximize the effectiveness of patient safety systems. The plan also advised the designation of a standardized format and terminology for identifying and reporting data related to medical errors.

In July 2005 President George W. Bush (1946–) signed into law the Patient Safety and Quality Improvement Act. Angela S. Mattie and Rosalyn Ben-Chitrit surmise in "Patient Safety Legislation: A Look at Health Policy Development" (*Policy, Politics, and Nursing Practice*, vol. 8, no. 4, November 2007) that the IOM calls for actions to improve patient safety in *To Err Is Human* are credited with heightening awareness of this issue and prompting Congress to pass legislation.

Who Is Responsible for Patient Safety?

Many federal, state, and private-sector organizations work together to reduce medical errors and improve patient safety. The CDC and the U.S. Food and Drug Administration (FDA) are the leading federal agencies that conduct surveillance and collect information about adverse events resulting from treatment or the use of medical devices, drugs, or other products. In "Estimates of Healthcare-Associated Infections" (May 30, 2007, http://www.cdc.gov/ncidod/dhqp/hai.html), the CDC estimates that every year 1.7 million patients are diagnosed with hospital- and health care–acquired infections and that these infections claim 99,000 lives. The CDC collaborates with state and local health departments, private-sector groups, academic medical centers, and health care providers to develop and implement other programs to reduce errors and adverse outcomes of care.

The Centers for Medicare and Medicaid Services acts to reduce medical errors for Medicare, Medicaid, and State Children's Health Insurance Program beneficiaries through its peer review organizations. Peer review organizations concentrate on preventing delays in diagnosis and treatment that have adverse effects on health.

The U.S. Departments of Defense and of Veterans Affairs (VA), which is responsible for health care services for U.S. military personnel, their families, and veterans, have instituted computerized systems that have reduced medical errors. The VA established the Centers of Inquiry for Patient Safety, and its hospitals also use bar-code technology and computerized medical records to prevent medical errors.

Safe medical care is also a top priority of the states and the private sector. In 2000 some of the nation's largest corporations, including General Motors and General Electric, joined together to address health care safety and efficacy and to help direct their workers to health care providers (hospitals and physicians) with the best performance records. Called the Leapfrog Group (http://www.leapfroggroup.org/), this business coalition was founded by the Business Roundtable, a national association of Fortune 500 chief executive officers, to leverage employer purchasing power that initiates innovation and improves the safety of health care.

The Leapfrog Group publishes hospital quality and safety data to assist consumers in making informed hospital choices. Hospitals provide information to the Leapfrog Group through a voluntary survey that requests information about hospital performance across four quality and safety practices with the potential to reduce preventable medical mistakes and improve health care quality. Leah F. Binder (April 16, 2008, http://www.leapfroggroup.org/news/leapfrog_news/4732651), the chief executive officer of the Leapfrog Group, explained in her testimony before the U.S. House of Representative's Committee on Oversight and Government Reform that the group is composed of major companies and other private and public purchasers of health care benefits for more than thirty-seven million Americans. Its mission is to promote health care safety programs and advocate innovative solutions to existing problems.

IMPROVING TEAMWORK TO PREVENT MEDICAL ERRORS AND IMPROVE PATIENT SAFETY. In November 2007 the U.S. Agency for Healthcare Research and Quality (AHRQ) and the Department of Defense launched TeamSTEPPS (http://teamstepps.ahrq.gov/abouttoolsmaterials.htm), a program that aims to optimize patient outcomes by improving communication and other teamwork skills among health care professionals. TeamSTEPPS

applies team training principles developed in military aviation and in private industry to health care delivery. Carolyn Clancy, the director of the AHRQ, asserts in "Physicians and Nurses Together Can Improve Patient Safety" (*Medscape Journal of Medicine*, vol.10, no. 2, 2008), that "nurses are trained to manage a variety of patient care situations, whereas physicians regard their role as having ultimate responsibility for the patients. In few instances do both nurses and physician train together, a disconnect that can be counterproductive to high-quality healthcare. In the new culture of medicine, teamwork should be the standard, not the ideal. As physicians, we can be leaders in the effort to instill teamwork where we practice and do right by our patients."

Professional societies are also concerned with patient safety. Over half of all the Joint Commission on Accreditation of Healthcare Organizations' (JCAHO) hospital standards pertain to patient safety. Since 2002 hospitals seeking accreditation from the JCAHO have been required to adhere to stringent patient safety standards to prevent medical errors. The JCAHO standards also require hospitals and individual health care providers to inform patients when they have been harmed in the course of treatment. The aim of these standards is to prevent medical errors by identifying actions and systems likely to produce problems before they occur. An example of this type of preventive measure, which is called prospective review, is close scrutiny of hospital pharmacies to be certain that the ordering, preparation, and dispensing of medications is accurate. Similar standards have been developed for JCAHO-accredited nursing homes, outpatient clinics, laboratories, and managed care organizations.

On January 1, 2004, the JCAHO began surveying and evaluating health care organizations using new medication management standards. The new standards revise and consolidate existing standards and place even greater emphasis on medication safety. The revised standards increase the role of pharmacists in managing appropriate and safe medication use and strengthen their authority to implement organization-wide improvements in medication safety.

HOSPITALS DESIGNED FOR SAFETY. Even though HealthGrades finds in *Third Annual Patient Safety in American Hospitals Study* (April 2006, http://www.healthgrades.com/media/dms/pdf/patientsafetyinamericanhospitalsstudy2006.pdf) that just 74% of hospitals surveyed had fully implemented a patient safety plan and 9% had no plan at all, some hospitals are taking extraordinary measures to reduce medical errors and enhance safety. As Gautam Naik reports in "Ounce of Prevention to Reduce Errors, Hospitals Prescribe Innovative Designs" (*Wall Street Journal*, May 8, 2006), novel approaches include hotlines to enable staff to anonymously report medical errors and architectural innovations such as slip-proof floors, special lighting to aid diagnosis, round rather than sharp interior wall corners, and standardized layout of equipment enabling staff to quickly and easily access needed equipment and supplies. Some hospitals have chosen to abandon the practice of recycling the air in the buildings to reduce the risk of spreading infections. Others have chosen to forgo vinyl coverings on external walls because it attracts infection-causing mold. Naik explains that at least one hospital that instituted facility-wide design and layout changes reports preliminary evidence that the changes it instituted have already reduced rates of infection, falls, and medication errors.

CLINICAL PRACTICE GUIDELINES

Clinical practice guidelines (CPGs) are evidence-based protocols—documents that advise health care providers about how to diagnose and treat specific medical conditions and diseases. CPGs offer physicians, nurses, other health care practitioners, health plans, and institutions objective, detailed, and condition- or disease-specific action plans.

Widespread dissemination and use of CPGs began during the 1990s in an effort to improve the quality of health care delivery by giving health care professionals access to current scientific information on which to base clinical decisions. The use of guidelines also aimed to enhance quality by standardizing care and treatment throughout a health care delivery system such as a managed care plan or hospital and throughout the nation.

Early attempts to encourage physicians and other health professionals to use practice guidelines was met with resistance, because many physicians rejected CPGs as formulaic "cookbook medicine" and believed they interfered with physician-patient relationships. Over time, however, physicians were educated about the quality problems resulting from variations in medical practice, and opinions about CPGs gradually changed. Physician willingness to use CPGs also increased when they learned that adherence to CPGs offered some protection from medical malpractice and other liability. Nurses and other health professionals more readily adopted CPGs, presumably because their training and practice was oriented more toward following instructions than physicians' practices had been.

The National Guideline Clearinghouse is a database of CPGs produced by the AHRQ in conjunction with the AMA and the American Association of Health Plans. The clearinghouse offers guideline summaries and comparisons of guidelines covering the same disease or condition prepared by different sources and serves as a resource for the exchange of guidelines between practitioners and health care organizations.

CPGs vary depending on their source. All recovery and treatment plans, however, are intended to generate the most favorable health outcomes. Federal agencies such as the U.S. Public Health Service and the CDC, as well as professional societies, managed care plans, hospitals, academic medical centers, and health care consulting firms, have produced their own versions of CPGs.

Practically all guidelines assume that treatment and healing will occur without complications. Because CPGs represent an optimistic approach to treatment, they are not used as the sole resource for development or evaluation of treatment plans for specific patients. CPGs are intended for use in conjunction with evaluation by qualified health professionals able to determine the applicability of a specific CPG to the specific circumstances involved. Modification of the CPGs is often required and advisable to meet specific, organizational objectives of health care providers and payers.

It is unrealistic to expect that all patients will obtain ideal health outcomes as a result of health care providers' use of CPGs. Guidelines may have greater utility as quality indicators. Evaluating health care delivery against CPGs enables providers, payers, and policy makers to identify and evaluate care that deviates from CPGs as part of a concerted program of continuous improvement of health care quality.

INFORMATION AND COMMUNICATION TECHNOLOGY

The explosion of communication and information management technologies has already revolutionized health care delivery and holds great promise for the future. Health care data can be easily and securely collected, shared, stored, and used to promote research and development over great geographic distances and across traditionally isolated industries. Online distance learning programs for health professionals and the widespread availability of reliable consumer health information on the Internet have increased understanding and awareness of the causes and treatment of illness. This section describes several recent applications of technology to the health care system.

Telemedicine

The term *telemedicine* describes a variety of interactions that occur by way of telephone lines. Telemedicine may be as simple and commonplace as a conversation between a patient and a health professional in the same town or as sophisticated as surgery directed by way of satellite and video technology from one continent to another.

In "Telemedicine Coming of Age" (January 13, 2005, http://tie.telemed.org/articles/article.asp?path=telemed101& article=tmcoming_nb_tie96.xml), Nancy Brown of the Telemedicine Research Center, a nonprofit public research organization, explains that there are two types of technology used in most telemedicine applications. The first type stores digital images taken with a digital camera and sends them from one location to another. The most common application of this kind of telemedicine is teleradiology—sending x-rays, computerized tomography scans, or magnetic resonance imaging scans from one facility to another. The same technology may be used to send slides or images from the pathology laboratory to another physician or laboratory for a second opinion. Another example of the use of digital image transfer is the rural primary care physician who, miles from the nearest dermatologist (physician specialist in skin diseases), can send a photograph of a patient's rash or lesion and receive an immediate, long-distance consultation from the dermatologist.

Another application of telemedicine that uses only the standard telephone line in a patient's home is transtelephonic pacemaker monitoring. (Cardiac pacemakers are battery-operated implanted devices that maintain normal heart rhythm.) Cardiac technicians at the other end of the telephone are able to check the implanted cardiac pacemaker's functions, including the status of its battery. Transtelephonic pacemaker monitoring is able to identify early signs of possible pacemaker failure and detect potential pacemaker system abnormalities, thereby reducing the number of emergency replacements. It can also send an electrocardiogram rhythm strip to the patient's cardiologist (physician specialist in heart diseases).

The second type of technology described by Brown is two-way interactive television, which uses video-teleconferencing equipment to create a meeting between a patient and primary care physician in one location and a physician specialist elsewhere when a face-to-face consultation is not feasible because of time or distance. Peripheral equipment even enables the consulting physician specialist to perform a virtual physical examination and hear the patient's heart sounds through a stethoscope. The availability of desktop videoconferencing has expanded this form of telemedicine from a novelty found exclusively in urban, university teaching hospitals to a valuable tool for patients and physicians in rural areas who were previously underserved and unable to access specialists readily.

Despite the promise of telemedicine, several obstacles have prevented Americans from realizing all its potential benefits. As of August 2008, many states did not permit physicians who are not licensed in their state to practice telemedicine, and the Centers for Medicare and Medicaid Services reimbursed for interactive teleconference services but would not pay for digital image transfer. Many private insurers have been reluctant to pay for telemedicine, and some physicians fear additional liability (medical malpractice suits or other litigation) arising from telemedicine. Finally, some of the communities that would benefit most from telemedicine do not have the telecommunications equipment necessary to deliver the bandwidth for telemedicine.

In "Perspectives on Medical Outsourcing and Telemedicine—Rough Edges in a Flat World?" (*New England Journal of Medicine*, vol. 358, no. 15, April 10, 2008), Sanjiv N. Singh and Robert M. Wachter observe increasing use of telemedicine, with projected annual growth rates of 15% to 20% and particularly strong growth in the fields of radiology, dermatology, mental health consultation, and home care. Singh and Wachter report that as many as three hundred U.S. hospitals and two-thirds of radiology practices use some form of teleradiology, and that the VA conducts nearly a quarter of a million teleconsultations per year.

Telemedicine appears to improve patient outcomes. For example, Andreas S. Morguet et al. find in "Impact of Telemedical Care and Monitoring on Morbidity in Mild to Moderate Chronic Heart Failure" (*Cardiology*, vol. 111, no. 2, 2008) that telemedical care and monitoring may reduce the frequency and severity of illness in patients with chronic heart failure (a condition in which the heart is unable to supply the body with enough blood). In "Telemedicine Facilitates CHF Home Health Care for Those with Systolic Dysfunction" (*International Journal of Telemedicine and Applications*, 2008), Pennie S. Seibert et al. find improved control of congestive heart failure when telemedicine was implemented.

Telemedicine has been used in schools to improve access to care, treat middle ear infections, and increase appropriate referral to specialists. It has also proven beneficial in helping to manage asthma in school-aged children. David A. Bergman et al. hypothesize in "The Use of Telemedicine Access to Schools to Facilitate Expert Assessment of Children with Asthma" (*International Journal of Telemedicine and Applications*, 2008) that asthma care would be improved through a telemedicine link between an asthma specialist and a school-based asthma program, which involved real-time video and audio conferencing between the patient and school nurse on-site at the school and the asthma specialist at San Francisco General Hospital. The researchers conducted the program in three urban schools to determine the feasibility of asthma-focused telemedicine. They find that the program produced significant improvements in health status outcomes and note that the use of telemedicine ensured that children identified with asthma received comprehensive assessments, action plans, and asthma education. Bergman et al. conclude that telemedicine "allowed for a more efficient use of the asthma subspecialist's time when contrasted with hospital-based asthma clinics."

Telemedicine has also proven to be a cost-effective alternative to emergency department visits. Kevin McKeever reports in "Telemedicine a Cost-Effective Alternative to ER Visits" (*HealthDay News*, May 9, 2008) on two presentations that were made at the May 2008 Pediatrics

Annual Societies meeting in Honolulu, Hawaii. The first presentation was by researchers from the University of Rochester Medical Center, which operates a Rochester-based telemedicine program that provides interactive, Internet-based pediatric health-care service. The researchers asserted that "telemedicine is a cost-effective way to replace more than a quarter of all visits to the pediatric emergency department." The second presentation noted that telelmedicine has the capacity to provide quality care at a lower cost—saving payers more than $14 per child per year.

Wireless Technology in the Hospital.

In "Ten Lessons from the Top 100" (*Hospitals and Health Networks*, July 2007), Alden Solovy asserts that the most wired hospitals have better outcomes than other hospitals on key measures including mortality rates, the AHRQ's patient safety measures, and average length of stay. Solovy's assertion is based on the results of the 2007 Hospitals and Health Networks Most Wired Survey and Benchmarking Study, which revealed a strong association between the implementation and adoption of IT and the quality and cost of patient care.

The top hospitals used technology to improve patient flow and to improve workflow by, for example, providing a central location for the nursing task list, so that all of a nurse's activities for an upcoming shift, including physician orders, reminders, and nursing interventions, are in one convenient place. Technology was also employed to measure and analyze process improvements such as "time to care"—the time between order placement and delivery of care. The most wired hospitals used technology to facilitate electronic ordering and bedside medication matching to reduce the number of potential medication errors. They also used "smart alerts"—real-time monitors that use information in the medical record to identify patients with potentially deteriorating conditions. Other uses of wireless technology include disseminating digital images, such as radiological images, to multiple sites, such as clinics and physicians' offices, and automating processes in the operating room.

Industry observers caution that IT is not itself a solution to the many problems plaguing the U.S. health care system. It is one of many tools for achieving process improvements that lead to better outcomes, and it must be used in combination with other tools and techniques to affect care. Solovy notes that the survey results reveal "an association between IT adoption and key quality measures, but association is not causality."

Online Patient-Physician Consultations

Even though no one is certain about the frequency with which online encounters or exchanges between physicians and patients occur, Harris Interactive reveals in "Few Patients Use or Have Access to Online Services for Communicating with their Doctors, but Most Would Like To" (September 22, 2006, http://www.harrisinteractive.com/news/allnewsbydate.asp?NewsID=1096) that a majority of respondents in a 2006 survey wanted access to a variety of electronic medicine (e-medicine) technologies in communicating with their doctors. For example, 77% wanted e-mail reminders of when a visit with their physician is coming up, 74% expressed the desire for e-mail communication with their physician, 67% wanted to receive diagnostic test results via e-mail, and 57% said they wanted to use a home monitoring device that sends information (blood pressure readings or blood tests) to their physician.

In "Communication between Physicians and Patients in the Era of E-Medicine" (*New England Journal of Medicine*, vol. 356, no. 24, June 14, 2007), John H. Stone observes that payers in Florida, California, Massachusetts, and New York reimburse physicians for Web consultations. In those states that do not reimburse physicians for Web consultations, such "electronic visits" typically cost between $10 and $25, and patients pay for them out of pocket. Other electronic communications between patients and physicians' offices include appointment scheduling, reminders of follow-up visits, prescription renewal requests, administrative functions (e.g., billing, insurance verification, and changes of address), and questions about test results, all of which are generally provided free of charge. Stone notes that "early studies indicate that e-medicine methods improve the productivity of providers, reduce the number of office visits, and save money."

One important advantage of electronic encounters (e-encounters) over telephone conversations is the patient's ability to communicate home monitoring results such as blood pressure or blood glucose levels in a format that is easily included as documentation in the patient's permanent (paper or electronic) medical record. Another advantage is that less time devoted to telephone calls improves the efficiency of the physician's office, thereby boosting productivity and potentially reducing practice expenses.

Concerns about e-encounters center on privacy and security of patient information exchanged and physician reimbursement for the time spent in electronic correspondence with patients. Besides legal and privacy issues, some industry observers suggest that guidelines should be developed for e-encounters to ensure that they are clinically appropriate and are not used as substitutes for needed, but more costly, face-to-face office visits.

Peter Stalberg et al. find in "E-mail Access and Improved Communication between Patient and Surgeon" (*Archives of Surgery*, vol. 143, no. 2, February 2008) that despite medicolegal concerns, providing patients undergoing elective surgery with e-mail access to their surgeons proves to be an effective means of improving patient-physician communication.

Despite promising research findings about the benefits of e-mail correspondence between patients and physicians as well as increasing consumer demand for electronic communication, most physicians are not engaging in online communication with patients. Alicia Chang reports in "It's No LOL: Few US Doctors Answer E-mails from Patients" (Associated Press, April 22, 2008) that a 2007 study found that just 31% of physicians e-mailed their patients. The American Medical Association cautions that e-mail should not be used as a substitute for face-to-face time with patients and advises physicians to talk with patients about the technology's limitations.

Is Applied Technology the Solution to the Nursing Shortage?

In "What Nurses Want" (Government Health IT, March 31, 2008), John Pulley explains that many efforts are being made to address the current nursing shortage in the United States. Instead of trying to recruit more nurses and nursing students, the American Academy of Nurses (AAN) is endeavoring to make better use of nurses, in large measure by using IT to improve their efficiency. With the assistance of the Robert Wood Johnson Foundation, the AAN Workforce Commission examined the work processes and environments of nurses and other health care providers at twenty-five sites throughout the United States.

The commission found that nurses and other health professionals sought IT solutions to assist with coordination and delivery of care, communication, discharge planning, documentation, patient transport, and supplies and equipment. Nurses want completely electronic medical records, which in 2007 were only used by an estimated 10% of the nation's health care providers; computerized order entry systems to eliminate problems arising from illegible handwriting; touch-screen or voice-activated technology for documentation; and automated networks to collect and download patient data. They are especially enthusiastic about hands-free tools and wireless technology. Other needs identified by the commission include nurses' desire for increased use of radio frequency identification technology to track people, supplies, and equipment, and greater use of robotics to deliver supplies. Nurses also endorse the use of smart beds that monitor patient movements and pressure sensors to help reduce the frequency of bedsores.

MORE STAFF, RATHER THAN TECHNOLOGY, IS KEY TO IMPROVING QUALITY OF CARE. Despite rapid advances in technology, many industry observers feel that it is not sufficient to solve the nursing shortage that the Bureau of Labor Statistics projects in the press release "Employment Projections: 2006–16" (December 4, 2007, http://www.bls.gov/news.release/pdf/ecopro.pdf), which will require over one million replacement nurses by 2016. In "Nurse Staffing in Hospitals: Is There a Business Case for Quality?" (Health Affairs, January–February 2006), Jack Needleman et al. report on their study of 799 acute care hospitals in 11 states. They find that U.S. hospitals could prevent an estimated 6,700 patient deaths, 70,416 complications, and 4.1 million hospital days of care by hiring more registered nurses and increasing the hours of nursing care per patient. Needleman et al. project that increased staffing would produce minimal increases in hospital budgets, ranging from 0.4% to 0.8%, when offset by savings realized by reducing rates of medical errors and hospital lengths of stay.

The American Hospital Association (AHA) reports in "America's Hospitals Confront Serious Workforce Challenges" (AHA News, August 21, 2007) that in 2006, 5,000 community hospitals alone were in need of 116,000 registered nurses to fill vacancies. In "Bill Would Ease Nurse Visa Backlog, Bolster Nurse Education" (AHA News, May 12, 2008), the AHA expresses its support for legislation to provide funds to help U.S. nursing schools expand the domestic supply of nurses and establish a three-year pilot program aimed at keeping U.S. nurses in the workforce. The bill, the Emergency Nursing Supply Relief Act (H.R. 5924), would also set aside twenty thousand employment-based visas per year for the next three years for foreign-educated registered nurses and physical therapists.

Promise of Robotics

One technological advance that promises to reduce hospital operating costs and enable hospital workers to spend more time caring for patients is the use of robots. Once relegated to the realm of science fiction, the twenty-first century has seen a resurgence of interest in automated machines such as self-guided robots to perform many routine hospital functions.

Mike Crissey describes in "Courier Robots Get Traction in Hospitals" (Associated Press, July 7, 2004) the "Robo-Cart," a motorized table that transports linens, medical supplies, x-rays, food, and other materials throughout a hospital. Another automated robot courier, a four-foot-tall cabinet with flashing lights and turn signals called "HelpMate," speaks in English and Spanish. The robots use wireless radio to call elevators and open automatic doors, and they communicate respectfully, saying "thank you" on entering an elevator and inviting hospital employees to "please examine my contents when making deliveries." According to Kawanza Newson, in "Robot Now Makes Tracks through Hospital" (Milwaukee Journal Sentinel, March 30, 2008), a robotic cart that looks like a train, warns onlookers to "pardon my caboose" when it backs up, and makes deliveries of oxygen monitors and feeding pumps was one of a hundred such robotic carts in use in U.S. hospitals in 2008.

Some robots are involved in more than simply routine, menial tasks. Barnaby J. Feder explains in "Prepping Robots to Perform Surgery" (New York Times, May 4, 2008) that a growing number of surgeons delegate much of their work to medical robots controlled from computer consoles. The robotic system allows a cardiovascular surgeon to perform heart surgery without touching the patient, or a urologist to ensure precise, tremor-free incisions to prevent damage to delicate nerves during prostate surgery. Seated at a console with a computer and video monitor, the surgeon uses handgrips and foot pedals to manipulate robotic arms that hold scalpels, sutures, and other surgical instruments to perform the operation. These robotic systems have been approved for use by the FDA, and in 2008 they represented a $1 billion segment of the medical device industry.

Robots do not, however, trump humans in all aspects of health care delivery. In "Enhanced Gait-Related Improvements after Therapist- versus Robotic-Assisted Locomotor Training in Subjects with Chronic Stroke. A Randomized Controlled Study" (*Stroke*, vol. 39, no. 6, 2008), T. George Hornby et al. of the University of Illinois, Chicago, compare the results of physical therapist–assisted training and rehabilitation of stroke patients with training provided by a robotic device. They find that therapist-assisted training produced greater improvement in walking speed and symmetry as well as in overall walking ability than did training provided by a robotic device. At the end of treatment, the increase in gait speed and the ability to stand using one limb was twice as high in the group of patients receiving services from physical therapists than in the group treated by robots.

The Future Is Here for Pioneering Hospitals

In 2008 many hospitals instituted new technology to help reduce errors, improve safety, and assist nurses to perform their responsibilities more easily, accurately, and efficiently. For example, the article "Survey Investigates Role of Pharmacy in Technology Use in Hospitals" (*Medical News Today*, February 26, 2008) notes that most U.S. hospitals and health systems use multiple complex health ITs to support patient medication use, but only some of them have integrated these systems.

In "Information Technologies and Improved Patient Safety: A Study of 98 Hospitals in Florida" (*Journal of Healthcare Management*, vol. 52, no. 6, November–December 2007), Nir Menachemi et al. examine the overall adoption of IT by hospitals and patient outcome measures. The researchers looked at a large sample of Florida hospitals, public and private, rural and urban, and used widely accepted patient safety indicators to measure the effect of IT systems on patient outcomes. Menachemi et al. find that patients are more likely to have better health outcomes when they are treated at hospitals using IT.

INNOVATION SUPPORTS QUALITY HEALTH CARE DELIVERY

The health care industry is awash in wave after wave of new technologies, models of service delivery, reimbursement formulae, legislative and regulatory changes, and increasingly specialized personnel ranks. Creating change in hospitals and other health care organizations requires an understanding of diffusion—the process and channels by which new ideas are communicated, spread, and adopted throughout institutions or organizations. Diffusion of technology involves all the stakeholders in the health care system: policy makers and regulatory agencies establish safety and efficacy, government and private payers determine reimbursement, vendors of the technology are compared and one is selected, hospitals and health professionals adopt the technology and are trained in its use, and consumers are informed about the benefits of the new technology.

The decision to adopt new technology involves a five-stage process beginning with knowledge about the innovation. The second stage is persuasion, the period when decision makers form opinions based on experience and knowledge. Decision is the third phase, when commitment is made to a trial or pilot program, and is followed by implementation, the stage during which the new technology is put in place. The process concludes with the confirmation stage, the period during which the decision makers seek reinforcement for their decision to adopt and implement the new technology.

Innovation to Improve Access

In April 2006 Massachusetts made national news when it enacted a compulsory health insurance plan intended to extend health coverage to every state resident by 2009. According to Christopher Rowland, in "Mass. Health Plan Seems Unlikely to Be US Model" (*Boston Globe*, April 14, 2006), other states have passed legislation aimed at providing universal coverage but none are as ambitious as the Massachusetts plan, which seeks to unite employers and health access advocates to achieve their shared objectives. In 2003 Maine passed a law to make coverage available for all residents by 2009, Hawaii requires all employers to contribute to health care coverage for their workers, and Illinois provides coverage for children up to age eighteen.

Conservative critics of the Massachusetts plan, which requires employers and individuals to purchase health insurance, consider the state mandate an unwelcome government intrusion on individual rights. Liberal skeptics fear that many individuals will suffer when forced to purchase insurance the state deems affordable, but still constitutes an unworkable proportion of their income.

Even though it is not yet known how well the plan will work to improve health care coverage and access or whether it will be a model for other states, which have higher proportions of uninsured residents (Rowland notes that in 2006 Massachusetts had just 10% uninsured, compared to the national average of 18%), many states may look more closely at some of the plan's other provisions, such as its requirement that hospitals fully disclose cost and quality measures to enable health care consumers and payers to choose quality, cost-effective providers of medical care.

Alice Dembner reports in "Subsidized Care Plan's Cost to Double" (*Boston Globe*, February 3, 2008) that by 2008,169,000 people had enrolled in the Commonwealth Care plan, which provides free or subsidized insurance for low and moderate income residents, at a cost of $618 million for the fiscal year ending June 30, 2008. According to Dembner, state officials estimated that the plan will double in size and expense over the next three years—to 342,000 people at a cost of nearly $1.4 billion annually—which means that the plan will have to scale back its ambitious goals in terms of coverage or pass the associated expenses along to taxpayers. These projections far exceed forecasts developed at the plan's inception. The state has requested assistance from the federal government to finance the plan from 2009 to 2011; however, as of August 2008, there was no assurance that the federal funds would be available.

Communicating Quality

In *Crossing the Quality Chasm: A New Health System for the 21st Century* (2001, http://www.nap.edu/books/0309072808/html/), the IOM sets forth six goals for improvement and ten rules for redesign of the U.S. health care system. These ten rules are:

1. Care is based on continuous healing relationships

2. Care is customized according to patient needs and values

3. The patient is the source of control

4. Knowledge is shared and information flows freely

5. Decision making is evidence based

6. Safety is a system priority

7. Transparency is necessary

8. Needs are anticipated

9. Waste is continuously decreased

10. Cooperation among clinicians is a priority

Rule number seven, which focuses on transparency, refers to the need for public accountability for the quality of the health care system. Health care consumers should be given information that allows them to make thoughtful, informed choices and decisions about health insurance plans and providers.

The requirement for transparency requires health care providers and plans to disclose information they previously did not share among themselves or with consumers. Furthermore, many health care plans and providers find that to compete successfully for health care consumers, they must demonstrate the ability not only to deliver health care services effectively but also to document and communicate measures of clinical quality and fiscal accountability.

The publication of medical outcomes report cards and disease- and procedure-specific morbidity rates (the degree of disability caused by disease) and mortality rates (the number of deaths caused by disease) has attracted widespread media attention and sparked controversy. Advocates of the public release of clinical outcomes and other performance measures contend that despite some essential limitations, these studies offer consumers, employers, and payers the means for comparing health care providers.

Some skeptics question the clinical credibility of scales such as surgical mortality, which they claim are incomplete indicators of quality. Others cite problems with data collection or speculate that data are readily manipulated by providers to enhance marketing opportunities sufficient to compromise the utility and validity of published reports. Long term, the effects of published comparative evaluation of health care providers on network establishment, contracting, and exclusion from existing health plans are uncertain and in many instances may be punitive (damaging). Hospitals and medical groups may be forced to compete for network inclusion on the basis of standardized performance measures.

The number of Web sites that rate physicians and hospitals continues to grow, with Angie's List and Vitals .com joining more established sites such as HealthGrades .com in 2008. The sites describe physicians' training, experience, certification, and any disciplinary actions taken against them, as well as patient ratings. They also encourage physicians to respond to patient comments. Some industry observers contend that the sites, especially those that use anonymous ratings, have the potential to further erode patient-physician relationships by prompting physicians to behave defensively. In "Online Ratings Irk Doctors" (*USA Today*, March 31, 2008), Kim Painter quotes Nancy Nielsen, the president-elect of the American Medical Association, as saying that even though "doctors care very much what patients think and welcome scientifically valid patient surveys, anonymous online ratings and rants can ruin reputations and destroy trust."

Despite legitimate concern about the reliability, validity, and interpretation of data, there is consensus that scrutiny and dissemination of quality data will escalate. As of August 2008, consumer interest focused on individual providers (local hospitals and physicians). When choosing between health plans involving the same group of participating hospitals and physicians, employers requested plan-specific information to guide their decisions.

Companies and employer-driven health care coalitions seeking to assemble their own provider networks relied on physician- and hospital-specific data, such as the quality data provided by HealthGrades, during the selection process.

The most beneficial use of the data is not to be punitive, but to be inspiring to improve health care delivery systematically. When evidence of quality problems is identified, health plans and providers must be prepared to launch a variety of interventions to address and promptly resolve problems.

CHAPTER 9
PUBLIC OPINION ABOUT THE HEALTH CARE SYSTEM

As with many other social issues, public opinion about health care systems, providers, plans, coverage, and benefits varies in response to a variety of personal, political, and economic forces. Personal experience and the experience of friends, family, and community opinion leaders (trusted sources of information such as members of the clergy, prominent physicians, and local business and civic leaders) exert powerful influences on public opinion. Health care marketing executives have known for years that the most potent advertising any hospital, medical group, or managed care plan can have is not a full-page newspaper advertisement or prime-time television ad campaign. It is positive word-of-mouth publicity.

The influence of the news media, advertising, and other attempts to sway health care consumers' attitudes and purchasing behaviors cannot be overlooked. A single story about a miraculous medical breakthrough or life-saving procedure can reflect favorably on an entire hospital or health care delivery system. Similarly, a lone mistake, an adverse reaction to a drug, or a misstep by a single health care practitioner can impugn (attack as lacking integrity) a hospital, managed care plan, or pharmaceutical company for months or even years, prompting intense media scrutiny of every action taken by the practitioner, facility, or organization.

Political events, the economy, and pending legislation can focus public attention on a particular health care concern, supplant one health-related issue with another, or eclipse health care from public view altogether. In 2005 Hurricanes Katrina and Rita focused attention on the U.S. public health and federal emergency management systems' capacities to effectively respond to disasters. At the same time, federal, state, and local government officials assessed disaster preparedness funding and plans for the possibility of an influenza pandemic arising from the H5N1 avian flu that had already swept through birds in parts of Asia and Europe and might arrive in the United States.

In *Economic Anxiety Surges in Past Year* (March 28, 2008, http://www.gallup.com/poll/105802/Economic-Anxiety-Surges-Past-Year.aspx), Lydia Saad of the Gallup Organization observes that the U.S. economy and health care were Americans' top concerns in the second quarter of 2008. Americans' concerns about the U.S. economy increased dramatically, from 39% in March 2007 to 60% in March 2008. (See Table 9.1.) The economic anxiety appears to have slightly dampened concerns about health care—during this same period the percentage of Americans naming health care as a major concern dropped from 63% of respondents to 58%.

In *Kaiser Health Tracking Poll: Election 2008—June 2008* (June 25, 2008, http://kff.org/kaiserpolls/h08_posr 062508pkg.cfm), the Henry J. Kaiser Family Foundation finds that rising health care costs continue to worry Americans, along with other economic concerns. Most (43%) respondents named paying for gas as a serious economic concern. Twenty-five percent of those polled said paying for health care and health insurance posed a serious problem, and about the same proportion (27%) was worried about getting a well-paying job. Nearly one out of five (19%) expressed concern about paying for food, and comparable percentages were worried about credit card or personal debt (16%), losing money in the stock market (15%), and rent or mortgage (14%).

According to Victoria Culver, in "Polls Show Health Care a Growing Concern" (*San Francisco Chronicle*, April 29, 2008), industry observers assert that the Kaiser poll underscores the fact that despite the mortgage crisis, rising gasoline prices, and growing economic uncertainty, health care remains high on the list of Americans' concerns. Observers also note that the Kaiser poll reveals the role of health care in lifestyle decisions. Culver indicates that 23% of survey respondents said they or a member of their household either switched or stuck with a job because of health benefits. Seven percent said health care coverage influenced their own or a household member's decision to marry during the past year.

TABLE 9.1

Poll respondents who worry about major national issues, March 2007–March 2008

[Percent who worry a great deal]

	March 2007	March 2008	Change
	%	%	pct. pts.
The economy	39	60	21
Unemployment	25	36	11
Energy	43	47	4
Crime and violence	48	49	1
Possible terrorism against the U.S.	41	40	−1
Race relations	19	18	−1
Drug use	45	43	−2
Social Security	49	46	−3
The environment	43	40	−3
Healthcare	63	58	−5
Illegal immigration	45	40	−5
Hunger/Homelessness	43	38	−5

SOURCE: Lydia Saad, "Recent Trend in Worry about Major National Issues," in *Economic Anxiety Surges in Past Year*, The Gallup Organization, March 28, 2008, http://www.gallup.com/poll/105802/Economic-Anxiety-Surges-Past-Year.aspx (accessed May 21, 2008). Copyright © 2008 by The Gallup Organization. Reproduced by permission of The Gallup Organization.

AMERICANS ARE CONCERNED ABOUT HEALTH CARE COVERAGE, COSTS, AND QUALITY

In November 2007 the Gallup Organization found that 26% of Americans named health care insurance costs and 30% named access to care as the most pressing health problems facing the country. (See Table 9.2.) Twice as many survey participants named health care system problems, as opposed to specific diseases, as the nation's most urgent health problems. Fourteen percent of respondents said cancer was the most urgent health problem facing the country and 10% felt it was obesity.

Americans' assessment of the quality of health care they receive remains relatively unchanged from past years. In November 2007 just 17% rated U.S. health care as "excellent" and the same proportion (16%) described it as "poor." (See Table 9.3.) Thirty-seven percent said it was "good," whereas 29% said the quality of U.S. health care was "only fair." Similarly, American's assessment of health care coverage has not changed in recent years. In November 2007 slightly more than a quarter of survey respondents felt that health care coverage in this country was "excellent" (6%) or "good" (21%), whereas 41% said it was "only fair" and 31% described it as "poor." (See Table 9.4.)

Some industry observers believe health care providers, policy makers, biomedical technology and research firms, and academic medical centers have fanned the flames of

TABLE 9.2

Public opinion about the most urgent health problem facing the nation, November 2007

WHAT WOULD YOU SAY IS THE MOST URGENT HEALTH PROBLEM FACING THIS COUNTRY AT THE PRESENT TIME? [OPEN-ENDED]

	A	B	C	D	E	F	G	H	I	J	OT	DK
	%	%	%	%	%	%	%	%	%	%	%	%
2007 Nov	26	30	14	10	2	1	1	*	—	1	7	9
2006 Nov	29	22	14	8	6	3	1	*	*	1	8	8
2005 Nov	25	17	15	9	6	4	10	1	*	1	5	7
2004 Nov	29	29	9	7	5	2	2	*	*	*	9	8
2003 Nov	27	25	13	7	8	3	*	1	1	1	8	6
2002 Nov	25	14	21	7	8	5	1	2	1	*	7	9
2001 Nov	14	8	19	4	7	6	1	1	22	1	9	8
2000 Sep	25	13	20	3	18	3	—	1	—	2	8	7
1999 Feb	13	1	23	1	33	5	—	3	—	2	13	6
1997 Oct	9	13	15	*	29	3	—	2	—	6	18	5
1992 Mar	30	—	5	—	41	2	—	—	—	—	18	4
1991 Nov	20	—	6	—	55	2	—	—	—	—	14	3
1991 May	10	2	16	1	45	2	—	*	—	5	15	4
1987 Oct	1	—	14	3	68	7	—	1	—	4	8	3

Key:

A. Health care/insurance costs.
B. Access to health care.
C. Cancer.
D. Obesity.
E. AIDS.
F. Heart disease.
G. Flu.
H. Smoking.
I. Bioterrorism/anthrax/smallpox.
J. Alcohol/drugs.
OT. Other.
DK. No opinion.

—Data not available.
*Less than 1%.

SOURCE: "What Would You Say Is the Most Urgent Health Problem Facing This Country at the Present Time? [Open-ended]," in *Gallup's Pulse of Democracy: Healthcare System*, The Gallup Organization, November 2007, http://www.gallup.com/poll/4708/Healthcare-System.aspx (accessed May 15, 2008). Copyright © 2008 by The Gallup Organization. Reproduced by permission of The Gallup Organization.

TABLE 9.3

Public opinion on the quality of health care, 2001–07

OVERALL, HOW WOULD YOU RATE — [ROTATED] — AS EXCELLENT, GOOD, ONLY FAIR, OR POOR?

A. The quality of health care in this country

	Excellent	Good	Only fair	Poor	No opinion
	%	%	%	%	%
2007 Nov 11–14	17	37	29	16	*
2006 Nov 9–12	16	37	32	14	1
2005 Nov 7–10	16	37	33	14	*
2004 Nov 7–10	20	39	28	12	1
2003 Nov 3–5	18	42	28	12	*
2002 Nov 11–14	14	41	32	12	1
2001 Nov 8–11	15	38	34	12	1

*Less than 1%.

SOURCE: "Overall, How Would You Rate—[ROTATED]—As Excellent, Good, Only Fair, or Poor? A. The Quality of Health Care in This Country," in *Gallup's Pulse of Democracy: Healthcare System*, The Gallup Organization, November 2007, http://www.gallup.com/poll/4708/Healthcare-System.aspx (accessed May 15, 2008). Copyright © 2008 by The Gallup Organization. Reproduced by permission of The Gallup Organization.

TABLE 9.4

Public opinion on health care coverage, 2001–07

OVERALL, HOW WOULD YOU RATE — [ROTATED] — AS EXCELLENT, GOOD, ONLY FAIR, OR POOR?

B. Health care coverage in this country

	Excellent	Good	Only fair	Poor	No opinion
	%	%	%	%	%
2007 Nov 11–14	6	21	41	31	1
2006 Nov 9–12	6	19	41	33	1
2005 Nov 7–10	2	19	43	35	1
2004 Nov 7–10	4	26	41	29	*
2003 Nov 3–5	5	23	42	29	1
2002 Nov 11–14	4	26	41	27	2
2001 Nov 8–11	5	25	43	26	1

*Less than 1%.

SOURCE: "Overall, How Would You Rate—[ROTATED]—As Excellent, Good, Only Fair, or Poor? B. Health Care Coverage in This Country," in *Gallup's Pulse of Democracy: Healthcare System*, The Gallup Organization, November 2007, http://www.gallup.com/poll/4708/Healthcare-System.aspx (accessed May 15, 2008). Copyright © 2008 by The Gallup Organization. Reproduced by permission of The Gallup Organization.

TABLE 9.5

Public opinion about total cost of health care, 1993 and 2001–07

ARE YOU GENERALLY SATISFIED OR DISSATISFIED WITH THE TOTAL COST OF HEALTH CARE IN THIS COUNTRY?

	Satisfied	Dissatisfied	No opinion
	%	%	%
2007 Nov 11–14	17	81	2
2006 Nov 9–12	19	79	2
2005 Nov 7–10	20	79	1
2004 Nov 7–10	21	78	1
2003 Nov 3–5	20	79	1
2002 Nov 11–14	22	75	3
2001 Nov 8–11	28	71	1
1993 May 10–12	8	90	2

SOURCE: "Are You Generally Satisfied or Dissatisfied with the Total Cost of Health Care in This Country?" in *Gallup's Pulse of Democracy: Healthcare System*, The Gallup Organization, November 2007, http://www.gallup.com/poll/4708/Healthcare-System.aspx (accessed May 15, 2008). Copyright © 2008 by The Gallup Organization. Reproduced by permission of The Gallup Organization.

The national economy and the rate of increase of health care costs, especially out-of-pocket expenses, also play important roles in shaping public opinion. When unemployment rates are high, the proportion of people without insurance increases, workers fear losing their jobs and their health care coverage, and dissatisfaction with the present health care system grows. Many surveys show a direct relationship between rising out-of-pocket expenses and dissatisfaction with the health care system. The recent spike in health care costs, coupled with survey findings that employers intend to pass off some of the increasing costs to their employees, will likely inspire renewed interest in health care reform.

The overwhelming majority of Americans remain dissatisfied with the total cost of health care. In November 2007, 81% of respondents were dissatisfied with health care costs, the highest percentage since May 1993, when 90% of respondents expressed dissatisfaction with health care costs. (See Table 9.5.) Despite increasing health care costs and overall dissatisfaction with the total cost of health care, when the Gallup Organization queried Americans about their satisfaction with what they pay for their own health care, the majority (57%) was satisfied with the total cost of their own health care, and the percent that was dissatisfied had dropped three percentage points from the previous survey, from 42% to 39%. (See Figure 9.1.)

The November 2007 Gallup poll found that 83% of respondents were covered by some form of health insurance and 16% had no coverage. (See Table 9.6.) Of those covered by insurance, 57% were covered by private insurance and 31% by Medicare or Medicaid. (See Table 9.7.) These proportions have remained relatively stable since 2001, although the percentage of respondents with private insurance has declined over this period.

consumer dissatisfaction with the health care system by overselling the promise and the progress of modern medicine and the U.S. health care system. They fear that the overzealous promotion of every scientific discovery with a potential clinical application has created unrealistic expectations of modern medicine. Health care consumers who believe there should be "one pill for every ill" or feel all technology should be made widely available even before its efficacy has been demonstrated are more likely to be dissatisfied with the present health care system.

FIGURE 9.1

Poll respondents who are satisfied with the total cost of health care, 2002–07

[Based on all Americans]

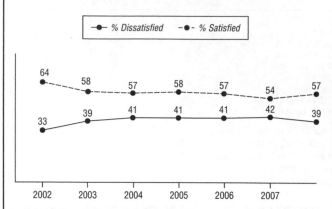

SOURCE: Jeffrey M. Jones, "Satisfaction with the Total Cost You Pay for Healthcare," in *Majority of Americans Satisfied with Their Healthcare Plans*, The Gallup Organization, November 29, 2007, http://www.gallup.com/poll/102934/Majority-Americans-Satisfied-Their-Own-Healthcare.aspx (accessed May 16, 2008). Copyright © 2008 by The Gallup Organization. Reproduced by permission of The Gallup Organization.

TABLE 9.6

Percent of Americans with health insurance other than Medicare and Medicaid, 2001–07

DO YOU CURRENTLY HAVE MEDICAL COVERAGE THROUGH SOME OTHER FORM OF HEALTH INSURANCE?

[Based on adults not insured by Medicare or Medicaid]

	Yes	No	No opinion
	%	%	%
2007 Nov 11–14	83	16	1
2006 Nov 9–12	84	15	1
2005 Nov 7–10	81	19	*
2004 Nov 7–10	84	16	*
2003 Nov 3–5	87	13	*
2002 Nov 11–14	83	17	*
2001 Nov 8–11	84	16	*

*Less than 1%.

SOURCE: "Do You Currently Have Medical Coverage through Some Other Form of Health Insurance? [BASED ON ADULTS NOT INSURED BY MEDICARE OR MEDICAID]," in *Gallup's Pulse of Democracy: Healthcare System*, The Gallup Organization, November 2007, http://www.gallup.com/poll/4708/Healthcare-System.aspx (accessed May 15, 2008). Copyright © 2008 by The Gallup Organization. Reproduced by permission of The Gallup Organization.

TABLE 9.7

Percent of poll respondents with private health insurance, Medicare/Medicaid and no insurance, 2001–07

DO YOU CURRENTLY HAVE MEDICAL COVERAGE THROUGH SOME OTHER FORM OF HEALTH INSURANCE?

	Private insurance	Medicare/ Medicaid	No insurance	No opinion
	%	%	%	%
2007 Nov 11–14	57	31	11	*
2006 Nov 9–12	57	33	10	*
2005 Nov 7–10	57	30	13	*
2004 Nov 7–10	59	30	11	*
2003 Nov 3–5	63	27	10	*
2002 Nov 11–14	61	27	12	—
2001 Nov 8–11	62	26	11	1

—Data not available.
*Less than 1%.

SOURCE: "Do You Currently Have Medical Coverage through Some Other Form of Health Insurance? [SUMMARY TABLE: HEALTH INSURANCE COVERAGE]," in *Gallup's Pulse of Democracy: Healthcare System*, The Gallup Organization, November 2007, http://www.gallup.com/poll/4708/Healthcare-System.aspx (accessed May 15, 2008). Copyright © 2008 by The Gallup Organization. Reproduced by permission of The Gallup Organization.

TABLE 9.8

Percent of poll respondents who have their health insurance premiums paid by themselves/someone in their household, their employers, or by a combination of both, 2001–07

WHO PAYS THE COST OF PREMIUMS ON YOUR HEALTH INSURANCE? DO YOU OR SOMEONE IN YOUR HOUSEHOLD PAY THE TOTAL COST, DOES AN EMPLOYER PAY THE TOTAL COST, OR IS THE COST SHARED BETWEEN THE EMPLOYER AND YOU OR SOMEONE IN YOUR HOUSEHOLD?

[Based on adults with private health insurance]

	Self/ household	Employer pays all	Costs are shared	None/ other (vol.)	No opinion
	%	%	%	%	%
2007 Nov 11–14	18	15	64	2	1
2006 Nov 9–12	20	15	62	2	*
2005 Nov 7–10	18	14	65	2	1
2004 Nov 7–10	18	17	64	1	*
2003 Nov 3–5	23	16	59	2	*
2002 Nov 11–14	21	19	57	2	1
2001 Nov 8–11	19	24	54	2	1

*Less than 1%.

SOURCE: "Who Pays the Cost of Premiums on Your Health Insurance? Do You or Someone in Your Household Pay the Total Cost, Does an Employer Pay the Total Cost, or Is the Cost Shared between the Employer and You or Someone in Your Household?" in *Gallup's Pulse of Democracy: Healthcare System*, The Gallup Organization, November 2007, http://www.gallup.com/poll/4708/Healthcare-System.aspx (accessed May 15, 2008). Copyright © 2008 by The Gallup Organization. Reproduced by permission of The Gallup Organization.

In November 2007, 64% of survey respondents shared the cost of their health insurance premiums with their employers, whereas 18% paid their own premiums and 15% reported their employers pay the total cost of their health insurance premiums. (See Table 9.8.) The percentage of respondents with employers that pay for all their health insurance premiums decreased, from 24% in 2001 to 15% in 2007. Similarly, the percentage of survey respondents that share costs with their employers rose, from 54% to 64% during this same period.

Among those respondents who pay for all or part of their health insurance premiums, 29% said their premiums had "gone up a lot" and 46% said their premiums had "gone up a little" when the Gallup Organization surveyed

TABLE 9.9

Poll respondents who felt their health insurance premiums increased, decreased, or stayed the same, 2003–06

OVER THE PAST YEAR, HAS THE AMOUNT YOU PAID FOR YOUR AND YOUR FAMILY'S HEALTH INSURANCE—[ROTATED: GONE UP A LOT, GONE UP A LITTLE, NOT CHANGED, GONE DOWN A LITTLE, (OR) GONE DOWN A LOT]?

[Based on adults who pay all or part of their health premiums]

	Gone up a lot	Gone up a little	Not changed	Gone down a little	Gone down a lot	No opinion
2006 Nov 9–12	29%	46	19	3	1	3
2005 Nov 7–10	28%	46	23	2	*	1
2004 Nov 7–10	28%	48	17	5	1	1
2003 Nov 3–5	31%	43	23	*	1	2

*Less than 1%.

SOURCE: "Over the Past Year, Has the Amount YOU Paid for Your and Your Family's Health Insurance—[ROTATED: Gone up a Lot, Gone up a Little, Not Changed, Gone Down a Little, (or) Gone Down a Lot]?" in *Gallup's Pulse of Democracy: Healthcare System*, The Gallup Organization, November 2007, http://www.gallup.com/poll/4708/Healthcare-System.aspx (accessed May 15, 2008). Copyright © 2008 by The Gallup Organization. Reproduced by permission of The Gallup Organization.

them in November 2006. (See Table 9.9.) Nineteen percent said their premiums were unchanged and 3% reported their premiums had "gone down a little."

AMERICANS WANT TO REFORM THE HEALTH CARE SYSTEM

Most Americans feel the U.S. health care system is plagued by problems. In November 2007, 56% of Gallup poll survey respondents said they felt the health care system was beset by major problems, 24% felt there were minor problems, and 17% said the health care system was in a state of crisis. (See Table 9.10.) Just 2% of survey respondents said the current health care system "does not have any problems."

Demographic changes, particularly the aging of the baby-boom generation (people born between 1946 and 1964) into Medicare eligibility, may also fuel concern and dissatisfaction with the health care system. If the health care futurists who have projected glaring deficiencies in the current system's capacity to meet the needs of the aging population are correct, this generation may become the largest and most vocal advocates for health care reform. In January 2008 a majority (72%) of Americans polled by Gallup were dissatisfied with the availability of affordable health care in the United States. (See Table 9.11.) Nearly two-thirds (64%) of Americans expressed dissatisfaction with Medicare and less than half (45%) said they were satisfied with the quality of medical care. (See Table 9.12.)

In November 2007 Americans were evenly divided about how to provide health care in the United States. Forty-one percent favored replacing the current U.S.

TABLE 9.10

Public opinion about the state of the health care system, 1994 and 2000–07

WHICH OF THESE STATEMENTS DO YOU THINK BEST DESCRIBES THE U.S. HEALTH CARE SYSTEM TODAY — [ROTATED: IT IS IN A STATE OF CRISIS, IT HAS MAJOR PROBLEMS, IT HAS MINOR PROBLEMS, (OR) IT DOES NOT HAVE ANY PROBLEMS]?

	State of crisis	Major problems	Minor problems	Does not have any problems	No opinion
	%	%	%	%	%
2007 Nov 11–14	17	56	24	2	1
2006 Nov 9–12	16	55	25	3	1
2005 Nov 7–10	18	52	28	1	1
2004 Nov 7–10	14	53	31	2	*
2003 Nov 3–5	14	54	30	1	1
2002 Nov 11–14	11	54	32	2	1
2001 Nov 8–11	5	44	47	2	2
2000 Sep 11–13	12	58	28	1	1
1994 Sep 6–7	17	52	29	1	1

*Less than 1%.

SOURCE: "Which of These Statements Do You Think Best Describes the U.S. Health Care System Today—[ROTATED: It Is in a State of Crisis, It Has Major Problems, It Has Minor Problems, (or) It Does Not Have Any Problems]?" in *Gallup's Pulse of Democracy: Healthcare System*, The Gallup Organization, November 2007, http://www.gallup.com/poll/4708/Healthcare-System.aspx (accessed May 15, 2008). Copyright © 2008 by The Gallup Organization. Reproduced by permission of The Gallup Organization.

TABLE 9.11

Poll respondents' dissatisfaction with national issues, January 2008

[Listed by net satisfied]

	Satisfied	Dissatisfied	Net satisfied
	%	%	Pct pts.
The acceptance of homosexuality in the nation	38	52	−14
The quality of public education in the nation	42	57	−15
The size and power of the federal government	41	57	−16
The role the U.S. plays in world affairs	40	56	−16
The moral and ethical climate	39	59	−20
The nation's campaign finance laws	26	50	−24
The state of the nation's economy	36	61	−25
The size and influence of major corporations	35	61	−26
The amount Americans pay in federal taxes	34	62	−28
The nation's energy policies	31	59	−28
The Social Security and Medicare systems	31	64	−33
The nation's efforts to deal with poverty and homelessness	26	69	−43
The availability of affordable healthcare	25	72	−47
The level of immigration into the country today	23	72	−49

SOURCE: Lydia Saad, "Issues with Which Majority of Americans are Dissatisfied," in *State of the Union: Both Good and Bad*, The Gallup Organization, January 24, 2008, http://www.gallup.com/poll/103918/Americans-State-Union-Ratings-All-Bad.aspx#1 (accessed May 16, 2008). Copyright © 2008 by The Gallup Organization. Reproduced by permission of The Gallup Organization.

health care delivery system and 48% felt the present system should be maintained. (See Table 9.13.) Eleven percent, the highest percentage in recent years, said they had no opinion or preference about replacing or maintaining the health care delivery system.

TABLE 9.12

Poll respondents' satisfaction with domestic issues, January 2008

	% Satisfied
Nation's policies to reduce or control crime	48%
Nation's laws or policies on guns	48%
Quality of the environment	47%
Quality of medical care	45%
Quality of public education	42%
Nation's energy policies	31%
Nation's campaign finance laws	26%
Availability of affordable healthcare	25%
Level of immigration	23%
Average	37%

SOURCE: Lydia Saad, "U.S. Public Satisfaction by Category—Domestic Issues," in *State of the Union: Both Good and Bad*, The Gallup Organization, January 24, 2008, http://www.gallup.com/poll/103918/Americans-State-Union-Ratings-All-Bad.aspx#2 (accessed May 16, 2008). Copyright © 2008 by The Gallup Organization. Reproduced by permission of The Gallup Organization.

TABLE 9.13

Public opinion on replacing the current health care system with a government-run health care system, 2001–07

WHICH OF THE FOLLOWING APPROACHES FOR PROVIDING HEALTH CARE IN THE UNITED STATES WOULD YOU PREFER — [ROTATED: REPLACING THE CURRENT HEALTH CARE SYSTEM WITH A NEW GOVERNMENT RUN HEALTH CARE SYSTEM, (OR) MAINTAINING THE CURRENT SYSTEM BASED MOSTLY ON PRIVATE HEALTH INSURANCE]?

	Replacing the current system	Maintaining the current system	No opinion
	%	%	%
2007 Nov 11–14	41	48	11
2006 Nov 9–12	39	51	10
2005 Nov 7–10	41	49	10
2004 Nov 7–10	32	63	5
2003 Nov 3–5	38	57	5
2001 Nov 8–11	33	61	6

SOURCE: "Which of the Following Approaches for Providing Health Care in the United States Would You Prefer—[ROTATED: Replacing the Current Health Care System with a New Government Run Health Care System, (or) Maintaining the Current System Based Mostly on Private Health Insurance]?" in *Gallup's Pulse of Democracy: Healthcare System*, The Gallup Organization, November 2007, http://www.gallup.com/poll/4708/Healthcare-System.aspx (accessed May 15, 2008). Copyright © 2008 by The Gallup Organization. Reproduced by permission of The Gallup Organization.

The November 2007 Gallup poll showed that 64% of Americans believed it is the responsibility of the federal government to ensure that they have health care coverage. (See Table 9.14.) One-third (33%) of survey respondents said it was not the federal government's responsibility to make sure all Americans have health care coverage. The proportion of Americans holding these views has remained relatively unchanged since 2000.

In anticipation of the 2008 presidential elections, in January 2008 the Gallup Organization asked Americans what kind of change they would like to see the next president of the United States bring about. The number-

TABLE 9.14

Public opinion on the federal government's responsibility to provide national health care coverage, 2000–07

DO YOU THINK IT IS THE RESPONSIBILITY OF THE FEDERAL GOVERNMENT TO MAKE SURE ALL AMERICANS HAVE HEALTH CARE COVERAGE, OR IS THAT NOT THE RESPONSIBILITY OF THE FEDERAL GOVERNMENT?

	Yes, government responsibility	No, not government responsibility	No opinion
	%	%	%
2007 Nov 11–14	64	33	3
2006 Nov 9–12 ^	69	28	3
2005 Nov 7–10 ^	58	38	4
2004 Nov 7–10 ^	64	34	2
2003 Nov 3–5 ^	59	39	2
2002 Nov 11–14	62	35	3
2001 Nov 8–11 ^	62	34	4
2000 Sep 11–13	64	31	5
2000 Jan 13–16	59	38	3

^Asked of a half sample.

SOURCE: "Do You Think It Is the Responsibility of the Federal Government to Make Sure All Americans Have Health Care Coverage, or Is That Not the Responsibility of the Federal Government?" in *Gallup's Pulse of Democracy: Healthcare System*, The Gallup Organization, November 2007, http://www.gallup.com/poll/4708/Healthcare-System.aspx (accessed May 15, 2008). Copyright © 2008 by The Gallup Organization. Reproduced by permission of The Gallup Organization.

one change respondents called for was an end to the war in Iraq (26%), and the second-most frequent response was "healthcare reform" (19%). (See Table 9.15.)

AMERICANS FEEL THEIR OWN HEALTH CARE IS BETTER THAN THE U.S. HEALTH CARE SYSTEM

Most Americans give much higher ratings to the care they receive than to the larger U.S. health care system. Respondents to the November 2007 Gallup poll gave failing and mediocre grades to the overall quality of the U.S. health care system; however, when it came to rating their own personal health care quality and coverage, the survey respondents seemed much happier with their health plan. The majority, a full 83%, rated the quality of health care they receive as "excellent" (33%) or "good" (50%), and just 15% said their own care is "only fair." (See Figure 9.2.) Similarly, 70% of respondents felt their health care coverage is "excellent" (25%) or "good" (45%).

MANY AMERICANS ARE CONCERNED ABOUT THEIR ABILITY TO PAY FOR HEALTH CARE

In view of escalating health care costs and increasing out-of-pocket expenses, it is understandable that Americans are extremely concerned about health care costs. Gallup surveys have repeatedly found that health care costs, which continue to rise much faster than inflation, top the list of health problems Americans believe beset

TABLE 9.15

Public opinion about the change Americans would like to see the next president bring about, January 2008

AS YOU MAY KNOW, A COMMON THEME IN THIS YEAR'S PRESIDENTIAL ELECTION HAS BEEN A DESIRE FOR CHANGE IN THIS COUNTRY. WHAT TYPE OF CHANGE WOULD YOU, PERSONALLY, MOST LIKE TO SEE THE NEXT PRESIDENT BRING ABOUT? (OPEN-ENDED)

	2008 Jan 10–13
End the war in Iraq/bring troops home	26
Healthcare reform	19
Fix the economy/create more jobs	18
Secure the country's borders/address illegal immigration issue	10
Change tax laws	7
Change U.S. foreign policy/improve the U.S. role in the world	6
Better honesty/ethics in government	6
More domestic spending; less international spending	6
Balance the budget/better fiscal discipline	5
Improve the schools	5
Lower gas prices/less dependence on foreign oil	4
Change in leadership from Bush/new direction	4
Increased morality/religion/spirituality/values	3
Fix the Social Security system	2
More help for the poor/address poverty issue	2
World peace	2
Address environmental problems/global warming	2
Less government intrusion/interference in personal lives	1
More help for the middle class	1
Overturn Roe v. Wade/end abortions/fewer abortions	1
Less corporate influence	1
More/better care for the elderly	1
Other	5
Nothing/no change (vol.)	2
Change everything (vol.)	1
No opinion	6

(vol.) = Volunteered response.
Note: Percentages add to more than 100% due to multiple responses.

SOURCE: Frank Newport, "As You May Know, a Common Theme in This Year's Presidential Election Has Been a Desire for Change in This Country. What Type of Change Would You, Personally, Most Like to See the Next President Bring About? (OPEN-ENDED)," in *Just What Types of Change Do Americans Want?* The Gallup Organization, January 17, 2008, http://www.gallup.com/poll/103783/Just-What-Types-Change-Americans-Want.aspx (accessed May 16, 2008). Copyright © 2008 by The Gallup Organization. Reproduced by permission of The Gallup Organization.

FIGURE 9.2

Poll respondents' assessment of the quality of health care and the coverage they received from their health care plans, 2007

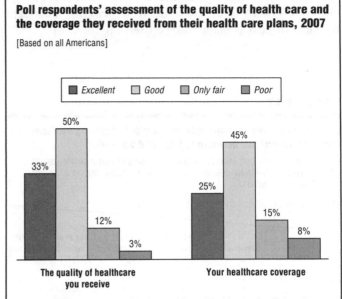

SOURCE: Jeffrey M. Jones, "Ratings of Own Healthcare Quality and Coverage," in *Majority of Americans Satisfied with Their Healthcare Plans*, The Gallup Organization, November 29, 2007, http://www.gallup.com/poll/102934/Majority-Americans-Satisfied-Their-Own-Healthcare.aspx (accessed May 16, 2008). Copyright © 2008 by The Gallup Organization. Reproduced by permission of The Gallup Organization.

TABLE 9.16

Percent of survey respondents who put off obtaining medical care because of concerns about cost, 1991 and 2001–07

WITHIN THE LAST TWELVE MONTHS, HAVE YOU OR A MEMBER OF YOUR FAMILY PUT OFF ANY SORT OF MEDICAL TREATMENT BECAUSE OF THE COST YOU WOULD HAVE TO PAY?

	Yes	No	No opinion
	%	%	%
2007 Nov 11–14	30	70	*
2006 Nov 9–12	30	69	1
2005 Nov 7–10	28	71	1
2004 Nov 7–10	26	74	*
2003 Nov 3–5	24	76	*
2002 Nov 11–14	25	75	*
2001 Nov 8–11	19	81	*
1991 Jan 3–6	22	77	1

*Less than 1%.

SOURCE: "Within the Last Twelve Months, Have You or a Member of Your Family Put off Any Sort of Medical Treatment Because of the Cost You Would Have to Pay?" in *Gallup's Pulse of Democracy: Healthcare System*, The Gallup Organization, November 2007, http://www.gallup.com/poll/4708/Healthcare-System.aspx (accessed May 15, 2008). Copyright © 2008 by The Gallup Organization. Reproduced by permission of The Gallup Organization.

the nation and are perceived as more urgent than threats of specific diseases.

In November 2007, 30% of Gallup survey respondents reported that they had put off some form of medical treatment because of concerns about costs. (See Table 9.16.) This percentage has risen since 2001. Among those who delayed or did not seek treatment, 15% said they put off treatment of a "very serious condition" and another 45% said they put off treatment for a "somewhat serious" condition. (See Table 9.17.)

Not unexpectedly, the Gallup Organization finds that wealthier Americans are less likely to postpone or defer seeking medical care because of cost. In *Three in 10 Have Postponed Medical Treatment Due to Cost* (December 14, 2007, http://www.gallup.com/poll/103261/Three-Postponed-Medical-Treatment-Due-Cost.aspx) Magali Rheault of the Gallup Organization observes that "Americans whose household incomes are under $50,000 (39%) are more likely than those whose incomes are at least $50,000 (23%) to say that they or a family member put off treatment." Similarly, younger survey respondents aged eighteen to forty-nine (37%) were more likely to report deferring care than those aged fifty and older (22%). Nearly twice as many respondents with children under age eighteen (40%) as those without children (24%) said they delayed seeking treatment because of cost considerations. (See Figure 9.3.)

TABLE 9.17

Percent of survey respondents who put off obtaining medical care, by severity of condition, 1991 and 2001–07

WHEN YOU PUT OFF THIS MEDICAL TREATMENT, WAS IT FOR A CONDITION OR ILLNESS THAT WAS—VERY SERIOUS, SOMEWHAT SERIOUS, NOT VERY SERIOUS, OR NOT AT ALL SERIOUS?

[Based on who put off medical treatment due to costs]

	Very serious	Somewhat serious	Not very serious	Not at all serious	No opinion
	%	%	%	%	%
2007 Nov 11–14	15	45	28	10	2
2006 Nov 9–12	10	48	32	9	2
2005 Nov 7–10	18	37	31	13	1
2004 Nov 7–10	16	44	30	10	*
2003 Nov 3–5	6	42	44	8	1
2002 Nov 11–14	16	43	31	9	1
2001 Nov 8–11	15	47	23	13	2
1991 Jan 3–6	15	37	37	10	1

*Less than 1%.

SOURCE: "When You Put off This Medical Treatment, Was It for a Condition or Illness That Was—Very Serious, Somewhat Serious, Not Very Serious, or Not at All Serious? [BASED ON WHO PUT OFF MEDICAL TREATMENT DUE TO COSTS]," in *Gallup's Pulse of Democracy: Healthcare System*, The Gallup Organization, November 2007, http://www.gallup.com/poll/4708/Healthcare-System.aspx (accessed May 15, 2008). Copyright © 2008 by The Gallup Organization. Reproduced by permission of The Gallup Organization.

AMERICANS UNCERTAIN ABOUT SOCIALIZED MEDICINE

The Harvard School of Public Health and Harris Interactive conducted a poll in January and February 2008 and reported the results in "Poll Finds Americans Split by Political Party over Whether Socialized Medicine Better or Worse Than Current System" (February 14, 2008, http://www.harrisinteractive.com/NEWS/all newsbydate.asp?NewsID=1278). The poll reveals that even though two-thirds of respondents said they understood the term *socialized medicine* (publicly or government-administered health care delivery in which all health workers and facilities are paid by the government) "very well" (34%) or "somewhat well" (33%), respondents' understanding of the term varied widely. More than three-quarters (79%) correctly associated the term with the statement that in a socialized medicine system, "the government makes sure everyone has health insurance." Seventy-three percent said they thought socialized medicine meant that the government would pay for all or most of the cost of health insurance and 32% of respondents opined that under socialized medicine the government "tells doctors what to do."

Among those who claimed to understand the term, 45% asserted that instituting socialized medicine in the United States would improve care and 39% felt it would worsen health care delivery. Four percent of respondents felt it would not change the current health care system and 12% said they did not know how it would influence the current system.

FIGURE 9.3

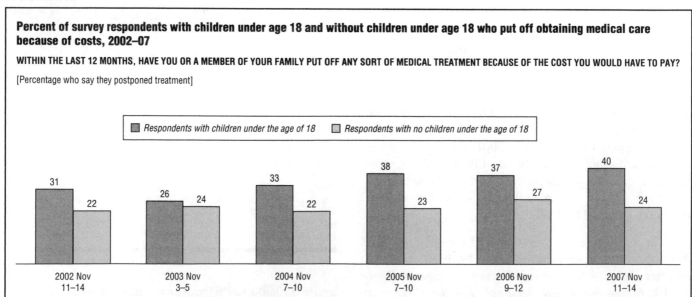

Percent of survey respondents with children under age 18 and without children under age 18 who put off obtaining medical care because of costs, 2002–07

WITHIN THE LAST 12 MONTHS, HAVE YOU OR A MEMBER OF YOUR FAMILY PUT OFF ANY SORT OF MEDICAL TREATMENT BECAUSE OF THE COST YOU WOULD HAVE TO PAY?

[Percentage who say they postponed treatment]

SOURCE: Magali Rheault, "Within the Last 12 months, Have You or a Member of Your Family Put off Any Sort of Medical Treatment Because of the Cost You Would Have to Pay?" in *Three in 10 Have Postponed Medical Treatment Due to Cost*, The Gallup Organization, December 14, 2007, http://www.gallup.com/poll/103261/Three-Postponed-Medical-Treatment-Due-Cost.aspx (accessed May 16, 2008). Copyright © 2008 by The Gallup Organization. Reproduced by permission of The Gallup Organization.

The poll reveals marked differences by political party affiliation. Most Republicans (70%) contended that socialized medicine would be worse than the current system, whereas the same proportion of Democrats (70%) said a socialized medical system would be an improvement. Independents were divided on the issue—43% thought socialized medicine would be better and 38% felt it would be worse than the present system.

Most American Physicians Favor National Health Insurance

Physician support for national health insurance appears to be increasing. Aaron E. Carroll and Ronald T. Ackerman surveyed physicians in 2002 and again in 2007 to assess their support for government legislation to establish national health insurance and universal coverage. The results of their research were published in "Support for National Health Insurance among U.S. Physicians: 5 Years Later" (*Annals of Internal Medicine*, vol. 148, no. 7, April 1, 2008).

In 2002 the researchers found that about half (49%) of physicians surveyed supported national health insurance legislation. In 2007 overall support for national health insurance increased to 59%. Support for national health insurance was highest among psychiatrists (83%), pediatric subspecialists (71%), emergency medicine physicians (69%), general pediatricians (65%), general internists (64%), and family physicians (60%) More than half (55%) of general surgeons supported national health insurance, nearly twice as many as favored it in 2002.

CONSUMER SATISFACTION WITH HEALTH CARE FACILITIES

Despite the problems that continue to plague hospitals, such as shortages of nurses and other key personnel, diminished reimbursement, shorter inpatient lengths of stay, sicker patients, and excessively long waiting times for patients in emergency and other hospital departments, consumer satisfaction with hospital services has remained relatively high. In fact, Press Ganey Associates Inc. reports in *Hospital Pulse Report: Patient Perspectives on American Health Care* (2008, http://www.pressganey.com/galleries/default-file/2008_Hospital_Pulse_Report.pdf), which considers the experiences of nearly 2.8 million patients treated at 1,946 hospitals nationwide, that overall patient satisfaction with inpatient hospital care has steadily increased since 2003.

Patient satisfaction with hospital care was linked to the hospital's success in meeting patients' spiritual and emotional needs. This finding, that satisfaction is associated with patient-centered care and intangible qualities of the hospital experience such as sensitivity, attention, and responsiveness to emotional needs, concerns, and complaints, underscores the fact that many health care

consumers assess the quality of service they receive in terms of the care and compassion displayed by hospital personnel.

Consistent with the findings that personal care and attention strongly influence satisfaction with hospital care, Press Ganey Associates finds that as the hospital size increases (in terms of number of beds) patient satisfaction decreases. Patient satisfaction was highest (87.5%) at hospitals with fifty or fewer beds, and satisfaction declined steadily to 83.4% in hospitals with six hundred or more beds. Presumably, this is because larger hospitals, and the health care workers they employ, find it more challenging to deliver the individual care and attention patients have come to associate with quality.

Other patient-related variables and hospital characteristics also influence satisfaction with care. Fewer patients admitted through the emergency department (82.5%) were satisfied, compared to those who did not have emergency admissions (85.2%). This difference may be attributed to the understandable stress and discomfort surrounding an emergency hospital admission, but it may also reflect dissatisfaction with specific hospital qualities such as long waits for admission.

Government Web Site Posts Patient Satisfaction Survey Data

In March 2008 the federal government posted the results of the Hospital Consumer Assessment of Healthcare Providers and Systems (HCAHPS) survey on the Hospital Compare Web site (http://www.hospitalcompare.hhs.gov/), which enables consumers to compare up to three hospitals. Robert Pear reports in "Study Finds Many Patients Dissatisfied with Hospitals" (*New York Times*, March 29, 2008) that 63% of hospital patients were satisfied with the care they had received—giving their hospitals a 9 or 10 rating on a scale of 0 to 10. An even higher percentage (67%) said they would definitely recommend the facility where they received treatment to friends and relatives.

Pear notes that the study, which encompassed more than twenty-five hundred hospitals, included questions about hospital cleanliness and noise levels as well as issues such as being treated respectfully and whether health care providers listened to patient concerns. In "Medicare Adds Patient Opinions to Hospital Comparison Web Site" (March 31, 2008, http://www.ihealthbeat.org/articles/2008/3/31/Medicare-Adds-Patient-Opinions-to-Hospital-Comparison-Web-Site.aspx?topicID=55), the California HealthCare Foundation indicates that many patients felt health care providers did not treat them with respect. Others said they did not receive adequate pain management after surgery. A quarter of survey respondents said nurses did not communicate well, and 20% said they did not receive written information about follow-up care when they were discharged.

Pear explains that there was some variation in patient satisfaction based on geography. For example, in Alabama 73% of patients gave hospitals high scores, whereas in Hawaii just 57% of patients rated their hospitals as nines or tens. According to Kevin Freking, in "Patient Ratings of Local Hospitals Online/Federal Survey Results Offered in Plain English" (Associated Press, March 29, 2008), patients rated their experiences at rural hospitals better than those in urban settings for several satisfaction measures. Freking notes that Herb Kuhn, the acting deputy administrator at the Centers for Medicare and Medicaid Services, attributed this finding to the communities served rather than specific hospital characteristics, opining, "I think that has to do with rural hospitals being more of a fabric of the community."

Consumer groups, employers, labor unions, and other government agencies applauded the dissemination of these data, asserting that it will help promote transparency and accountability. The California HealthCare Foundation notes that Gerry Shea of the AFL-CIO said, "It's a major step for consumers and not an easy step for hospitals. It puts them in the spotlight on how they are doing against the competition." Carolyn Clancy, the director of the Agency for Healthcare Research and Quality, agreed that patient satisfaction data are an important measure of the quality of health care delivery.

Some industry leaders question the study design and results. According to the California HealthCare Foundation, in "Experts Question CMS Web Site's Patient Satisfaction Information" (April 8, 2008, http://www.ihealth beat.org/articles/2008/4/8/Experts-Question-CMS-Web-Sites-Patient-Satisfaction-Information.aspx?topicID=89), Chip Kahn, the president of the Federation of American Hospitals, said the data are still preliminary, noting, "From an analytical standpoint, the numbers are not totally transparent." He added that the findings call for greater review of the data characteristics. Deirdre Mylod, the vice president of public policy at Press Ganey Associates, said "the survey accounts for differences in patient populations but that no adjustments were made for hospitals' characteristics." In "HCAHPS No Hiccup" (*Modern Healthcare*, vol. 38, no.15, April 14, 2008), Charles S. Lauer explains that Richard Umbdenstock, the president of the American Hospital Association, advises patients to consider a "variety of factors" when choosing a hospital and cautions them not to rely exclusively on the HCAHPS results.

A GROWING NUMBER LOOK FOR HEALTH INFORMATION ONLINE

Even though public trust in hospitals and personal physicians remains relatively high, and many people seek and receive health education from physicians, nurses, and other health professionals, a growing number of Americans are seeking health information online. Harris Poll researchers dub the millions of adults who seek information on the Internet about specific diseases or tips about how to maintain health "cyberchondriacs."

In "Harris Poll Shows Number of 'Cyberchondriacs'—Adults Who Have Ever Gone Online for Health Information—Increases to an Estimated 160 Million Nationwide" (July 31, 2007, http://www.harrisinteractive .com/harris_poll/index.asp?PID=792), Harris Interactive indicates that nearly three-quarters (71%) of American adults sought health information online in 2007. Typically, cyberchondriacs searched the Internet for health information 5.7 times per month, up from 5.1 times per month in 2004 and 3 times per month in 2001. The vast majority (88%) of cyberchondriacs said they found the information they were seeking on the Internet.

Harris Interactive finds that in 2007, 86% of cyberchondriacs felt the information they obtained on the Internet was reliable, down from 90% in 2005. More than half (55%) reported using the Internet to obtain information following discussions with their physicians.

Rachael King explains in "Here Come the Cyberchondriacs" (*BusinessWeek*, August 2, 2007) that some industry analysts posit that the growing number of consumers choosing to research medical conditions online is in part motivated by escalating health care costs and the proliferation of high-deductible health plans, which motivate consumers to assume greater responsibility for their care. Cyberchondriacs not only seek information about medical problems but also want to know how much treatment should cost and whether their physician has a good track record treating specific conditions or performing specific procedures. Furthermore, industry observers feel online consumers are seeking greater control over health care decisions, which will serve to incrementally change the nature of relationships between patients and physicians.

MARKETING PRESCRIPTION DRUGS TO CONSUMERS

Even though health care consumers continue to receive much of their information from physicians, nurses, other health professionals, and the Internet, many also learn about health care services and products from reports in the news media and from advertising. Media advertising (the promotion of hospitals, health insurance, managed care plans, medical groups, and related health services and products) has been a mainstay of health care marketing efforts since the 1970s. During the early 1990s pharmaceutical companies made their first forays into advertising of prescription drugs directly to consumers. Before the 1990s pharmaceutical companies' promotion efforts had focused almost exclusively on physicians, the health professionals who prescribe their products.

Since the mid-1990s spending on prescription drugs has escalated and has become the fastest-growing segment of U.S. health care expenditures. In 1997 the U.S. Food and Drug Administration released guidelines governing direct-to-consumer advertising and seemingly opened a floodgate of print, radio, and television advertisements promoting prescription drugs. Industry observers wondered if this upsurge of direct-to-consumer advertising had resulted in more, and possibly inappropriate, prescribing and higher costs.

Is Direct-to-Consumer Advertising Effective?

It stands to reason that pharmaceutical companies must be receiving significant returns on their direct-to-consumer advertising investments to justify increasing budgets for consumer advertising, but it is difficult to measure the precise impact of consumer advertising on drug sales. In "Drugmakers Not Asleep When It Comes to Advertising" (*Philadelphia Inquirer*, June 2, 2006), Rob Waters notes that spending on direct-to-consumer prescription drug advertising increased by 7% to $4.8 billion in 2005, even though the pharmaceutical industry agreed to adhere to Pharmaceutical Research and Manufacturers of America guidelines urging the inclusion of information about the risks as well as the benefits of the drugs in direct-to-consumer advertising.

William E. Boden and George A. Diamond observe in "DTCA for PTCA—Crossing the Line in Consumer Health Education?" (*New England Journal of Medicine*, vol. 358, no. 21, May 22, 2008) that direct-to-consumer advertising results in a favorable return on investment for more than 90% of brand-name drugs, and that ten of the leading twelve brand-name drugs with direct-to-consumer advertising campaigns had sales of more than $1 billion annually. Nearly three-quarters of the brand-name drugs advertised generated "returns in excess of $1.50 for every $1.00 invested and 35% of which had returns in excess of $2.50 for every $1.00 invested."

Is Direct-to-Consumer Advertising of Psychoactive Drugs Helpful or Harmful?

At what point does an understandable response to distressing life events become an indication for drug treatment—and a market opportunity?

—Barbara Mintzes, "Direct to Consumer Advertising Is Medicalising Normal Human Experience" (*British Medical Journal*, vol. 324, no. 7342, April 13, 2002)

In the landmark report *Mental Health: A Report of the Surgeon General, 1999* (1999, http://www.mental health.samhsa.gov/features/surgeongeneralreport/home .asp), the U.S. surgeon general estimates that about 20% of Americans experience mental health problems and that nearly half of all Americans with severe mental illness do not seek treatment, often because they fear the social stigma and potential loss of employment or health insurance that a diagnosis of mental illness might precipitate. The Substance Abuse and Mental Health Services Administration finds in *Results from the 2006 National Survey on Drug Use and Health: National Findings* (September 2007, http://www.oas.samhsa.gov/nsduh/2k 6nsduh/2k6results.pdf) that in 2006, 11.3% of all adults suffered from serious psychological distress (an overall indicator of past-year nonspecific psychological distress) and 15.8 million adults (7.2% of people aged eighteen and older) had suffered at least one major depressive episode (a period of at least two weeks when a person experienced a depressed mood or loss of interest or pleasure in daily activities and had symptoms that met the criteria for major depressive disorder) in the past year. Among adults aged eighteen and older who had a major depressive episode in the past year, 69.1% received treatment (i.e., saw or talked to a medical doctor or other professional or used prescription medication) for depression in the same time period.

Even though these studies rely primarily on self-report, they do suggest that the United States is in the throes of an epidemic of mental illness. However, some researchers argue that Americans' mental health is no worse than it was in past decades. They contend that the availability and aggressive marketing of psychopharmacological agents—prescription drugs aimed at mental health problems such as nervousness, anxiety, panic, and shyness—has prompted the overdiagnosis of mental health problems and conditions motivated primarily by the desire to increase drug sales.

There have been advocates and opponents of direct-to-consumer prescription drug advertising since its inception. According to Joel S. Weissman et al., in "Consumers' Reports on the Health Effects of Direct-to-Consumer Drug Advertising" (February 26, 2003, http://www.npcnow .org/resources/PDFs/W3-82Weissman.pdf), 35% of respondents discussed an advertised drug with their physician as a result of direct-to-consumer advertising, a finding that supports the contention that advertising exerts a significant influence on consumer preferences and behavior. Among patients prompted by consumer drug advertising to discuss a health problem with their physician, one-quarter received a new diagnosis and a new prescription. About four out of five patients who received a prescription drug and took it as prescribed reported they felt "much better" or "somewhat better" overall after taking the prescription medication. These findings were interpreted as supporting the premise that direct-to-consumer drug advertising increases awareness of specific health problems, provides reliable information, and encourages affected individuals to seek treatment.

Health care consumers favor advertisements for prescription drugs to treat mental health conditions. According to "The Public on Prescription Drugs and Pharmaceutical Companies" (March 2008, http://kff.org/kaiserpolls/upload/7748.pdf), a *USA Today*/Kaiser Family Foundation/Harvard School of Public Health survey that was conducted in January 2008, 60% of adults felt such advertisements "are mostly good because they improve understanding of these conditions and encourage people to seek treatment, whereas 36% think these ads are mostly bad because they encourage people without serious mental health conditions to think they need treatment."

Opponents usually contend that direct-to-consumer advertising is primarily intended to drive sales and that it:

- Increases prescription drug costs

- Does not provide the impartial, objective information that would enable consumers to make informed health choices

- Increases risk because, unlike other consumer goods, prescription drugs, even when administered properly, may cause serious adverse reactions

- Takes unfair advantage of vulnerable people facing difficult treatment choices, especially people who suffer from mental illness

- Aims to increase awareness and utilization of newer products to gain market share and recoup development costs (new drugs are not necessarily safer or more effective but are usually costlier, and often little is known about long-term risks)

- Does not enhance consumer awareness or public health because there is no evidence that advertising helps patients to make better choices about prescription drug use

- May unduly influence physician-prescribing practices; physicians often rely on manufacturers for information about drugs, rather than on independent sources, and many studies show that the physicians most influenced by pharmaceutical advertising tend to prescribe less judiciously

Richard L. Kravitz et al. contend in "Influence of Patients' Requests for Direct-to-Consumer Advertised Antidepressants: A Randomized Controlled Trial" (*Journal of the American Medical Association*, vol. 293, no. 16, April 27, 2005) that the consequence of direct-to-consumer advertising is that the medicines that generate profits for drug companies are often overprescribed. During 2003 and 2004 Kravitz et al. sent actors posing as patients to the offices of 152 family physicians and internists practicing in California and New York. The actors scheduled appointments with the physicians during which some described symptoms of major depression, a long-lasting mood disorder that is often treated with antidepressant medications. Others complained of symptoms of a less serious mental health problem, called adjustment disorder with depressed mood. This condition generally disappears within months without medication.

Among the actors who posed as patients describing symptoms of major depression, one group did not specifically request an antidepressant, a second group mentioned that they had seen a television show about depression that had prompted them to seek drug treatment, and a third group said they had seen a television commercial that advertised paroxetine (one of several drugs often used to treat major depression) and they specifically asked for that drug. Of the first group, 31% were prescribed medication. For the second group of actors, 76% received a prescription. In both of these groups, about 6% of the actors posing as patients who received a prescription were given a prescription for paroxetine. Of the third group, more than half were prescribed the drug they requested.

Concerning the actors posing as patients who presented with symptoms of adjustment disorder and did not mention antidepressant drugs, just one out of ten received a prescription for any medication. However, when the actors asked for medication, nearly 50% were given prescriptions. Most of the actors who specifically requested paroxetine received a prescription for that drug, whereas those who simply asked for some sort of medication were prescribed another antidepressant. Kravitz et al. conclude that "patients' requests have a profound effect on physician prescribing in major depression and adjustment disorder. Direct-to-consumer advertising may have competing effects on quality, potentially both averting underuse and promoting overuse."

Finally, critics of direct-to-consumer advertising, such as Elizabeth A. Almasi et al., in "What Are the Public Health Effects of Direct-to-Consumer Drug Advertising?" (*PLoS Medicine*, March 28, 2006), contend that the information in these advertisements is frequently biased and misleading and that direct-to-consumer advertising increases prescribing costs and has not demonstrated any evidence of health benefits. They also worry that the emphasis on advertisements for new drugs overshadows other vital public health messages about diet, exercise, addictions, social involvement, equity, pollution, climate change, and appropriate use of older drugs.

Still, many mental health professionals favor direct-to-consumer advertising, crediting it with informing consumers that there is effective treatment for potentially debilitating mental disorders and helping them to overcome reluctance to seek needed treatment. Anne McIlroy reports in "High Anxiety" (*Globe and Mail*, September 20, 2003) that Jaques Bradwejn, the chief of psychiatry at the Royal Ottawa Hospital, believes anxiety disorders remain underdiagnosed and claims he has never had a patient ask to be treated for an anxiety disorder who was not suffering from one.

According to Joel S. Weissman et al., in "Physicians Report on Patient Encounters Involving Direct-to-Consumer Advertising" (*Health Affairs*, April 28, 2004), a survey of 643 U.S. physicians, many physicians opine that pharmaceutical ads are a mixed blessing, simultaneously enhancing patient-physician communication and prompting patients to seek unnecessary treatment. Four-fifths of the survey respondents said direct-to-consumer advertising not only encourages patients to seek unnecessary treatments but also fails to fully convey the risks and potential adverse effects of drug treatment. Nearly three-quarters of the physicians surveyed said they thought direct-to-consumer ads inform people about medicines that might help them, and two-thirds of the doctors said ads stimulate dialogue. The physicians estimated that one-quarter of the ad-initiated patient-physician conversations lead to diagnoses of treatable problems that might have gone undetected.

IMPORTANT NAMES
AND ADDRESSES

**Accreditation Association for
Ambulatory Health Care**
5200 Old Orchard Rd.
Skokie, IL 60077
(847) 853-6060
FAX: (847) 853-9028
E-mail: info@aaahc.org
URL: http://www.aaahc.org/

Administration on Aging
Washington, DC 20201
(202) 619-0724
URL: http://www.aoa.gov/

**Agency for Healthcare Research
and Quality**
540 Gaither Rd.
Rockville, MD 20850
(301) 427-1364
E-mail: info@ahrq.gov
URL: http://www.ahrq.gov/

**American Academy of Child
and Adolescent Psychiatry**
3615 Wisconsin Ave. NW
Washington, DC 20016-3007
(202) 966-7300
FAX: (202) 966-2891
URL: http://www.aacap.org/

American Academy of Family Physicians
11400 Tomahawk Creek Pkwy.
Leawood, KS 66211-2672
(913) 906-6000
1-800-274-2237
FAX: (913) 906-6075
URL: http://www.aafp.org/

**American Academy of Physician
Assistants**
950 N. Washington St.
Alexandria, VA 22314-1552
(703) 836-2272
FAX: (703) 684-1924
E-mail: aapa@aapa.org
URL: http://www.aapa.org/

**American Association for Geriatric
Psychiatry**
7910 Woodmont Ave., Ste. 1050
Bethesda, MD 20814-3004
(301) 654-7850
FAX: (301) 654-4137
E-mail: main@aagponline.org
URL: http://www.aagpgpa.org/

**American Association for Marriage
and Family Therapy**
112 S. Alfred St.
Alexandria, VA 22314-3061
(703) 838-9808
FAX: (703) 838-9805
URL: http://www.aamft.org/

**American Association of Pastoral
Counselors**
9504A Lee Hwy.
Fairfax, VA 22031-2303
(703) 385-6967
FAX: (703) 352-7725
E-mail: info@aapc.org
URL: http://www.aapc.org/

American Cancer Society
2200 Century Pkwy., Ste. 950
Atlanta, GA 30345
(404) 816-4994
URL: http://www.cancer.org/

American Chiropractic Association
1701 Clarendon Blvd.
Arlington, VA 22209
(703) 276-8800
FAX: (703) 243-2593
E-mail: memberinfo@amerchiro.org
URL: http://www.amerchiro.org/

American College of Nurse Practitioners
1501 Wilson Blvd., Ste. 509
Arlington, VA 22209
(703) 740-2529
FAX: (703) 740-2533

E-mail: acnp@acnpweb.org
URL: http://www.acnpweb.org/

**American Counseling
Association**
5999 Stevenson Ave.
Alexandria, VA 22304
1-800-347-6647
FAX: 1-800-473-2329
URL: http://www.counseling.org/

American Dental Association
211 E. Chicago Ave.
Chicago, IL 60611-2678
(312) 440-2500
E-mail: membership@ada.org
URL: http://www.ada.org/

American Diabetes Association
1701 N. Beauregard St.
Alexandria, VA 22311
1-800-342-2383
URL: http://www.diabetes.org/

American Geriatrics Society
Empire State Building
350 Fifth Ave., Ste. 801
New York, NY 10118
(212) 308-1414
FAX: (212) 832-8646
E-mail: info@americangeriatrics.org
URL: http://www.americangeriatrics.org/

American Heart Association
7272 Greenville Ave.
Dallas, TX 75231
(301) 223-2307
1-800-242-8721
URL: http://www.americanheart.org/

American Hospital Association
One North Franklin
Chicago, IL 60606-3421
(312) 422-3000
URL: http://www.aha.org/

American Medical Association
515 N. State St.
Chicago, IL 60610
1-800-621-8335
URL: http://www.ama-assn.org/

American Osteopathic Association
142 E. Ontario St.
Chicago, IL 60611
(312) 202-8000
1-800-621-1773
FAX: (312) 202-8200
E-mail: info@osteotech.org
URL: http://www.osteopathic.org/

American Pharmacists Association
1100 Fifteenth St. NW, Ste. 400
Washington, DC 20005-1707
(202) 628-4410
1-800-237-2742
FAX: (202) 783-2351
URL: http://www.aphanet.org/

American Physical Therapy Association
1111 N. Fairfax St.
Alexandria, VA 22314-1488
(703) 684-2782
1-800-999-2782
FAX: (703) 684-7343
URL: http://www.apta.org/

American Psychiatric Association
1000 Wilson Blvd., Ste. 1825
Arlington, VA 22209
(703) 907-7300
E-mail: apa@psych.org
URL: http://www.psych.org/

American Psychiatric Nurses Association
1555 Wilson Blvd., Ste. 530
Arlington, VA 22209
1-866-243-2443
FAX: (703) 243-3390
URL: http://www.apna.org/

American Psychological Association
750 First St. NE
Washington, DC 20002-4242
(202) 336-5500
1-800-374-2721
URL: http://www.apa.org/

American Psychological Society
1133 Fifteenth St. NW, Ste. 1000
Washington, DC 20005-4918
(202) 293-9300
FAX: (202) 293-9350
URL: http://www.psychologicalscience.org/

Association of American Medical Colleges
2450 North St. NW
Washington, DC 20037-1126
(202) 828-0400
FAX: (202) 828-1125
URL: http://www.aamc.org/

Center for Mental Health Services Substance Abuse and Mental Health Services Administration
PO Box 42557
Washington, DC 20015
(240) 221-4021
1-800-789-2647
FAX: (240) 221-4295
URL: http://www.mentalhealth.samhsa.gov/

Center for Studying Health System Change
600 Maryland Ave. SW, Ste. 550
Washington, DC 20024
(202) 484-5261
FAX: (202) 484-9258
URL: http://www.hschange.org/

Centers for Disease Control and Prevention
1600 Clifton Rd.
Atlanta, GA 30333
1-800-232-4636
E-mail: cdcinfo@cdc.gov
URL: http://www.cdc.gov/

Centers for Medicare and Medicaid Services
7500 Security Blvd.
Baltimore, MD 21244-1850
(410) 786-3000
1-877-267-2323
URL: http://www.cms.gov/

Children's Defense Fund
25 E St. NW
Washington, DC 20001
(202) 628-8787
1-800-233-1200
E-mail: cdfinfo@childrensdefense.org
URL: http://www.childrensdefense.org/

Families USA
1201 New York Ave. NW, Ste. 1100
Washington, DC 20005
(202) 628-3030
FAX: (202) 347-2417
E-mail: info@familiesusa.org
URL: http://www.familiesusa.org/

Health Coalition on Liability and Access
PO Box 19008
Washington, DC 20036-9008
URL: http://www.hcla.org/index.html

Hospice Association of America
228 Seventh St. SE
Washington, DC 20003
(202) 546-4759
FAX: (202) 547-9559
URL: http://www.nahc.org/HAA

Joint Commission on Accreditation of Healthcare Organizations
One Renaissance Blvd.
Oakbrook Terrace, IL 60181
(630) 792-5000
1-800-994-6610

FAX: (630) 792-5005
URL: http://www.jcaho.org/

March of Dimes Birth Defects Foundation
1275 Mamaroneck Ave.
White Plains, NY 10605
URL: http://www.marchofdimes.com/

Medical Group Management Association
104 Inverness Terrace East
Englewood, CO 80112-5306
(303) 799-1111
1-877-275-6462
FAX: (303) 643-4439
E-mail: service@mgma.com
URL: http://www.mgma.com/

National Association of Community Health Centers
7200 Wisconsin Ave., Ste. 210
Bethesda, MD 20814
(301) 347-0400
URL: http://www.nachc.com/

National Association of Public Hospitals and Health Systems
1301 Pennsylvania Ave. NW, Ste. 950
Washington, DC 20004
(202) 585-0100
URL: http://www.naph.org/

National Association of School Psychologists
4340 East West Hwy., Ste. 402
Bethesda, MD 20814
(301) 657-0270
1-866-331-NASP
FAX: (301) 657-0275
E-mail: center@naspweb.org
URL: http://www.nasponline.org/

National Association of Social Workers
750 First St. NE, Ste. 700
Washington, DC 20002-4241
(202) 408-8600
E-mail: membership@naswdc.org
URL: http://www.socialworkers.org/

National Center for Health Statistics U.S. Department of Health and Human Services
3311 Toledo Rd.
Hyattsville, MD 20782
1-800-232-4636
URL: http://www.cdc.gov/nchs

National Committee for Quality Assurance
1100 Thirteenth St. NW, Ste. 1000
Washington, DC 20005
(202) 955-3500
1-888-275-7585
FAX: (202) 955-3599
URL: http://www.ncqa.org/

**National Institute
of Mental Health**
Science Writing, Press, and
Dissemination Branch
6001 Executive Blvd.
Rm. 8184, MSC 9663
Bethesda, MD 20892-9663
(301) 443-4513
1-866-615-6464
FAX: (301) 443-4279
E-mail: nimhinfo@nih.gov/
URL: http://www.nimh.nih.gov/

National Mental Health Association
2000 N. Beauregard St., Sixth Fl.
Alexandria, VA 22311
(703) 684-7722
1-800-969-6642
FAX: (703) 684-5968
URL: http://www.nmha.org/

**United Network for Organ
Sharing**
700 N. Fourth St.
Richmond, VA 23218

(804) 782-4800
1-888-894-6361
FAX: (804) 782-4817
URL: http://www.unos.org/

World Health Organization
Avenue Appia 20
Geneva 27, 1211
Switzerland
(011-41-22) 791-2111
FAX: (011-41-22) 791-3111
E-mail: inf@who.int
URL: http://www.who.int

RESOURCES

Agencies of the U.S. Department of Health and Human Services collect, analyze, and publish a wide variety of health statistics that describe and measure the operation and effectiveness of the U.S. health care system. The Centers for Disease Control and Prevention tracks nationwide health trends and reports its findings in several periodicals, especially its *Advance Data* series, *National Ambulatory Medical Care Survey*, *HIV/AIDS Surveillance Reports*, and *Morbidity and Mortality Weekly Reports*. The National Center for Health Statistics provides a complete statistical overview of the nation's health in its annual *Health, United States*.

The National Institutes of Health provides definitions, epidemiological data, and research findings about a comprehensive range of medical and public health subjects. The Centers for Medicare and Medicaid monitors the nation's health spending. The agency's quarterly *Health Care Financing Review* and annual *Data Compendium* provide complete information on health care spending, particularly on allocations for Medicare and Medicaid. The Administration on Aging provides information about the health, welfare, and services available for older Americans.

The Agency for Healthcare Research and Quality researches and documents access to health care, quality of care, and efforts to control health care costs. It also examines the safety of health care services and ways to prevent medical errors. The Joint Commission on Accreditation of Healthcare Organizations and the National Committee for Quality Assurance are accrediting organizations that focus attention on institutional health care providers including the managed care industry.

The U.S. Census Bureau, in its *Current Population Reports* series, details the status of insurance among selected U.S. households.

Medical, public health, and nursing journals offer a wealth of health care system information and research findings. The studies cited in this edition are drawn from a range of professional publications, including the *Journal of the American Medical Association*, *Annals of Internal Medicine*, *New England Journal of Medicine*, *Health Affairs*, *American Journal of Managed Care*, and *Journal of Nursing Administration*.

Gale, a part of Cengage Learning, thanks the Gallup Organization for the use of its public opinion research about health care costs, quality, and concerns. We also express appreciation to the Organization for Economic Cooperation and Development for permission to use information from its *Health at a Glance OECD Indicators 2007*. Our thanks also go to the many professional associations, voluntary medical organizations, and foundations dedicated to research, education, and advocacy about efforts to reform and improve the health care system that were included in this edition.

INDEX